AN ALLY AND EMPIRE

Two Myths of South Korea-United States Relations, 1945–1980

AN ALLY AND EMPIRE

Two Myths of South Korea-United States Relations,1945-1980

PARK TAE GYUN
Translator Ilsoo David Cho

THE ACADEMY OF KOREAN STUDIES PRESS

PUBLISHED BY THE ACADEMY OF KOREAN STUDIES PRESS

English translation copyright © 2012 by The Academy of Korean Studies
All rights reserved. Published in Korea by
The Academy of Korean Studies Press, 323 Haogae-ro, Bundang-gu, Seongnam-si,
Gyeonggi-do, 263-791, Korea
book.aks.ac.kr

Originally published in South Korea as *Ubanggwa Jeguk, Hanmigwangyeui
Du Sinhwa*(우방과 제국, 한미관계의 두 신화) by Changbi Publishers,
Paju-si, Gyeonggi-do, in 2006. Copyright © 2006 by Park Tae Gyun.

ISBN 978-89-7105-899-2 (paper)

Manufactured in Korea
First edition published 2012

Printed on Recycled Paper

PREFACE

US-South Korea relations have a special significance for scholars in Korea because of the special role the United States has played in the history of Korea since 1945. For Korea, particularly for South Korea, the United States was not just something that exerted its influence from the outside–because the United States has been an agent that has shaped the history of South Korea from the inside in just about every aspect.

Of course, the United States is not the first foreign agent in the history of Korea. Korea has a history of at least three thousand years according to Chinese historical records, and Korea was heavily influenced by China due to its geopolitical position for more than two thousand years of that history. In the first century BC, the Han dynasty of China even established a regional government in northern Korea. That, however, was a rare case. While Korea was heavily influenced by China's Confucianism and maintained a tributary relationship with China through the Sinocentric tributary system, Chinese were not an internal agent that created Korea's traditional society.

The Japanese colonial rule dating from 1910 to 1945 can be seen as yet another exception, as such a relationship constituted that of metropole-colony and not a diplomatic relationship between two nations. Perhaps the Japanese colonial rule was similar to that of the four commanderies established by the Han dynasty. That relationship did not continue after Japan was defeated in the Pacific War in 1945.

The United States, however, was different. While an "empire," it never created formal colonies. The Philippines, a former commonwealth of the United States, became an independent nation after the Pacific War. Although the United States had a plan for trusteeship in Korea in 1945, such plan did not succeed. While not encompassing the entire peninsula, the United States, in the end, sought to establish a republic in the southern half of Korea where an election under UN supervision was carried out. The Republic of Korea (South Korea) was an independent state with official recognition from the United Nations.

While the Republic of Korea was formally an independent country, it was not so in substance. In particular, the United States held on to operational control of the South Korean military forces. The fact that an independent nation released the power to control its own military forces to another nation holds a special meaning. Of course, the only party to problematize this fact was North Korea–most South Koreans never questioned it.

In addition, the Republic of Korea received economic aid from the United States from its birth in 1948 to 1975. For about a decade following the Korean War, the South Korean government could not have even survived without American aid. The South Korean and the United States governments collectively formed an organization to discuss South Korea's economic policy, and they decided on the general thrust of South Korea's economic policy and the ways to use aid materials through this organization. Of course, it was the United States that had the decisive agency in its workings.

Such military and economic influence led to political influence. The US ambassadors to South Korea were de facto "governor-generals" into the 1960s and were recognized as such. In other words, the people acknowledged that even the South Korean presidents should abide by the words of American ambassadors. In addition, the Korea branch of the Central Intelligence Agency located inside of the US Embassy in Seoul was often thought of as the "power behind the curtain" in Korean politics.

America's socioeconomic influence was also absolute. First of all, those who questioned the role of the United States or US forces in Korea were prosecuted for violating the National Security Law. Criticisms against the United States were taboo. In addition, the United States' cultural influence emanating from the clubs around the US military bases in Korea, American Forces Network Korea (AFKN) broadcasts, and Hollywood movies was also absolute. South Korea's schools taught American-style democracy as the most perfect political model, and the ultimate goal of those who sought jobs in academia was to obtain a PhD degree in the United States before securing a job at one of the major campuses in South Korea.

That is why the study of US-Korea relations was one of the most important goals for scholars interested in modern Korean history and society. Therefore, political scientists, economists, sociologists, and most recently historians of science, in addition to Korea's historians, have attempted to analyze US-Korea relations. How much power did the United States have in shaping modern Korean history and what sorts of mechanisms were at work? And do such mechanisms function the same way across time and space or not?

Historians were the first to be interested in US-Korea relations, and their interests initially focused on late nineteenth century. The US-Korea relations following the United States-Korea Treaty of 1882 differed from the relations Korea had with other empires. The treaty with the United States included a good office clause, and the attitude of the American diplomats–as well as a number of missionaries at the time–towards Korea was generally well-disposed. Given Korea's difficulties in managing its foreign relations between China and Japan and later Russia and Japan, the American attitudes toward Korea garnered much interest from historians.

Political scientists expanded the temporal bounds of analysis centered on the nineteenth century to the period after 1945, starting with analyses on the United States Army Military Government in Korea. While pioneering, Choe Sangyong's work published in the 1970s did not receive much exposure due to the political conditions under the Yusin system. *Haebang jeonhusaui insik* (An understanding of Korea's postwar history) was published following the Yusin system's collapse, and it stimulated an expansion of interests on US policy as well as conditions in Korea at the time of the US military government.

While such interest in the US military government appeared to have waned with the 1980 massacre in Gwangju and the new military government's establishment (the Fifth Republic), the publication and translation of Bruce Cumings's *The Origins of the Korean War, Vol. 1: Liberation and Emergence of Separate Regimes, 1945–1947* sparked a renewed interest. Attention to the United States' role in Gwangju in 1980, brought about by its operational control of the South Korean military units, spread to the revolutionary conditions of Korea in 1945. Political scientists, sociologists, and historians thereafter produced massive analyses on the US policy towards Korea and the policies of the US military government in the southern half of Korea for the years in and immediately following 1945. Of course, the publicization of American sources related to the US military government in the mid-1980s played an important role in this new renaissance of research activities.

However, a significant amount of time was needed for the research scope to expand into the period after the Korean War. This primarily had to do with the availability of sources. Without the release of the South Korean government sources that pertain to the US-Korea relationship, only the US sources were available for research. And that is why many researchers in the fields of history and sociology went to the US National Archives and Records Administration (NARA) and presidential libraries, where they started collecting sources on US-Korea relations.

Based on such foundational studies with these sources, works on US-Korea relations in the 1950s and the 1960s started to come off the press in the first decade of the twenty-first century. The work of Yi Jongwon, published in Japan during the 1990s, played an important role here. Yi Jongwon analyzed the relationships between the United States, Japan, and South Korea during the 1950s, and his work proved to be influential for political scientists, sociologists, and historians in the latter part of the 1990s.

The period that most interested Korean researcher during the first few years of the new millennium was the transitional period between the 1950s and the 1960s. This period, of course, includes critical historical moments such as the April Revolution (1960) and the May coup (1961). What role did the United States play in this critical period of transition? Would the April Revolution and the May coup have been possible without intervention from the UN Commander, who is also the commander of the United States Forces Korea and has operational control over South Korean military forces? Why did the United States remain silent during the May coup, given the American emphasis on the principles of democracy at the time of the April Revolution? Why did President Kennedy meet Park Chung Hee five months after the coup, given Park's illegal seizure of power as well as his position in an unconstitutional government?

Taking a step further, researchers then started to look at the role played by the United States in the execution of the South Korean economic development plan. Scholars started to argue that the changing of American policy towards developing nations during the Kennedy administration led to the success of the Park Chung Hee government's economic development plan and a successive series of American policies towards South Korea following the Kennedy administration made a successful nation-state out of South Korea.

This book is an extension of the abovementioned body of work produced on US-Korea relations in South Korea. I primarily relied on US policy papers in analyzing the US Korea policy, and I also used the document dispatches between the US Department of State and the US Embassy in Seoul to analyze the conditions in South Korea. The time period covered, from 1945 to the 1970s, also reflects the contemporaneous research trend in South Korea. Of course, some of the topics discussed in this book, such as the introduction of nuclear weapons during the 1950s, Rostow and the new US policy towards developing nations, a detailed analysis of the May 16 coup, the US policy in regards to the removal of Kim Jongpil, and the process of negotiation between the United States and South Korea on the dispatch of South Korean troops to Vietnam, are original topics that other researchers in South Korea have not yet touched upon. However, this book still should be considered an extension to the existing body of work given the emphasis on American sources.

What I aim to argue in this book differs from that of existing perspectives in South Korea. While older works of research focused on the specifics of US Korea policy in analyzing US-Korea relations, this book ultimately seeks to analyze "the level" of South Korean society in approaching the relations between the United States and South Korea. Despite the close military connection, why was the supposed alliance between the United States and South Korea so unequal? As nineteenth-century Japanese intellectuals sought to revise Japan's unequal treaties with the great powers into equal treaties, so too did South Korean intellectuals during the 1980s. If so, why did such a phenomenon develop? Was it because the United States was, as South Korea's democratization movement activists have argued, an imperialist nation? Was it because South Korea was a de facto colony of that imperialist nation?

In fact, the "level" of analysis on US-Korea relations in South Korea has been unilateral as is the case for the US-South Korea relations—only the analysis of the US Korea policy existed until the middle of the 2000s. I, however, have sought to observe South Korean government and society's responses to the US Korea policy. How did members of the South Korean government and society respond to the US Korea policy? How did the United States government evaluate such responses? Were such responses appropriate?

Such an analytical framework has two aspects of significance. One is viewing the relations between South Korea and the United States as something reciprocal. Considering the difference in national power, of course, equal reciprocity is not possible. Just as the March First Movement in colonial Korea stimulated a change in the method of ruling Korea for the Taishō democracy of Japan, the US Korea policy also was influenced by South Korean government and society's responses. And that American evaluations of such responses from South Korea significantly influenced the establishment of new us policies on Korea is a central hypothesis of this book. The discussion of Korea's democracy in the conclusion of this book is not out of the context—its significance is one of the most important arguments of this book.

Of course, this work does not include all of the most recent research that has been progressing in South Korea. Two phenomena appeared in the last few years of the first decade after the new millennium. One is that the temporal endpoint of research expanded to the periods after the 1970s. Now scholars have started to analyze the US-Korea relationship during the era of détente. Another phenomenon is that South Korean government documents from the past, which began to be released by the Roh Moo-hyun administration, started being used in research. Such introduction of new documents is enriching the project that Sin Ukhui has been carrying out–analyzing the thought on South Korea's foreign relations by South Korean agents. If the United States government sought to control the heads of state of its ally in the figures of Park Chung Hee and Syngman Rhee, why did it do so? What were the US-Korea relations like in the minds of Syngman Rhee and Park Chung Hee? What position in Asia did the two men want to place Korea, as an ally of the United States? Did their visions match US policy?

Initially limited to analyzing the speeches of Syngman Rhee and Park Chung Hee, research projects aiming to answer the abovementioned questions are making more progress with the introduction of South Korean documents. The South Korean government and Blue House documents have started to be released from the South Korean National Archives, the Presidential Library, and the Ministry of Foreign Affairs and Trade archives. While I have recently written articles on Park Chung Hee's and Syngman Rhee's thoughts on foreign policy, they are not included in this book. That is perhaps the greatest limitation this book has.

All fields of research evolve. The field of US-South Korea relations in South Korea also continues to evolve. This book is, in a way, representative of the state of the field in South Korea at the time of its publication in 2006. I am bold to argue that it functions as a bridge between the previous works of research and the still-evolving field after its publication. Would it be possible to define my book, although not free from the past achievements and limitations of the works on US-Korea relations, as something that sought to take a step further into the future?

August. 2012
Park Tae Gyun

CONTENTS

INTRODUCTION

1. Worries of the American Ambassador

In August of 1966, the US ambassador to South Korea sent the following telegram to the US Department of State:

> We have a very special relationship with the Koreans. The Republic would not exist had it not been for us. We make possible its military establishment. We participate in all major economic decisions of its Government. In the central sanctum of the Economic Planning Board there are always Americans. Each provincial Governor has an American advisor. We have unusual intelligence liaison arrangements. The American military review and pass on virtually every aspect of the Korean defense budget.
>
> Everywhere one goes in Korea there are Americans in key places. These men are frequently "advising" men senior to them and as competent as they are. Sometimes their major function is to provide a counterweight to undesirable Korean political pressures. Thus far, to the credit of all concerned, the relationships have been easy and mutually rewarding. We are still needed, and badly needed, in many places and on many problems.
>
> But it cannot be expected that this very intimate and special relationship, so pervasive and so all embracing, can continue, or indeed should continue, as the process of economic growth, political maturity, and international competence proceeds, particularly if it does so at the rapid pace which has characterized the last two years. The problem can perhaps be stated by saying that we have an abnormally close and abnormally good relationship with the Koreans.

How can we best move to a close and good relationship with the
Koreans that approximates more nearly the type that normally exists
between two friendly sovereign nations?[1]

This telegram was composed at the time when the South Korean
government dispatched its combat troops to Vietnam at the United
States' request. This was a time when US-South Korean relations
were at their best. Besides South Korea, no other country in
the world sent and sacrificed so many young men in aid of the
American war effort in Vietnam. South Korea was the only country
that directly aided the US military forces by dispatching two army
divisions to Vietnam.

The United States therefore treated South Korea more cordially
than at any other period of time in history, and the South Korean
government did not experience much conflict with the United States.
For the South Korean government, which continuously clashed
with the United States government on a number of issues since the
1961 coup d'etat, including the first economic development plan,
currency reform, the US plan to reduce armed forces in South
Korea, and South Korea-Japan normalization, the dispatching of its
combat troops marked the first moment in which the South Korean
government could demand things from the US with dignity.

The above-quoted telegram, sent exactly at the time of the high
point in US-South Korea relations, reveals their nature in important
ways. Americans were in all the important places in South Korea.
While the US role in South Korean policymaking was sometimes
checked by the South Korean government, Americans were
nevertheless involved in shaping all major state policies in South
Korea. Such interventions were to continue into the future.

"We have a very special relationship with the Koreans" is
therefore the phrase that best sums up the US-South Korea relations.
The relationship between two "abnormally close" sovereign states is
uniquely special, and thinking of the ways to turn that relationship
into one that "approximates more nearly the type that normally
exists between two friendly sovereign nations" was at the center of
the American ambassador's worries.

2. "Special" Relationship between South Korea and the United States

The nature of the "special" relationship between the United States and South Korea, as can be seen in the quoted telegram, defies explanations based on normal diplomatic protocols. The most obvious example of this is the fact that the United States has some of its military forces stationed in South Korea. The American military forces first landed in Korea following the Japanese surrender in 1945. With the period from June 1949 to June 1950 being the only exception, the American military forces remained stationed in South Korea for more than sixty years to this day. Even during the abovementioned one-year exception, five hundred military advisors, the largest of its kind in the world at the time, remained stationed in South Korea.

What is probably even more important is the fact that the United States Forces Korea has commanding authority over the South Korean armed forces, and that fact has not changed to this day. The commander-in-chief of the South Korean military forces, constitutionally speaking, is the president of South Korea. Having the power to control its own military forces is an obvious right of any sovereign state. The South Korean head of state, however, cannot move the South Korean armed forces at his or her will–that authority rests with the commander of the US forces in Korea.

There were, of course, instances of change. The commanding authority of the South Korean military at first rested with the United Nations Command. As the UN commander often was the commander of US forces in Korea, domestic and international critics frequently attacked the arrangement in different ways. In 1994, the United States released the peacetime operational control of South Korean armed forces to the South Korean head of state. The operational control in wartime, however, still rests with the US commander in Korea. While the Combined Forces Command formally exists to control and coordinate the military forces of both countries in South Korea, the highest commanding authority still rests with the American commander.

Because of this arrangement, a number of conflicts broke out between South Korea and the United States over the control of the South Korean military units. In 1952, President Syngman Rhee of South Korea sought to bring in troops from the front to the wartime capital Busan in order to survive a political crisis. The South Korean Army chief of staff, however, did not respond to the president's order. Because of the arrangement of command, which gave the UN commander the final authority, the South Korean Army chief of staff was able to refuse to abide by the president's orders.

President Syngman Rhee unilaterally ordered the release of anticommunist POWs on the day armistice between the United Nations forces and the North Korean and Chinese forces was to be signed. This release was carried out through the direct order from President Syngman Rhee to the South Korean military police, bypassing the United Nations commander. President Syngman Rhee had released control of the South Korean military to the UN commander immediately after the Korean War broke out. Rhee had therefore broken his own promise.

Faced with the crisis of the impending April Revolution of 1960, President Syngman Rhee sought to mobilize military units in order to repel the demonstrators rushing to Gyeongmudae, the president's official residence. While the South Korean military forces entered Seoul to maintain order, they did not fire upon the demonstrators. Though the president was the constitutional commander-in-chief, there was not much the president could do when the army did not listen to him.

Immediately after the May 16 coup d'etat of 1961, the United Nations commander visited the South Korean president and asked him to order the suppression of the coup forces. The president, however, was against the suppression. He believed that the coup merely removed the incompetent government that was already destined to fall. The UN commander reported to Washington that the suppression of the coup would be pointless without the South Korean president's acquiescence. Perhaps the UN commander did not want to suppress the coup forces himself—the commander could have used his authority to suppress the coup by using other South Korean military units had he so desired.

After three days, the US government recognized that the coup forces had successfully taken over the structure of power in South Korea. At that point, however, a heated argument broke out between the coup forces and the UN commander. There still was an unresolved problem between the two sides—the question of responsibility in moving military units without the United Nations Command's permission.

On December 12, 1979, the core members of the Hanahoe, led by Chun Doo Hwan, began a coup d'etat to take over the South Korean government. They gave orders to Korean military units without the American commander's approval. While certain members of the South Korean military then requested permission from the American commander to thwart the coup forces, their requests, in the end, were not granted. Later on, the commander of US forces in Korea publicly stated that the United States had nothing to do with the coup's success.

Civilian militia had taken over Gwangju in May 1980. The new military government, which had seized power through the December 12 coup d'etat in 1979, refused to negotiate with the civilian militia of Gwangju and ordered the army to suppress it. The commander of US forces in Korea approved the plan for the bloody suppression. The people of South Korea, who desperately desired democracy, argued that if the American commander approved the suppression, he (and the United States) was responsible for the shedding of blood in Gwangju. The US commander later recalled that he sought to minimize the violence by approving the mobilization of more "moderate" units to capture Gwangju. He added that the United States is not responsible for the massacre.

South Korea in June 1987 was captivated by the popular movement for democracy. Cornered and convinced that they were facing a real political threat, the Chun Doo Hwan government sought to mobilize the army for suppression. In the end, however, they could not do this. The special envoy sent from Washington had urged the Chun government not to do so, and the Chun government could not mobilize the military units without the consent of the American commander in Korea.

So far, I have only discussed major events that rose to the surface. More research would reveal additional instances of clashes over the issue of operational control over South Korean military units. The issue of control of the South Korean military forces is perhaps the most salient aspect of the special nature of US-South Korean relations.

3. Why Is the US-South Korea Relationship Special?

While the military aspect reveals the unique nature of US-South Korea relations in important ways, the unique nature of this relationship is certainly not limited to military issues. The American ambassador notes in the quoted telegram that Americans are involved in all major decision-making processes in South Korea. Americans were deployed at the centers of all important institutions of the South Korean government.

The telegram below shows the recorded conversation between the South Korean minister of foreign affairs Yi Dongwon and the US secretary of state. The conversation was titled "US Assistance to Pak's Election Campaign."

> The Foreign Minister then asked that the United States Government make some public gesture which would be interpreted in Korea as support for President Pak in his campaign for reelection. The Secretary asked if public opinion in Korea regarding the United States would be helpful to the government in the elections. Lee replied that this would definitely be the case and that the Secretary had seen for himself during President Johnson's recent visit to Korea the deep feeling for the United States which existed among the Korean populace. Ambassador Kim added that, in his opinion, the U.S. attitude toward President Pak and his administration will determine the results of the election. Later, as the Foreign Minister was leaving, he asked when the Secretary was planning to visit Seoul. The Secretary replied that he had no immediate plans for doing so inasmuch as he had just been there. The Foreign Minister urged the Secretary to consider the possibility of going to Seoul and publicly praising Pak's leadership, prior to the election.[2]

As seen in the telegram above, the special relationship between the United States and South Korea can be noted in domestic politics as well. The South Korean government here is asking for an American intervention in the upcoming election in South Korea, and it believes that such intervention would aid the government.

Foreign help or intervention on behalf of a certain candidate usually does not produce a positive effect. Such tendency is particularly true for nations with strong nationalistic sentiments. A candidate dependent on a foreign power is also likely to face domestic criticisms, as dependency can be seen as a sign of weakness as well as disloyalty to one's nation.

However, a historic truth in modern South Korean history is that American interventions in politics have often yielded positive outcomes. Criticisms against American control of the South Korean military units have long been taboo. Such facts testify to the unusual uniqueness of the US-South Korea relationship.

What caused the special relationship? At a glance, this question is not a difficult one. Korea was liberated through the American victory over Japan in the Pacific War. US intervention in the Korean War saved South Korea from communism. South Korean economic development would not have been possible without grants and loans from Washington. American interventions at key times in South Korean history obviously led to the special relationship between the United States and South Korea. For most people, the answer is obviously an easy one.

There is more to that answer, however. This point is particularly evident when the South Korean case is compared with other nations. In matters of security and economy, US-Japan relations also acquire a special character that rivals that of the US-South Korea relationship. Even so, however, there is not much evidence of the United States directly intervening in Japanese politics nor controlling the Japanese Self-Defense Forces. Of course, US policy documents reveal that Washington repeatedly exhorted Japanese remilitarization and acted in a number of ways to prevent the Japan Socialist Party (now better known as the Social Democratic Party of Japan) from taking over the government. There were, however, very few instances of outright and direct American interventions in internal matters of Japan.

One could claim that such disparity results from Korea's division and its geopolitical location at the Cold War's frontlines. This, however, also cannot be an entirely satisfactory answer—Japan also faces a significant security threat from China, North Korea, and Russia. The security threat generated by China's first successful nuclear weapons test in 1964 was one of the major factors that drove the once-reluctant Japanese government to complete the normalization of relations with South Korea. Japan's recent conflict with North Korea and China is a good example of the persistence of such a security threat to this day. Despite the security threat, however, Japanese-American relations remain different from the US-South Korea relationship.

The special nature of US-South Korea relations could have been caused by the global Cold War. However, the example of West Germany provides a good counterpoint here. The fact that West Germany directly bordered the Eastern Bloc during the Cold War provided an obvious reason and justification for the stationing of US military forces there. At a glance, the German example appears to be similar to that of the Korean case.

However, the United States did not acquire operational control over West German forces. In the case of war, the German forces come under the commanding authority of the North Atlantic Treaty Organization's Military Committee. As the supreme allied commander of NATO in Europe is an American, one could make an argument that such an arrangement is in fact similar to that of South Korea. However, while the German forces formally do come under the commanding authority of Allied Command Operations, one could also argue that Germany does not lose its control of its military forces due to the fact that the commander of the Allied Forces Central Europe is a German. In addition, a number of governments with critical stances against the United States' foreign policy came into power in Germany. Unlike South Korea, Germany refused to dispatch its troops to the war in Iraq.

Perhaps the closest example to the South Korean case was South Vietnam before the communist takeover. Washington was deeply involved in South Vietnamese politics to the point that it orchestrated military coup d'etats. The degree of American intervention in South Vietnam may have been greater than in the case of South Korea, and this fact is evident in the American planning and support for major economic development projects such as that of the Mekong River. In the end, however, the Vietnamese people rejected such interventions. The US forces had to withdraw from Vietnam, and the entire country became communized thereafter.

Then what is the reason behind the "special" relationship between the United States and South Korea? Why is it so different from the American relationships with other nations around the world? Can the relationship be accurately defined as a relationship between "allies"? Are the two nations "allies" to each other? As is the case with South Korea, the United States has signed mutual defense treaties with Japan, the Philippines, and a number of European nations. The US-South Korea relationship, however, displays special and unique qualities that do not exist in the cases of other bilateral relationships maintained by the United States. An investigation into this issue must involve a historical perspective, and this is one of the main reasons why I have decided to write this book.

4. Are South Korea and the United States Allies?

The term "alliance" is often used to describe the US-South Korea relationship. The existence of a military alliance, as defined by the bilateral mutual defense treaty between the two countries, confirms the suitability of such a definition. Given the asymmetric relationship, however, one cannot help but to question whether or not the term "alliance" is entirely suitable.

"Alliance" often stems from a bilateral relationship with a common interest. In particular, when the logic of power is involved, an "alliance" often involves a common enemy. In other words, alliances are formed between nations to defend, deter an invasion from, or launch an attack against a common enemy. In such cases, an "alliance" is formed between nations with similar levels of national power. The Triple Alliance between Germany, Austria-Hungary, and Italy during the era of high imperialism is a representative example.

With the end of an era of imperialism and beginning of the Cold War, alliances were formed between nations of unequal national power. Such development was a result of the global reorganization by the two superpowers–the United States and the Soviet Union. The two superpowers stood at the centers of their spheres divided by philosophies in government and economy, and each sought to weaken the other side by bringing more nations into their respective spheres. In so doing, the Soviet Union and the United States formed

How can we define the special relationship between South Korea and the United States? A photograph of Korean grade school students performing in front of U.S. marines during the Korean War.

alliances with nations with much weaker levels of national power. This is the point in time when alliances began to be formed between nations that were asymmetrical in national power.

However, two problems arise from such a development. One is the question of whether or not it is possible to use the term "alliance" to define such relationships. While these alliances still were born out of a common interest against a common enemy, the "size" of such common interest began to significantly differ. While a number of America's allies are participating in the Iraq War, their degrees of participation differ radically. Could we define all of America's alliances–including those with nations that did participate as well as those with nations that did not participate in the Iraq War at all– under the same theoretical umbrella?

The conditions of alliance also differ between nations with

different levels of national power, and we can easily discover this fact from the mutual defense treaty between the United States and South Korea. While one nation has the obligation to provide space for military bases for the other in its own territory, only the other country has the right to establish military bases in the other nation's land. One could argue that South Korea receives a security guarantee at the expense of providing military bases. If so, why did Syngman Rhee and Park Chung Hee persist in demanding the inclusion of the automatic intervention clause in the mutual defense treaty? Could we define such relationship as an "alliance"? Considering the asymmetry, the questioning of whether or not US-South Korea relations fit the generally accepted definition of "alliance" is valid.

Research on US-South Korea relations therefore started with analyzing the historical origins of such an asymmetric relationship. For example, research works based on the world-systems theory all began from such "problem-consciousness." While Choe Sangyong's pioneering work remained largely unnoticed under the censorship of the Yusin system,[3] the work of Bruce Cumings became the first landmark study that analyzed the origins of such asymmetry from the perspective of world-systems theory.[4] Cumings analyzed why Korea became divided using American documents, and in so doing he showed that US-South Korea relations actually were a dominant-subordinate relationship. In addition, Cumings showed the systematic hierarchy existing between the "core" and "peripheral" nations in modern East Asia.[5]

Cumings' work played an important role in explaining the historical origins of the US-South Korea relationship. Following his work, a number of researchers sought to discover the nature of US-South Korea relations around the time of Korea's division.[6] The scope of research gradually expanded onwards, covering the 1950s to the 1970s.[7] Yi Samseong's analysis of the 1980s was also conducted from the perspective of world-systems theory.[8] In addition, Jeong Iljun expanded the horizon of research into the realm of "soft power."

Perhaps the most noticeable among recent publications are those by Yi Jongwon, who expanded the perspective of analysis to include Japan.[9] Focusing largely on the 1950s, Yi Jongwon sought to analyze how US world policy took place in East Asia as a whole, arguing that due to the particular conditions of post–Korean War East Asia, the American policies in the region produced timely and spatially refracted results. While other works emphasized the "special" qualities of US-South Korea relations, Yi Jongwon's work stands out in that he analyzes the US-South Korea relationship in the larger context of American global policy.

However, the biggest issue with the works based on the world-systems theory is that such a perspective does not view the US-South Korea relationship *as an interaction*. Due to its emphasis on the asymmetric nature of US-South Korea relations, the focus remains largely on US Korea policy. To put it differently, such works miss out on how the South Korean side reacted to the US policies, and how such reactions changed the American policy towards South Korea.

Let's first examine the abovementioned work of Bruce Cumings. Cumings first analyzes how strong the South Korean leftist movements were. Cumings then analyzes the activities of Korean politicians on the ground in order to discern the dynamics of Korean politics. The overall flow of his work, however, shows that the internal dynamics of Korea did not change US Korea policy. Foreign policies of the all-powerful "core" nation were realized in Korea, directly resulting in the division of the country and the breakout of the Korean War. This perspective becomes stronger in the second volume of *The Origins of the Korean War* (1990) with greater emphasis being placed upon the international politics centered around the United States.

Another problem with the world-systems approach is that it often overemphasizes US-South Korea relations as something unique and particular. An important premise of such works of research is that the Korean Peninsula somehow was an all-important region for the United States. In other words, these works assume that the United States somehow focuses more on the Korean Peninsula than other parts of the world, and the special military arrangement between the United States and South Korea is often pointed out as the reason why.

Another noteworthy work on US-South Korea relations is that of Victor Cha.[10] Instead of the world-systems theory approach, Cha applies the concept of "alliance" in defining the nature of US-South Korea relations. He uses the concept of "quasi alliance" to define United States-South Korea-Japan relations. Of course, the "quasi alliance" concept refers to the relationship between that of South Korea and Japan, each of whom have a military alliance of its own with the United States. While South Korea and Japan do not have a military alliance with each other, Cha argues that their relationship is nevertheless defined by their military alliances with the United States.

Because of his emphasis on the concept of "alliance" (not domination) between the United States and South Korea, Cha focuses heavily on the role of Japan. He analyzes the shifts in South Korea-Japan relations according to the changes in US foreign policy.

In order for such a scheme to be analytically useful, however, an important and necessary premise has to be that the US-South Korea relationship must be somehow similar to that of the US-Japan alliance in terms of its content. Only then can South Korea-Japan relations be effectively analyzed as a part of the US-centered triangle. If the relationships between the three countries form a structure of hierarchy instead of a triangle, then the concept of "quasi alliance" cannot be analytically sustained. For example, Victor Cha argues that the crisis of South Korea-Japan relations during the period between 1972 and 1974 stems from the different interpretations of the Korea clause in the Nixon-Sato agreement. Because of this, Cha adds, the South Korean government recognized the danger of abandonment by Japan in terms of national security. This example can be seen in Cha's own admission that South Korea-Japan relations cannot be seen as something horizontal.[11]

Because of the prioritization of US Japan and Korea policies in the process of drawing out the concept of "quasi alliance," similar to the works based on the world-systems theory, Cha ends up viewing US-South Korea relations as something unilateral and dominated by the US Korea policy. The concepts of "abandonment" and "entrapment," as employed by Victor Cha, work only when the center of analysis is the US foreign policy.

Furthermore, a common "enemy" is necessary in explaining the relations between South Korea and Japan within the "quasi alliance" model. However, while the "enemy number one" for

South Korea has always been North Korea, the "enemy" of Japan during the Cold War was China. South Korea and Japan still face different "enemies" to this day, and the ways the two countries deal with foreign threat therefore differ. For example, while Victor Cha explains the conflicts between South Korea and Japan from 1972 to 1974 as differences in responding to détente, a better explanation should take account of the facts that, while relations between North and South Korea deteriorated, Sino-Japanese relations improved during the same period.

5. How This Book Has Been Written

This book, while considering earlier works of research, seeks to examine the historical conditions of the US-South Korea relationship in a different way. I have several goals in mind. First, I will focus primarily on important historical moments in US-South Korea relations. While I will consider the entire duration of the US-South Korea relationship, my analysis will be centered on the period from 1945 to 1980. Instead of covering the entire period equally, I will zoom in on significant moments in history to examine the larger trajectory of US-South Korea relations. Instead of theories, I will rely primarily on available sources. The main reason for the the book's coverage ending at 1980 is that the necessary primary sources are only available up to the early 1970s. My first and foremost goal is therefore to make an empirical analysis.

Some of the primary sources on US-South Korea relations are partially available for the periods beyond the early 1970s. However, because volumes of *Foreign Relations of the United States* (the officially published collection of US diplomatic papers) have not been published for the period after the early 1970s, it is still difficult to get a good grasp of the time period beyond the early 1970s. I therefore limited the analysis to the period before 1980.

Second, an emphasis will be placed upon the interaction between the United States and South Korea. While useful to a certain degree, the world-systems theory ends up producing a unilateral depiction of US-South Korea relations. I therefore will aim to display and examine how South Korean actions impacted the US-South Korea relationship. Such task is not an easy one given the relative lack of availability of South Korean sources. The importance of official record keeping only recently became recognized in South Korea. The National Archives of Korea has been established, and individual government agencies themselves have begun to systematically archive their own documents. However, the government-related documents the National Archives of Korea has are still quite limited in number. I therefore utilized Korean newspaper articles as well as US documents to track down the South Korean government's actions and movements. In so doing, I will attempt to reveal the interactions between the United States and South Korea. While the South Korean Ministry of Foreign Affairs and Trade began to release its diplomatic papers for the period after the 1960s in 2005, I will have to leave the analysis of those papers to a later date due to the publication schedule of this book.[12]

Third, I will locate the US-South Korea relations within the larger context of American foreign policy. Because of the stationing of American troops in South Korea, US-South Korea relations are destined to differ from relations between the United States and other nations. The existence of US forces in Korea forms the first fundamental reason for the "special" nature of the US-South Korea relationship. However, given the fact that the larger context of American foreign policy impacts the policy on the US forces in Korea, focusing exclusively on the particularities of the US-South Korea relations will prevent a thorough understanding of US Korea policy. Therefore, I will first examine the larger US foreign policy before analyzing the specifics of the US Korea policy. This point is evident in the fact that other works on US-Japan relations or US-Germany relations are conducted according to a similar trajectory of analysis.

Fourth, instead of analyzing the details of specific policies, I will focus on policymakers' thought processes that form the background of policymaking. A number of researchers already have analyzed the details and specifics of policies. However, there are not many works that analyze the thought processes of the policymakers themselves. My analyses of the thoughts of George F. Kennan, Paul Nitze, and Walt Whitman Rostow have to do with the larger goal of understanding the background of American foreign policy.

In explaining the characteristics and backgrounds of policies, researchers often focus on material interests. However, the power of thought sometimes has greater influence on decision making than is generally believed.

Fifth, I will make a distinction between South Korea as a society and the South Korean government. Earlier works of research often conflated the two in analysis, giving the impression that the interests of South Korea as a society and nation equaled that of the South Korean government. Such is only possible when the South Korean government is truly representative of South Korean society. In other words, the interests of a dictatorial government that has little concern for public opinion and values are not equal to that of South Korean society. The term "the South Korean government" is therefore useful in distinguishing the interests involved.

ONE

The Beginning of US-Korea Relations

Research on the US-Korea relationship in the postliberation era generally reaches either of two contradictory conclusions. One perspective insists that the US intervention destroyed Korea's revolutionary capability and resulted in the establishment of separate regimes. This perspective, best represented by the work of Bruce Cumings, views South Korea as being molded into a periphery of the new world order dominated by the United States. Through the process of peripheralization, it contends, much of the pre-1945 colonial order was revived.

Another perspective insists that, given the inevitability of division due to the Cold War's intensification, those who actively participated in the establishment of separate regime(s) were meant to win. Such perspective is often put forth by conservative South Korean scholars. They advance a consequentialist argument that those who participated in the division made a more realistic and (ultimately) discreet political decision.[1]

However, do these two perspectives objectively comprehend the conditions of the post-liberation era?

1. The United States in Korean Eyes, Korea in American Eyes

The US-Korea relationship officially began in 1882. However, back then, not only was the United States less involved in activities overseas, it was more interested in Manchuria than Korea. Unlike more active approaches taken by Qing China, Japan, and Russia, American activities in Korea involved more of a "soft power" approach. The American presence in Korea was largely confined to the dispatching of Christian missionaries and the projects carried out by those missionaries in education and medicine. Qing China, Japan, and Russia, on the other hand, sought to escape their own fall in international status or even colonization through the colonization of Korea. They therefore risked war to maintain their interests in Korea.

At a missionary meeting in the early twentieth century, United States president William H. Taft emphasized the political roles of Christian missionaries in the following way:

> You are pioneers in pushing Christian civilization into the Orient, and it has been one of the great pleasures of my life that I have had to do with these leaders of yours who represent your interest in China, India, the Philippines, and in Africa. These men are not only bishops and ministers, they are statesmen. They have to be.[2]

Because of the different approach taken by the United States, the Korean people viewed the United States in a different (and more positive) light. While the treaty with the United States was mediated by Qing China, its terms were not brashly unequal as were the treaties with other nations. In fact, the treaty with the United States was advantageous to Korea to a significant degree—it included a favorable tariff rate as well as the most-favored-nation clause. The "good office" clause also gave hope that Korea could rely on the United States in its efforts to escape foreign domination.

King Gojong trusted the United States. He dispatched a consul and later even sent a special envoy there to petition for Korea's independence. The United States government sometimes even behaved in a way so as to check the arrogant stances of Qing China and Meiji Japan in the early years of US-Korea relations. Horace N. Allen, a missionary who also worked as a minister in Seoul, diplomatically fought for Korea's independence despite the US government's opposition to such acts.

Perhaps the most important were the educational programs of American missionaries in Korea, including programs for Korean youth to study abroad in the United States. Baejae Hakdang, Ihwa (Ewha) Hakdang, Gyeongsin Hakgyo in Seoul, and Pyeongyang's

Sungsil Hakgyo were the most representative educational institutions established by American missionaries. These schools often taught about American thought and institutions as well as Christianity. Through these missionaries, small numbers of young Koreans even received a chance to study in the United States. Syngman Rhee is a representative example of such students. After failing at the civil service examination, Rhee chose to attend Baejae Hakdang. During the time of his stay there, Rhee was selected to study in the United States through the help of American missionaries and Eombi, one of King Gojong's favorite court ladies. Other well-known independence activists, such as Yeo Unhyeong, Kim Gyusik, and Bak Heonyeong, all sought to study abroad in the United States through the American missionaries in Korea. Only Kim Gyusik was able to complete his study in the United States—as Yeo and Bak remained in Shanghai and absorbed socialism there. Given the significant contributions made by American missionaries, it is not surprising that decisively pro-American sentiments became widespread in Korea.

Korean officials dispatched to the United States also played a role in generating pro-American sentiments. Bak Jeongyang, the first Korean minister to the United States, is representative in this regard:

> King Gojong asked, "Did the Americans treat you well during your stay?" Jeongyang answered, "The Americans truly disregard the level of power in managing diplomatic relations with other nations. They treat all peoples fairly. They are simple and homely in nature, and therefore treated us with respect. ..." King Gojong asked, "I hear that that country is very wealthy and powerful. Is that true?" Jeongyang answered, "The wealth and power of that country do not rest in the amount of material or the power of their military forces. The source of their wealth and power rests in the fact that they concentrate on fair home administration above all else. Speaking of its finances, they prioritize the tax from the ports first and the foremost. The land tax is next. They also take miscellaneous taxes, and the total amount they take is not small. ... Becoming rich and powerful are the priorities of each and all nations. The source of wealth and power, however, lies in the laws through which they rule by. Although the country is big in size, all parts of this country have firm rules that they all follow.

The people dare not disobey the laws. ... Because the United States is less than a hundred years old, it still has vast tracts of uncultivated land. It therefore emphasizes gathering people to increase the power of labor. Furthermore, because it prioritizes education as its primary policy goal, its people are simple and genuine."[3]

The King asked, "I hear that the laws of that country are cautiously thorough. Is that true?" Jeongyang answered, "Speaking of their officials, they consider state affairs as their own affairs at home. They are careful in abiding by the rules and are not lazy. Speaking of its people, they all concentrate on carrying out their respective duties without play. The number of people who are idle is small. Such are the sources of its wealth. Such are the sources of its circumspect laws."[4]

It is obvious from the quotes that Bak Jeongyang had a positive understanding of the United States. Such understanding is also evident in his travelogue to the United States, *Misok seubyu*.[5] He believed that the United States' wealth and power were greater than what they looked to be on the surface—they were based on a solid economic foundation. He also positively evaluated the American focus on its domestic affairs, as can be seen in his descriptions of the American people: "Speaking of their officials, they consider state affairs as their own affairs at home" and "speaking of its people, they all concentrate on carrying out their respective duties without play." He also positively evaluated the American emphasis on education and industrial development through proper methods of taxation.

Such positive perspective vis-à-vis the United States on the part of Korean people continued into the first decade of the Japanese colonial period. The Taft-Katsura Agreement, in which United States secretary of war William Taft unofficially recognized the Japanese sphere of influence over Korea and the Japanese prime minister Katsura Tarō (also unofficially) recognized the American sphere of influence over the Philippines, took place in 1905. But news of it did not reach Korea until years later. On the contrary, the United States was (yet again) seen as a country that could help Korea attain its independence when President Woodrow Wilson made his public call for self-determination of all nations during World War I. Such hopes led the Korean Provisional Government in Shanghai to dispatch its representatives to Washington and Paris to petition for Korean independence.

On the other hand, a sense of disappointment vis-à-vis the United States among the Korean intelligentsia also arose when they realized that it did not sign the Treaty of Versailles and the American rhetoric of self-determination only applied to those who were ruled by the Central Powers prior to the war's end. Ultimately, the United States viewed Korea as a part of Japan and did not consider its independence at the time. Divisions within the Korean Provisional Government in Shanghai and the increasing number of Korean activists seeking help from the Soviet Union were both connected to the crushing disappointment with Wilson's call for self-determination.

Choe Rin, a well-known Korean collaborator with Japanese colonial rule, was once one of the thirty-three national leaders of the March First Movement. He later expressed his disappointment towards American self-determinism in the following speech:

> Roosevelt! Listen to me if you have ears. I have been disloyal to the Japanese emperor after being tricked by Wilson's so-called self-determinism. An enemy worth gnashing one's teeth at! I will be fooled no more. I will now square myself with the past. Know that I have become a loyal subject of the Japanese emperor!

However, not all Korean activists gave up on the United States. The Korean Provisional Government in Shanghai continued to maintain representation in the United States and to argue for the cause of Korean independence there. After the breakout of the Pacific War, a number of intelligentsia sought to understand the global developments through the American radio program *Voice of America*.

As can be seen, while the Korean perception of the United States remained largely positive, the United States rarely considered Korea to be a significant factor. While strategic considerations on the Korean Peninsula were made by the US government with the breakout of the Pacific War in order to ultimately rearrange the international order in Northeast Asia, the strategic value of Korea did not change much. The contemporaneous American perception of Korea can be represented by the view of George Kennan, an advisor to President Franklin Roosevelt.

> So far as my limited observation qualifies me to judge, the average Korean spends more than half his time in idleness. Instead of cleaning up his premises during his long intervals of leisure, he sits contentedly on his threshold and smokes, or lies on the ground and sleeps, with his nose over an open drain from which a turkey-buzzard would fly and a decent pig would turn away in disgust.[6]

Of course, there were more moderate American perspectives that viewed the Joseon dynasty in a more positive light. Negative impressions, however, were more widespread. Such perception was based particularly on views that compared and contrasted Korea with the case of Japan, which apparently succeeded in modernization.

Such negative impressions of Korea can also be found among other prominent Americans. Missionary Homer B. Hulbert, who protested against the signing of the Eulsa Treaty (the Japan-Korea Protectorate Treaty of 1905) as King Gojong's special envoy to the United States and worked as an editor of the Korea Review, spoke of the American public's understanding of Korea:

> The American Public has been persistently told that the Korean people are a degenerate and contemptible nation, incapable of better things, intellectually inferior, and better off under Japanese rule than independent.[7]

Missionary Arthur Brown, who visited Korea twice as the head of the Presbyterian Church's Board of Foreign Missions, also wrote in his *The Mastery of the Far East* that "indolence is a national characteristic."[8]

Such American perception is based on the understanding that Korea did not have the capacity for self-rule. Korea never had a history of self-rule, and it therefore needed "foreign help" until it acquired such competence. Such understanding is in fact closely tied to the Japanese view of history that Korea had been a dependency of China in premodern times and achieved modernization only with the help of the Japanese after the Sino-Japanese War.

Divisions among Korean independence activists in the United States further tainted American perceptions of Korea. Korean independence activists had been active in the United States since the 1920s. However, the Korean activists were largely divided into the pro-Rhee and anti-Rhee camps, which tainted their activities in the eyes of the US government. The two camps often sent letters criticizing each other to the US State Department.

Considering Syngman Rhee to be at the center of this dispute, the State Department had a negative evaluation of Rhee and did not recognize him as a representative of the Korean people living in the United States. The State Department also did not recognize the Korean Provisional Government in Shanghai who named Rhee as its representative to the United States. One of the reasons why the State Department refused to recognize the Korean Provisional Government in Shanghai was that it was not the sole representative body of Korean independence activists.[9] Even after the 1945 liberation, the US State Department cited factionalism as a key reason for not allowing speedy repatriation of Korean Provisional Government officials, including Syngman Rhee. While Syngman Rhee was able to quickly return to Korea due to his connections to the Office of Strategic Services (hereafter OSS; it later became the Central Intelligence Agency, hereafter CIA), other officials of the Korean Provisional Government were forced to wait three months before being able to return back to Korea.

2. The United States' Reason for Trusteeship

Such mutual understanding between the United States and Korea became an important premise for the post-1945 relationship between the two nations. Pre-1945 understandings, in part, explain why the Korean intelligentsia could not openly embrace the policies of the United States Army Military Government in Korea (USAMGIK) even as they welcomed the Americans as liberators. They also explain why the United States opted for trusteeship despite the fall of Japanese rule in Korea. A noteworthy point is the process of how the United States government broached the issue of trusteeship vis-à-vis Korea.

Trusteeship was first raised by President Franklin D. Roosevelt at the Yalta Conference, six months before the Japanese defeat:

> THE PRESIDENT then said he wished to discuss the question of trusteeships with Marshal Stalin. He said he had in mind for Korea trusteeship composed of a Soviet, an American and a Chinese representative. He said the only experience we had had in this matter was in the Philippines where it had taken about fifty years for the people to be prepared for self-government. He felt that in the case of Korea the period might be from twenty to thirty years.
>
> MARSHAL STALIN said the shorter the period the better, and he inquired whether any foreign troops would be stationed in Korea.
>
> THE PRESIDENT replied in the negative, to which Marshal Stalin expressed approval.
>
> THE PRESIDENT then said there was one question in regard to Korea which was delicate. He personally did not feel it was necessary to invite the British to participate in the trusteeship of Korea, but he felt that they might resent this.
>
> MARSHAL STALIN replied that they would most certainly be offended. In fact, he said, the Prime Minister might "kill us." In his opinion he felt that the British should be invited.[10]

Why did Roosevelt consider trusteeship for Korea while not doing the same for Japan? In the case of Austria, which was under US-Soviet trusteeship for ten years from 1945 to 1955, one could make the case that Austria was a defeated nation that participated in the Second World War on the side of Germany. Why did Korea, who had little to do with the war as an active participant, receive the same treatment?

In the quoted conversation, Roosevelt compares the case of Korea with the case of the Philippines. While Roosevelt states that only twenty to thirty years of trusteeship would be sufficient for Korea, which was around half of the time the Philippines experienced, Roosevelt saw no difference between the two countries in the sense of them being incapable of self-rule.

The United States government, however, did not consider trusteeship for the defeated nations of Japan and Germany aside from temporary military rule. The US government sought to justify its plan for trusteeship in Korea claiming that it was considering the same for other nations that came under fascist rule. Austria, while an aberration, was not simply an "occupied" nation under Germany and can be understood differently. Furthermore, trusteeship was not considered anywhere else besides Korea.

In conclusion, there were four general reasons why the US government opted for trusteeship in Korea. First, it believed that Korea did not possess the capacity for self-rule. As mentioned already, such perception was based on its pre-1945 understanding of Korea. The United States also saw Korea as a historical dependency of China, which further rationalized American understanding of Korea as a country without a history of self-rule.

Second, economic concerns also played an important role. The US government officials questioned whether or not Korea's economy could survive on its own after being detached from the economy of Japan. If Korea failed to survive on its own, its fall would create a negative impact on the region.

Third, Korea did not constitute an important factor in the US global strategy after World War II. While the US government immediately began plans for military rule in Germany and Japan, it did not pay much attention to Korea's future. Instead, the US government planned for an indirect rule using Korean underlings. A plan for trusteeship was raised as a method for such indirect rule.

The final concern for the United States government was the socialistic propensity of the majority of Korean independence activists. Immediately before the Japanese surrender, the US government received an intelligence report from the Chinese Nationalists that some twenty thousand Korean communists were being trained by the Soviet Union in Siberia. Considering the fact that Korean conservatives remained relatively weak, the US government believed that an infusion of Soviet-supported Korean communists into Korea after 1945 would produce a decisively pro-Soviet regime in Korea. Therefore, given the state of affairs in China around 1945 that favored the Chinese Nationalists, the United States government believed that the four-power trusteeship (involving the United States, the Soviet Union, China, and Great Britain) would allow a 3:1 numerical advantage in establishing a capitalist (read pro-American) government in Korea.

Considering the internal affairs of Korea, however, certain members of the US government expressed opinions that trusteeship may not be the best option for Korea. They argued that, given the stronger position of socialists in Korea, indirect rule, such as trusteeship would result in the creation of a socialist regime. As will be discussed in greater detail later, such opinions were raised by the members of the US military government in Korea who actually experienced Korea firsthand. Their perception of the conditions in Korea can be seen in the following telegram.

> Southern Korea can best be described as a powder keg ready to explode at the application of a spark. ...
> Although the hatred of the Koreans for the Japanese is unbelievably bitter, it is not thought that they will resort to violence as long as American troops are in surveillance. ...
> The removal of Japanese officials is desirable from the public opinion standpoint, but difficult to bring about for some time. They can be relieved in name but must be made to continue in work. ...
> The most encouraging single factor in the political situation is the presence in Seoul of several hundred conservatives among the older and better educated Koreans. Although many of them have served with the Japanese, that stigma ought eventually to disappear. Such persons favor the return of the "Provisional Government" and although they may not constitute a majority they are probably the largest single group.[11]

The above telegram was sent by H. M. Benninghoff, a political advisor for the US military government in Korea, a week after the Americans reached Korea. It shows the difficulties the US military regime faced due to Korea's internal conditions. The telegram also argues that, despite Korea's liberation from Japanese colonial rule, Korean collaborators to the Japanese as well as Japanese officials themselves should continue to be employed for governance of the country. This was the dilemma the US military government faced, and it also constituted a reason for establishing direct rule over

©NARA

The beginning of U.S.-South Korea relations. The U.S. military government in Korea began when Hinomaru was replaced by the American flag. September 9, 1945.

southern Korea.

The first US policy in Korea was to refuse to recognize Korean independence activist groups. Such a stance is clearly displayed in the first general order issued by the Allied high command on September 2, 1945:

> b. The senior Japanese commanders and all ground, sea, air and auxiliary forces within Manchuria, Korea north of 38 north latitude and Karafuto shall surrender to the Commander in Chief of Soviet Forces in the Far East.
>
> c. The senior Japanese commanders and all ground, sea, air and auxiliary forces within the Andamans, Nicobars, Burma, Thailand, French Indo-China south of 16 degrees north latitude, Malaya, Borneo, Netherlands Indies, New Guinea, Bismarcks and the Solomons, shall surrender to (the Supreme Allied Commander South East Asia Command or the Commanding General, Australian Forces—the exact breakdown between Mountbatten and the Australians to be arranged between them and the details of this paragraph then prepared by the Supreme Commander for the Allied Powers).[12]

The US command stipulated that only the Allied Powers can receive surrender from the Japanese, meaning that only the American, Soviet, and Chinese forces can disarm and receive Japanese surrender in Northeast Asia. This suggestion was accepted by the Soviet Union and the Chinese Nationalist regime.

While General Order Number One is best known and remembered for the demarcation of the thirty-eighth parallel, perhaps the more important repercussion of it was that it stripped the Korean activists of the right to receive surrender from the Japanese in Korea. According to this logic, all Korean activities against the Japanese in Korea and China were to go unrecognized in the postwar settlement. This order also prevented all Korean organizations for self-rule such as the Committee for Preparation of Korean Independence and the People's Committee from taking executive and legal powers from the Japanese colonial government. This order paved the way for the US military government in denying the legitimacy of the Korean People's Republic of the political left as well as the Korean Provisional Government of the right.

Such a policy differed significantly from how the United States dealt with the conditions in Europe. The United States government recognized the French regime in exile. It also recognized Josip Tito's guerilla activities against the Germans in Yugoslavia. Despite Tito's socialistic and nationalistic tendencies that did not translate favorably for the United States, it nevertheless recognized Tito's wartime activities.

The fact that the United States did not recognize the Korean independence movement can be linked to the fact that the United States government did not allow inclusion of Korea as a victor nation in the San Francisco Treaty in 1951. Of course, Japan played the most significant role in excluding Korea as a victor nation. Conservative politicians of Japan actively lobbied against including Korea as a victor nation out of the fear that hundreds of thousands of Zainichi Koreans (Korean residents in Japan) would become citizens of a victor nation. It was easy for the United States government to accept the demand of conservative Japanese politicians—the US government already had determined the postwar status of Korea in General Order Number One.

3. Reorganizing Korean Political Forces 1: Let's Strengthen the Conservatives

Perhaps the biggest concern for the United States government upon entering Korea was Korea's political landscape. Informed on the situation in Korea by members of the Japanese colonial government, the US military government did not trust the Koreans. Not only were most Koreans supposedly leftist, they were also seen as "most narrow, selfish and confused in their political thought."[13] William R. Langdon, a political advisor of the US commander John R. Hodge, described the Koreans as the following:

> After one month's observation in liberated Korea and with background of earlier service in Korea, I am unable to fit trusteeship to actual conditions here or to be persuaded of its suitability from moral and practical standpoints, and, therefore, believe we should drop it. It is thought wrong because the Korean people have always been a distinct nation except for 35 years of Jap rule and have high literacy, cultural and living standards judged by Asiatic and Middle Eastern standards. … In the Korean People are certain bad traits that cannot be overcome except by actual experience of their evil consequences: Division, obsequiousness, inordinate self seeking, strong sectional rivalries and intolerance of opposition. The Japs did not give the Koreans the opportunities to work these faults out of their system.[14]

On the one hand, Langdon believed at the time that trusteeship was not the best option for Korea given Koreans' relatively high level of education as well as Korea's experience of being an independent nation. On the other hand, however, Langdon also believed that negative characteristics of Koreans presented a troubling dilemma to the US military government in Korea.

Perhaps a more significant problem to the US military government was that rational and conservative politicians (in the US government's eyes) remained few in Korea. Such a perspective is evident in the above-quoted telegram sent by Benninghoff. In southern Korea at the time, the Korean Democratic Party constituted perhaps the only organized conservative political force. The Korean Democratic Party, however, lacked popular support due to the joining of a significant number of known collaborators as well as landlords. On the left, the Korean Communist Party led by Bak Heonyeong and the Korean People's Party of Yeo Unhyeong constituted well-organized political forces with substantial popular support. According to the US military government's own evaluations of the Korean political scene, while it could at least deal with Yeo Unhyeong, it could not do the same with the Korean Communist Party at all. While the Yeo Unhyeong faction seized the first initiative through the Committee for the Preparation of Korean Independence, the Korean Communist Party soon dominated the political scene with its organizational power. With its history as an organization dating back to 1925, the Korean Communist Party soon recovered its broad and powerful machinery in southern Korea.

The US military government sought to change the abovementioned political topography in Korea. The question of trusteeship was secondary to this primary objective. If the pro-US forces remained weak in Korea, the trusteeship would not produce positive results for the United States and its Korea policy. The US military government therefore established two strategic goals in order to change the landscape of Korean politics. First was the strengthening of the Korean political right, and the Korean Democratic Party became the primary target for this program. Another was to weaken the political left.

The first US attempts at weakening the Korean left were its refusal to recognize the Korean People's Republic as a legitimate state and the appointment of a body of advisors to the US military government in Korea. The US military government appointed eleven prominent Koreans as its advisors in October 1945. Seven were from the Korean Democratic Party and included Kim Seongsu and Song Jinu. Yeo Unhyeong was the only political moderate who was appointed. Of course, Yeo refused to join an advisory committee with a Korean Democratic Party majority. Another moderate figure, Jo Mansik of the Joseon Democratic Party, could not join as he was located north of the thirty-eighth parallel. The plan for the advisory committee was ultimately dissolved after much criticism against it as an organization in support of the Korean Democratic Party and composed largely of ex-collaborators to the Japanese.

The US military government then took a more active step. It decided to bring in influential Korean conservatives from overseas in order to strengthen the political right in Korea. Benninghoff, a political advisor of John Hodge in southern Korea, sent the following telegram to Commander Douglas MacArthur in Tokyo on September 15, 1945:

> Consideration be given to returning the Chungking Government in exile to Korea as a provisional government under Allied sponsorship to act as figureheads during occupation and until Korean people stabilize to where there can be an election.[15]

This telegram shows how desperate the US military government in Korea was at the moment. While the United States government had decided not to recognize the Korean Provisional Government in Shanghai before 1945, it now considered bringing them back in order to make use of them for political purposes. In other words, the US military government sought to strengthen the right-wing political forces in Korea by bringing back the members of the Korean Provisional Government while recognizing their authority to a certain degree. However, not only was it difficult to recognize the Korean Provisional Government without recognizing the Korean People's Republic, the US military government also could not entirely trust the Korean Provisional Government members either. The Korean Provisional Government included left-wing nationalists under the support of the Chinese Nationalists. Conservative politicians of the Korean Provisional Government, led by Kim Gu, also were strongly nationalistic. The US military government therefore could not entirely trust them even while supporting them.

The US military government's first targets were Syngman Rhee and members of the Korean Provisional Government. Syngman Rhee was considered particularly important. As discussed earlier, prior to 1945, the US State Department had viewed Syngman Rhee in a negative light. Rhee, however, had strong support within the US government. Due to his lobbying, Rhee had established a viable connection with the OSS (the aforementioned predecessor of the CIA) in 1944. It was therefore easy for Rhee to gain access to the US military government.[16]

While the State Department refused his visa, Syngman Rhee was able to make his way back to Korea with the OSS's help. On his way back to Korea, Rhee also had a chance to meet with Commander Douglas MacArthur in Tokyo. Commander John Hodge was also in attendance at the meeting. The three men discussed ways to reorganize the political landscape in Korea. The following telegram, sent by George Atcheson of the US military government, shows the content of this meeting.

> 1. Syngman Rhee reportedly visited Tokyo October 13 unaccompanied en route to Korea.
> 2. For some time I have delayed recommending that Dept seriously consider whether situation in Korea is not such that we should commence to use some progressive, popular and respected leader, or small group, to act as a nucleus of an organization which in cooperation with and under the direction of our military government could develop into an executive and administrative governmental agency. Such nuclear organization would not need to be called "The Korean Provisional Government," but might be given some title as "National Korean Peoples Executive Committee" and the Advisory Council which General Hodge has set up could either act as advisers to such committee or, if circumstances should so dictate, might in due course be integrated into the Committee. From what has been reported as to the respect with which Syngman Rhee is held by the Korean people in our zone, such committee might at least in initial stage be formed around him, Kim Koo and Kim Kiu [Kimm Kiusic] (...)
> 4. General Hodge asked to see me October 13 and after talking with him I do not think he would be opposed to this point of view ... the suggested Committee could be set up as adjunct to our military Govt.[17]

The "National Korean Peoples Executive Committee" was to be created in order to strengthen the Korean conservative political forces around the key figures Syngman Rhee, Kim Gu (Kim Koo), and Kim Gyusik (Kimm Kiusic). The inclusion of an advisory committee into this organization was also political. While this organization was meant to be an affiliate of the US military government, it also was to function as a quasi government in southern Korea.

This plan materialized further by November 1945. Stating that trusteeship was not a realistic option in Korea, Langdon proposed the following plan with the changing of the name of the National Korean Peoples Executive Committee into the Governing Commission. An important transformation can be noted here–the US government began to pay more attention to Kim Gu after realizing that Syngman Rhee's influence did not meet its expectations.

(1) The Commanding General directs Kim Koo to form a council in MG representative of the several political groups to study and prepare the form of government of Korea and to organize a Governing Commission; MG provides facilities, advice and working funds for such commission.

(2) The Governing Commission is integrated with MG (presently rapidly being built up as an all Korean organization).

(3) The Governing Commission succeeds MG as interim government, with Commanding General retaining power of veto and of appointing such American supervisors and advisors as he deems necessary.

(4) Three other powers concerned are requested to supply some supervisors and advisors in Governing Commission in place of American.

(5) Governing Commission hold selection of head of state.

(6) Government formed by elected head of state recognized treaties made with and missions accredited to it, and Korea admitted to UNO.

Note: Somewhere in the transition, perhaps between (4) and (5), negotiations to be signed with Russia for mutual withdrawal of troops and extension to Russian zone of Governing Commission's authority. Russia should be informed in advance of above plan and invited to further it by allowing persons in Russian zone nominated to Governing (Commission by council to proceed to Seoul, but if Russian participation is not forthcoming plan should be carried out for Korea south of 38th parallel.)[18]

A shocking thing here is that the Governing Commission, appointed by the US military government, was to select the Korean head of state. As can be seen in earlier American perceptions of the Koreans, the US government at the time judged that political democracy was impossible in Korea.

Langdon's plan in a way foresaw the establishments of separate regimes. The plan suggested the formation of the Governing Commission south of the thirty-eighth parallel before expanding its coverage to the north through negotiating with the Soviets. Given that the Soviet acquiescence to such a plan was unlikely, it was in fact for the establishment of separate regimes in Korea. Of course, the Cold War had not yet actualized in 1945 and US-Soviet cooperation was still in place. Nevertheless, this plan had the effect of strengthening pro-American political forces south of the thirty-eighth parallel regardless of their stance on trusteeship. The US military government's major policies from this point on largely abided by Langdon's outlines.

While the US military government insisted that trusteeship was unrealistic, the US State Department continued to maintain that trusteeship was the priority of US Korea policy. In the end, the US government submitted a proposal for trusteeship at the Moscow Conference of Foreign Ministers in December 1945. The continued insistence on trusteeship, however, did not mean an abandonment of Langdon's suggestions. Regardless of trusteeship, the US government believed that pro-American conservatives must take control of politics in the South in order for its Korea policy to succeed.

The US military government therefore took active steps in strengthening the Korean conservatives. First, following Atcheson's suggestion, the US government sought to strengthen the political right around Syngman Rhee and the Central Council for Rapid Realization of Independence. This attempt, however, did not succeed. Most Korean politicians avoided the Central Council for Rapid Realization of Independence due to Syngman Rhee's exclusive stance vis-à-vis the left as well as his equivocal attitude towards known collaborators with the Japanese.[19]

The efforts in establishing the Governing Commission began with the so-called Korean Citizens' Representative Democratic Commission. Following the Moscow Conference of Foreign Ministers, the Korean right was carrying out anti-trusteeship campaigns in its struggle against the left. The Korean Provisional Government faction, led by Kim Gu, dominated the right in this process. Using this political momentum, Kim Gu sought to unify the right-wing forces around the Korean Provisional Government through establishing an organization called the Emergency Citizens' Convention.

On the other hand, the United States sought to absorb Kim's organization into the plan for the Governing Commission. When the Emergency Citizens' Convention appointed the twenty-eight-man "High Council of Political Affairs," the US military government changed its name to the "Democratic Council" and turned it into an advisory committee via Commander John Hodge's request. The former OSS agent Preston Goodfellow played a pivotal role in this process. After helping bring Syngman Rhee back to Korea, Goodfellow lobbied for the rights for ship transport after the Republic of Korea's establishment.[20] As a political advisor to the US military government in Korea, Goodfellow met with leaders of the Korean right in order to persuade them to transform the High Council of Political Affairs into the Democratic Council. In the end, he played a pivotal role in the Democratic Council's establishment with Syngman Rhee as its leader.

This process reflected the worsened relationship between Kim Gu and the US military government over the assassination of Song Jinu and the anti-trusteeship demonstrations. The US military government believed, without any proof, that Kim Gu had something to do with Song's assassination.

4. America's Dilemma: Policy Change due to Anti-Trusteeship Demonstrations

The US military government in Korea faced another obstacle as it sought to strengthen the Korean conservatives while the conservatives themselves began to challenge the US policy in their demonstrations against trusteeship. The US military government judged that trusteeship was not an appropriate policy for American interests in Korea. It also believed that trusteeship would generate significant popular resistance on the part of the Korean people as well. These are the reasons why the US officials on the ground, such as Langdon, strongly argued against trusteeship.

However, the US government nevertheless pushed for the

trusteeship plan at the 1945 Moscow Conference of Foreign
Ministers. It also won Soviet and British acquiescence for trusteeship
in Korea at the Moscow Conference. The US proposal at the
Moscow Conference can be summarized as follows:

> 1. In American draft it was proposed for first period to form in
> Korea unified administration headed by two military commanders
> who were to exercise administration of Korea until establishment of
> trusteeship. Along with this it allowed for participation of Koreans in
> administrative organs of military commanders only as administrators,
> consultants and advisers. Establishment of national Korea government
> in this period was utterly unprovided for in American draft. ... 2.
> In American draft it was proposed for establishment of trusteeship
> in Korea to create four power administrative organ (US, USSR,
> Great Britain, China) which should exercise its powers and functions
> through High Commissioner and Executive Council of representatives
> of these four states. ... 3. In American draft it was proposed to
> establish trusteeship in Korea for period of 5 years and extension of
> trusteeship for 5 more years was allowed.[21]

However, as is well known, the agreement at the Moscow
Conference did not directly translate into trusteeship in Korea.
While the agreement included the plan for trusteeship, it also
provided a possibility of Korean participation in shaping their
future in the establishment of the "Korean Democratic Provisional
Government." According to the Moscow Agreement, while the issue
of occupation was to be dealt by the US-Soviet committee, other
issues, including that of the trusteeship, were to be handled by the
Korean Democratic Provisional Government (made up of Koreans)
through a consultation with the four powers.[22]

Even so, however, the Moscow Agreement's third article stated
that trusteeship was going to last in Korea for a maximum of five
years. Korean conservatives immediately began their protest against
the trusteeship. The group whom the US military government in
Korea sought to support now opposed the American policy. On the
other hand, the left and moderates began expressing their support
for the Moscow Agreement.

Members of the Korean Provisional Government led the protests against trusteeship, declaring a general strike on December 30, 1945. On this day, they issued orders in the name of the Korean Provisional Government urging a strike. Even some of the Koreans who worked at the US military government joined in, causing its operations to temporarily shut down. The US military government labeled this Kim Gu–led movement a coup attempt. The US military government called him in and harshly warned him in person. It also sent a telegram to Washington stating that Kim Gu attempted to commit suicide.

The US military government in Korea now had no choice but to abandon the plan to strengthen the conservatives around Kim Gu. While the US military government in Korea had believed trusteeship to be an unrealistic policy option, Washington had established trusteeship under US-Soviet cooperation to be the cornerstone of its Korea policy. The US military government therefore had no choice but to "change horses."

While the US military government realized that it had chosen a "wrong horse" in Kim Gu, Kim now controlled the Korean conservatives through the anti-trusteeship demonstrations. On the other hand, Syngman Rhee had a difficult time in establishing himself in the Korean political scene after his initial efforts went astray. At this point, the US military government sought to radically change the political landscape of Korean conservatives by appointing Syngman Rhee as the Democratic Council's chairman while placing Kim Gu and Kim Gyusik as vice-chairmen.

The US military government, however, entered into another dilemma with the US-Soviet Commission. As stipulated in the Moscow Agreement, the US-Soviet Commission was to organize the Korean Democratic Provisional Government with representative Korean leaders and handle the issue of trusteeship with them. Due to the Korean right's resistance against the trusteeship, however, it became difficult for the United States to organize the Korean Democratic Provisional Government to their liking. The formation of the Democratic Council was meaningful for the purpose of preparing for the US-Soviet Commission. However, both Syngman Rhee and Kim Gu of the Democratic Commission were against the idea of trusteeship, and the Korean Democratic Party remained passive. As can be seen from the fact that the assassination of Song

©NARA

Photograph of Lieutenant General Stikov, a Soviet representative at the US-Soviet Commission, making a speech. The United States and the Soviet Union confronted each other over the issue of trusteeship. On January 16, 1946 at Deoksu Palace in Seoul.

Jinu, the first head of the Korean Democratic Party, took place at the time of his public insistence on the need to tone down the anti-trusteeship demonstrations, the Korean Democratic Party did not have much room to maneuver. These conservative forces all refused to participate in the US-Soviet Commission as well as the Korean Democratic Provisional Government.

The assassination of Song Jinu is still a subject of many questions. While the US military government's high officials and the Gyeonggi Province's chief of police Jang Taeksang believed that the anti-trusteeship forces led by Kim Gu were behind the assassination, there is no solid evidence to prove such a claim. Considering the Korean political landscape at the time as well as the fact that Song Jinu remained close to the US military government in Korea, there is little chance that Kim Gu ordered the assassination. In other words, there was little reason for Kim to risk it. While Song's bodyguards were discovered to be the assassins, we do not yet know who was behind them.[23]

The Soviet Union, in its participation in US-Soviet cooperation, insisted that those who stood against the Moscow Agreement be excluded. The Soviet Union's insistence was a reasonable one–those who stood against the Moscow Agreement could not be expected to cooperate in carrying it out. From the US military government's perspective, however, holding the US-Soviet Commission without anti-trusteeship forces would result in a leftist takeover of Korean politics. Caught in a dilemma, the US military government declared its decision to delay the US-Soviet Commission in May 1946.

In the end, the anti-trusteeship demonstrations brought about a change in the American Korea policy. Anti-trusteeship movements became the first case in which the power of the periphery, consolidated through the logic of national self-determination that appealed to the masses, changed the core's policy. Of course, one must also consider the charge that the US military government, which was against trusteeship in Korea in the first place, used the anti-trusteeship forces to its own advantage. The most important thing here, of course, is that Washington could not abandon the Moscow Agreement it worked out with the Soviet Union and Great Britain nor execute the plan for the US-Soviet Commission that would have favored the Korean left. Ultimately, the US State Department could no longer pursue a policy designed to strengthen the Korean conservatives. Washington also began questioning whether or not the Moscow Agreement really was a policy favorable to the American interests. Washington and the US military government in Korea now had to devise a new policy for Korea.

5. Reorganizing Korean Political Forces 2: Let's Weaken the Leftists

Around the time the first US-Soviet Commission broke down in May 1946, the US military government organized a commission for left-right cooperation and began actively supporting it. Given the rupture of the US-Soviet Commission due to the anti-trusteeship activities of the Korean conservatives, the US military government needed an organization that was free from the influences of anti-trusteeship movements. Not only did the Democratic Council fail to garner popular support, it also did not play a constructive role vis-à-vis the US-Soviet Commission. It therefore could not become a viable alternative to the Governing Commission.

The US military government in Korea now had to find a new political force that could support the US Korea policy while also accepting the Soviets. This new force was to aid the United States in gaining a more favorable position vis-à-vis the Soviet Union when the US-Soviet Commission reopened. The US military government now laid its eyes on the moderates in Kim Gyusik and Yeo Unhyeong. Kim was a devout Christian and a graduate of Roanoke College in Virginia. He was well-known for his gentlemanly attitude and disposition since his time in the United States. The US military government judged that, while too much of an intellectual, Kim Gyusik was a politician with an "American" sense of rationality.

> There are only a limited number of Korean leaders who have an unselfish interest in Korea at heart and the General (Arnold) places Kim Kiu Sik high on the list. Lyuh Woon Heung he regards as brilliant and personable, but irresolute. Kim Koo has lost out completely. Syngman Rhee, while powerful, is completely self-seeking.[24]

Yeo Unhyeong (Lyuh Woon Heung) was similar to that of "chicken ribs" in the eyes of the US military government. While popular, the US military government could not openly support him due to his close connections to the Korean left. Although the US military government had invited Yeo to organizations such as the political advisory committee and Democratic Council, he had repeatedly refused to join. The fact that those organizations were populated by well-known Japanese collaborators of the Korean Democratic Party made it difficult for him to become a part of them.

After the US-Soviet Commission's breakdown, the US military government no longer had reason to wait. Despite Yeo's leftist disposition, the United States military government judged that American support for him and his cooperation with Kim Gyusik would generate favorable conditions for the United States while also receiving support of the Soviet Union. The Moscow Agreement was impossible without cooperation with the Soviet Union.

The US State Department had suggested the need for left-right cooperation around major middle-of-the-road Korean political figures prior to the US-Soviet Commission, for which the US State Department had high hopes.[25] At the point of its rupture, the State Department proposed the following new plan to overcome the deadlock:

> It is the intention of the United States Government to achieve its objectives in Korea within the framework of the Moscow Agreement and to this end to do all in its power to achieve the fulfillment of the terms of the Agreement and in particular the attainment of Korean independence at the earliest possible date. ...
> With a view to preparing Koreans for early independence and winning popular Korean support for United States policies and thus strengthening the United States position in future negotiations with the Soviet Union, the Commander of United States Forces in Korea, pending the establishment of a nation-wide Provisional Korean Government, shall broaden the basis for Korean participation in the administration of Southern Korea. Insofar as the following can be accomplished, without impairing the maintenance of the necessary military control, he shall:
> Establish through broad electoral processes an advisory legislative body which shall supersede the present Representative Democratic Council of Southern Korea and shall have the duty of formulating and presenting to the United States Commander draft laws to be used at his discretion as a basis for political, economic and social reforms in the southern zone, pending the establishment of a Provisional Korean Government. The Commander of the United States Forces in Korea shall put into effect such draft laws except when they are inconsistent with basic United States objectives or the Moscow Agreement.[26]

The quote is a part of the conclusion of the telegram sent to the US military government in Korea by the US Department of State after gaining approval from the US Army and Navy. The telegram's dispatch date is June 6, 1946, a month after the US-Soviet Commission's breakdown. Declaring the Democratic Council to be no longer useful, the telegram argues for a new political organization for Korea. Instead of an alliance of politicians like the Democratic Council, the new organization was to acquire legitimate representativity through an election and carry out more duties, including advising on legislation.

How then should this plan be carried out and who should participate? An addendum to the above-quoted telegram explains,

> In particular, the holding of elections to choose an advisory legislative body should enable us to create a Korean leadership in the south which is more truly representative of all Korean political opinion than is the leadership of the present Representative Democratic Council of southern Korea, which includes no leftists of any kind. Such a new leadership should prove to be not only stronger but also more acceptable to the Soviet Union than the present Council and, therefore, a factor strengthening rather than weakening the possibility of agreement with the Soviet Union. ...
>
> Agreement not only between the Soviet and United States authorities but also between the various factions in southern Korea would also be greatly facilitated if certain personalities who have been the storm centers of recent political controversy in Korea were to retire temporarily from the political scene. There is reason to interpret the collapse of negotiations in the Joint Commission as the result of a clash between United States insistence upon respect for the principle of freedom of speech and Soviet determination to prevent certain avowedly anti-Soviet Korean leaders from participation in a Provisional Korean Government. These leaders constitute a group of older émigré Koreans who have returned to Korea since the capitulation of Japan.

The addendum suggests that, instead of supporting Syngman Rhee and Kim Gu, who obstructed the US-Soviet Commission, the United States should support new faces and organization to more effectively carry out its Korea policy. The State Department's plan was to have the new political forces take control of the Korean political scene while pushing the likes of Syngman Rhee and Kim Gu into retirement.

There are a number of noteworthy points in the telegram. First, there was a significant difference in perspectives of the US military government in Korea and the US State Department. While the US military government on the ground believed trusteeship and the US-Soviet Commission to be unrealistic, Washington continued to pursue the US-Soviet Commission based on the 1945 Moscow Conference of Foreign Ministers. The telegram therefore includes an exhortation from Washington that the US military government should not misunderstand the aim of US Korea policy and work towards the success of the US-Soviet Commission.

Second, the US State Department's Korea policy at the time was entirely based on an American rationale and point of view. The US State Department believed that a government established through an election south of the thirty-eighth parallel would automatically produce new political leaders as well as a democratic system of governance with popular support. The State Department believed that it could use the new popular government south of the thirty-eighth parallel to pressure the Soviet Union into agreeing with the American agendas.

Such judgment, however, was faulty and based on a lack of understanding of the developments south of the thirty-eighth parallel. Such a US military government-led election was impossible considering the conditions of the postliberation period. Even if such elections did take place, the new leaders could not make the Soviet Union budge—the left and the right already had separate and semi-exclusive support bases, and an election led by the one side would not be accepted nor supported by the other.

Under Washington's order, the US military government in Korea organized a commission for left-right cooperation. It included five members from the right's Democratic Council and five members from the left's Nationalist National Front. Yeo Unhyeong and Kim Gyusik worked respectably as representatives of the left and the right. First Lieutenant Leonard Bertsch, a former lawyer and a graduate of Harvard Law School, played the role of mediator between the commission and the US military government.

The commission, however, revealed a decisive difference of opinion on the matter of the legislative body. With the US military government determined to empower only those who abided by its plans, Kim Gyusik could not convince Yeo Unhyeong, who wanted to create a new pan-national political body encompassing those from the North, into agreeing with the US military government. In addition, both the left and the right clamored to the commission for it to only accept conditions that were favorable to them. They ultimately wanted to obstruct more moderate Kim Gyusik and Yeo Unhyeong from exercising leadership. In the end, the important political forces in the Korean Democratic Party and the Korean Communist Party left the commission. When the US military government unilaterally decided to create a temporary legislative body on its own, moderates, including Yeo Unhyeong, also left the commission.

The US military government thereafter organized a temporary legislative body without the Yeo Unhyeong faction. It was made up of ninety members, with half selected by the US military government and the other half selected through an indirect election. While a number of moderates were appointed due to Kim Gyusik's influence, those elected through the indirect election included a number of conservatives who supported Syngman Rhee and the Korean Democratic Party.

Due to a miscommunication, Jeju Island actually elected people's committee members for the legislative body. When the Jeju representatives arrived in Seoul, they were shocked by its composition. The Jeju representatives, in the end, refused to join after being contacted by the recently founded (and widely popular) South Korean Labor Party. Given the initial infusion of moderates, the temporary legislative body presented bills for punishment of Japanese collaborators and land reform. However, the right-wing majority ensured that such legislative bills would never pass. The legislative body could not become the new political organization the US military government hoped for—it became an alliance of organizations in support of Syngman Rhee and Kim Gu.

The US military government now gave up on creating a new political organization. It then began a sustained effort to weaken the left and strengthen those whom they saw as rational and conservative. The biggest losers here were members of the South Korean Labor Party, which succeeded the Korean Communist Party, and the middle-of-the-roader Yeo Unhyeong. While the US military government displayed a moderate stance at first— it even sent a representative to the South Korean Labor Party's inauguration ceremony–it began attacking the communists soon after the first US-Soviet Commission broke down in May 1946. The US military government already caused Jo Bongam to change his political stance and publicly denounce the Korean Communist Party through political maneuverings in March and April of 1946. It now charged Jeongpansa, the publisher of the South Korean Labor Party's mouthpiece newspaper *Haebang ilbo*, for printing counterfeit money and started investigating it.[27] The US military government also suspended three other leftist newspapers. When the communists sought to fight back with a strike, the US military government ordered their arrest. The South Korean Labor Party's leadership now had to flee to the North.

The US military government also began its secret political maneuvering against Yeo Unhyeong. In addition to cooperating with Kim Gyusik, one of the reasons why the US military government brought Yeo Unhyeong into the left-right cooperation commission was also to separate the Korean right into the more moderate Yeo Unhyeong faction and the more radical Bak Heonyeong faction. The US military government also manipulated Yeo's Korean People's Party, causing Yeo Unhyeong's brother to leave it and create a new party called the Social Democratic Party with American support. All such maneuverings were carried out by First Lieutenant Leonard Bertsch.

The US military government also investigated Yeo Unhyeong's background in order to discover evidence of collaboration during the Japanese colonial period. In the end, the US military government could not find any evidence of collaboration on Yeo Unhyeong's part. The only testimonies the US military government could obtain from the investigation was that Yeo Unhyeong did not cooperate with the Japanese.

The US military government's policy to weaken the Korean left nevertheless was a big blow to Yeo Unhyeong. The activities of the commission for left-right cooperation became the impetus that severely strained Yeo's relationship with Bak Heonyeong. Yeo Unhyeong could no longer work with the Korean communists. A number of significant events broke out during the time of the commission–the general strike in September, the Daegu Incident in October, and the South Korean Labor Party's founding. The conflict between Yeo and Bak became particularly intense at the time of the South Korean Labor Party's founding.

Troubled, Yeo even announced his retirement from politics. Bak's faction criticized Yeo for his collaboration with the US military government in setting up the temporary legislative body. While the loss of Yeo, who still had significant popular support, was a blow to the Korean left as a whole, the South Korean Labor Party leadership did not mind it as long as it could dominate the Korean left.

Yeo Unhyeong ultimately became politically isolated. While he allied with the anti-Bak leftists in the process of reorganizing the Korean People's Party into the Working People's Party, he could no longer garner substantial support due to his role in left-right cooperation. While Yeo once again tried to unite the Korean left and the right prior to the resumption of the US-Soviet Commission in 1947, he was gunned down before his efforts bore fruit.

The assassination of Yeo Unhyeong precluded political alternatives for both the US military government in Korea as well as Korean political forces. Yeo Unhyeong was not only the one person who could have mediated between the left and the right, he was also the only person both the right and the left could accept as the leader of a unified government. While the US military government did reopen the second US-Soviet Commission after the assassination of Yeo, it was merely part of a procedural sequence towards abandoning the Moscow Agreement and transferring the Korea problem to the United Nations in order to establish a separate government in southern Korea. In the end, the second US-Soviet Commission merely became a statement that such a commission was no longer useful.

From that point on, the United States actively supported establishing a separate regime south of the thirty-eighth parallel with the Korean Democratic Party in control. However, the United States ran into another unexpected snag when Jang Deoksu, the "brain" of the Korean Democratic Party, was assassinated. Jang was practically leading the party after the assassination of Song Jinu, and Jang's death paralyzed it to the point that it could not expect to lead in the elections south of the thirty-eighth parallel. The US military government actively investigated the murder. While there definitely was a political conspiracy in the case of Jang's assassination, the US military government's investigation was yet another politically manipulative move on the part of the Americans. Immediately after the death of Jang, the US military government reported to Washington in a telegram that Jang Deoksu was assassinated soon after fighting with Syngman Rhee. This line implied that the US military government understood Jang's death to be related to Syngman Rhee and his political interests. The death of Jang Deoksu and the weakening of the Korean Democratic Party left the US military government with no choice but to (re)select Syngman Rhee as the leader for southern Korea.

The arrow of investigation, however, pointed to Kim Gu. The US military government demanded that Kim Gu appear at the trial of Jang's assassin. Although just a murder case, the US military government even had President Harry Truman write a letter to Kim Gu asking him to appear at the trial. Faced with the impending South-North negotiations, Kim Gu had no choice but to do so. It was a great blow to Kim's image as a politician. While the assassination of Jang Deoksu remains a mystery, it appears most likely that it was yet another instance of political manipulation on the part of the US military government in Korea.[28]

The main agenda of US Korea policy from 1945 to 1948 was to establish trusteeship in the entire Korean peninsula for some time. Despite the US military government's opinion to the contrary, the US State Department labored to carry out the Moscow Agreement up to a certain point in 1947. Despite the steady escalation of tension between the United States and the Soviet Union during this time, the US policy papers of this period show that the United States government did not intend the division of Korea until the middle of 1947.

Important turning points in the US Korea policy were interviews of the US military government officials in Washington from late 1946 to early 1947 and Syngman Rhee's visit to the United States. Through interviewing major figures of the US military government in Korea, Washington gradually realized the unfeasibility of trusteeship in Korea. Syngman Rhee strongly argued for the need to establish a pro-American government south of the thirty-eighth parallel during meetings with important figures of the US Department of State and the Department of Defense. The United States government transferred the issue of Korea to the United Nations immediately after the US-Soviet Union Commission failed. It then carried out an election in the South and established the Republic of Korea (South Korea). If so, did the US Korea policy in fact succeed?

Looking at the conditions of post-liberation Korea, one could say that the US Korea policy was successful to a certain degree. Despite the initial dominance of the left in Korean politics, the United States was able to successfully establish a regime dominated by the Korean right through political manipulation. On the other hand, however, the US plan to establish a pro-American regime for the entire country failed. The plan for trusteeship also did not work out. Its plan to strengthen the Korean conservatives around Syngman Rhee and Kim Gu also failed due to the anti-trusteeship demonstrations. Therefore, when Syngman Rhee did become the president of South Korea under the constitution based on a presidential system, Arthur C. Bunce, an economic advisor to the US military government in Korea, grumbled in pessimism.

The failure of the US military government, first and foremost, had to do with the dynamics of power within Korea. Post-liberation Korea featured political forces of all spectrums. Regardless of their differences, most of them could agree that they could not accept the establishment of separate regimes in Korea. While the Republic of Korea (South Korea) was established by the United States, those who supported its foundation were relatively few at the time– Syngman Rhee and the Korean Democratic Party. A few followers of Kim Gu who joined in were mostly arrested in the National Assembly Spy Incident in 1949. In the end, the US Korea policy was only half-successful. The internal strength of Korean politics ended up dictating the other half.

I've argued that widespread American perception that Koreans were unable to rule themselves marked the beginning point of the US Korea policy. It is difficult to judge whether or not such perception at the time was objective or accurate. The Koreans, however, could not accept such judgment about their future. Such rejection formed the basis of the strength that obstructed the American policy in Korea. It is a representative example that the US Korea policy could not be unilaterally executed.

TWO

Not Giving Up the Korean Peninsula

Certain works of research on the United States Department of Defense in the 1950s suggested American (over)emphasis on economic aid over military aid as a reason for its "failure" in the Korean War. Other researchers have suggested the withdrawal of American forces from the Korean Peninsula in June 1949 and Secretary of State Dean Acheson's public statement excluding Korea from the American defense perimeter in January 1950 as the most important reasons for the Korean War's breakout.

Why did the United States withdraw its forces from Korea in June 1949? Does this mean that the United States "gave up" on Korea? Was it trying to place greater weight upon the US forces in Japan for the Japan-centered regional strategy? If so, why did the United States plan massive economic aid to South Korea in 1949 and 1950?

1. Why Did the United States Forces Withdraw?

George F. Kennan, who worked at the Policy Planning Staff of the United States State Department, began shaping US foreign policy during the Cold War's intensification. He put forth his concept of containment in order to check the expansion of communism and Soviet power.

Kennan's containment is particularly noteworthy in its emphasis on economic and psychological aspects. Unlike traditional thought that focused on matters of military and politics, Kennan's plan emphasized psychological victory through economic means in checking communism. If capitalism can give people the assurance of material prosperity, Kennan reasoned, they did not have to resort to communism.

The Marshall Plan, which took place in Europe on a massive scale in 1947, was based on Kennan's theory. The Marshall Plan sought to block the Soviet Union's westward advance by stimulating economic growth in Europe. It was based on an understanding that helping the people of Europe to economically overcome the devastation of World War II was the best way to destroy the appeal of communism. If capitalism could lead Europe back to prosperity, there was no need for communism.[1]

There were, of course, several important underlying premises in Kennan's emphasis on economic and psychological means. The first was the American monopoly on nuclear weapons. First used in 1945, the atomic weapons displayed their enormous power of destruction to the world at Hiroshima and Nagasaki. The United States was able to maintain its military superiority vis-à-vis the Soviet Union based on this monopoly until 1949, when the Soviet Union also acquired its own nuclear weapons. There was no pressing need for the United States to strengthen its conventional military forces to contain the Soviet Union during that time.

Second, Kennan also paid attention to the limitations of the Soviet system itself. Working at the US Embassy in Moscow from 1944 to 1946, Kennan acquired an expert-like understanding of Soviet politics and society. Based on his firsthand experience of the country, Kennan sent what is widely known as the "long telegram" back to Washington. Through his analysis of the Soviet communist system, Kennan argues in this telegram that the Soviet system is not as strong as it appears to be on the surface. While maintained by the power of its ideology, Kennan believed that it was not as effective in providing the stability that could unite its people. Therefore, there was no reason to pressure the Soviet Union using political and military means. Doing so would be a waste of resources.

According to Kennan's logic, containment using excessive military means would only strengthen the internal cohesion of the Soviet Union. Such understanding can also be applied to the US North Korea policy, as it failed to bring about fractures within the North

Korean society itself. Kennan also expected internal fissions within the Communist Bloc. As was with the case of Yugoslavia, Kennan correctly predicted that China would also break away from the Soviet influence.

Kennan, best known for his role in establishing the policy of containment. He argued that communism will not spread if one can convince the people that capitalism will provide better living.

The problem, however, was that Kennan's plan required enormous funding. After spending astronomical sums in winning the Second World War, the United States now had to carry out expensive programs for reconstruction as well as for stimulating economic revivals in Europe and Asia. Although the United States was the only major power that did not suffer direct damage from World War II, it could not bear all this burden by itself. Kennan therefore adjusted his theory. He now sought to concentrate aid to a handful of strategically important places around the world.

Kennan designated give strategic regions around the globe. The United States and Great Britain formed the centers of Western Europe. Central Europe was centered on Germany. Japan and the Soviet Union also formed respective regions in Kennan's scheme. Kennan believed that the United States could be under substantial military and political threat even if just one of such regions outside of the Soviet Union itself went pro-Soviet. Kennan also believed that guaranteeing prosperity in the other four spheres would contain the expansion of the Soviet Union. He therefore insisted that the United States should focus its aid to Western and Central Europe and Japan to create core areas that could form the basis of a new capitalist world order that could outcompete the Soviet Union. Limiting the number of nations/regions that would receive aid also made the program feasible for the United States.

Kennan's containment theory began to be reflected in American foreign policy in 1947. The first task was to select the target nations for American aid. After extensive discussions, the US Joint Chiefs of Staff made the following conclusion:

21. In view of this general consideration of the areas of primary strategic importance to the United States in the event of ideological warfare, it appears that current assistance should be given if possible to the following countries arranged in order of their importance to our national security: 1. Great Britain, 2. France, 3. Germany, 4. Belgium, 5. Netherlands, 6. Austria, 7. Italy, 8. Canada, 9. Turkey, 10. Greece, 11. Latin America, 12. Spain, 13. Japan, 14. China, 15. Korea, 16. The Philippines. ...

31. An initial step in this study was to list the countries of the world to which assistance should be given in order of urgency-of need. For this purpose documents of the Department of State prepared in connection with a preliminary similar study- for the State-War-Navy Coordinating Committee have been consulted (J.C.S. 1769-SWNCC 360). These documents support the following listing of countries in order of the urgency of their need: 1. Greece, 2. Turkey, 3. Italy, 4. Iran, 5. Korea, 6. France, 7. Austria, 8. Hungary, 9. Great Britain, 10. Belgium, 11. Luxembourg, 12. Netherlands-N.E.I., 13. The Phillipines, 14. Portugal, 15. Czechoslovakia, 16. Poland, 17. Latin American Republics, 18. Canada.[2]

The Joint Chiefs of Staff submitted the report above to the State-War-Navy Coordinating Committee (SWNCC) in order to obtain final coordination.[3] The report lists Japan at number eight, right behind the nations of Western Europe. Greece and Turkey are the exceptions here, as they have been designated as strategically important in blocking Soviet advances to southern Europe and the Middle East. These two countries were also subjects of the Truman Doctrine of March 1947.

Because of Kennan's influence in determining priorities in containment and foreign aid, the nations outside of the list ended up receiving less attention than they did before. Korea was a representative case of a country that dropped down on the priority ladder despite the presence of the US troops in the country. The representative nations that the United States established military governments in after World War II were Japan, Germany, Austria, Italy, and Korea. While the first four nations were the defeated powers of the Second World War, Korea was not. Korea was seen as merely a colony of Japan. Korea was also the only country out of the five that was not included in the five strategic regions designated by Kennan. Based on these facts, Kennan most likely believed that Korea was a place the United States could abandon as long as Japan could be defended. Kennan believed that, as was the case before 1945, Japan should become a check against the Soviet Union in East Asia. In other words, Kennan wanted the United States to get out of Korea as soon as possible.[4]

Korea aid therefore became relatively sidelined in terms of geostrategic importance. This point can be seen in Korea's place in the report quoted above. While Korea ranked fifth in terms of "urgency" of need, Korea's final place was thirteenth. Such were the reasons why the United States could not actively aid Korea despite the establishment of an American military government there. The US military government south of the thirty-eighth parallel remained severely underfunded despite the pressing need for funds for governing southern Korea. The US military government had difficulty collecting taxes in the waves of postliberation turmoil, and Washington shied away from financial support. The US military government in Korea had no choice but to print more money. Expansion of the money supply soon resulted in massive inflation.

As can be seen in table 1, prices of commodities skyrocketed tenfold during the span of three years between liberation in 1945 to the establishment of the Republic of Korea (South Korea) in 1948. The fivefold expansion of the money supply played the most important role in stimulating such radical inflation during this period. The US military government soon had to abandon the free-market policy it implemented at the beginning of its rule and resort to controlling the supplies of vital commodities. Extreme inflation also turned the public opinion against the US military government. While the general strike of September 1946 and the Daegu Insurrection of October had to do with the Korean Communist Party's activities, they also were desperate responses to the worsening living conditions under the US military government's rule. Particularly bad were the shortages of rice, abandonment of free rice markets, and resumption of rice collection.

Despite the conditions in Korea, the US government began contemplating reducing its Korea aid. The first item of discussion was the withdrawal of American military forces in Korea. The

Table 1. Major economic indicators of the late 1940s

	Price index	Amount of currency in issue index
June 1945	2.5	52.6
August 1945	100.0	100.0
January 1946	116.5	111.5
March 1947	527.1	215.3
June 1948	957.1	376.0
September 1948	1059.4	387.4
June 1949	1185.9	494.7
September 1949	1527.1	597.0
December 1949	1705.3	893.6

Source: Kim Donguk, "1940~1950 nyeondae Hanguk ui inpeulleisyeon gwa anjeonghwa jeongchaek" (PhD diss., Yeonse Daehakgyo, 1995), 52.

maintenance of US forces abroad made up the largest portion of American foreign aid, and it exerted perhaps the largest pressure on the US government's finances. Given the level of priority of Korea at the time, it was natural that the United States government began contemplating withdrawing American forces from Korea.

Furthermore, there were assertions that the stationing of American forces in Korea was problematic from the perspective of military strategy. Because of Korea's mountainous topography and cold winters, the US Joint Chiefs of Staff believed that Korea was an unfavorable location to fight the Soviet Union. Americans would be at a disadvantage in Korea in fighting the Soviets forces, which were trained in cold and harsh terrains.

Of course, a more basic reason was the legitimacy of the occupation itself. The fundamental reason why the Soviet and American forces occupied Korea was to obtain surrender from the Japanese forces on the Korean Peninsula. The establishments of Korean regimes in 1948 therefore made the continued stationing of the US forces difficult to justify. With the withdrawal of the Soviet forces from Korea in 1948, Washington was left without a choice.

A noteworthy assertion on this issue is that the withdrawal of the American forces from Korea had to do with the threat of northward advance on the part of Syngman Rhee. If the US forces were stationed in South Korea at the time of the northward attack from the South Korean forces, not only would the United States become involved in a war, the United States would be subjected to international criticism for aiding an aggressor nation. The mobilization of the United Nations would also become impossible.

This assertion can also be considered together with the American policy of limiting the size of the South Korean military forces. As can be seen in the National Security Council Report 8 (NSC-8), Washington forbade South Korea from having more than an eighty-thousand-man army and navy. The South Korean air force, founded by Syngman Rhee, was also scaled down by Washington. As the South Korean forces were maintained by American aid at the time, it was impossible for Seoul to create additional military units or increase the size of its forces without American acquiescence. While the South Korean air force was formed in 1950, it was not created with official US recognition. These policies can be interpreted as an effort on the part of Washington to obstruct the attempts of northward advance from South Korea.

The decision to withdraw from South Korea became official. The problem, however, was the condition of South Korea. Could it survive on its own without additional safeguards? That was the main concern of the United States at the time. While the Republic of Korea (South Korea) was established in 1948, it could not even hold an election on Jeju Island due to the April 3 Insurrection. The Yeosun Incident of September showed that even its army could not be entirely trusted. While staunchly anticommunist Syngman Rhee became South Korea's president, the National Assembly had a substantial number of independent assemblymen who did not always agree with Rhee's virulent anticommunism. They threatened the members of the police who had a history of collaboration with the Japanese by forming the Committee of Antinational Activities (Banmin Teugwi). Some assemblymen even submitted a resolution for the withdrawal of American forces from Korea.

The US State Department believed that there was a substantial chance that the South Korean government could collapse from the inside. It also believed that the withdrawal of the US forces at the time South Korea was facing militarily superior North Korea was no different from allowing the entire Korean Peninsula to fall into communist hands. Another problem here was the dispositions of the Koreans themselves:

> The efforts of the U.S. to foster the establishment of a democratic and sovereign government in Korea are handicapped by the political immaturity of the Korean people. The tendency of Korean political elements to polarize into extremes of right and left and to pursue their ends through the use of violence acts as a serious deterrent to the achievement of political stability on a democratic basis in Korea.[5]

While withdrawal of the US forces from Korea became inevitable due to the establishment of the Republic of Korea and the withdrawal of Soviet forces, different agencies of the US government started to disagree on the appropriate timing of the withdrawal. While the State Department wanted to delay it as long as possible, the Joint Chiefs of Staff wanted just the opposite. NSC-8 was released during this process of contention. Submitted on April 24, 1948, this document notes three primary American goals in Korea.

> (1) To establish a united, self-governing, and sovereign Korea as soon as possible, independent of foreign control and eligible for membership in the UN.
> (2) To ensure that the national government so established shall be fully representative of the freely expressed will of the Korean people.
> (3) To assist the Korean people in establishing a sound economy and educational system as essential bases of an independent and democratic state.
> To these may be added the derivative objective of terminating the military commitment of the U.S. in Korea as soon as practicable consistent with the foregoing objectives.[6]

The "broad objectives" listed in NSC-8 display the US Korea policy's characteristics well. First, the United States sought to establish a pro-American regime for the entire Korean Peninsula even at the time when separate regimes were coming into place. The expression "united, self-governing" clearly illustrates this goal, which became the context of the American decision to move the United Nations forces across the thirty-eighth parallel in October 1950 after the success of the Incheon Landing.

Second, the United States wanted to establish a state independent from the major powers surrounding Korea. Of course, the major powers here not only included the Soviet Union but also Japan. The United States government had been expressing its intention to establish a state independent from the influence of Japan since 1945. While such an objective collided with the Department of Defense and the Joint Chiefs of Staff's goal of establishing a Japan-centered regional order in Asia, it continues to reappear in US policy papers right into 1950.

Third, the US forces in Korea were to be withdrawn from the Korean Peninsula. While this goal is added as a secondary objective to the three primary goals, it nevertheless shows that the withdrawal itself was important. It shows that the withdrawal of the US forces in Korea could not be delayed any longer given the conditions within Korea as well as US global policy.

NSC-8 also emphasizes the need to solve Korean issues through the United Nations. This is also a particularity of the US-Korea relationship as well. Beyond the bilateral relationship, the United States sought to maintain a façade of legality in its intervention through the United Nations. While the 1953 mutual defense treaty between the United States and South Korea established direct relationship in military matters, the US intervention in Korea thereafter still often wore the mask of the United Nations.

Organizations such as the United Nations Temporary Commission on Korea (UNTCOK), the United Nations Commission on Korea (UNCOK), the United Nations Committee for the Unification and Rehabilitation of Korea (UNCURK), and the United Nations Korean Reconstruction Agency (UNKRA) are good examples of American intervention in Korea that took place under UN cover. The United States also dispatched its forces under the United Nations banner in the Korean War, and the United Nations Command is maintained to this day despite the reduction of its duties to that of armistice maintenance. Not only did the United States seek to acquire an aura of legality for its actions in Korea, it also sought to justify its Korea policy through the United Nations.

Considering the pattern, there is a strong chance that the United States will utilize the United Nations in solving the nuclear issue in

North Korea. This may be the biggest difference between the Iraq case and the North Korea case–whether or not the United Nations (and the international community) are involved. Probable involvement of the international community in the North Korean case may also make the use of extreme measures unlikely, as China will not tolerate unilateral American actions against North Korea.

Under these goals, the United States withdrew its forces from Korea in June 1949. While a five-hundred-man military advisory group remained in order to provide training to the South Korean forces, the regular forces withdrew entirely. The one-year span from June 1949 to June 1950 was the only time since 1945 to the present day that US forces did not remain stationed in Korea. But as can be seen from the US policy objectives above, withdrawal of its forces did not mean an end of American interest in Korea, which the United States maintained through other methods.

2. Massive Aid

A substantial change occurred in US Korea policy with the establishment of the Republic of Korea. Along with the withdrawal of US forces, the American Mission in Korea (AMIK) was established.[7] Responsibility for Korea aid was also transferred to the Economic Cooperation Administration (ECA). The AMIK was in a "country team" form, as were most American missions abroad. The AMIK was largely made up of three core components: the United States Embassy in Seoul, the ECA Korea division headquarters, and the Korean Military Advisory Group (KMAG). Each component was to report, respectively, to the US Department of State, the ECA headquarters, and the US Department of Defense. The United States ambassador to Korea John J. Muccio was to oversee AMIK as a whole.

An important aspect of the US Korea policy at this time was Korea aid, as described in NSC-8. The amount of aid was to be $185 million, and the objective of aid was to stimulate "rehabilitation," not just "relief." "Relief" refers to supplying consumer goods to help a region overcome damages inflicted by war or natural disasters. "Rehabilitation," on the other hand, refers to aid aimed at creating a self-sustaining and viable economy of its own. "Rehabilitation" entails aiding capital goods.

A day after the Republic of Korea's establishment, on August 16, 1948, President Truman ordered the US government's departments to determine which organization could best carry out the program for Korea aid. Through Arthur C. Bunce's research,[8] Truman ordered the transferring of responsibility for Korea aid from the US Army to the ECA. This move meant that the Korea aid was to be carried out at the level of the Marshall Plan.[9] The Department of State first submitted a three-year plan for Korea aid to the ECA.[10] When the responsibility of Korea aid was finally transferred to the ECA, effective January 1, 1949, research projects on economic conditions in Korea and the actualization of Korea aid began in February 1949.

Korea aid was increased to $196 million in NSC-8/1, submitted on March 16, 1949. NSC-8/1 also defined the need to legislate a Korea aid plan for the 1950 fiscal year and extend and actualize the yearlong aid plan for 1949 into a three-year one. NSC-8/2 also added in technological aid as well as efforts for increasing efficacy in exchange programs in information, culture, and education.

The ECA was initially formed as an organization under the direct control of the president to execute the Marshall Plan in Europe. Unlike programs such as the United Nations Relief and Rehabilitation Administration (UNRRA) and Government and Relief in Occupied Areas (GARIOA) that focused on providing relief to the damages of war–such programs fall within the boundary of defense aid, not economic aid–the ECA focused on providing capital goods and facilities in order to stimulate recovery.[11]

The nature of ECA aid to Korea reveals itself in the speeches high American officials gave to Congress. President Truman made it clear that Korea aid sought recovery, not merely relief. Truman argued that only recovery can create a self-supporting economy in Korea, and that Korea aid was going to reach the level of US aid in Europe.[12] Furthermore, Deputy Secretary of State James E. Webb, in his congressional speech, argued that investment in Korea would be "capital investment."[13] The ECA president Paul G. Hoffman made it clear in his testimony at the Senate that the ECA activities aimed for recovery, not just relief.

Until 1948, the ECA was only responsible for China in its activities in Asia. The program for relief in US–occupied Japan was under the Department of Defense. After the communist victory in China in September 1949, Korea became the only country receiving ECA aid and support in Asia. The ECA gradually sought to expand its coverage to Southeast Asia.

In order to secure necessary funds for Korea aid, all unused funds initially designated for recovery in the occupied areas were transferred to the ECA through Public Law No. 793. Then the United States carried out research of economic conditions in South Korea. Research on South Korean economy were carried out by the advisors of the Day & Zimmermann company, who were asked to do so by the Syngman Rhee protégé Preston Goodfellow, as well as US army technicians, who researched electric power, the Allis-Charlmers company, which researched tungsten mines, and members from the Pittsburgh station of the US Bureau of Mines, who researched the coal mines. The ECA also carried out its own research on the ground from March 11, 1949, to March 28, 1949.

The research and planning for Korea aid that took place beginning in February 1949 soon bore fruit. The detailed plan was laid out by April, and the designated amount of aid was submitted to the Department of Treasury. After receiving its approval, the plan for Korea aid was finally confirmed through reviews of the reports to be submitted to the Department of State and Congress.

The final amount provided was $150 million, which was substantially less than the amount designated in NSC-8/1 ($195 million). Because of its failure to receive initial ratification from Congress in 1949, the final amount was further reduced to $120 million when it finally received ratification in 1950.[14] The detailed plan, as prepared by the ECA, is listed in table 2.

There are several noteworthy points in the plan. First, aid for recovery made up a large portion of the overall budget. Only food, fertilizer, agricultural pesticides, petroleum-based products, and medicine were included as "relief" aid, among which petroleum-based products were also intended to increase the production of the rubber industry.[15] In all, "relief" aid did not make up more than 35 percent of the total aid plan. On the other hand, items related to "recovery" aid amounted to more than 50 percent of the overall aid in raw materials, half-finished goods, industrial equipment, supplies, recovery plan, investigation plan, technological assistance, and expenditures of administration (the ECA administration costs).

Second, foods and textiles were not part of the aid plan for the fiscal year 1951. This shows that the ECA Korea plan was aiming to increase textile and food production in South Korea through supplying agricultural pesticides and fertilizers and increasing the Japanese-made textile plants' rate of operations. The ECA was planning to make South Korea self-sufficient in food and textile production.

Third, items for the recovery plan made up more than a quarter of all aid in capital goods. Based on the data reported to the US Congress, construction of fishing boats made up the largest portion of the recovery plan's budget, followed by electricity, cement plants, railroad construction, coal carriers, construction of roads and bridges, land reclamation, and communication.[16]

Another interesting aspect of the recovery plan is that a

Table 2. Overall ECA aid program (unit: 1 dollar)

	1950 budget	1951 budget	Difference
Food	119,000 (0.09%)	–	−119,000
Fertilizer and pesticide	32,851,000(27.3%)	42,223,000	9,372,600
Petroleum-based products	7,862,000(6.5%)	4,670,000	−3,182,000
Medicinal products	226,000 (0.18%)	–	−326,000
Raw materials and half-finished goods	27,702,000(23.1%)	19,292,400	−8,409,600
Industrial equipment and supplies	3,973,000(0.3%)	2,765,000	−1,208,000
Recovery plan	33,958,000(28.2%)	25,085,000	−8,873,000
Investigation plan	1,980,000(1.6%)	↘1,625,000	−355,000
Technological assistance	3,512,000(2.9%)	2,779,000	−633,000
Ocean freight	55,244,000(4.4%)	60,000	−5,184,000
Administrative expenditures	1,650,000	1,500,000	−150,000
Reserve fund	923,000	–	−923,000
Total	120,000,000	100,000,000	−20,000,000

Source: Hong Seongyu, *Hanguk gyeongje ui jabon chukjeok gwajeong* (Seoul: Goryeo Daehakgyo Asea Munje Yeonguso, 1965), 282.

substantial investment was made for the purchase of fishing boats. Such a policy aimed at increasing the amount of fish caught in order to stimulate South Korean exports to Japan while reducing South Korea's trade deficit with that country. The noticeably high portions of the budget taken up by fertilizers and pesticides, as can be seen in table 2, also suggest that the ECA was going to push South Korea beyond self-sufficiency. The ECA was even foreseeing Korean food exports to Japan.

Investments related to social overhead capital (SOC) also take up a substantial portion of the aid plan. Construction of railroads, electricity, and communication are relevant items here, and they constitute the foundation for the success of the recovery plan. The ECA also had ambitious plans for construction of cement and fertilizer plants. Its biggest priority was the construction of fertilizer plants. A substantial sum also was to be invested in the development of coal mines. Greater coal output would increase the generation of electricity, ultimately allowing construction and operation of fertilizer plants. Construction of railroads was also discussed in tandem with the transportation plans for coal and fertilizers. The ECA was planning to complete the construction of its fertilizer plant by the fiscal year 1952.[17]

While it is questionable whether or not the ECA plan was feasible, the designated objectives at the time were the following:

- rice production: 2.3 million tons in 1948, 2.7 million tons in 1950, and 2.8 million tons in 1952.
- power production: 50 million kW in 1948, 82 million kW in 1950, and 120 million kW in 1952. Without much change in waterpower, the amount of power generated by barges was to increase by two to three times and thermal power was to increase by three times.
- anthracite production: 75,000 tons in 1948, 140,000 tons in 1950, and 230,000 tons in the fiscal year 1951 (production of bituminous coal, in contrast, was going to be reduced).
- fishing production: Recover to the 1940 level. 550,000 tons by 1952, which is twice as much as in 1948.

Ultimately, the ECA plan aimed to create a self-sustaining economy in South Korea through its recovery plan. It was to be carried over a three-year span from the latter half of 1949 to the first half of 1952.

3. Economic and Psychological Containment—the Starting Point for Korea Policy

Why did the United States plan such massive aid? Was South Korea that important to the United States? Did the United States have a certain economic interest in South Korea? To find answers, we must start with the particularities of the US Korea policy itself.

The United States government planned a program for South Korean economic recovery from late 1946 to early 1967, and it was to take place under the policy for decolonization.

> a. The ultimate objective of the United States with respect to Korea is to foster conditions which will bring about the establishment of a free and independent nation capable of taking her place as a responsible and peaceful member of the family of nations. The achievement of this objective will require the progressive elimination of all vestiges of Japanese control over Korean economic and political life and the eventual substitution of independent Korean governmental, economic and social institutions. ...
> c. You will make it clear to the Korean population that your administration of civil affairs in Korea is intended principally:
> (1) To insure compliance with the surrender by the Japanese armed forces in Korea;
> (2) To effect a complete political and administrative separation of Korea from Japan and to free Korea from Japanese social, economic and financial control;
> (3) To facilitate the development of a, sound Korean economy devoted to peaceful pursuits.[18]

Based on this policy, the US military government in Korea devised a plan for independent industrial development in southern Korea. Industrialization plans that were developed by the economic advisor to the US military government Arthur Bunce in February 1946 as well as the plan developed by a special committee in February 1947

all stem from the abovementioned policy philosophy.[19] Of course,
due to the failure of the military government's economic policy,
the recovery plan was not carried out at all. Furthermore, given
the impending end of its rule with the international trusteeship
or establishment of a new Korean government, the US military
government was not in a position to actively carry out a program of
economic development. Even so, the US Korea policy continued to
seek ways of creating an independent and self-sustaining (postcolonial)
economic structure in Korea by severing the economic connection
between South Korea and Japan.

Considering the abovementioned aspects of US Korea policy,
Bruce Cumings's assertion that the US policy in Asia resulted in
a resurrection of colonial relations after World War II should be
revised.[20] While Cumings's assertion makes sense when one considers
the American strategy of regional consolidation *after* 1950, the US
policy up to the Korean War displays substantial differences. Of
course, the United States reverted to the so-called reverse course
that sought Japan's remilitarization and economic revival in 1948.
The "reverse course," however, did not immediately translate into a
Japan-centered strategy of regional consolidation.

On the contrary, President Truman actively pursued a program
for economic recovery in Korea and did not consider South Korea
as an economic extension of Japan. President Truman suggested the
following four points in his message to Congress on June 7, 1949,
before the House overview of Korea aid. Here's a summary of his
four points:

1. The Korean Peninsula is in fact a "testing ground" in which
democratic ideals in South Korea compete with North Korea's
communism.
2. South Korea's survival and progress towards a self-sustaining and
stable economy will broadly influence the people of Asia.
3. The case of South Korea will inspire the people exposed to
communist propaganda in South Asia, Southeast Asia, and the Pacific
Islands.
4. The understanding that the success of democracy and adamancy of
South Korea can serve the function of a "lighthouse" for the people
of North Asia in their struggle against communism.[21]

President Truman's plan for massive Korean aid was also connected to the so-called Point Four plan, which was revealed in his New Year's speech to the nation in January 1949.[22] The core idea of this plan was to provide technological support to the underdeveloped regions of the world. The logic of the Point Four plan was based on an understanding that the economic recovery plan for Europe can also be applied to underdeveloped nations. That is why this plan was also called "the Asian Marshall Plan."

Officials who constructed the ECA aid program with President Truman also had a positive stance towards massive economic aid to South Korea. This point is also evident in the discussions held at the House Commission on Foreign Relations. Edgar A. J. Johnson, the ECA division director who was also responsible for its Korea plan, testified that Korea had a substantial number of factories and equipment left behind by the Japanese that were still underutilized at the time. He argued that only about a half of all factories in South Korea were in use, and the rate could go up to around 80 percent with the supply of new equipment from the United States.[23] Of course, it is questionable whether or not such assessment of the South Korean economy was objective. We also do not know whether or not such an opinion was representative of all US officials working on South Korea.

There were several reasons why Truman and the State Department officials so strongly emphasized ECA aid. First, President Truman and the State Department officials were well aware that, without such aid, South Korea could collapse from the inside. This aspect is perhaps the most important in understanding the ECA aid plan. Military and economic aid listed in the NSC-8 series were also aimed at preventing the self-destruction of South Korea.[24] The US CIA also evaluated, "When the Rhee Government took over responsibility for the infant Republic of Korea, thoughts in the United States began to turn to a more positive aid programme which would assist in making the newly created republic progressively less dependent on foreign subsidization, would make it into a factor of stability in Asia, and into 'a display window of democracy.'"[25]

Second, the US Korea aid, in a way, was a response to North Korean economic development. The United States at the time was under pressure due to the ongoing North Korean economic growth and development, and it most likely felt the need to stimulate economic growth and development in the South. Although limited, the US government at the time nevertheless believed that the North Korean economy was substantially developing.[26] This also was an important ideological and psychological reason to fund economic recovery and development in South Korea. An official who worked for the United Nations Commission for the Unification and Rehabilitation of Korea (UNCURK) explained the US Korea policy by saying that the United States sought to transform South Korea into a force of stability in Asia through aid plans. The United States ultimately wanted to transform South Korea into "a display window of democracy."[27]

Third, another important factor at play was the need to reduce the burden upon the US government's budget. The Truman Doctrine, the Marshall Plan, and the recovery plan for Japan exerted enormous pressure on US government finances. As already mentioned, financial pressure was the main factor that caused the US government to prioritize its aid targets. The pressure became more acute in late 1948 when the US economy started to show signs of trouble. The US government was under even more pressure to reduce aid.

The Department of State and the ECA's programmers for Korea aid believed that, while it would initially be a financial burden, creating a self-sustaining South Korea would ultimately reduce America's burdens in the long run. Calling himself a "businessman" rather than a bureaucrat, the ECA president Paul Hoffman stated that his focus was to reduce aid from a businessman's perspective. He argued that the ECA aid for Korea would go down to $35 million by 1953.[28] Truman also argued that it is in American national interest to elevate the living standards in aid-receiving countries such as South Korea.[29] Such thinking on the part of Truman was revived by Walt Rostow in the 1960s.

Although a bit late in timing, the US government began to carry out the ECA recovery aid beginning in early 1950. Table 3 shows the uses of aid money in the latter part of 1949 (the first part of the 1950 fiscal year).

Looking at table 3, one can see that the amount of aid for recovery is substantially less than the planned amount. The initial

Table 3. ECA aid uses in the latter half of 1949 (the first half of the 1950 fiscal year) (unit: 1 million dollars)

Items	Amount of aid
Fish	0.2
Fertilizer and pesticide	23
Petroleum-based products	5.8
Medicinal products	0.226
Raw materials and half-finished goods	13
Industrial equipment and supplies	1.4
Recovery plan	5.5
Investigation plan	0.978
Technological assistance	2.4
Overseas freight	5.7
ECA administrative expenses	1.5
Others	0.175
Total	60

Source: Daehan Minguk Gongbocheo, "Gyeongje wonjo wa saneop geonseolchaek," *Jubo* 58, May 11, 1950.

sum designated for the ECA plan for the 1950 fiscal year was $33,958,000. The amount spent, however, was only $5,500,000. Of course, research and planning do take up a significant amount in the beginning phase of recovery programs. The amount, however, is still radically smaller than what was projected. The 1949 rejection at Congress and the problem of inflation played major roles here.

While the overall amount was cut down, as can be seen in table 4, the recovery plan still was carried out as planned. Looking at the details, the funds were concentrated in key areas in social overhead capital, including bridge building, railroad construction, farmland development, water control, power plant construction, and coal carrier introduction; export industry support, including the development of mines and purchasing of fishing boats; and import substitution projects, including construction of cement factories and fertilizer plants.

Another noteworthy point is that the plan for the construction of fertilizer plants was moved early into the fiscal year 1950.

Table 4. Actual uses of the recovery plan (unit: 1 million dollars)

Items	Expenditures
Danyang wind power plant	▄ 1.25
Sangdong tungsten mine	▄▄▄ 3.34
Dangan-ri power plant boiler	▄ 0.74
Bridge construction	▄▄▄▄▄▄▄▄▄▄ 10.99
Irrigation works	▄▄▄▄▄ 5.89
Salt pond construction	▄ 0.66
Coal mine	▄▄▄▄▄ 5.94
15,000 kW power plant	▄▄ 2.8
30,000 kW power plant	▄▄ 2.24
Seomjin River hydroelectric power plant	▄▄▄▄ 5.32
Railroad construction	▄▄▄▄▄▄ 7.63
Fishing boats	▄▄▄▄▄▄ 7.05
Cement plant service expenditures	▄ 0.5
Fertilizer plant service expenditures	▄ 1
Total	50

Source: Same as table 3.

Bukpyeong was considered as the site for construction, and the new plant was to produce some three hundred thousand tons of fertilizer per year (around one-third of the demand in South Korea at the time). The expenses would to amount to $382,000 in 1950, $7,000,000 in 1951, and $13,918,000 in 1952. Discussions for an additional $6 million to $7 million for the fertilizer plant project were taking place in May 1950.[30]

4. The Reason Why ECA Aid Failed

In the end, however, the ECA plan for Korea was never carried out as planned. There were several important reasons at play here. First, the plan for Korea was severely hampered when it initially failed to receive ratification from the Congress. While both the Senate and House committees on foreign relations accepted the ECA aid plan, it failed to garner enough votes in both the Senate and the House.[31] Korea aid was therefore enacted through another budget bill. For the $150 million proposal submitted by the ECA for the 1950 fiscal year, the Senate and the House passed a third expenditures budget called "H.R. 5360" on October 6, and $30 million from it were set aside for Korea. The ECA planned to spend a total of $60 million for Korea aid from July 1949 to February 15, 1950.[32] In conclusion, the ECA plan could not be carried out as planned until the budget proposal of $100 million was passed by the US Congress on June 5, 1950.[33]

One of the reasons why the American lawmakers at the time saw the Korea aid plan in a negative light was their concern that investment towards Korea may overlap with that of Japan in Northeast Asia. Those with a pro-Chinese Nationalist stance also questioned the issue of equity between US support towards South Korea and US support towards the Republic of China (Taiwan).

The problem of overlap was most strongly asserted by the Department of Defense, which was in charge of the occupation of Japan at this time. Headed by General Douglas MacArthur, US forces occupied Japan until 1951. Undersecretary of the Army William H. Draper and the MacArthur command, in particular, strongly argued for a Japan-centered regional order.[34]

Such discussions began to appear on US policy papers starting from late 1949. This was also the time China went communist, stimulating important and sweeping changes in US foreign policy. Such changes are most evident in the NSC-48 series that comprehensively defined the American Asia policy. The sections on economy at 48/1 and 48/2 included plans to transform the economic order in Asia centered on Japan and India.[35]

The policy papers that intensified the discussions can be found in the NSC-61 series, submitted by Assistant Secretary of the Army Tracy Voorhees. NSC-61 argued most strongly for a Japan-centered reorientation of Asian economy. The core idea of NSC-61 was for Japan to be the location for the purchase of aid commodities in Asia, providing the bulk of aid dollars to Japan. It essentially displays a perspective for the regional integration of Asian economies centered on Japan.

Voorhees also dispatched a team of researchers to East Asia in

January 1950. The researchers further worked on NSC-61 after visiting eleven Asian nations, including Japan and South Korea, over a period of approximately two months. The team suggested reorganizing and adjusting production structures of different Asian countries for the purpose of vertical integration among them, using aid as a means to stimulate such regional integration and establishing a centralized headquarters that could manage US aid for Asia as a whole.

A Korea-related point discussed was the construction of fertilizer plants in South Korea, pushed forth by the ECA. Stanley Andrews, a foreign relations expert of the US Department of Agriculture and a member of the research team organized by Voorhees, argued against what he considered to be the inefficient waste of reducing Japanese fertilizer exports for the sake of increasing fertilizer production in South Korea. He argued for a comprehensive regional view over nation-specific goals. Combining the ECA aid and the Point Four, Export-Import Bank of the United States, and World Bank loans, Stanley argued that $100 million would be enough for South Korea for the fiscal year 1950-51.[36] His assertion was in effect a refutation of the ECA's Korea plan.

The NSC-48 series, the NSC-61 series, and Andrews all envisioned a Japan-centered regional order. Their core idea is that, given the "loss" of China and Manchuria, there was a need to transform other parts of Asia into Japan's economic "backyards" in order to reconstruct Japan as the center of Asia. Voorhees wanted more than 70 percent of all aid goods for Korea to be produced in Japan. The plan to construct fertilizer plants in Korea, of course, did not make sense to him given the existing productive capacity of Japan.

This issue was also discussed in the US Congress. At the Senate Commission on Foreign Relations in 1949, Senator Elbert D. Thomas of Utah argued that Japan should become the center of Asia and that the economies of South Korea and Taiwan should be considered as supplements to the Japanese economy.[37] The same issue became a topic of discussion at the House Committee on Foreign Affairs in March 1950 over the budget of the 1951 fiscal year. Voorhees argued that the plan should be rethought as a comprehensive picture of the economies of Japan and South Korea, and Bunce responded by saying that Japan-made products would account for about 36 percent of all South Korean imports (some $50 million) and much of the ECA aid goods for Korea would be procured in Japan.[38]

The US officials working on the ground in South Korea also presented their opinions on the matter. David M. Bane, who worked on South Korea-Japan trade negotiations, argued that there was little chance of the Korean economy acquiring self-sustenance even if US aid continued after the end of the ECA plan in 1952. Not only was there a slim chance of unification in Korea, Bane also argued that substantial private investments would not take place given the instability in the country. The ECA plan to transform Korea from an agricultural economy to an industrial one, therefore, was a misguided one. Bane argued that the most efficient option was economic integration with Japan.

Bunce and his men, however, presented a memorandum arguing against this position. They contended that the South Korean economy could create a basis for self-sustenance with ECA Korea aid by 1952, holding that the existing facilities and equipment in textiles, machinery, and excavation south of the thirty-eighth parallel made for a substantial potential for industrial development in South Korea. They also argued that, instead of being an effort to hastily transform an agricultural economy into an industrial one, the ECA plan was merely aiming to take full advantage of the existing industrial potential, equipment, and domestic resources already available in South Korea. On the point of economic integration with Japan, they argued that resumed Japanese influence over Korea would generate widespread resistance in the country. Koreans, they argued, may even choose Soviet protection instead of being dominated by the Japanese again.[39]

In the end, discussions surrounding the ECA aid ended with the victory of Truman, the Department of State, and Bunce. A Japan-centered regional strategy was not yet in place at this time, as evident in the rejection of NSC-61's proposal to concentrate US Asia aid on Japan. Therefore, the release of NSC-61/1 was limited to the part on creating an aid coordinating organization, a reflection of the US State Department's wariness that the resurgence of Japan would have negative political and psychological effects on other

Asian nations. The State Department felt uncomfortable with Japan-centered aid so soon after World War II. Therefore, it was not until the mid-1950s, when it experienced a revival of its economy through the Korean War, that Japan resumed its trade and aid vis-à-vis Asia.

The second reason why the ECA Korea aid was not carried out as planned was the level of inflation in South Korea. The inflation problem of the US military government in Korea was not solved with the South Korean government's establishment. As can be seen in table 1, inflation was the most serious social problem of the US military government era. Without sufficient financial support from Washington, the US military government in Korea had no choice but to print more money.

The vicious inflation carried over to the South Korean government, which also could not find a solution to the problem of inflation. In order to curb inflation, it needed to stop the overprinting of money at the same time increasing the supply of daily necessities. In other words, the South Korean government needed to increase its tax base while expanding its manufacturing facilities. Given the instability of the postliberation era, however, it was impossible for the South Korean government to secure a steady tax base.

The number of unemployed overflowed, and the factories could not operate properly due to the shortage of technicians as well as resources. The severing of connections with Japan in 1945 resulted in the loss of Japanese technicians and resources. The South Korean government then tried to sell the "enemy property" of the Japanese settlers who were living in Korea before the surrender. Even that did not go well.

Enemy property was one of the South Korean government's most valuable assets. Japanese properties in southern Korea were confiscated by the US military government through ordinance number 33 in December 1945, and they were later transferred to the South Korean government with its establishment in 1948. In the negotiations between South Korea and Japan during the 1950s, the Japanese delegation argued that the confiscation of Japanese property in Korea went against the body of international laws promulgated through the 1907 Hague Conference. The Japanese demanded their return, and the battle over this issue raged on between the two countries for the next decade.

While the South Korean government sought to sell enemy property, there were not enough people in Korea who had sufficient funds to buy them at the time. The South Korean government had an even harder time getting businessmen to buy its confiscated factories given the unstable supply of resources and the large pool of unemployed who continued to depress the consumer market.

In the end, vicious inflation continued into the 1950s. The ECA aid could not be carried out as planned, as its plan would have entailed a substantial increase in the money supply. While the Syngman Rhee government prepared a five-year economic development plan of its own, it also could not be carried out due to inflation. The US government criticized Rhee's plan as incohesive as well as unrealistic.

Inflation in South Korea was a social problem dating from the US military government era. The US State Department, however, saw it as a specific problem of the South Korean government itself and believed that it could result in the South Korean government's collapse. The US government understood the 1949 defeat of the Chinese Nationalists in mainland China in a similar fashion. It saw similar signs in the South Korean government under Syngman Rhee and believed that the South Korean failure to curb inflation in late 1949 placed the regime under the threat of collapse.[40] The United States therefore strongly urged the Syngman Rhee government to stabilize its finances.

In January 1950, a collective economy commission between the United States and South Korea became established with the goal of curbing South Korea's vicious inflation. The commission declared fifteen principles for economic stability in March 1950, aiming to check government expenditures and money supply in order to curb inflation. Having succeeded in a similar program in Japan, the United States government sought to apply the same principles to South Korea. The South Korean government revised its budget accordingly, and the South Korean minister of finances released a statement declaring that its recovery plan would be adjusted as well.[41]

The Korea Bank Act also was meant to contribute to this

economic stabilization policy. Coming into effect in February 1950, the Korea Bank Act was devised by an expert in the US Federal Reserve Bank. Its main long-term aim was to stabilize the value of currency, and by consistently maintaining a reserve fund, it sought to control and standardize credit control activities in the short term.[42]

Inflation in South Korea started to stabilize. While the rise of rice prices could not be stopped, the problems of the budget deficit and the expansion of the money supply started to come under control. Military expenses were sharply cut, and the amount of collected taxes began to soar with increased efficiency in tax collection. The money supply decreased from around 74 trillion won in January 1950 to around 55 trillion won in June 1950.[43]

Furthermore, the ECA positively evaluated the growths of Korean industry during the first quarter of 1950. Compared against 1947, the ECA found that South Korean industry grew by 80 percent. It also judged that, despite the rising price of rice, the food supply in South Korea had become sustainable. The ECA also saw a substantial increase of productions in fishing, mining, electricity, textiles, railroad construction, agriculture, and exports.[44]

Once the problem of inflation began to stabilize, the South Korean government began to use the counterpart fund for its recovery plan as well as loans and subsidies for industrial reconstruction. Due to the 1948 Comprehensive Agreement regarding Economic Technical Assistance between the United States and South Korea, the counterpart fund could not be used without American consent. These funds were generally used to cover government deficits until early 1950 for the purpose of reducing the money supply and checking inflation. With inflation coming under control in early 1950, the counterpart fund could now be used for the purposes of economic recovery and industrial development.

Bunce, who was an economic advisor of the US military government in Korea and the head of the ECA delegation to Korea after the South Korean government's establishment, allowed the counterpart fund to be used in eighteen projects as either loans or subsidies. The projects included railroad construction, irrigation works, development of mines, building of thermoelectric and hydroelectric power plants, water control, purchasing of fishing supplies, and production of peat. The amount was around 10 trillion won. About 3.5 trillion was to be distributed as direct subsidies to government–controlled companies as dictated by the ECA delegation and the rest was to be distributed as loans through the South Korean government agencies and banks. Of course, distribution was to cease in case inflation soared. The uses of counterpart funds included foundation work for the building of mines as well as cement and fertilizer plants.[45]

Breaking out within a month after the ECA plan's beginning was actually announced, the Korean War made its execution impossible. Looking at the records of counterpart funds used after ECA aid ended, it is evident that the ECA plan was not carried out as planned. Looking at the Bank of Korea's research in 1954 after the war's end, while none of the funds were spent on the military, most were used to compensate for the South Korean government's deficit. Only around 5 percent (1.03 million Korean hwan) was used for the economic recovery plan, and they were concentrated on the rebuilding of airfields and ports, production and development of peat, management of fishery resources, and the recovery of shipbuilding. Such numbers show that the Korean War's breakout irreversibly obstructed the ECA plan in South Korea.[46]

With the Korean War's breakout, the United States transferred all Korea aid activities to the United Nations Command. Under the conditions of war, US aid to Korea changed to a military-based aid. All Korea aid was now carried out by the United Nations Civil Assistance Corps Korea (UNCACK). And despite the name "civil assistance," its activities largely concentrated on military-related matters.

Considering the US Korea policy at the time, we can be confident that the assertions that the withdrawal of the US forces in June 1949 meant an American abandonment of South Korea or that the United States sought to induce the communist attack through the withdrawal of its forces are false. While the American withdrawal on the one hand represents the conditions of the US global strategy at the time–which could not strongly commit to South Korea– the real reason that the United States chose to withdraw its forces from South Korea was that it could no longer legitimize stationing them there with the South Korean government's establishment and the withdrawal of Soviet forces from North Korea. Moreover, the United States displayed its strong commitment to South Korea through the ECA plan.

While several factors caused the delay of the ECA plan, and the Korean War's breakout caused its ultimate fall, it is nevertheless significant for a number of reasons. First, it shows that the United States was not committed to re-creating a Japan-centered regional order prior to 1950. The ECA plan included components that overlapped with Japan's industrial policy, and that is the reason why so many of the Department of Defense officials who played a role in the occupation of Japan resisted it. Industrial development (such as the building of fertilizer plants) in South Korea meant a loss of market for Japanese economic growth. The US government nevertheless pushed for it, only to be stopped by the Korean War.

Second, although never fully carried out, the ECA plan shows the two policy objectives the United States had established in South Korea at the time. One was that the Korean Peninsula was to become an ideological battleground between the two types of systems in the Cold War's context. Another was that, despite its commitment, Washington felt the need to reduce its burden in supporting South Korea. The former becomes more evident after the 1960s, and the latter becomes clearer after the Korean War with the New Look policy. The latter, in particular, was carried out as a way of transferring the American burden to Japan in the context of a Japan-centered regional order and the strengthening of the alliance between Japan and the United States.

Third, it shows yet another instance of the US Korea policy being delayed or obstructed due to the internal conditions of Korea. If the US military government's policy up to 1948 failed due to the dynamic relationships between the various political forces in southern Korea at the time, the ECA plan was delayed due to South Korea's internal instability and obstructed because of the breakout of the Korean War.

Considering the Korean Peninsula's conditions today, we can easily perceive how effective (and successful) the containment policy based on economic means has been. Kennan's method of containment ultimately delivered victory to the free world on the Korean Peninsula as well as around the world. From this perspective, it is questionable how effective the current US North Korea policy would be in the long term. To put it differently, wouldn't strong political and military pressures against North Korea only strengthen its force of internal cohesion? Why would not the United States government recall the history lesson that the changes of the Soviet Union and the rest of the communist world arose not from such methods of containment? Although Kennan died and the Cold War ended, his theory of containment is still alive.

THREE

The Korean War and the 1950s

The US-South Korea relationship of the 1950s started with the Korean War. The United States immediately intervened in the Korean War under the flag of the United Nations and concluded the mutual defense treaty with South Korea when it ended. This military alliance became the fundamental factor in defining the US-South Korea relationship thereafter. The South Korean government provided military bases and released control of its military forces to the United States in return for this security guarantee.

The US-South Korea relationship, however, did not progress so smoothly. The US government even established a plan to remove President Syngman Rhee during the war. While such a plan was revised in 1953 and again in 1954, it was never carried out. Why? Why did the United States, which could not remove Syngman Rhee throughout the 1950s, change its stance once the 1960 April Revolution broke out?

1. Jumping into the War

When the news of war first reached Washington, President Harry Truman was at his private residence in Missouri, and Secretary of State Dean Acheson was also on vacation at a farm in Maryland. President John F. Kennedy and Secretary of State Dean Rusk were also on leave when the May 16 coup d'etat broke out in 1961.

Washington, however, reacted with speed, almost as if it had been waiting for the war. On June 25, 1950, US time, Secretary of State Dean Acheson obtained the US president's approval to discuss the Korean War at the United Nations Security Council. The resolution was presented to the UN Security Council even before President Truman returned to Washington. The resolution contended that North Korea must cease hostile acts in defiance of peace and return to the other side of the thirty-eighth parallel immediately. North Korea was marked as an international aggressor then, which provided the justification for the formation of the UN forces.

The problem, however, was that there was no clear evidence that North Korea was the invader. North Korea claimed that the war started with aggressive acts by the United States and South Korea, with South Korea and the United States claiming the opposite. In the end, the United Nations selected the report submitted by the United Nations Commission on Korea's (UNCOK) military observers on the ground as evidence. The report did not discuss many details beyond noting that South Korea's military strongholds were arranged defensively. The rapid southward advance of the North Korean forces served as additional proof that North Korea had launched a unilateral and surprise invasion. General Douglas MacArthur also played an important role in the decision making of the United Nations. MacArthur personally visited Suwon on June 29 to observe the situation and report to the White House. MacArhur's report played an important role in Washington's decision to intervene on June 30.

How did the United States react so fast? How did the United States, which had maintained a passive Korea policy with the exception of the activities of the Economic Cooperation Administration (ECA), end up intervening in Korea? How did the United States, which had proclaimed that it could abandon the Korean Peninsula according to George Kennan's strategy of maintaining important geographical and political points, intervene so quickly?

Prior to the Korean War, the United States essentially maintained a passive Korea policy. While the ECA aid can be seen as an exception, the United States nevertheless was passive in its military policy vis-à-vis South Korea. While the two countries established a mutual defense assistance agreement in January 1950, this did not mean that there was a military alliance between the United States and South Korea. Furthermore, the United States already had limited the size of the South Korean military in the National Security Council (NSC) 8 series. While ECA aid was maintained, it appeared as if the United States was abandoning South Korea militarily. Military strategists often opined that the Korean Peninsula was not a suitable place to fight the Soviet Union due to its unfavorable topographical conditions.

The United States, however, quickly intervened. It did not spend time in strategic calculations or considering its foreign policy interests. An understanding of the transformation of American foreign policy in 1949, which entailed significant changes to Kennan's strategy, is therefore necessary in understanding the American decision to intervene in June 1950. There were two major events that triggered this transformation.

The first was the successful communist revolution in China. After years of civil war, the Chinese Communist Party had (temporarily) formed an alliance with the Chinese Nationalist Party during the Second World War to fight off the Japanese invaders. The civil war, however, resumed between the two sides after the Japanese surrender. While the US-supported Chinese Nationalists initially maintained superiority, the Chinese Communist Party began to turn the tide in 1947. Widespread corruption in the Chinese Nationalist Party, which alienated the masses, and the Chinese Communist Party's pro-peasant policy played important roles in the ultimate victory of the communists in China.

The United States sent two envoys to China in 1946 and 1947 to gauge the developments in China (Wedemeyer envoy). The United States realized then that the tide was turning against the Chinese Nationalists, and, in response, Washington began contemplating a transformation of its Asia policy. The United States had considered China to be its most important ally in post–World War II Asia, which led the US policy makers to relatively deemphasize the prime importance of Japan in American Asia policy. Therefore, the initial US Japan policy emphasized demilitarization and democratization of Japan to ensure that it could not make war in the future. With the "communization" of China, however, Japan became the only remaining alternative for the United States in stopping communism in Asia. As can be seen in Kennan's strategy, at that time, Japan was the only country in Asia with substantial military and industrial base.

Best known as the "Reverse Course," the new US Japan policy aimed for Japanese political and economic revitalization including its remilitarization. Japan was to become America's only real "partner" in Asia. Foes of the Second World War now became new friends.

> Turning to the question of security, the General outlined his views on the position of the Pacific area in the pattern of our national defense. He said that the strategic boundaries of the United States were no longer along the western shores of North and South America; they lay along the eastern shores of the Asiatic continent. ... In the past the center of our defense problem had lain farther south, in the neighborhood of the Philippines. It had now shifted to the north.
> The General then described the area, of the Pacific in which, in his opinion, it was necessary for us to have striking force. This was a U-shaped area embracing the Aleutians, Midway, the former Japanese mandated islands, Clark Field in the Philippines, and above all Okinawa. Okinawa was the most advanced and vital point in this structure. From Okinawa he could easily control every one of the ports of northern Asia from which an amphibious operation could conceivably be launched. This was what was really essential. ...
> For these reasons, he attached great importance to Okinawa, and felt it absolutely necessary that we retain unilateral and complete control of the Ryukyu chain south of Latitude 29.[1]

MacArthur believed that the western shores of the United States should now stretch to the eastern shores of Asia, turning the Pacific into an American lake. The eastern shores of Asia meant Japan. Japan was militarily and economically important to the United States. Considering the magnitude of Japanese power, the Soviet control of Japan would be disastrous to the United States and its foreign policy interests.[2]

The "Reverse Course" vis-à-vis Japan was therefore designed to check the Soviet Union's influence in Asia. The Reverse Course was not exclusive to the economy. Although limited to self-defense, the Reverse Course also entailed Japan's remilitarization. Japan established the Japan Self-Defense Forces soon after the San Francisco Treaty and began remilitarizing. Of course, as mentioned in the second chapter of this book, the Japan-centered US Asia policy was not fully realized until the Korean War.

If Japan becomes the last bastion in Asia in containing the Soviet Union, the Korean Peninsula assumes an important role in ensuring Japan's security. Given the geographical proximity, the Korean Peninsula under Soviet influence would pose a direct threat to Japan. When Japan perceived its economic interests with the Korean Peninsula in a negative light during the normalization talks with South Korea in the 1960s, the United States convinced Japan to reconsider by emphasizing the security interests between Japan and South Korea. The United States therefore had to intervene for the sake of Japan's security when a war broke out on the Korean Peninsula.

Secretary of State Dean Acheson had already emphasized in 1947 the importance of Korea in prioritizing Japan.

[I]n the event of general hostilities, "Korea would be a military liability" and thus the United States had "little strategic interest in maintaining troops or bases in Korea." Nonetheless, "control of all Korea by Soviet or Soviet-dominated forces ... would constitute a strategic threat to U.S. interests in the Far East." In particular, this "would constitute an extremely serious political and military threat" to Japan.[3]

Perhaps the even bigger shock to the United States than the communization of China was the first successful nuclear weapons test by the Soviet Union in 1949. While the United States government has been expecting it, it had predicted the test to come in the early 1950s. The sudden news of the Soviet nuclear weapons test caused Washington to reevaluate its global foreign policy.

Prior to the successful nuclear weapons test, the United States did not pay much attention to the Soviet Union's military capabilities. While tensions arose with the Soviet Union following the Second World War in places like Berlin, Greece, and Turkey, the United States still had confidence in military matters. The source of such confidence, first and foremost, was the American monopoly over nuclear weapons. As long as the United States maintained this monopoly, the Soviet Union could not compete with the Unied

Stated solely with conventional weapons.

The American monopoly was now broken with the Soviet Union's successful nuclear weapons test. While the United States could rely on the Soviet fear of nuclear reprisal before, the United States now faced the numerically superior Soviet military forces without such an advantage. The Soviet Union had continued to expand its conventional military forces out of its fear of American nuclear weapons into 1949, which gave it an edge against the United States by the time Moscow acquired its own nuclear weapons.

The communization of China and the Soviet acquisition of nuclear weapons therefore forced the United States to revamp its foreign policy. The United States quickly organized the North Atlantic Treaty Organization (NATO) and sought to shut down further transfer of technology to the Soviet Union and the Eastern Bloc by limiting trade with them. Then, the still-controversial Rosenberg case occurred, in which civilians Julius and Ethel Rosenberg of New York were convicted and executed in 1953 for passing information about the atomic bomb to the Soviet Union. The conviction fueled a phenomenon generally referred to in American history as "McCarthyism"–widespread and hysterical anticommunist pursuits against the supposed agents of the Soviet Union.

The change in US foreign policy was also reflected in a personnel change that led to the abandonment of containment strategy with its emphasis on economic and psychological aspects. Paul Nitze replaced George Kennan as the director of policy planning in the State Department, reflecting the rise of strong American isolationism and statism in American politics against the background of McCarthyism.[4] Nitze was a hard-liner who insisted on confronting the Soviet Union. Nitze soon composed a policy document to reshape American foreign policy–National Security Council Report 68 (NSC-68).

NSC-68 is one of the most important and representative texts of the US containment policy. NSC-68 emphasized not only the need for the active containment of the Soviet Union, but also the need to minimize Soviet influence itself. In addition to Kennan's emphasis on economic and psychological factors, NSC-68 also underscored the military aspect. NSC-68 stressed that the containment policy could not be successful without military might.

As for the policy of "containment," it is one which seeks by all means short of war to (1) block further expansion of Soviet power, (2) expose the falsities of Soviet pretensions, (3) induce a retraction of the Kremlin's control and influence and (4) in general, so foster the seeds of destruction within the Soviet system. ... One of the most important ingredients of power is military strength. In the concept of "containment," the maintenance of a strong military posture is deemed to be essential for two reasons: (1) as an ultimate guarantee of our national security and (2) as an indispensable backdrop to the conduct of the policy of "containment." Without superior aggregate military strength, in being and readily mobilizable, a policy of "containment"—which is in effect a policy of calculated and gradual coercion—is no more than a policy of bluff.

At the same time, it is essential to the successful conduct of a policy of "containment" that we always leave open the possibility of negotiation with the U.S.S.R. A diplomatic freeze—and we are in one now—tends to defeat the very purposes of "containment" because it raises tensions at the same time that it makes Soviet retractions and adjustments in the direction of moderated behavior more difficult. It also tends to inhibit our initiative and deprives us of opportunities for maintaining a moral ascendency in our struggle with the Soviet system.[5]

The quote above illustrates well the concept of containment as maintained by NSC-68–any policy vis-à-vis the Soviet Union would not be effective without American military superiority. NSC-68's perspective therefore diverges significantly from Kennan's perspective that the containment against the Soviet Union was possible simply through economic and psychological means.

In addition, NSC-68 was critical in that some US military structures overemphasized defense. It argued that containment cannot be successful with such defensive stance:

U.S. military capabilities are strategically more defensive in nature than offensive and are more potential than actual. It is evident, from an analysis of the past and of the trend of weapon development, that there is-now and will be in the future no absolute defense. The history of war also indicates that a favorable decision can

Nitze, who emerged in the American political scene with the rise of McCarthyism. A hard-liner against the Soviet Union, Nitze argued for superior military power over the Soviet Union in addition to economic and psychological containment.

only be achieved through offensive action. Even a defensive strategy, if it is to be successful, calls not only for defensive forces to hold vital positions while mobilizing and preparing for the offensive, but also for offensive forces to attack the enemy and keep him off balance. The two fundamental requirements which must be met by forces in being or readily available are support of foreign policy and protection against disaster. To meet the second requirement, the forces in being or readily available must be able, at a minimum, to perform certain basic tasks.[6]

NSC-68 therefore argues for a more proactive containment policy. The problem, however, was that a more aggressive policy would require additional spending. As NSC-68 prescribes, the expansion of armaments was necessary in order to attain American military superiority vis-à-vis the Soviet Union.

NSC-68 was also more emphatic with the necessity of foreign economic aid than Kennan. It argued for a more broader and more comprehensive aid to places beyond those Kennan had promoted:

> With a high level of economic activity, the United States could soon attain a gross national product of $300 billion per year, as was pointed out in the President's Economic Report (January 1950). Progress in this direction would permit, and might itself be aided by a build-up of the economic and military strength of the United States and the free world; furthermore, if a dynamic expansion of the economy were achieved, the necessary build-up could be accomplished without a decrease in the national standard of living because the required resources could be obtained by siphoning off a part of the annual increment in the gross national product. ...
> 2. Intentions. Foreign economic policy is a major instrument in the conduct of United States foreign relations. It is an instrument which

can powerfully influence the world environment in ways favorable to the security and welfare of this country. It is also an instrument which, if unwisely formulated and employed, can do actual harm to our national interests.

(1) assistance to Western Europe in recovery and the creation of a viable economy (the European Recovery Program);

(2) assistance to other countries because of their special needs arising out. of the war or the, cold war and our special interests in or responsibility-for meeting them (grant assistance to Japan, the Philippines, and Korea, loans and credits by the Export-Import Bank, the International Monetary Fund, and the International Bank to; Indonesia, Yugoslavia, Iran, etc.)

(3) assistance in the development of under-developed areas. (The Point IV program; and loans and credits to various countries, overlapping to some extent with those mentioned under point 2)

(4) military assistance to the North Atlantic Treaty countries, Greece, Turkey, etc.;

(5) restriction of East-West trade in items of military importance to the East;

(6) purchase and stockpiling of strategic materials; and

(7) efforts to re-establish an international economy based on multi-lateral trade, declining trade barriers, and convertible currencies (the GATT-ITO program, the Reciprocal-Trade Agreements program, the IMF-IBRD program, and the program now being developed to solve the problem of the United States balance of payments).[7]

NSC-68's foreign policy therefore entailed a massive increase of government expenditures. As can be seen in the seven items quoted above, Nitze's plan includes underdeveloped regions that were not included in Kennan's plan. Massive increases of government expenditures were necessary in order to fund both military armaments as well as foreign aid. For additional funding, however, taxes had to be increased.

NSC-68 proposed four options that the United States could select for its containment policy: continuation of Kennan's policy, isolationism, war, and a rapid increase of the political, economic, and military power of the Free World. The document supported the most expensive alternative in the fourth option. Given the unsatisfactory progress of the revival program for Europe, Nitze argued that the existing plan would not be enough to contain the Soviet Union. While there were also calls for war, Nitze argued that it may not produce a favorable result for the United States given the contemporaneous conditions of the Free World.

Given the enormous increase in government expenditures, one has to question whether or not Nitze considered the state of US fiscal policy. Was it part of his calculations? Yes. In fact, Nitze actually saw his plan as a solution to the economic problems the United States was facing at the time. He emphasized that the United States in 1949 was already experiencing what could be seen as postwar economic stagnation:

> B. ECONOMIC
> 1. Capabilities. ... Furthermore, the United States could achieve a substantial absolute increase in output and could thereby increase the allocation of resources to a build-up of the economic and military strength of itself and its allies without suffering a decline in its real standard of living. Industrial production declined by 10 percent between the first quarter of 1948 and the last quarter of 1949, and by approximately one-fourth between 1944 and 1949. In March 1950 there were approximately 4,750,000 unemployed, as compared to 1,070,000 in 1943 and 670,000 in 1944. The gross national product declined slowly in 1949 from the peak reached in 1948 ($262 billion in 1948 to an annual rate of $256 billion in the last six months of 1949), and in terms of constant prices declined by about 20 percent between 1944 and 1948. ...
> Despite certain inadequacies and inconsistencies, which are now being studied in connection with the problem of the United States balance of payments, the United States has generally pursued a foreign economic policy which has powerfully supported its overall objectives. The question must nevertheless be asked whether current and currently projected programs will adequately support this policy in the future, in terms both of need and urgency.[8]

Given the economic state, what sorts of consequences would such an increase in military expenditures bring? Was it not dangerous to increase military expenditures at a time of recession? Such concerns were the reasons for Truman's refusal to approve NSC-68 when it was first presented to him in early 1950. It was not approved until after the Korean War. How did NSC-68's author seek to overcome the issue of expenditures?

> Essential as prerequisites to the success of this program would be (a) consultations with Congressional leaders designed to make the program the object of non-partisan legislative support, and (b) a presentation to the public of a full explanation of the facts and implications of present international trends. ... The United States is currently devoting about 22 percent of its gross national product ($255 billion in 1949) to military expenditures (6 percent), foreign assistance (2 percent), and investment (14 percent), little of which is in war-supporting industries. ... In an emergency the United States could devote upward of 50 percent of its gross national product to these purposes (as it did during the last war), an increase of several times present expenditures for direct and indirect military purposes and foreign assistance.
>
> From the point of view of the economy as a whole, the program might not result in a real decrease in the standard of living, for the economic effects of the program might be to increase the gross national product by more than the amount being absorbed for additional military and foreign assistance purposes. One of the most significant lessons of our World War II experience was that the American economy, when it operates at a level approaching full efficiency, can provide enormous resources for purposes other than civilian consumption while simultaneously providing a high standard of living. After allowing for price changes, personal consumption expenditures rose by about one-fifth between 1939 and 1944, even though the economy had in the meantime increased the amount of resources going into Government use by $60 $65 billion (in 1939 prices).[9]

The above quote provides clues for perhaps the actual motive behind NSC-68. While emphasizing the military aspect, NSC-68's ultimate goal was to overcome post–World War II economic stagnation.

In this aspect, NSC-68 also displays an important characteristic of US foreign policy at large. A significant number of high-ranking policymakers serving in areas related to the military have worked in fields connected to finance or investment. For example, Paul Nitze had worked at an investment bank prior to his government career. Robert McNamara, who oversaw the US war in Vietnam during the Kennedy administration, was once the president of Ford Motor Company. Secretary of Defense Donald Rumsfeld was president of a pharmaceutical company before he was CEO of General Instrument.

In other words, US policymakers in the military often play the role of a synthesizer–balancing out interests of foreign affairs, military, and government finances. While Nitze worked at the Policy Planning Council, one of his main concerns had to do with connecting American foreign policy with the goal of reviving the US domestic economy.

The quote above shows that NSC-68's writers believed that an active policy of increased spending in military and foreign aid would revitalize the American economy. It was an archetypal Keynesian fiscal policy–one which aims to expand demand through an increase in government spending. An increase in government spending would increase the amount of money in circulation, which would stimulate an increase in individual spending throughout the country. An increase in individual spending would then revitalize the American economy.[10] The Keynesian policy did not necessarily seek to create government projects to reduce unemployment; its ultimate goal was to increase overall demand in the economy. In other words, the point of providing the unemployed jobs was to revitalize overall consumption by providing them money.

NSC-68 was essentially an extension of the Keynesian logic to the realm of foreign policy. Of course, as mentioned earlier, the two major events in the communization of China and the successful nuclear test by the Soviet Union played important roles in providing the background in which NSC-68 emerged. It also meant, however, that Keynesian thought was beginning to play an even bigger role in shaping the philosophy of the US government. Increases in military expenditures meant an enlargement of the war industry, which created more jobs. This point is also evident in NSC-68's emphasis on conventional weapons as well as nuclear weapons in confronting the Soviet Union. While an expansion of strategic nuclear weapons would be more effective and less costly, only the expanded production of conventional weapons could generate jobs on a massive scale.

In order to prove the suitability of his policy, Nitze reminded the readers that the time of World War II was one of the most prosperous eras in American history. The Second World War, of course, was a time of emergency. While American military expenditures increased manyfold, the US economy remained prosperous. Nitze argued that an expansion of military expenditures could prove an opportunity for overcoming the economic stagnation at the time.

The approval of NSC-68 also changed the US Korea policy. Under the Kennan's policy, Korea was a place that the United States could abandon, and such a stance produced two sharp debates on the Korean Peninsula in Washington between 1948 and 1950. According to NSC-68, however, the Korean Peninsula was a place that the United States could not abandon. As can be seen in the quote on foreign economic aid, the Korean Peninsula was now somewhere that the United States should take an active stance in aiding.

The Korean War broke out at the moment when such change in policy was taking place, and the United States therefore sent its military forces there. While American participation in the Korean War tripled US military expenditures, policymakers in Washington believed that such increase would not have a negative impact on the American economy. The United States therefore jumped into the war as soon as it started.

The US intervention in Korea also became the first application of the domino theory in American foreign policy. The domino theory contended that if one state in a region came under the influence of communism, the surrounding countries would follow in a domino-like fashion. The loss of South Korea, which the United States had defended in the United Nations, would be a morale blow to the nations under American support and aid. The loss of South Korea also meant a serious security threat to Japan, now the centerpiece of US foreign policy in Asia.

NSC-68, approved soon after the breakout of the Korean War, ironically lost its effectiveness at war's end. The Eisenhower administration selected the New Look policy, aiming to reduce military expenditures and balance out the government budget. The content of NSC-68, however, was revived in the 1960s under the Kennedy administration. Some scholars therefore refer to the Kennedy administration's policies as the "Keynesian Revolution."

2. The Plan to Remove Syngman Rhee and the Plan EVERREADY

(1) The Plan to Remove Syngman Rhee

In June 1952, when fighting raged across the thirty-eighth parallel during the ongoing negotiations for armistice, the following telegram arrived from the Joint Chiefs of Staff to the Far Eastern Command in Tokyo:

> The Joint Chiefs of Staff to the Commander in Chief Far East (Clark)
> TOP SECRETWASHINGTON, June 25, 1952-3:50 p. m.
> OPERATIONAL IMMEDIATE
> JCS 912098. From JCS. Reur CX 504162 and Muccio's 1395.
> CINCUNC pass to Muccio.
> Part I. As Def and State now view polit sit created by Rhee, two different gen lines of development appear possible.
> 1. First, there may not be any sudden or critical development requiring, on purely mil grounds, direct intervention, or providing adequate justification for direct intervention upon polit grounds. This appears to be present sit in which only feasible action appears to be intensification of polit measures. Ur suggestions wld be most helpful as to what addl dipl and mil representation cld be applied to whatever degree possible to resolve polit crisis.
> 2. Second, sit may deteriorate to point where, in order prevent interference with UN mil opns, direct intervention in sit cannot be avoided. As this action may be forced upon us suddenly by one or more incidents, Depts desire you confer with each other earliest in order develop and submit to Wash for approval detailed polit and mil plan accordingly. Depts concur that premature disclosure of existence such plan cld be extremely embarrassing to United States Govt, therefore, UNCURK participation in ur planning shld be to extent to which you mutually determine to be necessary.

Part II. To facilitate ur planning folg guidance is furnished:

3. It is hoped that necessity for implementation of plan can be foreseen sufficiently in advance to permit implementation to be on decision by highest govtal authy. However, in event of sudden outbreak of violence, civil disorder or an emerg necessitating immed action, CINCUNC will be authorized to implement the plan without further authy, reporting his action expeditiously.

4. Under› less emerg conditions the plan shld contemplate action along folg lines:

a. If circumstances permit, UNCURK, Emb and CINCUNC shld present appropriate demand that Rhee or other responsible official take such immed action as, in judgment of UNCURK, Emb and CINCUNC, is required to restore sit.

b. If circumstances do not permit making foregoing demand or if requested action is not immediately taken by ROK Govt, CINCUNC, preferably at UNCURKs request shld recommend to United States Govt that intervention be authorized.

5. On authorization by United States Govt to intervene as exec agt for UN, CINCUNC shld take action along folg lines:

a. Direct ROKA Ch of Staff to assume cmd of all ROKA Forces, quasi mil forces and such elements of natl or local police as CINCUNC may deem necessary, and thereafter to administer and direct martial rule in Pusan area. As matter of policy utilization of UN troops other than Korean shld be avoided or minimized to greatest extent possible.

b. Administration of martial rule shld be such as to preserve to maximum possible extent authy and functioning of an ROK Govt organization as a symbol of ROK sovereignty. Orders issued to ROKA Ch of Staff under these circumstances shld be of such nature as to envisage local martial rule in Pusan area, supplemented by ROK civil govt agencies which are capable of continued functioning. These orders shld clearly provide for preservation of constitutional govt and early restoration of civil power where such power is necessarily suspended. Appropriate individuals and organizations of ROK Govt shld be given full protection and, as soon as order is restored, they shld be encouraged to take such action as necessary to effect continuation of normal functioning of constitutional govt.

c. While foregoing contemplates use of ROK forces only, and while that is desirable from viewpoint of world opinion, there is no restriction on use of other UN forces shld sit require.

6. Re this request appraisal as to dependability of ROKA Ch of Staff, and ROKA forces, under these conditions, particularly shld Rhee as an anticipatory measure, rescind his order of 14 Jul 50 which placed ROKA under CINCUNCs cmd.

7. In implementation of foregoing there shld be maximum coordination between CINCUNC, UNCURK and American Amb.

8. Request ur comments.[11]

The quoted telegram is ordering a coup d'etat in South Korea using South Korean military units. The most important part of this document is that Syngman Rhee caused a crisis which made an emergency action necessary on the part of the United States government. An emergency action, of course, meant a coup d'etat to be accomplished with South Korean military forces. The telegram orders that an intervention should take place if the pressure from the United Nations Commission for the Unification and Rehabilitation of Korea (UNCURK), the US Embassy in Seoul, and the United Nations Command do not move Syngman Rhee to normalize conditions. Intervention would take the form of a coup d'etat by South Korean forces overseen by the United Nations Command. It was a plan to remove Syngman Rhee from power.

The plan becomes even more concrete in the next document, describing in detail how Syngman Rhee would be removed from power:

a. Pres Rhee wld be invited to visit in Seoul or elsewhere–anywhere to get him out of Pusan.

b. At an apptd time the UNC comdr wld move in to the Pusan area and seize between 5 and 10 key ROK officials who have been ldrs in Rhee's dictatorial actions, protect all UNC installations and ROK installations deemed advisable, and take over the control of martial law through the Chief of Staff, ROK Army, until it is lifted.

c. Rhee wld then be informed of the action taken as a "fait accompli." He wld be urged to sign a proclamation lifting martial law, permitting Natl Assembly freedom of action and estab freedom of the press and radio without interference fr his various strong armed agencies.

d. If Pres Rhee wld not agree to issue the proclamation, he wld be held in protective custody incommunicado and a similar proclamation wld be presented to Prime Min Chang Taek-Sang.

e. It is believed here that Prime Min wld agree. However, if he does not, it wld then be neces to take further steps approaching a UNC interim govt.

f. In the event that either Rhee or Chang agree statements wld be released to the press to the eff that it had been neces for mil rsns and (if appropriate) at the rqst of the nations participating in the conflict for the UNC to step in and remove certain individuals who had been taking illegal actions which interfered with the United Nations Mission. There statements wld stress the fact that the ROK Govt was taking the action and was being assisted by the UNC.[12]

The quoted simulation flows almost like a soap opera. It would entail arresting and confining Syngman Rhee and his associates in order to make them accept the UN Command's demands. If Rhee still did not concede, the United Nations forces would directly intervene and resolve the crisis itself. Why was this plan formulated? Despite this concrete and detailed planning, why was it not carried out?

(2) Syngman Rhee's First Challenge: Against the Institutions of Free Democracy

The political landscape in South Korea did not change much even after the breakout of the Korean War in June 1950. Given the constitutional clause that gave the power to select the president to the National Assembly, the election on May 30, 1950 that saw a significant number of independent candidates elected placed Syngman Rhee in a politically unfavorable position. Despite being in a war, voices of criticism against the president by the members of the National Assembly grew ever louder. While the intervention by the United Nations eventually turned the tide of war, revelation of a number of corruption scandals placed the Syngman Rhee government on the defensive. There was even an incident of South Korean troops attacking national assemblymen. The National Defense Corps Incident in the winter of 1950-51 and the Geochang massacre were some of the most blatant examples of Rhee's misgovernance.

The National Defense Corps were the reserve forces that were to be drafted to reinforce the South Korean army. Its officers were made of pro-Rhee anticommunist youth groups, and men between the ages of seventeen and forty were inducted into it. The problem, however, was that tens of thousands of young men drafted into the National Defense Corps either escaped or died from cold and starvation even before they made it to the battlefield. Some fifty thousand trainees died, and another three hundred thousand were physically maimed from beatings and starvation.

The South Korean National Assembly immediately sought an investigation that subsequently revealed that significant portions of the budget were embezzled by the officials of anticommunist youth groups, with evidence that some of these funds were pocketed by politicians in the pro-Rhee camp. The investigation, however, was cut short by the Rhee government's obstruction. The incident closed with executions of five commanding officers of the National Defense Corps.

The Geochang massacre was one of the largest civilian massacres of the Korean War. The massacre was carried out by South Korean military forces stationed at Geochang with orders to subjugate the communist guerillas in the area. Convinced that the people of Geochang were colluding with the guerillas, the commander on the ground ordered punitive killings of the locals. Because guerillas were relying on the locals for food, the South Korean military forcefully removed the people living in the mountainous areas, and a significant number of civilians including children, elderly, and women were killed in the process of relocation.

When the story of the Geochang massacre became known, the South Korean National Assembly immediately organized a research group to investigate. On its way to Geochang, however, the research group was attacked by the guerillas. Further investigation revealed that the supposed guerillas who attacked the research group were in fact soldiers of the South Korean army, compelling the National Assembly to strongly demand the punishment of those responsible. While the commanding officer of the Geochang massacre was executed, Kim Jongwon, the man who led the attack on the national assemblymen, was freed and later became the minister of home affairs.

On the other hand, however, the investigation team's leader Seo Minho was arrested and imprisoned for killing a soldier in uniform. When an officer of the South Korean military had approached and threatened Seo Minho with a gun, Seo killed the officer in a fight. While such an incident could be read as self-defense, Seo was imprisoned for eight years until the April Revolution in 1960.

The South Korean national assemblymen generally became convinced that President Syngman Rhee should no longer have dictatorial powers, and some of them began taking concrete steps to neutralize Rhee's power and establish a new political system. While they were not necessarily all liberal in their political orientations, they collectively agreed that Syngman Rhee, who had denied the basic principles of democracy and done nothing to protect the status of national assemblymen, should no longer be president.

Cornered, Syngman Rhee organized his circle of supporters in the National Assembly into the Liberal Party in 1951. Posing as the "founding father" since his return to Korea in 1945, Syngman Rhee had so far refused to create or lead a particular political party or organization. Rhee wanted to appear as someone beyond the realm of politics. Given his minority position in the National Assembly, however, Rhee created a political party of his own in order to be reelected.

Contrary to what Rhee had hoped for, however, the Liberal Party became a party without much presence in the National Assembly. The National Assembly only had a few assemblymen who supported Rhee, and most assemblymen refused to join the Liberal Party. On the contrary, many assemblymen created their own "Liberal Party" inside the National Assembly and pushed for the establishment of the parliamentary system, which would allow assemblymen to weaken the post of president and give the prime minister the authority to govern the country.

However, because of the nature of the constitution at the time, there was no real need for the assemblymen to change it. The constitution allowed the National Assembly to select the president, and all the anti-Rhee forces had to do was to vote for another person who could replace Rhee. The dilemma, however, was that the anti-Rhee forces did not have a leader with enough charisma and leadership qualities to replace Syngman Rhee. The only alternative was to revise the constitution from a presidential system to a parliamentary one. The Democratic National Party, the successor of the Korea Democratic Party, also supported the proposal for the constitutional revision. Over two-thirds of the National Assembly supported the idea. The proposal was now put forth.

In response, Syngman Rhee ordered the assemblymen under his control to submit another constitutional revision for a system of direct election of the president. Rhee also mobilized pro-government demonstrations against the assemblymen in support of the parliamentary system. Rhee, who already had obtained a support group outside of the National Assembly through the 1952 election for local government, mobilized the group to pressure the assemblymen by accusing them of being traitors.

At this point, the US ambassador to Korea John J. Muccio sent the following telegram to Washington:

> It is pretty clear that fate has not dealt us a good hand of cards in the coming election. As we pointed out in our telegram, Rhee is becoming increasingly recalcitrant and senile. While he is president no one else seems to have the guts to stand up to him. Two of the other possible candidates, Yi Pom-suk and Sin Ik-hi, are pretty crummy from our point of view. The best two, Chang Myon and Ho Chong, lack popular followings and are somewhat weak.
>
> A trade of Rhee's re-election for a system of cabinet responsibility to the National Assembly would be one way of cutting Rhee down to size in the absence of another strong candidate. Rhee wouldn't have it, however, and I think it would be "out of the frying pan, into the fire," since the Koreans, I feel certain, would be totally unable to make a parliamentary system work.
>
> Chang Myon's chances in an election by the National Assembly are probably our best hope. As we mentioned in our telegram the fact that the United States is thought to like him is perhaps his greatest strength within the Assembly. ...
>
> If this is not wholly effective, however, the opportunity exists for us to take a very firm stand with Rhee and others in his Government on the observance of the principles of constitutional government and the holding of free elections. They must be made to understand the

serious consequences of their use of political intimidation and realize that totalitarian tactics would be bound to prejudice future United Nations support for the ROK.[13]

Muccio believed that the developments of South Korean politics were reaching a dead end. The State Department had earlier inquired whether or not there were political forces that could replace Syngman Rhee, and the telegram above was the reply to that inquiry. The problem, however, was that coming up with a viable alternative was equally difficult. The United States was already worried about the negative consequences that an intervention into South Korean politics could produce.

The South Korean National Assembly continued to push for the constitutional revision for a parliamentary system into 1952. At that point, Syngman Rhee summoned some of the South Korean army units from the front and declared martial law in the area around Busan. While the pretext for martial law was that there were communist guerillas in the area, there was no evidence of that being the case. Following the declaration of martial law, a bus carrying the lawmakers to the National Assembly was captured and towed away. Some of the assemblymen on board were arrested under the charges that they had something to do with the so-called International Communist Party. The South Korean legislature now ceased to function.

The United States reacted immediately. Along with the United States, the embassies of the nations who participated in the United Nations forces, international representatives of UNCURK, the US Embassy in Seoul, the United Nations Command, and Washington poured in protests to the South Korean government. They argued that the purpose of fighting in this war–protection of free democracy–went out of the window with the South Korean government's blatant stomping of democratic principles.

The US officials on the ground met with Syngman Rhee on a number of occasions to pressure him. US officials even threatened that the UN forces could retreat from South Korea unless Rhee free the lawmakers and allow the government to operate according to the constitution. Syngman Rhee, however, refused to accept the American demand. Rhee knew that the Americans could not pull

High-ranking officials of South Korea and the United States in the Korean War's early stage. American Ambassador Muccio is in the middle, the man left to Muccio is the defense minister Sin Seongmo, and the man right to Muccio is the foreign minister Im Byeongjik. The man holding Taegeukgi (the flag of South Korea) is the Commander of the U.S. forces in Korea, Walton Walker.

out of South Korea regardless of what he did.

Such actions on the part of Syngman Rhee, what American officials referred to as "brinkmanship," reoccurred several times during moments of conflict with the United States. In 1955, one year before the South Korean presidential election, Syngman Rhee drove out US ambassador William Lacy only five months after he arrived. Rhee also declared the severing of trade with Japan in 1955 when the Japanese government began sending ethnic Korean residents in Japan to North Korea. While this declaration had to be lifted due to the economic losses it caused South Korea, Syngman Rhee knew well that the US government could not rashly intervene in South Korea due to the risks of political instability. Rhee, who spent much of the Japanese colonial period in the United States, was also well aware of how sensitive Washington was to world public opinion.

The United States finally developed the plan to remove Syngman Rhee. The United States could no longer carry out the war under the United Nations banner as long as Rhee continued to threaten the democratic institutions in South Korea. Washington was also discontent with how Rhee called in the troops from the front to carry out the martial law in the rear. Washington decided that the only solution was to remove Syngman Rhee.

The plan, however, was not carried out. This plan is also known to have involved the Army Chief of Staff Yi Jongchan, the Director of Intelligence Yi Yongmun, and several field-grade officers including Park Chung Hee. The document below shows that Syngman Rhee was aware of Yi Jongchan's involvement in the plot against him.

Rhee then mentioned he had some news which he knew wld make the Gen unhappy. He said that, unfortunately, word had reached him that Chief of Staff Gen Lee was implicated in the plot against him and that he wld have to be removed. Gen Van Fleet expressed incredulity at this because he was convinced, as result long association Gen Lee, that Gen Lee's principal interest in life is in building up ROK and that he was sure Gen Lee completely loyal to Korea and Pres Rhee. Furthermore, it was almost an obsession with Lee to remain aloof from internal politics, a principle he had tried to inculcate throughout the ROKA. Rhee held out some papers, which he said were messages from Gen Lee to Gen Won and other officers, in effect countermanding oral understanding made with Pres last week and ordering the martial law commander to take no action except under instrs from himself. Gen Lee is expected Pusan in morning but Rhee seemed to have already made up his mind to fire him. Gen Van Fleet asked that Gen Lee be given chance to answer these charges which he (Gen Van Fleet) was most hopeful would be answered satisfactorily. However, in event the Pres was convinced that change must be made, Gen Van Fleet pointed out the necessity of obtaining very best man available to take his place. After some discussion of candidates, Gen Van Fleet said he felt best man would probably be Gen Paek Sun-Yop, altho it would be a loss to take the best fighting general away from the Third Corps.[14]

In the end, the United States opted for a compromise that

essentially amounted to giving in to Syngman Rhee. On the other hand, a "compromise" was reached between the two proposals for constitutional revision in the name of "selected revision." With policemen and soldiers surrounding the National Assembly, the proposal for constitutional revision passed without a single dissenting vote. This incident is called the Busan Incident of 1952. While "selected revision" meant that the new proposal "selected" important parts of the two proposals in a compromise, the content of it was largely for a system of direct election of the president. The only portion that came from the other proposal was to reform the National Assembly into a bicameral system. Even so, the clause for a bicameral legislature never materialized until the April Revolution of 1960.

The result was a triumph on the part of Syngman Rhee. He defeated the United States government in a tug-of-war. The United States could no longer pressure Rhee with the rhetoric of democracy. While Rhee had agreed to the American request to remove some of his associates in support of his dictatorship as a part of the compromise, Rhee handled them in a way he wanted–Rhee removed his biggest political opponent in Yi Beomseok at the Liberal Party national convention held immediately after the Busan Incident.

While Yi Beomseok had been supporting Syngman Rhee in the Liberal Party, Yi had the potential to become the number-one rival of Syngman Rhee. Formerly a member of the Korean Independence Army, Yi Beomseok was free from charges of collaboration with the Japanese and also had the prestige of being associated with the Korean Provisional Government. He also received much support from the country's young by founding the Korean Youth Corps after liberation. Jang Junha of *Sasanggye* and Prime Minister Baek Dujin were once members of the Korean Youth Corps. In addition, the Korean Youth Corps was the only youth group that received support from the United States Army Military Government in Korea. Yi Beomseok therefore had the potential to threaten Syngman Rhee with the support of the United States.

After removing Yi Beomseok, Syngman Rhee filled the Liberal Party with people who were more loyal to him. Led by Yi Gibung, Rhee loyalists soon dominated the party and captured the majority in the National Assembly in the 1954 general election. The pro-

Rhee forces soon carried out yet another constitutional revision in 1954, the so-called *Sasaoip* Incident ("the rounding off to the nearest integer" incident). The two constitutional revisions carried out by the pro-Rhee forces became the cornerstone of strengthening Rhee's dictatorship.

The second presidential election in South Korea took place on August 15, 1952, soon after its National Assembly passed the "selected" constitutional revision. This election was *the* first election in Korean history in which the citizens selected their own leader. The result of this wartime election, however, was easily foreseen. Nobody denied that Syngman Rhee was going to be reelected, and so he was. Rhee's dictatorial power now appeared unstoppable.

While the presidential election was held in wartime, it nevertheless reveals an important aspect of the US-South Korea relations as a whole—the United States had trouble deciding between democracy and anticommunist dictatorship. Democracy, as a symbol of American liberalism, was a sufficient condition for maintaining diplomatic relations. Anticommunism, however, was the necessary condition for maintaining the US-centered world order. The problem, however, was that American-style democracy was difficult to maintain along with anticommunism in the Third World. While this contradiction was partially resolved with the emergence of the new ideology of developmental dictatorship in the 1960s, it continued to cause confusion in the US policy vis-à-vis the Third World.

South Korea was not an exception here. The United States often had trouble prioritizing between the two goals through both the Syngman Rhee and Park Chung Hee regimes. While the United States ultimately did led its support for democracy, it still supported anticommunist dictatorships until such regimes were no longer sustainable.

(3) Syngman Rhee's Second Challenge and Another Attempt to Remove Him: The Plan EVERREADY

On May 4, 1953, Washington developed another plan to replace Syngman Rhee with a new government in South Korea. The plan composed by the Eighth United States Army Commander Maxwell Davenport Taylor was as follows:

(1) Send for Chief of Staff, ROKA, and instruct him to secure enforcement of orders.

(2) Confer with commanders of disaffected units,

(3) Relieve disloyal or recalcitrant leaders and replace them by commanders personally loyal to CG, Eighth Army.

(4) Dispatch teams of loyal ROK officers to present the UN cause orally to ROK units.

(5) Notify recalcitrant units that continuation of logistical support is conditioned on full compliance with UN policy.

(6) Discontinue supply of fuel and munitions to the disaffected units and move arms and munitions from ROK supply channels to US installations.

(7) Request CINCUNC to make a demand for compliance on the President of Korea.

(8) Recommend to CINCUNC a declaration of UN policy and reasons therefore to be given the Korean people and Army via:

(a) US radio facilities.

(b) Vehicle and airborne loudspeakers

(c) Preempted Korean radio facilities.

(d) Placards, handbills, and leaflets.

(9) Withdraw supporting artillery and air support, including the grounding of the ROK Air Force by arrangement with CG, Fifth Air Force.

(10) Demand return of US supplies and equipment in hands of ROKA.

(11) Cut off all communications between disaffected units of ROKA, their headquarters, and the ROK Government.

(12) Secure control, within Army area, of Korean civil and military communications, to include telephone, telegraph, radio, bus, railroad, and water transportation.

(13) Seize, divert, and secure in US installations all supplies in hands of dissident elements.

(14) Proclaim and establish martial law in the name of the UN.

(15) Secure custody of the dissident military and civil leaders.

(16) Proclaim military government in the name of the UN.[15]

Unlike the earlier plan in 1952, the 1953 plan was named "Plan EVERREADY," meaning that it is a plan that should be ready for implementation at any time. Also unlike the 1952 plan, the 1953 plan included establishment of a military government under the United Nations command. How did the United States establish this plan given the international criticisms it would face?

The problem began when the US assistant secretary of state for Far Eastern affairs Walter S. Robertson received a memorandum from the South Korean ambassador to the United States Yang Yuchan on April 24, 1953, around the time when the negotiations for a cease-fire were at their final stage. The South Korean ambassador visited Assistant Secretary Robertson in person at 2:45 in the afternoon. The memorandum included (1) a newspaper article arguing that the United States could allow the stationing of Chinese forces in North Korea following the cease-fire and (2) Syngman Rhee's responses to the news.

The memo showed that "President Syngman Rhee is preparing to withdraw the ROK (Republic of Korea) military forces from the UNC (United Nations Command) when, and if, the UN (United Nations) makes with the Communist aggressors any agreement which, after a cease-fire agreement, would either permit or allow Chinese Communists to remain south of the Yalu River, the northernmost boundary of the Republic of Korea."[16] President Rhee, in addition, released such statement to the public.[17]

Without a way to know whether or not such a statement was merely rhetoric or reflected an actual intent, the United States government was thrown into disarray. If the South Korean forces broke away from the United Nations Command and acted on their own, it would then be difficult to justify the American intervention in Korea. The independent South Korean operations at the front would also endanger ongoing negotiations to end the war, which was one of Eisenhower's core presidential election pledges in 1952.

Syngman Rhee had argued against the armistice throughout the process of negotiations and had stated that the South Korean forces could advance to the North on their own. Pro-government demonstrations against the armistice negotiations had been ongoing since the exchange of wounded POWs on April 11, 1953.

The United Nations commander judged that he needed an emergency plan in case the South Korean forces left the UN Command and acted on their own. He therefore ordered the commander of the Eighth Army to compose the above-quoted emergency plan. In the case the South Korean forces under the order of Syngman Rhee broke out of the United Nations Command and acted to sabotage the cease-fire negotiations, the plan stipulated an immediate severing of support for those units and the UN takeover of power in South Korea. The details, however, were not presented.

The conditions, however, worsened as the armistice negotiations went on. On May 22, 1953, Syngman Rhee recalled General Choe Deoksin, the South Korean representative to the cease-fire negotiations. It was an expression of protest by Syngman Rhee to the fact that the United Nation forces accepted the North Korean and Chinese demands related to neutral nations conducting the evaluations of POWs without consulting Seoul. The United Nations commander and the US ambassador then met with Syngman Rhee on May 25 to sound out the South Korean government. After the meeting, the two men concluded that Syngman Rhee would not change his stance.

> Although aide-memoire suggested in separate message should be submitted soonest in order that Rhee may have clear and unmistakable record of US position, I do not believe that this will significantly alter Rhee's attitude already adopted described herein and in previous telegrams.
>
> In fact, it now seems probable that at early date Rhee may issue public statement, perhaps along line indicated previous telegram, denouncing today's armistice proposal and reiteration ROK determination fight on alone.[18]

Convinced that it could no longer neglect the conflict with Syngman Rhee, Washington went on to actualize the emergency plan. The plan was revised in cooperation among the Department of State, the Joint Chiefs of Staff, and the Department of Defense, with the part on the establishment of military government by the UN forces edited out.[19]

In the end, however, the United States government decided to make a deal with Syngman Rhee rather than have a head-on collision with him. Washington decided to partially accept Syngman Rhee's original stipulation that he could accept the armistice if the

©NARA

President Eisenhower doing a spot inspection of the Korean front before his inauguration in December 1952. He made swift ending of the Korean War a presidential election pledge.

United States could ensure South Korea's security in the future.[20] The US government was initially disinclined to accept Rhee's stipulation. It was believed that the signing of the mutual defense treaty between the United States and South Korea could negatively impact the armistice negotiations.[21] In the end, however, Washington decided to partially accept Rhee's demand in order to avoid uncertainties that could arise from carrying out the emergency plan.

The US government decided to inform the South Korean government that it was ready to sign a mutual defense treaty with South Korea in late May of 1953.[22] Rhee was informed of this in early June.[23] Rhee, however, did not immediately accept the American offer. He demanded continued maintenance of twenty South Korean army divisions, the strengthening of the South Korean air force and navy, and the immediate signing of the treaty. In addition, Rhee unilaterally released anticommunist POWs.

The US government was shocked at Rhee's reactions. The

unilateral release of the anticommunist POWs was particularly concerning to the United States, as the South Korean units responsible for it moved independently under the order of Rhee instead of the United Nations Command.

As will be discussed in greater detail later on, a major issue of contention between the United States government and the South Korean military government at the time of the May 16 coup d'etat was over the fact that the South Korean military units were moved by the coup forces without the approval of the UN commander. The same issue was also raised with Rhee. The US government maintained that a mutual defense treaty was only possible with the official recognition that the South Korean military units' operational control remained with the United Nations commander.[24]

Even with the unilateral release of anticommunist POWs, however, the United States did not execute the emergency plan against Rhee. Instead, a special envoy was dispatched to Seoul to both pressure and persuade the South Korean government to agree with the armistice. While pressuring the South Korean government with the threats of the military withdrawal, the envoy also convinced it that the United States could accept the South Korean demand for security.

The special emissary to South Korea was Assistant Secretary Robertson. He emphasized to Rhee that various kinds of aid and cooperation would take place after the armistice. He also threatened that US aid to South Korea would be severed if Rhee refused to cooperate.

In the end, Rhee accepted the American demand, saying that while he would not sign the armistice, he wouldn't prevent the cease-fire either. Rhee's demand of an "automatic intervention" clause, however, ultimately was not accepted by the United States. The terms stipulated that the American intervention in the case of North Korean invasion would still require the ratification of the US Congress, and the United States would not intervene at all if the South was the aggressor.

(4) Learning Effect

a. The United States' Learning Effect: Let's Develop New Leadership
The plans to overthrow Syngman Rhee did not perish even after the

war's end. The US government could not let its guard down given his repeated calls for northward advance after the armistice. When the conflict between South Korea and the United States resumed over the issue of operational control of the South Korean military forces in 1954, Washington once again contemplated overthrowing Syngman Rhee, and such a plan had been maintained at least since that time.[25]

That being the case, why was the plan not carried out? According to the relevant US documents, the lack of South Korean political leaders capable of replacing Syngman Rhee was the biggest single reason for American hesitation. Given the ongoing war, the United States needed a strong and charismatic anticommunist leader in South Korea. In the American eyes, there was no better-known and charismatic leader in South Korea than Syngman Rhee. The US agencies had evaluated Rhee as someone who was capable of effectively controlling the South Korean society using anticommunist ideology.[26] Such capability, however, was not entirely based on Rhee's charisma–Syngman Rhee was simply the best-known politician in a society that was still fairly restricted and limited in terms of information flow.

Things might have developed differently had Kim Gyusik survived his kidnapping to North Korea during the Korean War. But the South Korean society at the time still did not have a leader who could replace Syngman Rhee. While some recommended the former South Korean ambassador to the United States Jang Myeon and the Democratic National Party's Sin Ikhui, they were still relatively unknown to the South Korean public. While they enjoyed certain degrees of popularity among politicians, they did not have the hold on the people to the extent that Rhee had. Jang was known for his gentlemanly attitude towards others, but he was also known to be weak. Sin had political capabilities, but he lacked in popular support. Sin's pre-1945 political career was also suspicious as he was also involved in the Korean Provisional Government even after the establishment of the US military government in Korea as well as in sending terrorists into North Korea in 1946.

There were, of course, reasons other than domestic conditions in South Korea. The US government was also concerned with other possible repercussions, including international criticism, wartime social disturbances in South Korea, and the reactions of certain members of the US military establishment who were against removing Syngman Rhee. The most important reason, however, was the fact that there was no leader in South Korea who could replace Rhee even after 1953.

There are two important things to note about this plan. First, the United States government began recognizing the need for a leadership replacement in a concrete way through its experiences with Syngman Rhee from 1952 to 1954. The document produced on November 8, 1954 to supplement the existing plan for Rhee's removal displays this aspect of US Korea policy:

> Contacts with Korean political and mil leaders will be increased and to the extent deemed appropriate they may be informed that Rhee's continued refusal to cooperate with US may rqr reexam of US attitude toward Rhee Govt, incl consideration of possible altn situations which might be brought about by Koreans themselves; that the US could only consider supp leaders who rep broad segment of political opinion in Korea, have the supp and cooperation of ROKA, and can dmst their ability to cooperate together and With US; and that US would consider prov political asylum in US mil instl on an indiv basis to extent US auth are sat that it is essential and wrnt by circumstances.[27]

This aspect is also evident in the letter from the Joint Chiefs of Staff to the Secretary of Defense on December 7, 1954:

> To develop the basis for select and encourage covertly the development of new South Korean leadership prepared to cooperate in maintaining the armistice, and if Rhee initiates or is about to initiate unilateral action, to enable assist such new leadership to assume power, by UNC resort to martial law if necessary means not involving overt U.S. participation until and unless U.S. overt support is necessary and promises to be decisive in firmly establishing such new leadership.[28]

As can be seen in the quotations, the United States government realized the need to prepare for post-Rhee leadership in South

Korea. In other words, conflict with Syngman Rhee always was a possibility, and such potential for conflict could only be resolved by replacing him with a new leadership more amendable to the United States. Plans were made for deep intervention into South Korean politics.

This plan appears to have been carried out to an extent during the process of the third South Korean presidential election in 1956. While not clearly evident in the declassified US documents, there was a significant rumor circulating in Seoul that the new US ambassador William Lacy was sent from Washington to engineer Rhee's fall in the upcoming third presidential election in South Korea.[29] Lacy had intervened deeply in the 1953 presidential election in the Philippines prior to his stop in South Korea. The US agencies in the Philippines at the time played a pivotal role in helping pro-American conservative Ramon Magsaysay win the election.

Syngman Rhee protested Lacy's appointment as the US ambassador by seizing the properties of Americans in South Korea. The US-South Korea relations therefore worsened with Lacy's appointment. In the end, Ambassador Lacy went back to the United States after spending less than a year in the country. Walter C. Dowling replaced him.

The plan, however, was not yet over. The US agencies on the ground in South Korea began making contacts with important South Koreans through diverse channels. The first group of men to be contacted by the American agencies for the upcoming 1956 election included Yi Gibung, technocrats from the Liberal Party, and major figures in the South Korean military forces who were friendly to the United States.

The US agencies on the ground in South Korea at the time predicted that the Liberal Party would win the 1956 presidential election by a comfortable margin. The vice president would become particularly important in this case, as the octogenarian Syngman Rhee might not be able to fulfill his term to the end. In other words, the United States wanted to prepare for the post–Syngman Rhee era. The US government preferred the Liberal Party moderates who possessed a certain amount of technical and professional expertise. In order to physically support them, of course, the United States also made contacts with certain senior officers of the South

Korean military establishment.

The prediction made by the American agencies, however, proved to be wrong–Jang Myeon in the end defeated the Liberal Party's vice presidential candidate Yi Gibung. The US government and its agencies were probably shocked by the election result. They soon had to opt for a new strategy.

An interesting point is that the US agencies in South Korea preferred Yi Gibung and other technocrats from the Liberal Party over the anti-Rhee politicians of the Democratic Party. The Democratic Party members were not only more conservative than the Liberal Party members, but they tended to be more pro-American. The Democratic Party was close to the United States since the time of US military government, and it included conservatives with strong ties to the United States, such as the former South Korean ambassador to the United States Jang Myeon. When Sin Ikhui died prior to the 1956 presidential election, some of the South Korean Democrats had even supported Syngman Rhee over Jo Bongam of the Progressive Party.

Even then, however, the United States did not trust the Democratic Party. The following quote is an American evaluation of the particularities of Korean politics. It also shows the US agencies' negative perception of the Democratic Party.

> It is very difficult to assess with any degree of accuracy the attitude of the Korean public toward the Democratic Party. That there is a very considerable amount of popular enthusiasm for it is indicated by the large attendance which has been reported at promotional and organizational meetings throughout the Republic. This enthusiasm probably is based on the premise that anything would be better than the party in power. Nevertheless, many people–especially the younger ones–recall with distaste the excesses and abuses of which the predecessor Democratic Nationalist Party was considered guilty during the early days of the Republic, when it wielded considerable power in the police, in government enterprises, in the Assembly, and in certain ministries; these people fear that if the Democratic Party were to take control of the government it would revert to the same corruption, inefficiency, and use of force which it is now imputing to the present Administration.

Korean political attitudes typically are based in large part upon (1) factionalism–"my clique against their clique"; (2) pragmatism–"what is in this for me and my family"; (3) disillusionment–"all governments are bad"; "the situation of Korea is hopeless"; "you can't trust anybody"; (4) individualism–"you can't do this to me"; (5) personal loyalties to individual leaders, rather than to abstract ideals; (6) the desire to be a "big shot"; (7) the desire for Korean unification; (8) nationalism, or more accurately, race-consciousness; (9) residual influence of the traditional Confucian ideals; and (10) influence of Western political theory. A healthy dislike and distrust for Communism has been added since 1950.

These attitudes have the results that (1) Koreans are slow to throw in their lot with a new group, and quick to distrust it; (2) they are readily frightened away from their somewhat confused ideals in pursuit of short-run safety or satisfaction; (3) they can only with difficulty be made to support a group which cannot offer them prompt and tangible rewards. ...

A French diplomat neatly summed it up with the remark, "The Koreans are too glorious." Perhaps this immaturity is inevitable in a people so recently relieved of the yoke of a foreign colonial government. Signs of progress are in evidence; even such a degree of coherence as the Democratic Party has attained would have been impossible five years ago. But Korean politics are still a far cry from American politics; the Democratic Party in Korea is not to be compared with the Democratic Party in the United States in any but an ideal sense.[30]

As can be seen in the quote, the United States held a negative perception vis-à-vis the Democratic Party, evaluating them as feudal and without effective leadership. The US government had paid attention to the potential new leadership centering around Jang Myeon at the time of the Busan Incident in 1952. The US hopes, however, dissipated when Jang Myeon fled to a UN hospital ship and other anti-Rhee politicians of the Democratic Party did nothing except to lean on the United States. The US government in the 1950s evaluated Jang Myeon as both gentlemanly as well as indecisive and lacking in leadership.

The negative US perceptions of the opposition centering on the

Democratic Party continued into the 1960s. The US government judged that it would be dangerous to allow the faction-ridden Democratic Party to take over the government in South Korea. This perception repeated itself in the constitutional amending of 1969 and in the "Seoul Spring" of 1979-80. Given South Korea's strategic place as a front line against the North Korean and Chinese powers, the US government decided that it would be even more dangerous to allow the weak Democratic Party to take over.

The US agencies on the ground therefore paid more attention to the role of the Liberal Party's technocrats. Although many of them had collaborated with the Japanese colonial government before 1945, the US agencies nevertheless believed that their expertise was necessary in "modernizing" or "Americanizing" Korean politics.

In the end, however, this perception of the United States proved to be wrong. Yi Gibung and the Liberal Party's technocrats, whom the US government entrusted with the post-Rhee era, eventually became the hard-liners within the Liberal Party after 1956. They also played a key role in rigging the March 15 election. The US misperception was caused by overlooking their past histories as collaborators with the Japanese. Because of their "tainted" past, they had to rely on the leadership of Syngman Rhee for survival rather than use their expertise to modernize Korean politics.

On the other hand, the US agencies on the ground also made contacts with younger technocrats in order to prepare for a long-term solution in South Korea. The US Embassy in Seoul often held regular seminars for councilors, inviting many young and promising South Korean technocrats to the meeting. Seminars involved heated discussions of a wide variety of topics, including Korean politics, society, and the economy.

The seminar was often led by the US Embassy counselor Edwin Cronk. Those who participated in the seminar at the US Embassy in Seoul later played significant roles in important government organs such as the Ministry of Finance and the Economic Planning Board. The members often called themselves the "thinkers," and played key roles in the government into the Yusin era of the 1970s. As will be written in greater detail later on, the United States pressured Seoul to utilize these technocrats when the US government and the South Korean military government had conflicts over economic policies.

b. Syngman Rhee's Learning Effect

Conflicts with the United States from 1952 to 1954 also provided "learning effects" for the Syngman Rhee government. Rhee must have realized during the Korean War that the United States had plans to remove him from power. From the Busan Incident, in particular, he realized that the United States could support his political opponents in an effort to remove him–Rhee had heard that the United States government was trying to replace him with Jang Myeon.

In the end, however, the United States did not execute the plan to overthrow Rhee. Syngman Rhee must have realized that the United States did not have alternatives to his strong leadership based on fierce anticommunism. Such experience must have been important in convincing Rhee that he could challenge the United States by unilaterally releasing the anticommunist POWs in 1953. Syngman Rhee must have realized that he could still hold onto power regardless of whether or not there were conflicts with the United States in its Korea policy. It is not difficult to surmise that Rhee's "brinkmanship," mentions of which can be found in the US documents from the 1950s, comes from such belief.

Syngman Rhee did not shy from coming into conflict with the United States on issues over exchange rates and South Korea-Japan relations. The exchange rate was pivotal in determining the amount of aid South Korea was going to receive from the United States. Upward evaluation of the South Korean currency meant more aid from the United States, and downward evaluation meant less. If we suppose that the costs of maintaining the South Korean military forces amounted to 100 million Korean hwan, the South Korean government could receive US$200,000 with the 500 hwan–to–1 dollar rate, while the 1000 hwan–to–1 dollar rate would only leave US$100,000.

US aid for South Korea was determined largely by calculating how much money would be necessary to maintain South Korean military forces. The South Korean government therefore could receive more aid the higher the South Korean currency was evaluated in relationship to the US dollar. Some researchers view such a policy as a strategy for import substitution industrialization. Given the negative stance Syngman Rhee had for economic development plans, however, the policy's aim was merely to receive "more dollars" from the United States in order to cover budget deficits.

As will be discussed in greater detail later, the US government of the 1950s pursued the New Look policy. One of the New Look policy's goals was to reduce foreign aid. The exchange rate issue with South Korea therefore was an important part of achieving this goal.

The South Korean government at the time focused on evaluating the South Korean currency to the maximum extent upwards to receive as much aid as possible. On the morning of Lunar New Year's Day in 1953, the South Korean government publicized its currency reform. While currency reform was in part absolutely necessary given the enormous inflation generated by the war,[31] the main aim was to fix the exchange rate. The South Korean government, through this reform, set 100 won as 1 hwan, and it also sought to fix the exchange rate to 180 hwan to 1 US dollar.

The US government strongly opposed the South Korean government's policy. In the case of Japan, for example, the Japanese government maintained a reduced budget and a tight control over currency circulation after the declaration of the Dodge Line in 1949. Such policies allowed a fixed exchange rate between the Japanese yen and the US dollar. South Korea, however, could not maintain a fixed exchange rate because of the increasing money supply. The war produced a high rate of unemployment in South Korea and the South Korean government had a hard time collecting taxes. It had no choice but to keep increasing the money supply to meet government expenditures. The South Korean government of the 1950s also pursued the building and maintenance of major fertilizer plants, glass plants, and steel works in addition to maintaining an enormous six-hundred-thousand-man military. The South Korean economy could not handle these expenses, and the South Korean government chose to make up the deficit by increasing the money supply.

Many of the pacts concluded between the United States and South Korea around the time of the armistice had to do with the exchange rate and aid. For example, the 1952 Agreement on Economic Coordination (also known as the Meyer Agreement)[32] and the 1953 Combined Economic Board Agreement for a Program of Economic Reconstruction and Financial Stabilization were signed in order to adjust the exchange rate and facilitate effective uses of the counterpart fund generated from US aid and exchange rate adjustment. Through the negotiations, the US government created the Office of Economic Coordinator in South Korea in order to allow the UN commander's economic advisors to oversee the uses of US Korea aid. The US government also pushed for a program for financial stability to curb the South Korean government from increasing the money supply.

In addition, the United States government created a stipulation allowing it to control the exchange rate when the value of South Korean currency dropped by more than 30 percent of its value due to an increase in money supply. The currency reform that set the exchange rate at 180 Korean hwan to 1 US dollar was later adjusted to 500 hwan to 1 dollar in 1955. Immediately before the 1960 April Revolution, the exchange rate was again adjusted to 650 hwan to 1 US dollar.

The rates, however, were merely official. Actual exchange rates at the market approximately doubled the official rate–1,280 Korean hwan to 1 US dollar. While the US government continued to pressure the South Korean government to actualize the exchange rate, Syngman Rhee did not back down. Rhee obsessed over the foreign currency to the point that he himself would approve each outflow of dollars from the country.

According to Song Insang, then the minister of prosperity, the president's personal approval was necessary even when students or government officials exchanged money for their study abroad.[33] The South Korean government also differentiated its exchange rate. Exchange rates all differed for missionaries exchanging money, the UN Command exchanging money, and businessmen exchanging money.

While the program for financial stability, pushed after 1957 when US aid to South Korea dropped significantly, reduced the expansion of the money supply and curbed inflation, the gap between official and market exchange rates remained. And because of this, there was a widespread rumor in South Korea that the new US ambassador to Korea Walter McConaughy, who was appointed in July 1959,

©National Archives of Korea

Photograph of Lieutenant General Stikov, a Soviet representative at the US-Soviet Commission, making a speech. The United States and the Soviet Union confronted each other over the issue of trusteeship. On January 16, 1946 at Deoksu Palace in Seoul.

came to South Korea to handle the exchange rate problem.[34] Regardless of his intentions, McConaughy nevertheless played an important role in Rhee's resignation by informing him that the United States no longer supported him at the time of the April Revolution in 1960. Additionally, the exchange rate changed three times during his stay in South Korea as the US ambassador (from July 1959 to May 1961). The official exchange rate even reached the market rate during the Democratic Party rule. But Syngman Rhee, however, maintained his "brinkmanship" on the issue of exchange rate until the day he was removed by the April Revolution.

Another issue of contention between the United States and South Korea in the 1950s was South Korea-Japan relations. The Eisenhower administration actively encouraged the normalization of relations between the two countries in order to "pass off" some of the US financial burden in supporting South Korea to Japan. The negotiations for normalization began soon after the Japanese government reasserted sovereignty through the conclusion of the Treaty of San Francisco with the Allied Powers in 1951.

However, the difference of opinion on the Japanese colonial period in Korea between the two countries made the negotiations particularly difficult. The two issues in particular that caused conflict between them were the 1953 statement by Kubota Kanichiro and the beginning of Japanese repatriation of ethnic Koreans to North Korea in 1959. The Kubota statement refers to the public remarks by Kubota Kanichiro, one of the Japanese representatives in the negotiations, in which he claimed that the Japanese colonial rule was beneficial to Korea. His statement caused the South Korean government to shut down negotiations, and there was no progress for the next five years.

While the Kubota statement constituted an important obstacle to the negotiations on the surface, perhaps the bigger issues of contention were the question of reparations and the Syngman Rhee Line. While the South Korean government contended that it should be compensated for the Japanese colonial period's damages, the Japanese government maintained that there was no need for compensation given the Korean confiscation of Japanese property in Korea. The Japanese government even asserted that it should be compensated for the confiscation. The Syngman Rhee Line refers to the unilateral South Korean declaration of maritime boundary vis-à-vis Japan beyond the borders designated by international law. While the roots of the two issues were based on the policies of the US military government and the Far Eastern Command, the United States did not make an effort to explain and resolve them as it encouraged the normalization of relations between South Korea and Japan.[35]

The repatriation of ethnic Koreans to North Korea raised sharper issues of contention. Seoul was vehemently against the repatriation. Syngman Rhee, who had refused to accept Japan-made products even as aid goods from the United States, ordered the immediate severing of economic exchanges with Japan. While the South Korean side was to suffer heavier losses from this act due to the difference in sizes of the two economies, Syngman Rhee nevertheless pushed for the trade embargo. He did not abandon the powerful (and useful) anti-Japanese "ideology" in controlling the Korean people.

While the US government continued to pressure South Korea for the normalization of relations, Syngman Rhee did not back down to the end. The US-South Korea conflict over this issue was so serious that the US government in part welcomed the 1960 April Revolution and subsequent overthrow of Syngman Rhee as a chance to resolve the normalization issue once and for all.

In the end, US plans to remove Syngman Rhee from 1952 to 1954 provided a "learning effect" for Syngman Rhee that he could stand up to the United States in managing the US-South Korea relations. Believing that South Korea should become "another Japan with active US support," there were times that Syngman Rhee did not back down from his "brinkmanship."

3. Changes in US Korea Policy through the New Look

(1) A Nuclear Korean Peninsula

On January 8, 1958, Assistant Secretary of State for Far Eastern Affairs Walter S. Robertson sent the following telegram to the Assistant Secretary of Defense for International Security Affairs Mansfield Sprague.

> The timing of the introduction of the Honest John and 280mm gun battalions into Korea with the concurrent introduction of related materials authorized in DEF 933850 and DEF 933889, is, as you know, of great interest to us. Although we have mutually agreed to move the battalions into Korea without publicity, we can expect the Koreans to give this action considerable play in official statements and in the press upon arrival of these weapons in Korea or soon thereafter.
>
> In view of this anticipated reaction in Korea and the effect the movement of dual-capable weapons into Korea can be expected to have in Japan and other countries in the Far East it is important that the Department of State be fully informed on the plans regarding the timing of these introductions. It would be appreciated, therefore, if you would keep me informed on the exact timing of the introduction of these items.[36]

DEF 933850 (December 11, 1957) was the telegram sent by Assistant Secretary Sprague to the United Nations Commander George Henry Decker. It recommended that the South Korean military forces of 676,995 men be reduced by 60,000 and Honest John rockets and 280-millimeter guns be deployed to South Korea.[37] DEF 933889 (November 11, 1957) is a still-classified Department of Defense document that argues that the deployment of the two weapons should not coincide with a reduction of South Korean military forces.

At the request of the Department of State, the Department of Defense notified the Department of State in the name of Assistant Secretary John Irwin on January 16 of the same year that the One Hundredth Artillery Battalion (equipped with Honest John rockets) and the 663rd Artillery Battalion (with 280-millimeter guns) would be deployed in South Korea by January 31. However, due to the objections of the South Korean government and the United Nations Commander Lyman Lemnitzer[38]–not against deploying of new weapons but the reduction of South Korean military forces–the Department of Defense, in the name of Assistant Secretary Sprague, responded by stating that the weapons would be deployed in the fourth quarter of the 1958 fiscal year (April, May, and June of 1958) and that eighteen months would be required for their full installation on the ground.[39]

While this process was supposedly carried out by the US and South Korean governments, as expected, the South Korean government soon leaked the information to the media. A newspaper article arguing that the United States would deploy nuclear weapons in South Korea appeared in the morning paper of January 29, 1958.[40] The First Corps of the US military forces revealed the cannon and the Honest John rockets, both capable of delivering nuclear warheads, on February 3, 1958. The two weapons were field-tested on the central front on May 1 of the same year. This was the second time nuclear weapons were deployed in the Far East, the first being the Honest John rockets placed in the Far Eastern Command in Japan in August of 1955. While the South Korean forces did not receive Honest John rockets until June 3, 1971, the South Korean media at the time made a great fuss about the fact that the South Korean military now possessed weapons that could deliver atomic warheads.

The first two months of 1958, during the deployment of these weapons, were a tumultuous time for the Korean Peninsula. The so-called Progressive Party Incident broke out immediately after the year began. Jo Bongam and other officers of that party were arrested on January 13 in an effort to rig the outcome of the upcoming general election. North Korea and China released special statements on February 5 and 7, stating that the Chinese forces would soon withdraw from North Korea and that they were hoping that the other foreign military forces would do the same. The United States, representing the United Nations forces, stated that it had no desire to withdraw its forces from Korea until its reunification. A South Korean airplane was skyjacked on February 16, and the North Korean government proclaimed on February 17 that it had safely landed in North Korea. The Military Armistice Commission spent over a year negotiating the return of the passengers and crew.

What is striking is that the incidents of the first two months of 1958 all had to do with the Korean armistice. First, while the Progressive Party Incident was political, it also became an important issue during the trial of a double agent named Yang Myeongsan. Yang Myeongsan was both an agent of South Korea's Headquarters Intelligence Detachment (HID) and also associated with its North Korean counterpart. Such covert intrigues were violations of the conditions of armistice that stipulated that all North-South contacts be made through the Military Armistice Commission. The issues of withdrawal of foreign forces and the skyjacking were discussed as part of the agenda of the Military Armistice Commission.

However, the most important issue regarding the armistice was the deployment of a new and far more destructive weapon that had not been used during the time of the Korean War, a clear violation of clause (d) of article 13. The relevant part of the armistice agreement reads as follows:

Cease the introduction into Korea of reinforcing combat aircraft, armored vehicles, weapons, and ammunition; provided however, that combat aircraft, armored vehicles, weapons, and ammunition which are destroyed, damaged, worn out, or used up during the period of the armistice may be replaced on the basis piece-for-piece of the same effectiveness and the same type.

Clause (d) of article 13 stated that the Neutral Nations Supervisory Commission should monitor ten ports in North and South Korea to prevent introduction of new types of weapons into the Korean Peninsula. Sinuiju, Cheongjin, Heungnam, Manpo, and Sinanju were the five designated ports in North Korea, and Incheon, Daegu, Busan, Gangneung, and Gunsan were the ports designated in South Korea. The Neutral Nations Supervisory Commission's Neutral Nations Inspection Teams were to monitor the ten ports and report to the Armistice Commission. Given the regulations, how could the United States reveal the deployment of new weapons?

(2) The United States' Preparatory Work: The Departure of Neutral Nations and Invalidation of Clause (d) of Article 13

In reality, the US government was already doing preparatory work to rescind clause (d) of article 13 even before the deployment of nuclear weapons in South Korea. One such effort was to abolish the Neutral Nations Supervisory Commission's Neutral Nations Inspection Teams. The establishment of Neutral Nations Inspection Teams had been a thorny issue even from the time of the 1951 armistice negotiations. The North Korean and Chinese side saw such surveillance as an effort to obstruct reconstruction and politically interfere in North Korea, while the United Nations side insisted on it to maintain its superiority in air power by overseeing all improvements in military establishments and increases in military strength.

After much dispute, both sides agreed on the establishment of Neutral Nations Inspection Teams–the communist side withdrew its demand to include the Soviets in the inspection teams and the UN side withdrew its insistence on overseeing the new construction of airfields. While some issues continued to linger, both sides agreed that the inspection teams were to be made up of representatives from Sweden, Switzerland, Poland, and Czechoslovakia. The inspectors were also to receive legal guarantees from each side so that they could inspect freely.

After the signing of the armistice, however, the United States began displaying signs of skepticism toward the inspectors' activities. The problem started with the composition of neutral nations involved. The United States maintained that because Poland and Czechoslovakia are de facto satellite states of the Soviet Union, their participation would only obstruct the UN forces' activities. The United States government continued to insist that Polish and Czechoslovakian representatives were spying. US insistence became stronger after the Soviet crushing of the Hungarian Revolution of 1956. The United Nations commander already had reported to the Joint Chiefs of Staff in June 1954 that the Neutral Nations Inspection Teams were obstructing the activities of the UN forces to a significant degree. He argued that the inspection teams must be withdrawn, suggesting that the United States should induce self-withdrawals of the Swedish and Swiss representatives in order stimulate the complete withdrawal of the inspection teams.[41]

The UN commander's opinion was accepted by the US government and it subsequently sought to shut down the inspection activities by first persuading the Swiss and Swedish representatives to withdraw. The US ambassador notified the South Korean government of this course of action[42] and sought to tame the South Korean demonstrations against the inspectors. In order to stop the inspectors' activities on the other side, the US government's course of action was to publicize through British and French media outlets that the Swedish and Swiss inspectors were having difficulties carrying out inspections in the North.[43]

On the other hand, the South Korean government had been critical of the inspectors since the middle of 1954. Basing itself on the armistice agreement, the South Korean government continuously argued for the complete withdrawal of inspectors from the 1954 Geneva Conference.[44] The South Korean government even proclaimed a deadline, urging the Polish and Czechoslovakian representatives to leave the country by August 13, 1955.[45] The South Korean government also organized large demonstrations against them by mobilizing its citizens. Such demonstrations began in early August of 1955 and continued into December of the same year. According to newspaper reports, some 9 million people participated in them.[46] These demonstrations even included Chinese-Korean participators from Incheon as well as those working in the service trade.[47] There were a number of car accidents and the demonstrators even clashed with Americans in uniform.[48]

While the United States and the South Korean government were both against the inspectors' activities, they nevertheless differed in their methods in achieving the withdrawal. Syngman Rhee, as he did during the negotiations for armistice, organized massive and fierce demonstrations, which differed from the American strategy and even conflicted with it. Mass demonstrations against the Military Armistice Commission's decision only made things difficult for the United States in the international media.

In the end, Secretary of State John Foster Dulles notified the South Korean government that such demonstrations were not conducive to US policy. Dulles instead sought to resolve the issue without providing propaganda material for the communist side.[49]

This development was similar to what happened during the armistice negotiations when Syngman Rhee challenged the negotiations by ordering mass demonstrations.

In the 1955 policy document NSC 5514, the United States established the policy aim to "[w]idely publicize the fact that the Communists, with the connivance of the Communist members of the Neutral Nations Supervisory Commission, have violated the provisions of the Armistice Agreement since its inception."[50] This course of action meant invalidating the legitimacy of the inspectors' activities themselves.

Another obstacle for US policy was the Swedish and Swiss representatives' noncooperation. Believing that the American demands would cost them unnecessary trouble with the communist countries, they instead suggested passing on more responsibilities to the Military Armistice Commission while reducing the inspectors' roles. Switzerland and Sweden had diplomatic relations with both the Soviet Union and China. They did not want to suffer diplomatically over the issues of inspection in Korea. Despite US pressure through the Swedish ambassador to the United States,[51] Sweden and Switzerland maintained their stance against the complete withdrawal and reduced the number of inspection teams to one each.[52]

The United States government insisted through meetings with the fifteen other nations of the United Nations forces that there was no alternative to the complete withdrawal of inspectors. The sixteen nations also argued for limiting the activities of inspectors to the neutral zones, including the Joint Security Area.[53] Then at the seventieth meeting of the Military Armistice Commission on May 31, 1956, General Robert G. Gard declared the inspections to be a failure. He blamed the sources of this failure on the noncooperation of North Korean and Chinese forces in the North and the abnormal activities of Polish and Czechoslovak inspectors in the South. He concluded that he would stop all inspection activities in the South as long as the communist side continued to violate the terms of armistice.[54]

Starting with the Polish and Czechoslovak inspectors working in Busan on June 6, all inspectors began withdrawing from their posts in South Korea to Panmunjeom in June 1956.[55] Inspection activities by neutral nations therefore permanently ended. This meant that both sides could increase their military capabilities in Korea without any restraint.

Second, the United States followed the withdrawal of inspectors with a declaration of annulment invalidating clause (d) of article 13. While the debates on the inspectors were ongoing, the United Nations Command strongly protested to the Military Armistice Commission that the communist side was strengthening its military forces in North Korea. The inspectors reported the introduction of additional airplanes into North Korea on February 11, 1954, and the South Korean government protested using the intelligence information provided by escapees from North Korea about the introduction of three hundred MiG aircraft into North Korea as well as the training of three thousand Soviet troops there. The South Korean government contended that this was a clear violation of the armistice–particularly clause (d) of article 13.[56]

On January 31, 1955, in the midst of heated debates surrounding the violation of clause (d) of article 13, United Nations Commander John Hull suggested that the Department of Defense annul it in addition to the withdrawal of inspectors. Hull insisted that the United States should push for its annulment even if the other fifteen nations of the United Nations forces disagreed.[57] On February 5 of the same year, the US Department of State dispatched a message saying that while it agreed with the UN commander's perspective, a unilateral action on the part of the United States would not be best considering the political and legal ramifications. The State Department also stated that a list of evidence proving that the communist side violated clause (d) of article 13 was also necessary.[58]

The US Department of State closely coordinated with the other fifteen nations of the UN forces on the issues surrounding the annulment of clause (d) of article 13 at an international meeting held in February 1955. The Department of State, of course, had stated that a unilateral call for annulment as described by the Department of Defense was not suitable.[59] However, the Department of State nevertheless argued at the meeting of sixteen nations on February 24 that an increase of military capabilities in South Korea was necessary given the violations by the communist side. Such discussions for the political and legal justification of clause (d) of article 13's annulment continued into the 240th National Security Council meeting in which the US president, secretary of defense, and the chairman of the Joint Chiefs of Staff participated.[60]

On April 21, 1955, United Nations Commander Hull attended the National Security Council meeting. At the meeting, the UN commander emphasized the violations of the armistice on the part of communists. According to Hull, the Soviets were delivering new weapons into North Korea via routes other than the ports. The longer clause (d) of article 13 was maintained, the worse it was for the United States and its allies. While the United States also needed to introduce new weapons into Korea, Hull insisted that the United States was "too big" to imitate the communists by secretly doing so.[61] Clause (d) of article 13 therefore needed to be annulled.

Despite the rounds of discussions, different agencies of the US government could not reach a consensus for the annulment. While they could easily agree on the issue of inspectors given the fact that Poland and Czechoslovakia were "enemy" nations, it was far more difficult to provide a solid list of evidence that the communists had violated clause (d) of article 13 without the satellites and high-performance reconnaissance planes available today. Secretary of State Dulles even expressed that the clause should not be a policy priority. Dulles also believed that the conditions on the Korean Peninsula were not urgent.[62]

President Eisenhower also stated that, unlike the disbanding of inspection teams, the annulment of the clause could not be carried out without the agreement of the other fifteen nations.[63] Even after a year of discussions, the Department of State continued to maintain that neutral nations would not accept the evidence provided by the Joint Chiefs of Staff.[64]

The only solution was to discover hard evidence that the communist side had been violating the armistice in order to persuade the other fifteen nations. State Department officials met with the officials of the British and French Embassies on May 13 and 21 of 1955 to find ways to persuade the other nations. Such discussions continued irregularly with the foreign embassy personnel in Washington.

Criticisms against the inspectors from the United Nations forces and the South Korean military forces continued unabated. The South

Korean chief of staff Jeong Ilgwon visited the Department of State with the attaché to the South Korean Embassy Yi Hurak during his visit to Washington in June 1955. During their meeting, Jeong stated that the communists had violated the armistice in five areas, including the introduction of airplanes, tanks, and flamethrowers.[65] The US representative, General Harlan Parks, argued at the sixtieth Military Armistice Commission meeting that the North Korean and Chinese forces had violated the armistice agreement in serious ways. Parks particularly pointed to the introduction of MiG fighters and the North Korean attempts at cover-up.[66] The subsequent Military Armistice Commission meetings became stages in which the UN forces denounced the communist side's armistice violations.[67]

Finally, Secretary of State Dulles declared at a press conference on May 14, 1957 that the United States would deploy "more modern, more effective" weapons in South Korea. Secretary of Defense Charles Wilson reconfirmed that the weapons to be deployed in South Korea might include "dual capability" weapons such as guided missiles.[68] On June 21 of the same year, General Homer Litzenberg of the United States declared at the Military Armistice Commission meeting that clause (d) of article 13 was invalid until the communist side displayed a willingness to abide by it.[69]

Two preparatory steps, the disbanding of the inspectors and the annulment of clause (d) of article 13, were pivotal in the US introduction of new weapons in South Korea. As can be seen from the discussions that went on inside the US government, the two provisions of the armistice were significant political and legal obstacles to the new US military strategy surrounding the Korean Peninsula.

These two steps, of course, were not exclusive to each other. The inspection work at the South Korean ports would become unnecessary if clause (d) of article 13 became invalid. The cessation of inspection activities would also render that clause irrelevant, as there would not be anyone to carry it out. An invalidation of one provision therefore would lead to an automatic invalidation of the other.

Questions, however, do remain. The abovementioned preparatory work was the endpoint of discussions that went on inside of the US government since 1954. What is puzzling is that such declarations suddenly were made when no real consensus has been reached after three years of debate between the Department of State, the Joint Chiefs of Staff, and the United Nations Command. The debate on clause (d) of article 13 suddenly stopped after the unilateral declaration by the United Nations forces at the seventieth Military Armistice Commission meeting in March 1956. What caused such change? Did the United States acquire the sweeping concurrence of the other fifteen nations? Did the United States catch the communists introducing new weapons into North Korea red-handed?

(3) Nuclear Weapons are the Best Way to Reduce Military Expenses

Another important factor was at play in the midst of the cutoff of US aid to South Korea, the reduction of US forces in Korea and the South Korean forces, and the modernization programs that accompanied the reductions. As mentioned earlier, the Eisenhower administration focused on reducing government spending abroad under the banner of the New Look policy from its beginning in 1953. The New Look policy's number-one priority was to resolve the enormous budget deficit generated by the Korean War.[70] The "New Look" meant a new direction in governance and signified that the Eisenhower administration's philosophy differed from that of the Keynesian Truman administration.

For the Eisenhower administration, the first step in cutting the government budget meant reducing of US military forces stationed abroad in order to reduce military expenses. The US forces in Korea became a target of this new policy direction. After reaching its peak at 320,000 men at the time of the Korean War's armistice, the US forces in Korea went through a steady reduction throughout the 1950s. Four army divisions left South Korea in 1954. Another left in 1956. The US forces in Korea stood at around seventy thousand men by the end of the 1950s.[71]

The US government also sought the reduction of South Korean military forces. Cutting of foreign aid was unavoidable in resolving the problem of budget deficit. It meant that South Korea, the number-one recipient of US aid during the 1950s, was going to receive less from the United States. Given the fact that most US aid was used in maintaining the South Korean military forces, the reduction of the South Korean military forces was necessary. The US Joint Chiefs of Staff, however, vigorously argued against the reduction given that the Korean War had just ended and that Chinese forces were still stationed in North Korea. Nevertheless, the Eisenhower administration pushed for the reduction.[72]

Most conflicts between the United States and South Korea during the 1950s stem from the American desire to reduce spending there. Perhaps the most representative conflict of the 1950s was the abovementioned collision over exchange rates. Another relevant example was the discussions dating from 1955 that led to the signing of the Treaty of Friendship, Commerce, and Navigation between the United States and South Korea in 1956. The US aim in signing this treaty was to reduce government spending on aid to South Korea by increasing direct investment on the part of civilian investors from the United States. Of course, the reduction of South Korean military forces also had to do with reducing the amount of US aid to South Korea. Despite Seoul's protests, the US government reduced aid to around two-thirds of the previous level after 1957. The Syngman Rhee government's offers to dispatch South Korean military forces to Indochina, Indonesia, and Laos on three occasions in 1954, 1958, and 1959 stem from a desire to stop the reduction of South Korean military forces.[73]

The new direction taken by the US government is evident in perhaps all Korea-related policy papers from the Eisenhower era. While the 1954 Agreed Minutes and Amendment between the United States and South Korea defined the size of US aid to Korea and the South Korean military forces, the reduction of forces in South Korea and methods for persuading the South Korean government to accept it became important agendas of the US government after the writing of NSC-5514 in 1955.

NSC-5702 of early 1957 assumes a particular importance in this aspect.[74] This document presents a number of options for reducing the South Korean military forces and points to the pros and cons of the different options. It also shows that the reduction of South Korean military forces was unavoidable despite the resistance on the part of the US Joint Chiefs of Staff. According to this document, reduction of the South Korean military forces had become inevitable by the second term of the Eisenhower administration.

The US government, however, could not push for the reduction without countermeasures. It had to consider the fact that Chinese forces were still stationed in North Korea. Washington sought to reconcile this situation with the weapons modernization program for both South Korean and US military forces in Korea. The modernization of military equipment and weapons could not only recoup the losses of military capabilities coming from the reduction, but also persuade the Syngman Rhee government to accept the US plan.[75] While personnel expenses required constant expenditure, weapons modernization would only entail modest maintenance costs after the initial investment. The US ambassador actually persuaded Syngman Rhee to accept the reduction in exchange for new weapons. While the total reduction only amounted to two divisions (around thirty thousand men), such reduction was absolutely necessary in order to reduce spending on the part of the United States.

The weapons modernization plan could not be carried out without annulling certain provisions of the armistice agreement. This is the reason why the discussions on clause (d) of article 13 stopped once the US government agencies agreed on reducing South Korean and US forces in Korea. In other words, the armistice provisions related to the introduction of new weapons had to be annulled once Washington made the decision to introduce new weapons into South Korea in exchange for reducing the South Korean and US forces there. This explains the cessation of discussion on clause (d) of article 13 by 1957.

The contentions that the communist forces were violating the armistice of course constitute an important background to the annulment of the relevant provisions of the armistice. However, given the fact that the Chinese forces withdrew from North Korea in 1958, the military conditions in Korea faced by the United Nations forces were certainly not urgent. This point is evident in the UN commander's report to President Eisenhower during the 245th National Security Council meeting in April 1955. He reported that, with the reduction of the number of troops, the communist forces were assuming a defensive formation.[76] In conclusion, the background of the annulment of certain provisions of the armistice can be found in the changes of US Korea policy in the 1950s.

The US-South Korea relationship of the 1950s began with the massive intervention of the United States in the Korean War and ended with the April Revolution in 1960. The United States dispatched its military forces to South Korea immediately after the breakout of the Korean War. When conflicts with the South Korean government ensued with the Busan Incident and the South Korean sabotaging of the armistice, the US government devised plans to remove Syngman Rhee from power. While the plan was never carried out, both the US and South Korean governments acquired much "learning effects" from the process. The United States government realized the need to cultivate leadership alternatives in case further conflicts with the Syngman Rhee regime become unbearable. The South Korean government, on the other hand, realized that it could challenge the United States at times in securing its interests due to the strategic importance of the Korean Peninsula.

However, the Syngman Rhee government did not fully understand the changes in US foreign policy under the Eisenhower administration. Unlike the Keynesian Truman administration, which allowed rapid expansion of foreign aid, the Eisenhower administration actively sought to reduce it under the banner of New Look. The ensuing conflicts between the Syngman Rhee government and the Eisenhower administration intensified with time. In the end, the US ambassador to South Korea recommended to Syngman Rhee in the midst of the April Revolution of 1960 that he resign.

On the surface, the conflicts in US-South Korea relations in the 1950s can be interpreted from a nationalistic perspective—the nationalist Syngman Rhee resisting the US world policy for the sake of Korean interests. Syngman Rhee certainly did seek more aid from the United States for South Korea. Rhee also sought to maintain the size of the South Korean military forces to deter possible aggression moves from the North. Rhee also meant to make South Korea "another Japan" in order to ensure its place in Asia. Syngman Rhee's resistance to US foreign policy reminds one of Park Chung Hee's conflict with US Asia policy after 1968.

However, it is difficult to state that the Syngman Rhee government dealt with the United States in the most ideal way possible as the Rhee regime also lost much from its dealings with the United States. While Rhee did squeeze out more aid from the

United States, the resulting conflict led to the depiction of South Korea as a "problem child" without the potential for development in US policy papers. The US government no longer trusted the South Korean government. Its Korea policy was covertly carried out thereafter.

The US government's stance was that consultation with the South Korean government was pointless as long as the South Korean president maintained his "brinkmanship." Instead of consultation, the primary objective of US Korea policy became persuading Syngman Rhee. The "learning effect" the United States government obtained through its dealings with the Syngman Rhee government continued into the 1960s. As will be discussed in greater detail in later chapters, the US government preferred persuasion and threats over consultation in its dealings with the Park Chung Hee government. Instead of becoming partners as did the United States and Japan, South Korea remained a "hot potato" for the United States.

In conclusion, the seemingly "nationalistic" stances of the Syngman Rhee regime vis-à-vis the United States caused more harm than good to South Korea's national interests. It failed to gain the US government's trust even as it relied on the United States for its everyday survival and security. Can we evaluate a regime that released the control over its military forces in exchange for more aid as simply "nationalistic"?

FOUR

The Military Government and the United States

The 1960s was an era of great change. In the United States, President John F. Kennedy established the United States Agency for International Development (USAID), proclaiming that the 1960s would be the "decade of development." In modern Korean history, the 1960s is conventionally understood as a decade of "hope," which stands in sharp contrast to the "darker" 1950s. The South Korean government established the Economic Planning Board and carried out economic development plans for the first time. In spirit of cooperation and development, the South Korean government signed a normalization treaty with Japan after fourteen years of discord and dispatched combat troops to Vietnam. On the surface, South Korea-United States relations appear to have been smooth.

However, South Korea-United States relations during this period were complex and ridden with dissent and gropings. A number of important questions can be asked with a simple comparison of the two eras. Why did South Korea achieve economic growth during the 1960s when it was receiving loans and not during the 1950s when it was receiving outright grants? Is it because the Park Chung Hee administration was more competent than Syngman Rhee's? Why did the United States, with its emphatic stance on democracy, watch with folded arms as the constitutionally legitimate Jang Myeon government fell? Why didn't the United States further aid South Korea when the military government was cornered with the rice shortages in 1963?

1. Background to Changes in US Korea Policy: Walt Whitman Rostow

(1) Why Rostow?

Walt Whitman Rostow is best known as an economist. His "take-off" model of economic growth has been enormously influential not only among the educated, but the general population as well. In Korea, if Ragnar Nurkse's "balanced growth" theory and "vicious cycle of poverty" captivated the intelligentsia during the 1950s, Rostow's "take-off" model functioned as the guide to economic growth for the South Korean people during the 1960s and 1970s through its appearance even in middle and high school textbooks and on college entrance exams.

After being first introduced through the *Seoul sinmun* on March 9, 1960 ("Bi gongsandang seoneon–pamun eul ireukin Roseutou hakseol" [Non-communist manifesto–Rostow's stirring theory] by Choe Hojin), Rostow became well-known as the author of the book *The Stages of Economic Growth*. This book was subtitled *A Non-Communist Manifesto*, which immediately drew strong reactions and attention from a generation of people influenced by the Marxist stages of economic growth since the colonial period.

Rostow's theories were introduced by a number of scholars and received severe criticisms from many, including world-class scholars such as Simon Kuznets, Paul Baran, Eric Hobsbawm, and Albert Fishlow.[1] In Korea, Bak Huibeom and Byeon Hyeongyun criticized Rostow's work.[2] In particular, Bak Huibeom criticized Rostow by arguing that Rostow's work "defends imperialism." Given Rostow's impact on Park Chung Hee and his administration, it appears ironic in hindsight that Bak Huibeom was critical of Rostow. As an economic advisor to Park Chung Hee after the May 16 coup d'état, Bak Huibeom carried out monetary reform and the establishment of the Industrial Development Corporation. Bak was one of the few people Park trusted into the 1970s.[3]

Perhaps more than his fame as an economist, Rostow's role as a policymaker in shaping American foreign policy (and South Korea-United States relations) needs to be examined. Rostow worked in important foreign policy positions in the Kennedy and Johnson administrations, and he was deeply involved in formulating American policy towards Asian nations.[4] Walt Rostow was the

George Kennan and Paul Nitze of the 1960s.

Rostow's work in policymaking is especially important because he espoused active intervention in the so-called Third World nations, including South Korea. He played a particularly important role in the Vietnam War. Given the weight and impact of this conflict in modern American history, Rostow could not avoid harsh criticisms due to his active role in it. Another captivating point is that Rostow's theories were implemented in South Korea almost without change. Sometimes his theories almost appear to be "evidence" of American interventions in South Korean economic development as well as South Korean society and politics.

Walt Rostow was born in New York City to a Russian-Jewish immigrant family in 1916. The first irony of his life was that his parents were once active socialists, and as a student Rostow himself was once an assistant to progressive economist Gunnar Myrdal. Rostow understood communism as an "epidemic" and searched for ways to contain it as a scholar throughout the 1950s. Therefore, it is surprising that Rostow grew up in a household with social democratic influences and worked for Gunnar Myrdal, who sympathized with Third World nationalisms and the inequalities that begot them. A widely used method in analyzing a historical figure is to review influences one received from home and school. In Rostow's case, such influences had an opposite.

Rostow graduated from Yale University when he was eighteen. At that point, Rostow found the unitary Marxist explanation of history inadequate. He later recalled that Marx's theories were imperfect in his own time and in this century were now completely obsolete. After graduating from Yale, Rostow studied at the University of Oxford in England with a prestigious Rhodes scholarship for two years. He received his doctorate in 1940 at age twenty-eight. Perhaps the most pivotal experience of his life was his work in the Office of Strategic Services (the predecessor of the Central Intelligence Agency) and the Economic Commission for Europe, a part of the State Department. It is likely that Rostow's perspective towards the Third World was influenced by George Kennan's containment policy during his time at the State Department. Kennan argued for a policy of psychological containment using economic aid to prove the "superiority" of capitalism. While there are significant

©National Archives of Korea

Doctor Rostow shaking hands with the public information minister Hong Jongcheol in his visit to South Korea in 1965. Rostow's "take-off" theory became a motto for the South Korean society thereafter.

strategic differences between the two, as Kennan focused on Europe and Japan while Rostow's policy of economic development aid was aimed toward the Third World, certain similarities also can be found.

It is conceivable that Rostow's experience at the State Department deeply influenced him. Although Rostow later turned to academia in 1946 and joined the faculties of the University of Oxford and Cambridge University, his experiences as "a young man picking bombing targets in World War II"[5] appear to have made a deep impact on his future goals and research. Rostow was widely regarded as one of the most outstanding amongst his peers and was considered "one of the most effective young officers" of the State Department.[6] Wherever he went, Rostow's work was outstanding and captivating.

Rostow returned to the United States in 1950 to become a faculty member of the Massachusetts Institute of Technology (MIT).

He was an active member of the Center for International Studies at MIT as an economic historian. Similar to other research institutions that worked on American foreign policy during the 1950s, the Center for International Studies looked at different global regions as research subjects, particularly focusing on the characteristics of Third World Asian nations.

During the 1950s, Rostow's interest was limited to the mainland Chinese Communist Party and the Kuomintang in Taiwan. His focus, however, gradually broadened to encompass all of Asia and later the entire Third World. This broadening of Rostow's research interests was connected to the Center for International Studies researchers' fieldwork in diverse parts of Asia.

At that time, the Center for International Studies at MIT had two distinctive characteristics. First, the center worked with the Central Intelligence Agency. American foreign policy of the 1950s largely aimed to avoid open intervention and maintain the status quo in the Third World. Such policy in turn, however, strengthened the CIA covert operations in the Third World, evidenced by documented CIA activities in the Philippines, Iran, and Nicaragua. During this period, the CIA collected information about target regions through active cooperation with university research centers. The Center for International Studies was also involved in such strategic activities. Rostow's two book publications in the 1950s, *A Proposal: Key to an Effective Foreign Policy* (with Max F. Millikan, 1957) and *An American Policy in Asia* (1955), espoused new foreign policy and strategy toward the Third World and reflected the research activities of the Center for International Studies.

Second, scholars from diverse disciplinary backgrounds worked together at the Center for International Studies. Economist Benjamin Higgins, for example, recalled the Center for International Studies' activities in the 1950s as follows:

> Were years of keen intellectual excitement at CENIS, with virtually non-stop interdisciplinary seminars and discussion groups, in which not only CENIS staff but almost all of MIT's anthropologists, economists, political scientists and sociologists participated in varying degrees ... [with] a community of scholars arriving at the same broad analytical framework. ... [There were economists such as] Richard

Eckhaus, Paul Rosenstein-Rodan, Benjamin Higgins, and Evsey Domar[;] ... political scientists such as Guy Pauker, Jean Mintz, Hugh McVey, Lucien Pye and Ithiel Poole; sociologist Dan Lerner; economic geographer Karl Pelzer; anthropologists Betty Pelzer and Clifford Geertz.[7]

Higgins called Rostow a "true light" even among such a stellar group of scholars. Spirit of interdisciplinary study and cooperation among the abovementioned scholars is further evident in Rostow's article, "My Life Philosophy" in the *American Economist*, in which Rostow defined himself as a "biologist." He described himself as not just a pure economist who makes his or her arguments based on a set of laws. Rostow believed that it is not sufficient to work with economics alone but also considered "political, social, cultural, and other non-economic forces" to be essential.[8] For Rostow, working with a number of renowned social scientists at the Center for International Studies when he was in his thirties, a time when a scholar is often most vigorous in his or her research, was decisive in shaping his scholarly projection.

Rostow began to participate in politics while at the Center for International Studies. An academic "star" of Cambridge, Massachusetts, home of Harvard University and MIT, Rostow began to advise then-senator John F. Kennedy in the mid-1950s and later joined the Kennedy presidential election campaign in 1960. Through this process, the so-called "Kennedy Gang," also known as the "Cambridge Group" and "Charles River Group," was born. A number of other stellar scholars from Harvard and MIT also joined this group. The MIT Center for International Studies, along with the RAND (Research and Development) Corporation and Rockefeller Foundation, played a key role in it.[9]

Perhaps most noteworthy in Rostow's advising to Kennedy was the passing of the Kennedy-Cooper Resolution, which provided American aid to India. The US government previously understood the Indian policy of nonalignment as an unfriendly gesture towards the United States and did not consider economic aid for India. However, moved by Rostow's advice, President Kennedy passed legislation to aid India in consultation with the US ambassador to India John Cooper. Such a move was based on Rostow's policy theory for the Third World–to use India as a check against China.[10]

Rostow also turned his theory into policy through his participation in the Task Force on Foreign Economic Policy, an ad hoc policy group created soon after Kennedy's victory in the presidential election. He was also appointed as the deputy assistant to the president for national security affairs (deputy national security advisor). While National Security Advisor McGeorge Bundy took charge of newly independent nations, such as the Republic of the Congo, Rostow focused on Asia.

However, Rostow's career was not without trial. Rostow was appointed counselor in the Department of State and chairman of the department's Policy Planning Council. Although Rostow actively and vigorously formulated new long-term foreign policies, he was eventually removed from the center of decision making due to his clashes with Kennedy. Implicitly, oral records from the Lyndon Baines Johnson Library and Museum suggest that Rostow was removed due to his differences with President Kennedy and the military in policymaking for Vietnam and Laos.[11]

Similar to how Harry Truman's succession to the presidency helped George Kennan to ascend the decision-making ladder, Rostow received his second chance with the assassination of President Kennedy and the succession of Lyndon Johnson.[12] Presidents Truman and Johnson were both laymen in foreign policy and needed foreign policy specialists like Kennan and Rostow next to them to provide advice and guide American foreign policy.

In February 1964, President Johnson appointed Rostow as US representative of the Inter-American Committee on the Alliance for Progress (ICAP). ICAP was created in 1961 to promote Latin American development, and it was one of the most critical agencies in US foreign policy towards Latin America. Succeeding McGeorge Bundy, Rostow was named assistant for national security affairs (now known as the national security advisor) on March 31, 1966. Rostow met with foreign national leaders, appropriated information, and formulated American foreign policy in this post as perhaps the closest associate to President Johnson. When criticisms against the Vietnam War began to rise, Rostow established even stronger links with President Johnson with optimistic reports on the war and comments of support for the president. A golden age for Rostow's career in foreign policymaking was starting.[13]

Rostow's views on guerilla warfare in Southeast Asia also prove that Rostow was not simply an economist. The reason why Rostow was assigned to Laos and Vietnam was that he had expert knowledge on communist guerillas of Asia. In criticizing the Department of Defense's guerilla policy, Rostow argued that antiguerilla warfare must be coupled with his "modernization theory."

Such a stance on Vietnam was already evident in Rostow's 1955 book, *An American Policy in Asia*. Rostow had contended that the war in Vietnam should not be avoided, and the best time to attack is when the Vietnamese people are most prepared against guerillas. He argued for active response against guerilla warfare, which would necessarily involve military aid as well as massive amounts of economic aid. Arthur M. Schlesinger, the author of the 1965 book *A Thousand Days: John F. Kennedy in the White House*, even remembers Rostow as the one who preached the "gospel" of antiguerilla warfare.[14]

Rostow, having already argued for bombing North Vietnam back in June 1961, insisted on greater military pressure against North Vietnam in June 1964. He later called for a naval blockade against North Vietnam for aiding the National Liberation Front (the Viet Cong) in South Vietnam in November 1964. Rostow's rationale behind American intervention in the Vietnam War was the domino theory–if Vietnam falls, so will the rest of Southeast Asia, Australia, and the western Pacific. For his hawkish stance, Rostow encountered over a thousand protestors during his visit to Japan. Rostow lectured at over a hundred colleges and universities beginning in May 1965 in defense of the US government and its foreign policy.

Based on his perception of the German precedent from World War II, Rostow called for sweeping full-scale bombings against North Vietnam and acted as the strongest supporter of such a strategy.[15] Along with President Johnson, Rostow continued to argue for consistent bombing of North Vietnam even when Secretary of Defense Robert McNamara expressed his skepticism about the war in Vietnam in 1967. Rostow continued to reject anything except full-scale bombings against North Vietnam, even when Johnson formed a new policy group under Secretary of Defense Clark

Clifford to reconsider the war following the 1968 Tet Offensive (which lasted from the end of January to early February). Johnson, however, partly stopped the bombings in March for negotiations.

Rostow's illustrious role as a policymaker during the 1960s ended with Lyndon Johnson's announcement that he would not run for reelection in 1968. Criticized for his part in the Vietnam War, Rostow could no longer play any significant role in the centers of power in Washington. What exactly were Rostow's theories and ideas? How does the take-off model, the most well-known of Rostow's theories, fit into the entirety of Rostovian thought?

(2) Let's Use Nationalism

Simply put, Rostow's foreign policy can be described as "modernization theory." Rostow's policy was aimed above all at stopping communist revolution in any given country through modernization, and it was not limited to the economy–it included a sweeping reconstruction of society and politics. Therefore, Rostow's theory is not limited to economics and encompasses different areas of social science. Rostow accepted both George Kennan's expressed need for containment using economic means and Paul Nitze's domino theory. He argued that the domino effect, the spreading of communism on a global scale, is inevitable unless it is globally "contained."

A particular characteristic of the Rostovian modernization theory is that it considers both "stability" and "instability" as byproducts of the modernization process. While modernization theory in general views modernization as an entirely positive thing, Rostow argued that the "stability" that modernization brings will only come in the long run, and "instability" will exist until then. Therefore, while Rostow referred to the transition to a modern society as the great transition, he nevertheless argued that "the world community is becoming both more interdependent and more fluid than it has been at any other time in history, a condition which presents us with both a great danger and a great opportunity."[16]

Rostow understood that economic development efforts will inevitably dismantle the established society and create instabilities.[17] Modernizing societies are therefore exposed to communist threats, and Rostow suggested a need to eliminate such danger through active intervention. Based on this theory, Rostow argued for active

intervention against communist guerillas in Vietnam, a nation
Rostow described then as being at the "take-off" stage. Rostow
drew parallels between the South Vietnam of the late 1960s and the
South Korea of the early 1960s and believed that active intervention
was necessary.

In the end, the "instabilities" of the modernization process are
something every society must inevitably go through. On the other
hand, however, if a society cannot successfully overcome the stage of
"instabilities," it cannot muster the social and psychological strength
to defeat the "epidemic" of communism. Such a stance leads to the
prioritization of economic development over democracy, and Rostow
insisted on using nationalism as an effective cohesive force to unite
society.

The second characteristic is Rostow's emphasis on the "psychological
factor." This point is similar to Kennan's highlighting of psychology
in containment. In carrying out the Marshall Plan, Kennan had
argued that the most important factor in stopping Soviet advances
was the European confidence in their system. Rostow also insisted
that the "instabilities" of the modernization process produce
favorable conditions which the "epidemic" of communism can
exploit, and only a "psychological remedy" can stop its spread. In
other words, weapons and armies are useless if there is no will to
use them. There must be a change in terms of values.[18]

Rostow pointed out that to think of revolution and resistance as
the product of "hunger and poverty" is a grave misunderstanding
that leads to mistaken policies that focus simply on feeding and
clothing the population. Rostow saw that "communists focus
on where there is hope, not where there is no hope." In other
words, the so-called Free World was not responding well to the
psychological factors communists exploited.

Based on such an understanding, Rostow went on to criticize
grant-type aids of the Eisenhower administration. According to
Rostow, grant-type free aid not only did not inspire confidence
among the people of the Third World, it instead created a lethargic
environment in favor of the status quo. Instead of the consumer
goods of grant-type aid, Rostow believed that loans made of capital
goods would help to inspire a faith in economic progress among
the people of the Third World. In addition, Rostow argued that

such psychological effect could create economic development plans' necessary premise–popular consent and support among the people.

Although Rostow and Kennan are similar in the sense that they both focused on the psychological factor, Rostow could go further than Kennan because he took note on the characteristics and role of nationalism in the Third World. By focusing on "strongholds," Kennan argued for efficient uses of limited resources by discriminating between "core" and "peripheral" regions. On the other hand, as can be seen since his early research on Asia, Rostow focused on the Third World, particularly Asia. He argued that the new stage of the Cold War would involve Asia and warned that the power of nationalism could function as another Cold War ideology.

In hindsight, Rostow's warning regarding the power of nationalism was a prophetic analysis. Since the collapse of the Soviet Union and Eastern European regimes and the introduction of market systems in those countries, the main conflict on a global scale is that between the hegemonic power of the United States and the nationalisms of the Third World.

Until the 1950s, Third World nationalism was synonymous with communism in the American perspective. The nonalignment of India and Egypt and the revolution of Cuba are good examples of this perception. Even Kim Gu's nationalism, which was in conflict with the United States Army Military Government in Korea, was little different from communism from the American liberalist perspective regardless of its actual ideological leanings, because nationalisms of the Third World were essentially resistant to the expansion of American power abroad. For Rostow, however, the Third World's nationalism are particular products of nations that experienced colonization. He believed that, depending on American foreign policy, the third World's nationalism can be both antagonistic to American liberalism as well as a pro-American force that can deliver economic development. Rostow even contended that nationalism can be morphed into an enemy of communism.

India was suggested as an example in *A Proposal*. According to Rostow, Indian nationalism is important as a push for the Indian economic development plan as well as for a sense of rivalry against the growth of communist China.[19] In addition, Rostow also pointed out in the same book that nationalism does not often buy into the international characteristic of communism.[20] In other words, Rostow located the sources of conflict between communism and nationalism of the Third World. In the case of Korea, while one axis of nationalism coupled with the left, the other axis united with anticommunism and functioned as an ideological force of cohesion in the process of capitalistic economic development.

(3) Paying Attention to the Military Officers of Developing Nations

An important feature of the Rostovian modernization theory is that it emphasizes the active efforts on the part of Third World nations themselves. Such a characteristic distinguishes the Rostovian view from American foreign policy precedents, and the theory provided an ideological justification for intervention throughout the 1960s.

In criticizing prior aid efforts, Rostow argued that American aid will not be effective regardless of its quality and quantity unless the Third World acquires what Rostow called "absorptive capacity." According to Rostow, a developing nation typically does not (or cannot) reach the "preconditions for take-off stage" on its own. It therefore experiences forced colonization in the initial stage of development. Once a nation becomes free from colonial rule, it needs new types of leaders.[21] Newly independent nations need new and vigorous leaders who are detached from the premodern establishment and can actively carry out much-needed social reforms. Social reforms by the new leadership can provide the energy and drive in planning and carrying out economic development plans. It can be a win-win situation for all.

As a potential social class, Rostow initially paid attention to the educated intelligentsia from the cities. However, as in the case of India, most of the educated intelligentsia were children of the establishment, and they were usually educated abroad. Because of their lack of knowledge and understanding of their own societies, they could not earn the trust of the masses. Therefore, Rostow focused on the role of military in developing nations:

> The army is frequently important to economic and political growth for three reasons. First, a military career is often the only way to positions of leadership and responsibility open to members of the less privileged classes and especially to men with rural backgrounds.

... Second, the army is often the only career in which a man has an opportunity to acquire both technical and administrative skills. Many of these skills are easily transferable to such civilian tasks as the building of roads and communication systems or the organization of a local community for improved sanitation. Third, military service provides vocational training which gives the peasants the skills needed in industry. Countries which have adopted military conscription might well pay more attention to the constructive potentialities of such a system.[22]

Rostow argued in *The Stages of Economic Growth* that the old landlord ruling class should be replaced by a new ruling class and that military men are essential in the transition period. In the end, however, Rostow pointed out that it is impossible to create a new ruling class exclusively made up of soldiers. He therefore believed that a union of military men, businessmen, and intellectuals was necessary.

Rostow wrote of this policy perspective in a document entitled "Our Doctrine of the Role of the Military" during the Kennedy administration.[23] In this document, Rostow argued that military officers of developing countries are capable of modernizing their nations. If their efforts are sufficiently united and supported by external aid, military officers of underdeveloped nations can act as deliverers of Western thought and values to their societies. Presenting the cases of Japan and Turkey as examples, Rostow argued that the roles of military officers can be institutionalized. Military officers, according to Rostow, can transform and align their countries in accordance with American foreign policy objectives.

In conclusion, Rostow argued that the new ruling class will lead the social reforms suitable to their societies and raise their absorptive capacities. By delegating the responsibilities of development and reform to the respective countries, the United States was to only "help those who help themselves."[24] Rostow's contention became the basic principle of the United States Agency for International Development (USAID). USAID was established in 1961 to replace and surmount the relative inefficiencies of the International Cooperation Agency (ICA) of the 1950s. USAID's operating principles clearly reflected Rostow's ideas toward the Third World.

Of course, allowing "self-help" did not mean that the United States was not going to be involved. However, the most important aspect of Rostow's policy towards the Third World was that the United States should only intervene to cultivate those nations' self-help abilities. Rostow was emphatically against the United States appearing to intervene in the Third World out of self-interest.

Rostow's contention thus far sounds as though he almost predicted the rise of the military officers who carried out the May 16 coup d'état in South Korea. Park Chung Hee, who grew up poor in the Korean countryside, formed a new ruling group with other military officers who also benefited from the modern education the South Korean military establishment provided with aid from the United States. The military officers, taking advantage of South Korea's strong nationalism, created a new state apparatus with powerful control mechanisms.

Park Chung Hee–style social control and state interventions in the economy stand against the fundamental values of American liberalism. Rostow, however, reconciled the fundamental contradiction of his approach by arguing that inelastic commitment to democratic principles can be harmful to economic growth–the most important and primary task of developing nations.[25] Therefore, according to Rostow, democratization was to be relegated as a task *following* economic development, and democracy can naturally arise or not in the economic development process. Max Millikan and Rostow stated, "Not only is economic growth a prerequisite for political, cultural, and social improvement, it can also be an engine of such improvement."[26]

Rostow's stance is the basic form of the "developmental state" model and can be related to Samuel Huntington's *Political Order in Changing Societies*. Additionally, Rostow articulated his stance within the particulars of the Third World. Because democratization is not an important issue there, it is unnecessary and even dangerous to force American democratic institutions and practices upon Third World countries. In other words, democracy in the Third World is to have country-specific qualities–Park Chung Hee's Yusin system justified itself as a "Korean-style democracy." Rostow wrote,

Asian democracy is linked to a system of private capitalism that assumes the existence of a large responsible middle class capable of performing the task of saving, initiating new methods, efficient management, tax paying, and so on. Asian societies generally do not have such a middle class. This fact, combined with the special difficulties of Asian economies in transition, makes private capitalism much less automatically an adjunct to democracy there than here. Generally speaking, we must expect a more powerful and especially more direct state control of economic activities in Asia than in the United States.

Further, the existence of widespread hunger, poverty, disease, and illiteracy strongly influences Asian ideas about the most important tasks for the democratic process. Free elections and the other purely political mechanisms for democracy appear less important to Asians than the relief of social and economic evils.[27]

(4) What should the United States Do?

What would the modernization theory for the Third World, as outlined above, bring to the United States? In addition to this question, it is most important to consider that a far greater amount of money would be needed to carry out such plans. Although this strategy signifies a triumph of the New Look over that of National Security Council Report 68 (NSC-68)[28] and the Keynesian counterattack against the New Look,[29] the policymakers had to convince the taxpayer-conscious members of Congress to appropriate an enormous amount of money for the Third World.

The strategy Rostow chose to convince Congress was similar to that of the Economic Cooperation Administration (ECA) director Paul Hoffman's approach in persuading it of the validity of aid towards Korea in 1949. Hoffman explained to the Congress's pro-Taiwan and pro-Japan members that he was not simply a government official, but a businessman. He argued that he would not ask for appropriations for something that would not be productive in the long run. A significant amount of investment would eventually reduce the amount of aid, and it would be beneficial to US finances.[30]

Rostow was even more straightforward than Hoffman. Long-term aid for economic development of the Third World, according to Rostow, was part of a method to create a world environment in which American society can continue to prosper and be secure–the two ultimate goals of American foreign policy. Therefore, the aim of development was not only to help subjected nations to accumulate enough capital of their own, but also so "the economies of the industrialized countries of Europe and Japan, as well as the United States, could continue to grow."[31] It was impossible to expect consumers of underdeveloped nations to buy cars and electronics from the United States and other industrialized nations if they did not have paved roads and power plants.

> In the long run, as the underdeveloped countries develop and become industrialized, their participation in world trade can become quantitatively much more important to total world-trade flows. Fears that as they develop they will become competitors of presently industrialized countries and thus reduce export opportunities should be quieted by the history of industrialization. As standards of living rise in a country, the growth in the magnitude and variety of it demand much more than compensates as a rule for such reduction as occurs in those limited types of imports it now produces at home.[32]

To achieve the abovementioned aim, the United States needed to develop several important policies. First, policymakers had to convince the US Congress to approve a long-term plan, as short-term initiatives were often inadequate. In addition, Rostow preached the need to establish an organization not solely relying on the United States for contributions, but also supported by other industrialized nations to collect and distribute the aggregated funds. In *A Proposal*, Rostow argued for an organization similar to the Special United Nations Fund for Economic Development (SUNFED). Reorganizing and expanding the Organisation for European Economic Co-operation (OEEC) to the Organisation for Economic Co-operation and Development (OECD) and broadening its sphere of activity from Europe to the rest of the world were also aimed at supporting Rostow's goals. Rostow was now insisting that the nations that experienced economic revival during the 1950s needed to participate in the global initiative of the United States as partners.

Second, the United States needed to take a more active stance in interventions. As already mentioned, the success of economic development aid was dependent upon the beneficiary country's "absorptive capacity." Although such capacity was to be self-attained by the new leadership's reform efforts, the United States could not simply wait with folded arms. Rostow expressed it as "made motivation"–the United States needed to actively motivate those struggling behind. The suspicion of whether or not the United States, which later staged the 1963 South Vietnamese coup, was involved in the May 16 coup d'état stems from such an interventionist stance in foreign policy.

Additionally, Rostow argued that the United States should make use of technical aid delegations in interventions. Such delegations were to assist the developing nations drafting economic development plans as well as various rules and regulations so that they could effectively absorb external aid and resources. In the case of South Korea, since 1963 USAID advisors actively advised the South Korean government on the revision of its economic development plan as well as interest rate and export promotion policies. When disclosed, currently undisclosed USAID documents from the 1960s will further reveal the activities of its advisors.

Third, underdeveloped nations should be allowed to use advanced nations' capital. Rostow argued that capital from advanced nations can allow underdeveloped nations that are suffering from lack of internal capital to invest in industrial development and in forming links between developing nations and advanced nations.[33] The US government's objection to the South Korean military government's domestic capital-based economic development plan and monetary reform for capital mobilization can be understood according to this stance.

Such a stance is based on the logic that developing nations, even after a certain degree of industrial development, should not become entirely self-sufficient. In other words, those nations should not be separated from the international division of labor.

[I]t seems reasonable to assume that for countries in the precondition stage of development, virtually all of the additional capital needed to launch the growth process must be supplied from the outside.[34]

Rostow pointed out that the course of economic development

aid should not be uniform for all nations. In other words, the quantity and quality of economic development aid distribution was to be dependent upon the subjected country's level of development. Here is where Rostow's "take-off" model comes in. The policy papers Rostow produced during the early part of the Kennedy administration categorize different countries' level of economic development according to his "take-off" model and emphasize the need to distribute economic aid accordingly. Based on his categorization of economic development, Rostow argued in another document that aid towards South Korea, Taiwan, Turkey, Greece, and the Philippines should be more economic than military. In the case of Iran, Rostow argued for the overall reduction of aid.[35]

Rostow's policy direction shows that his "take-off" model was part of his work in foreign policy. He was more than just an economic historian. His academic work in economic history was used to support his modernization theory.

(5) Rostow, South Korea, and Japan

Rostow visited South Korea a number of times beginning in 1965, and his visits occurred at the most important moments in South Korea-United States relations. His first visit took place in 1965 when the whole country was trembling due to the normalization treaty with Japan and the dispatch of combat troops to Vietnam. His second visit in the late 1960s took place during the time when the relationship between the United States and Park Chung Hee governments was deteriorating and Park Chung Hee was shifting his economic development policy from export-oriented and labor-intensive light industry to export-oriented heavy industry. Rostow's third visit in 1982 occurred at a time when the new military government was having trouble with foreign loans and overlapping investments in heavy chemical industry. His visit in 1965 was particularly important–it occurred when the South Korean government was having a difficult time dealing with negative popular opinion against the normalization treaty with Japan.

Rostow had two important meetings during his two-day visit to South Korea in 1965. One meeting was with Park Chung Hee. There is a memo Rostow wrote during this meeting at the Johnson Presidential Library and Museum. This hastily written memo contains several mathematical equations and his view on economic development. Although it is difficult to surmise what exactly went on between Rostow and Park during the meeting, it is obvious that Rostow advised Park Chung Hee on matters related to Korean economic development.

Immediately following his meeting with Park Chung Hee, Rostow went to Seoul National University for another important meeting. Perhaps the second meeting was more important to the direction Korean society took afterwards. Rostow delivered a lecture and engaged in a discussion on the topic of Korean economic development at Seoul National University. He declared to the students and faculty members that South Korean society was already at the "take-off" stage.[36] It is not clear that the declaration accurately reflected all the factors related to the economy, such as the state of industries, ruling class, investments, and national "will." However, his declaration had a huge impact on South Korean society. On the one hand, Rostow's declaration instilled a sense of trust and confidence to the South Korean people that their society was now ready for "take-off." On the other hand, it provided an important measure to the Park Chung Hee government in its plan for economic development.

What impact did Rostow's theory exactly have on US Korea policy? There is almost no serious discussion of South Korea in his books and policy papers. Rostow's comments on the Hugh Farley report, which caused a sensation in Washington during the early days of the Kennedy administration and the South Korean military government immediately after the May 16 coup d'état, are almost the only exceptions. In *A Proposal*, South Korea is even mentioned along Taiwan and Vietnam as a case in which his model of economic growth could *not* be effectively applied.[37]

However, developments in South Korea during the 1960s followed the schedule outlined in *A Proposal* and *The Stages of Economic Growth*. Park Chung Hee, a man from a poor rural background, seized political power through a military coup d'état, and the military officers associated with Park were critical of the widespread corruption in the military establishment. A new ruling class, separate from premodern modes of production, seized state power through a coup and bonded with businessmen, intellectuals, and government officials. South Korean development followed Rostow's model almost exactly at the time Rostow began to play an important role as a policymaker in Washington.

In a magazine interview in 1992, Rostow claimed that he had convinced President Kennedy to reconsider the Korean military government at a time when Kennedy was unsure about it.[38] Furthermore, Rostow even reported to President Kennedy that South Korean military officers in politics should be separated from the regular military establishment, and those military officers should be involved in the civil government after the transfer of power in mentioning principles of American diplomacy. Such comments gave the impression that Rostow perhaps had foreknowledge of what would happen in South Korea later.

Rostow's impact on South Korea is clear. The country in the early 1960s was at a crossroad. Although economists differed on the direction of economic development, a popular consensus for an economic development plan already existed by the late 1950s. Certain economists called for economic development based on the free market system. Others called for economic growth based on the balanced growth theory, while reformists preached the need for social democratic economic growth.[39] Among the different views, the balanced growth theory, which argued for a well-rounded and even growth of all industries, emerged as the dominant position. The reason why the military government's proclaimed economic development plans in 1961 and 1962 echo the balanced growth theory has to do with both Park Chung Hee's personal disposition as well as that of South Korean society at large. In addition, the balanced growth theory was a common route that many of the recently decolonized nations took.

However, external factors also shifted the South Korean path towards balanced economic growth. Although the first such factor came from Dr. Charles Wolf during the Jang Myeon administration (1960-61), the more potent one arose from Rostow's policy. The US government strongly opposed the military government's economic development policies from 1961 to 1963 because they emphasized the use of domestic capital instead of foreign capital. Early economic policies of the military government went against Rostow's theory, which called for the use of large amounts of foreign capital and the maintenance of economic links with the advanced nations through unbalanced growth. Although the US government also pointed to the lack of consultation with Washington, the main point of dissension was that the South Korean policy was overly "socialistic" and "nationalistic."[40] Of course, the American appraisal of South Korean economic policy and pressure against the military government was based on Rostow's theory.

Rostow's focus, according to declassified documents from the Kennedy administration, appears to be on other regions of Asia, particularly Japan and Southeast Asia. His vast knowledge on Asia as well as his deep interest in China and Japan are evident in the book *An American Policy in Asia*, the sequel to *The Prospects for Communist China*.[41]

Rostow's view continued to impact foreign policy in the Johnson administration. First, Rostow argued for active countermeasures against communist forces in Asia. Such insistence resulted in active American involvement against guerilla activities and disturbances in the Philippines and South Vietnam. In addition, Rostow insisted on establishing the means to perpetuate American economic and political power in Asia for an extended period of time. Advanced nations of the free world were to participate in it.[42] Rostow above all argued for Japan's active participation.[43]

Such views materialized with the establishment of the Asian Development Bank and active Japanese participation in Asian issues.[44] In the process, Rostow continuously participated in regular meetings with Japanese policymakers and emphasized the need to connect Japan's overseas trade to the needs of Southeast Asia.[45] Rostow particularly feared the establishment of trade relations between Japan and communist China, and focused on Southeast Asia as the export and import market for Japan. During the process, Rostow concluded that "[i]n such a regional effort it would have to be established in detail what Asian natural resources are suitable for economic development as Japanese imports" and "[t]hose Asian nations prepared to contribute to the development of exports to Japan would certainly have to receive additional loans for national development purposes."[46]

(6) No Aid Without Economic Development: Changes in US Korea Policy During the Kennedy Administration

The Kennedy inauguration in 1961 marked the beginning of change in US Korea policy. As mentioned before, Rostow's role and contentions within the Kennedy administration played an important role.

The Kennedy administration, which already considered reshaping US foreign policy even before the inauguration, began to seriously reconsider US Korea policy after reading the South Korea report submitted by Hugh Farley of the US Operation Mission in Korea (USOM/K).[47] Farley argued in the report that, although government corruption had decreased somewhat, fundamental reform was still desperately needed a full year after the May 16 coup d'état. He argued that South Korea, with continuous social unrest, was still in a desperate situation.[48]

To solve the abovementioned problems in South Korea, Farley argued that inefficiencies of US aid distribution must be resolved. Additionally, the United States needed to actively intervene in South Korean political processes and economic policymaking. Farley suggested dispatching a special ambassador to pressure the South Korean government and contact various political forces including students, intellectuals, journalists, national assemblymen, military officers, businessmen, and even Jang Myeon to bring discontented groups into the sphere of legality and create a national movement for reform.

Although an earlier report on South Korea jointly produced by the CIA, Department of State, and Joint Chiefs of Staff pointed out the weakness of the Jang Myeon regime, the rise of the socialist movement, and burgeoning interest in nationalistic neutralization of the Korean peninsula before the Farley report,[49] did not have as great of an impact. Although American officials posted in South Korea as well as those in the Department of Defense and the Department of State all agreed that South Korea had a number of problems, they did not consider them to be as serious as Farley did, and considered his recommendations to be unrealistic.[50] Surprisingly, however, US Korea policy following the submission of the Farley report adhered to its recommendations.

Rostow suggested to President Kennedy that a "fresh look"

towards Korea was necessary after receiving the Farley report,[51] and urged the State Department to submit a set of recommendations related to South Korea as soon as possible.[52] Robert Komer's report on March 15, 1961, in particular, illustrates well Kennedy administration officials' view of South Korea. Komer's report argued for appropriating the money saved from the reduction of South Korean military personnel to economic development and the need for active intervention by the United States in South Korean affairs. It also included a labor-intensive and light industry–oriented economic reconstruction plan with an emphasis on the public sector.[53] The content of the report formed the substance of later US Korea policy documents.

The US government efforts to reformulate its Korea policy materialized with the formation of the Presidential Task Force on Korea (Korea Task Force) by the order of President Kennedy. It was headed by Assistant Secretary of State for East Asian and Pacific Affairs Walter McConaughy and created during the 483rd meeting of the National Security Council on May 15, 1961.[54] The Korea Task Force, after a number of discussions, produced a report for the National Security Council based on four drafts produced between May 15, 1961 and June 1, 1961. After several reviews, the report to the National Security Council was submitted on June 5, 1961.[55] Its content was certified after a review by the National Security Council on June 12, 1961, and it was submitted as the official US Korea policy on June 13, 1961.[56]

Although slightly revised during the discussions, the content of the report nevertheless suggested that the United States should establish and support a national development plan, reorganize the American Mission in Korea, and begin researching and discussing the reduction of South Korean military personnel. Although the Joint Chiefs of Staff expressed concern that the reduction of South Korean military personnel could negatively impact the South Korean economy by increasing the number of unemployed, considering the expenses of maintaining these forces, it agreed to the reduction.[57]

Reduction of the American deficit was not the main purpose of reducing the size of South Korean military, as the money saved would be appropriated for Korean economic development. The first clause of the "What needs to be done?" article in the document written in preparation for the first Korea Task Force meeting suggests economic development as an answer.[58] Social reforms, including dissolving administrative organs impeding economic development and resolving the unemployment problem, were considered necessary to achieve the goal. Additionally, the importance of labor-intensive industry to take advantage of South Korea's human resources, the only major industrial resource South Korea had at the time, was particularly emphasized.[59] Although the reduction of the South Korean military was continuously discussed, it never materialized due to political considerations regarding the military government's internal stability,[60] financial considerations that urged its delay of discussion until after economic stabilization,[61] and regional security considerations. In addition, clashes on the border in 1963 also helped to delay arms reduction.[62]

Although the document's content can be understood as a part of the larger US policy towards the Third World, the US Korea policy was more forcefully carried out than those elsewhere. As a short-term goal, the Korea Task Force emphasized the need to establish a strong South Korean government within the next three to five years. Another point deserving of attention is that active US intervention was considered essential. According to the first draft of the Korea Task Force report, the United States was South Korea's "elder brother."

"Relative Priority of Military vs. Reconstruction: Focus in Korea,"[63] another policy document submitted around the time of the submission of the Korea Task Force report, argues that the US Korea policy of the 1950s failed because the Eisenhower administration focused on sustaining the South Korean military establishment instead of creating a self-sustaining economy. Komer, the author of the document, argued that with the withdrawal of the Chinese forces from North Korea, greater emphasis should have been on internal issues rather than external threats. American perception of the small chance of a North Korean invasion became a basic factor leading to a concentration on internal issues facing South Korea, particularly its economic development.[64]

Changes in the US Korea policy during the Kennedy administration can be considered as the materialization of Rostow's policy contentions. The new US Korea policy had the following

characteristics that distinguished it from the Korea policy of the
1950s. First, it prioritized planning and the carrying out of an
economic development plan by the South Korean government
with US support. Contrary to policies during the 1950s, private
investments by foreigners were no longer emphasized. Of course,
such measures did not aim to stop the flow of private capital into
South Korea. However, the new policy no longer pursued and
encouraged the participation of private capital with incentives as it
did back in the 1950s.[65]

Second, it accentuated sweeping social reforms. Secretary of
State Dean Rusk, in a directive to Ambassador Samuel Berger on
August 1, 1961, stressed that the priority should be South Korea's
internal matters.[66] As also can be seen in the Farley Korea Task
Force reports, the most important concern for the US government
was corruption.[67] Corruption was listed as *the* first impression of
South Korea in the first Seoul Embassy correspondence the Korea
Task Force consulted.[68] Therefore, reform of officialdom through
salary increases and the establishment of a clean and professional
machinery to carry out the economic development plan were among
the key points of the new US Korea policy.

An important additional point related to social reform was that
such a reform was not to be limited to institutional change and
should encompass mental reform. It would entail the "[u]ndertaking
of long-range social planning including the definition and public
promulgation by national leaders of national goals and ideals,"
"achievement of better relations with students, intellectuals, and the
press," and "enhancement of Korea's national image."[69] The first
provision was meant to change South Korean ways of thinking
through a top-down reform. To achieve such "human progress,"[70]
people should be educated to believe in state myth, and the US
government should intervene to help.[71] The Korea Task Force
report draft therefore spoke of the need to establish institutions for
economic and social reform.

Strong emphasis on social reform resulted from US officials'
negative perception of Korea. The National Security Council and
Korea Task Force documents typically included assessments of
Korean society and history, and they were mostly very negative.
Nationalistic prejudices, historic dependency, factionalism, rampant

slandering of others, agitations by intellectuals, and exposure to communism were typically mentioned as "Korean" traits and were reflected in the policy documents.[72] Such negative perceptions led to the suggestion of mental reform by US officials as an important premise for economic development.

The United States during the 1950s made consistent efforts to instill a positive image of itself in developing nations through educational aid and exchange programs.[73] Such efforts were strengthened during the 1960s, and in the case of South Korea, they were conducted as a part of a plan for social reform. The Fulbright-Hays Act of 1961 (the Mutual Educational and Cultural Exchange Act of 1961) institutionalized the US government's cultural efforts and provided additional support for new exchange programs, the translation of American books and journals into languages other than English, centers for American studies abroad, and international academic congresses.[74] The United States began dispatching members of the Peace Corps to developing nations around the world beginning in 1961, and a significant number went to South Korea. Although the dispositions of the Peace Corps members varied, the US government sought to both improve the image of the United States held by the citizens of developing nations and reform the developing nations' citizens' ways of life.[75]

Domestically, *Jaegeon Gungmin Undong Bonbu* (the Citizenry Headquarters for National Reconstruction) of the military government played an important role in social reform efforts in South Korea. Its connection to the United States is unclear at the moment. However, its goals of improving living conditions, promoting diligence, advancing production and constructive attitudes, raising the level of culture, encouraging thought refinement, and improving national physique were similar to the US Korea policy. In addition, its main participants–educators, journalists, publishers, and religious leaders–constituted members of the new leadership as prescribed by the new US policy towards the Third World.

Third, normalization of relations with Japan was more strongly emphasized than during the 1950s.[76] Immediately after inauguration, President Kennedy directed the secretary of state to speedily normalize the relationship between South Korea and Japan.[77] Walter McConaughy, the head of the Korea Task Force, mentioned in a clear statement that the relations between South Korea and Japan needed to be normalized within a year.[78] Additionally, the Japan section of the May 1963 summary of foreign policies produced by the Policy Planning Council contends that the United States should "[s]timulate it [Japan] to take larger role in development of underdeveloped countries." In the Korea section of the same document, it is suggested that the United States should "[p]romote establishment of normal relations with Japan."[79]

American wishes for the normalization of South Korea-Japan relations can be understood as part of the larger US regional coordination strategy since the late 1940s, which sought to pass on some of American burdens in South Korea to Japan. The more active stance of the Kennedy administration on this matter is in part due to Japan's economic revival during the 1950s, which increased Japanese capabilities to play an important economic and military role in the region.[80] Additionally, the need of Japanese capital and Japan as a market for the export of South Korean goods for the country's economic development was also taken into consideration.[81] The American perception that the Japanese economic revival was complete was an important premise in the normalization of the relationship between South Korea and Japan.[82]

A background paper for the National Security Council meeting in May 1962 points to the following reasons for speeding the normalization of relations between South Korea and Japan:

a. Rapid Korean economic development, crucially necessary for stability, would be materially accelerated by Japanese economic aid additive to continued U.S. aid.

b. Korea would gain greater access to Japanese markets for her exports, thus providing further major stimulus to Korean economic development.

c. A significant impediment to Free World unity and strength in Asia would be removed.

d. ROK prestige would be bolstered in the increasingly serious competition with the Communist North Korean regime.[83]

The statements above explain the reasons why the United States actively pushed for normalization between the two countries at this time.

Such changes in US Korea policy are in line with the new US Third World policy as theorized by Rostow. Another attention-grabbing point is that the South Korean military performed the desired role of the military in the Third World as Rostow had stated–almost as if Rostow himself had written the script of the May 16 coup d'état. Is it possible that the United States was behind the May 16 coup?

2. The May 16 Coup d'État and the United States

(1) Was the United States behind the May 16 Coup d'État?

As the commanding authority of South Korean military units rests with the United States Armed Forces commander in Korea (who is also the United Nations commander), support (or string-pulling) of the United States was the first and foremost precondition for the success of a coup d'état in South Korea. To put it differently, if the United Nations commander supported (or ignored) movements of military units seeking to launch a coup d'état and restricted movements of military units trying to suppress it, a coup could easily succeed. Considering that only 3,500 men were mobilized for the May 16 coup d'état–a mere 0.5 percent of the entire South Korean armed forces–it is easy to see how the question of American involvement is often raised.

Theories suggesting American involvement in the May 16 coup d'état have been put forth since the time of the coup itself. The presence of American military advisors in the South Korean military down to the battalion level[84] and the so-called Kreper incident[85] are examples typically cited to argue that the Americans were involved in the coup. In particular, the recently discovered Kreper incident reveals several important characteristics of US Korea policy.

The "Kreper Incident" is closely related to the "Ijudang Incident," an "anti-revolutionary" episode that occurred immediately after the coup. Kim Jongpil later testified that the Kreper incident was a US effort to overthrow the Jang Myeon government before the May 16 coup d'état.[86] Kim Jongpil, then the head of the Korean Central Intelligence Agency, obtained information that Washington was planning a coup to overthrow Jang Myeon. Colonel Kreper (a member of a US non-CIA secret service unit), Jang Myeon's political advisor Whittaker, and Army Chief of Staff Jang Doyeong were at the center of the scheme. The military government deported them for setting up the Ijudang Incident, and the CIA Korea Branch director de Silva was transferred to a post in Hong Kong. This is what has been discovered so far.

Based on the declassified telegrams sent from the US Embassy in Seoul and the Korea Task Force, it appears likely that the United States attempted a coup in South Korea before that of May 16. Negative perceptions of the conditions in South Korea were frequently raised in the Kennedy administration, and the US government sought a decisive breakthrough.

The possibilities of new radical developments, including a coup d'état, and the necessity of prompt US responses, were mentioned again at the Korea Task Force meeting in regards to determining US Korea policy. Another document titled "A Proposal to the Presidential Task Force on Korea,"[87] written by an unknown author, was submitted for a preliminary Korea Task Force meeting four days before the May 16 coup.[88] Two important statements can be found in its table of contents. One is on the counsel and flexibility in replacing the prime minister or the administration, and the other is on the need to identify politicians who will replace them in the process of overthrowing of the government.

The quoted proposal above is obviously insisting on the need to find a replacement for Jang Myeon and his government. Although the document is unclear on whether the United States should find and support a replacement or establish a link with those who already want to overthrow Jang, it is clear that the US government was preparing for new and radical developments in South Korea.

If the United States perceived the need to replace the incompetent Jang Myeon government with something else, the above mentioned Kreper incident may not be merely a rumor and be of actual substance. In particular, the mentioning of Jang Doyeong as a key figure on the South Korean side is important. As confirmed by a number of testimonies, Jang Doyeong, a close friend of Yi Gibung (close protégé of Syngman Rhee and vice president during the First Republic), was targeted during a purge of the military in the Jang Myeon government. However, Jang Doyeong was nevertheless supported by the United States and was later promoted as the army chief of staff to replace Choe Gyeongrok, who had clashed with the United States.[89]

However, it is difficult to prove that the United States was behind the May 16 coup d'état as there are no available documents related to the Kreper incident and the main participants of the May 16 coup d'état were not part of it. There are other reasons for doubt. First of all, KCIA Director Kim Jongpil, who first spoke of the Kreper incident, did not maintain a good relationship with the US government. Although it was Kim Jongpil who successfully negotiated with United Nations Commander Carter Magruder after the May 16 coup d'état,[90] the US government was highly suspicious of Kim, suspecting that he may be a socialist or a radical nationalist. Would the United States trust someone who they did not trust or considered favorably? Furthermore, if Kim Jongpil was part of the American scheme, Kim would not have disclosed it to the public.

(2) The US Government and Jang Myeon's Knowledge of the Coup d'État

Even so, what is clear is that the US government knew about the coup d'état on May 16, 1961. The *FRUS, 1961–1963* volume on Northeast Asia includes information related to the May 16 coup that was collected before it was actually staged. Here is an excerpt of the report that CIA Director Allen Dulles sent to President Kennedy:

[less than 1 line of source text not declassified] CIA commencing 21 April reported on plans for a coup d'état in Korea by Major General Pak Chong-hui as follows:

21 April–[less than 1 line of source text not declassified] reports that one of two existing coups to overthrow ROK Government is led by Major General Pak Chong-hui, Deputy Commanding General, Second ROK Army. The other is led by Yi Pom-sok and members of the Racial Youth Corps. Plans discussed throughout ROK Army down to and including division commanders. Army leaders look upon the present politicians as corrupt and weak and believe they have either caused or permitted situations to exist whereby the military, collectively and individually, have been hurt.

21 April–[less than 1 line of source text not declassified] summary on possibility of a military coup. Definite threat exists; however, increased political stability, absence of violence and civil disorder and strengthening of the police would tend to thwart any coup attempt.

23 April–[less than 1 line of source text not declassified] believes there is sufficient evidence to gauge that a significant grouping exists which is actively and seriously talking and planning a coup and that the grouping is largely made up of elements which are bitter, rash, purposeful and quite capable of abrupt and violent action.

23 April–The plot is supported by ROK Army, student groups and reformists. Leader believed to be General Pak Chong-hui, and General So Chong-ch'ol, Commanding General of VI Military District Command is also a close supporter. Much detail contained on military supporters.

24 April–Views of ROK Army Chief of Staff, Chang To-yong on military plot. Chang desires arrest Pak Chong-hui but has lack of evidence. Believes arrest might trigger coup. Chang believes Racial Youth Corps and Yi Pom-sok may support coup.

25 April–ROK Army CIC is investigating the coup. If the coup is not attempted on 26 April, group will await a more opportune time. As of 24 April, according to Chang, Chang Myon was unaware of the coup; however, newspaper publisher planned to advise him on 25 April.

25 April–[less than 1 line of source text not declassified] had one-hour meeting with ROK Army Chief of Staff Chang To-yong on 24 April and told Chang that information on coup had been volunteered our office, that General Magruder would be advised at first opportunity and that thereafter General Magruder would probably discuss this matter with Chang. Chang mentioned that Pak had talked to him one week earlier. Chang states that he believes no action imminent.

26 April–Prime Minister Chang Myon is aware of rumors circulating to the effect that a group of malcontents within the Army may be plotting some kind of coup. He attaches little importance to these stories and believes that the situation is by no means dangerous. Chang Myon is satisfied with the performance of ROK Army Chief of Staff Chang To-yong. He believes that General Chang is forceful and able and enjoys the respect of his American counterparts. He

plans to retain General Chang for a full two-year tour.[91]

US intelligence agencies, the United Nations commander, the South Korean Army chief of staff, and the South Korean prime minister Jang Myeon, all knew about the coup plan before it was carried out. They even dispatched an informant to Park Chung Hee's home to keep an eye on Park.[92]

Although the document above shows that the US government sensed Park's coup about a month before it was staged, words about the coup were already in circulation by April. Many papers written by academics and journalists on the May 16 coup d'état ask, "why didn't they respond to the coup?" However, wouldn't this be a simple question to answer if the very people capable (and responsible) of arresting the conspirators were supportive of the coup? In this case, the blame goes to Army Chief of Staff Jang Doyeong, the United Nations Command, and somebody responsible in a US intelligence agency.

Is there a possibility that a US agency in South Korea was in contact with the conspirators? As stated in the document above, Secretary of State Dean Rusk ordered the US agencies on the ground to establish channels with different factions in South Korea in addition to the usual information gathering. It is easy to speculate that the US intelligence agencies established contacts with the coup forces after they found out about the impending coup d'état.

Let us try to imagine what the contents of still-undisclosed papers from the 795B series documents (RG 59, General Records of the Department of State, Central Decimal File, Box 2182–2189) might be. One May 11, 1961 document and four May 15, 1961 documents are still categorized as "X-Security Classified Information" and therefore as of yet undisclosed. Nearly all the documents from the 795B series from January 1961 to May 1961 are available to the public. Why are these five documents still classified? Could these still-classified documents reveal the connection between the US government and the May 16 coup?

In the end, however, this is guesswork. A number of American documents emphasize the political neutrality of the South Korean army. A document produced in preparation for a Korea Task Force meeting on May 9, 1961, mentions the role of the South Korean military as follows:

> Agree to minimum ROK force levels consistent with ROK security
> and domestic stability and with U.S. policy objectives in the area.
> Promote understanding among the ROK military leadership of the
> desirability of political neutrality and responsibility for assistance to
> the civilian economy to the extent consistent with primary military
> responsibilities.[93]

Another piece of evidence that could refute the theory of
American involvement before the coup is that although many US
officials had negative opinions about the Jang Myeon government,
documents drafted well into May 1961 argued that the US
government should continue to support Jang. The first draft of the
Korea Task Force report, written on May 15, 1961–a day before
the May 16 coup d'état–shows such an attitude on the part of US
government officials:

Recommendations:

1. That the President request an individual of the stature of Harry S.
Truman to Visit Korea, via Japan, accompanied by a top official of a
selected planning advisory organization during the first week of June
to dramatize an intended new direction in United States support to
economic development of Korea and as an earnest of our expectation
of a settlement between Japan and Korea.

2. That the President utilize imminent visits of the Prime Ministers
of Japan and Korea to urge the earliest possible bridging of the
economic and political gaps in relations between the two countries,
while avoiding an active United States role in the negotiation.....

3. That the President urge upon Prime Minister Chang the crucial
importance of imaginative and forceful leadership to capture and
direct the tide of Korean aspirations towards national development;
that he be more courageous in pressing for economic and social
reform.

4. That the President approve in principle and publicly announce
during Prime Minister Chang's visit the United States intention, in
concert with other nations of the Free World, to provide external
resources required to carry out a soundly administered R.O.K. Five

Year National Development Plan;

5. That the President commit the United States specifically, and so announce publicly during the visit of Prime Minister Chang, to finance the foreign exchange costs of developing an additional 400,000 Kw. of electric power capacity over the next five years as the first and most basic step in the R.O.K. Five Year National Development Plan. ...

Planning and Leadership

... Unfortunately, the present Prime Minister, though sincere, intelligent and hardworking, is not a strong leader. He lacks physical courage, and does not have a sense of drama or popular appeal. At present, however, there is no clearly identifiable alternative leader. Therefore Chang's leadership capacities should be developed to the maximum; the best possible talent associated with him on a teamwork basis; and the image of government leadership before the people enhanced. The United States, through appropriate informal contacts and advice, should sharpen the Prime Minister's awareness of these needs and assist him in meeting them. At the same time, we should be on the lookout for alternative leadership. We should not play an active role, either overtly or covertly, in bringing about a change of leadership unless serious signs of instability appear; but we should be prepared to support an emerging leadership group which will advance our objectives for Korea, when the local situation is ripe for change.[94]

As mentioned above, up to a day before the coup, Washington officials continued to discuss ways to help strengthen the Jang Myeon regime, while also discussing possible new leadership.[95] By this time, the coup forces were already on the move.

Such policy documents make the readers' judgments difficult. As far as the currently disclosed documents show, there is almost no chance that the US government was supporting the May 16 coup d'état behind the scenes. Considering many other factors, however, there is a possibility that the US government, although not actively supporting the coup, already had a link with the conspirators. The presence of American military advisors in South Korea, dispatched down to the battalion level, allow a number of different hypotheses about the US role in the coup d'état.

(3) Prime Minister Jang Myeon's Call to the US Embassy in Seoul

Most testimonies on the May 16 coup d'état point out that the United Nations commander, who had the commanding authority over South Korean military units, had a strong intention to suppress the coup using the First Army led by General Yi Hanrim.[96] However, there are also a number views to the contrary that argue that United Nations Commander Magruder had a negative perception of the Jang Myeon government and had no desire to actively suppress the coup.[97] What then was the stance of the UN commander, who had the actual means to physically suppress the coup?

The exact time that the news of the coup reached Washington via the US chargé d'affaires ad interim Marshall Green was on May 15, 5:21 in the afternoon, which was May 16, 6:21 a.m. Korea time (via document number 1524, sent at 5:00 a.m.).[98] This telegram arrived five hours and thirty-one minutes after the report about the opposition candidate Kim Daejung's election victory in the by-election.

JUST INFORMED BY CINCUNC THAT ATTEMPTED COUP D'ETAT NOW IN PROGRESS REPORTEDLY HEADED BY MAJOR GENERAL PAK CHONG-HI SUPPORTED BY ONE OR TWO RESERVE DIVISIONS AND SOME TROOPS FROM FIRST MARINE BRIGADE. IT MORE CERTAIN THAT LATTER INVOLVED;
ARMY CHIEF STAFF CHANG DO-YONG ASKED CINCUNC FOR COMMITMENT U.S. FORCES TO HELP PUT DOWN COUP. CINCUNC REPLIED THAT HE WOULD NOT RELEASE THEM. I AGREE WITH THIS DECISION, ALTHOUGH WE OF COURSE SUPPORT DULLY CONSTITUTED AUTHORITIES HERE, AND WILL MAKE THIS CLEAR.
FROM 1405 HOURS SMALL ARMIES FIRING COULD BE HEARD IN EMBASSY RESIDENCE COMPOUND. FIRING APPARENTLY COMES FROM ROK ARMY HEADQUARTERS SOUTH PART OF SEOUL.

Although it is difficult to be certain about the United Nations commander's stance, he nevertheless made it clear that the US forces would not be mobilized in a suppression. Although most testimonies from those involved in the coup d'état argue that the UN commander had a strong intention to suppress the coup using US forces,[99] the UN commander made it clear early on that the American forces would not be mobilized. However, not mobilizing US forces does not mean that the UN commander approved the coup. As mentioned in chapter 3 of this book, the US military in Korea had also emphasized that only South Korean forces should be mobilized for the plan to remove Syngman Rhee back in 1952 as well.

The United Nations commander sent a telegram to the Joint Chiefs of Staff chairman General Lyman Lemnitzer to report about the coup in South Korea. Twenty-four minutes after Green's report arrived in Washington, General Lemnitzer received the following message:

> 6.(C) At Gen Magruder's request, Gen Chang visited Gen Magruder in his office at approximately 0630 hours. At this time Chang gave Gen Magruder the impression that he was not a party to the revolution, but desired to negotiate with the revolutionaries to prevent bloodshed. Chang stated he wished to talk to military cmdrs to get assurance they would back him in opposing revolution. ...
>
> 7.(C) In later talk with Magruder, Chang [Doyeong] indicated he was still negotiating with Pak in an endeavor to get Pak to operate through the ROK Government. Chang requested Pak to make his demands known to the government.

Immediately after the coup d'état was staged, the United Nations commander confirmed that Army Chief of Staff Jang Doyeong was not part of the coup forces. Although Jang did not support the coup, he nevertheless indicated his willingness to negotiate instead of engaging in outright suppression.

After meeting with Jang Doyeong, the United Nations commander and the US chargé d'affaires issued the following joint statement:

> 11.(C) At approx 1018 hours, the following statement was released by PIO EUSA: General Magruder, in his capacity as Commander in Chief of the UNC, calls upon all military personnel in his Command to support the duly recognized Government of the ROK headed

Prime Minister Jang Myeon meeting with the U.S. Ambassador McConaughy and the UN Commander Magruder just days after his appointment as the prime minister in August 1960. A coup broke out in South Korea less than a year after taking this photograph.

by Prime Minister Chang Myon. General Magruder expects that the Chiefs of the Korean Armed Forces will use their authority and influence to see that control is immediately turned back to the government authorities and that order is restored in the armed forces. 12.(C) Almost concurrently the following statement of Minister Marshall Green, Charge d'Affaires, American Embassy. The position taken by the Commander in Chief UNC in supporting the freely elected and constitutionally established Government of the ROK is [one with] which I fully concur. I wish to make it emphatically clear that the US supports the constitutional Government of the ROK as elected by the people of the Republic last July and as constituted by the election last August of a Prime Minister.

The statement by the UN commander and the US chargé d'affaires signified that they were against the coup d'état and supported the Jang Myeon government. The stance of the United Nations commander, who held commanding authority over South Korean forces, could decisively influence the coup's outcome.

However, the events unfolded in a complex manner. No Korean commander except First Army Commander Yi Hanrim expressed a firm intention for suppression.

13.(C) After reading General Magruder's statement, Gen Lee Han Lim, CG FROKA, stated that he will obey the ROK Government. That if his troops were called upon to put down the insurrection, there might be a few who would not fight the insurrectionists, but most would. Gen Lee has alerted certain troops for possible movement. FROKA has not been alerted.

14.(C) At approx 1030 hours KST Lt General Chang, Chief of Staff, ROKA, went to visit the President of the Republic of Korea who is under no restriction and the Minister of National Defense, who is under house arrest. The President told General Chang that he does not desire martial law to be established in Korea and that he does not desire any firm action to eliminate the revolutionary movement. The Minister of National Defense stated that he does not desire that FROKA troops be used to put down the revolutionary movement.

15.(C) At about 1115 hours, Lt Gen Choi Kyung-muk, CG ROKA, was in communication with General Magruder. He advised that he remained loyal to and would support the government; further he had recalled to their barracks elements of 2 engineer bns which had taken control in Taegu and they had withdrawn.[100]

South Korean politicians, usually highly responsive to American policy and stance, were surprisingly lukewarm toward suppression of the coup d'état, even after the US agencies on the ground publicly spoke against the coup.

At this moment, Prime Minister Jang Myeon called the US Embassy.

During course morning both Primin and minister foreign affairs telephoned the embassy. Formin indicated that he was at his home and had apparently not been arrested. Primin told me that he was "not far away" but for obvious reasons we did not discuss his exact whereabouts. I informed him of statements (transmitted embtel

1528) which CINCUNC and I proposed issue. He responded with expressions deep gratitutde and urged that CINCUNC "take charge of situation."....

Generals Chang and Pak, and possibly other officers of revolutionary committee, and other service chiefs or staff met with President Yun approximately 1100 hours.

Primin phoned emb at 1130, reported he was safe and asked political counselor or pass this word his cabinet.

Charge has just left for meeting with president at Blue House at latter's request.

Magruder concluded by emphasizing that any usurpation of governmental authority by small insurgent group at gunpoint would be disastrous for future of Korea.

I [Green] then referred to statements issued by General Magruder and myself earlier this morning (Embtel 1528) and stressed that I supported the constitutionally established government of ROK and that we believe, as General Magruder stated, that any change in government brought about at gunpoint would have dangerous long-term implications for the survival of ROK democratic institutions which had been won at great cost. Coups invited further coups. I further remarked on effect which success of such coup would have on Korea's international standing and emphasized that Korea's democratic institutions and free-elected government are her greatest assets in confrontation with Communist totalitarianism in North.[101]

Prime Minister Jang Myeon called the embassy after seeking refuge in a nunnery and passed on his authority to the United Nations commander. In Jang Myeon's view, the United Nations commander now held all the keys. However, the UN commander needed justification as well as an order from Washington.

(4) Yun Boseon vs. the United Nations Commander

The UN commander and the US chargé d'affaires decided to meet President Yun Boseon. They had already heard the news that the coup forces would meet with President Yun, and they needed to discuss countermeasures with the Korean president, who constitutionally held the highest position in the South Korean government. When they arrived at the Blue House at 11:30 in the morning, Park Chung Hee and Yu Wonsik of the coup forces already had stopped by.

> Magruder concluded by emphasizing that any usurpation of governmental authority by small insurgent group at gunpoint would be disastrous for future of Korea. ...
> I [Green] then referred to statements issued by General Magruder and myself earlier this morning (Embtel 1528) and stressed that I supported the constitutionally established government of ROK and ... government brought at gunpoint would have dangerous long-term implications for the survival of ROK democratic institutions which had been won at great cost. Coups invited further coups. I further remarked on effect which success of such coup would have on Korea's international standing and emphasized that Korea's democratic institutions and free-elected governments are her greatest assets in confrontation with Communist totalitarianism in North.[102]

The topic US chargé d'affaires Green brought up to President Yun was the significance of democracy in South Korea. According to Green, despite South Korea's limited economic power, South Korea's democracy was its greatest asset against North Korea. The reason why Green mentioned democracy was that he had already heard of President Yun's stance from General Jang Doyeong.

However, the president's stance was different–not dissimilar to how today's South Korean society has begun to forget about the hard-won value of democracy.

> President responded that his evaluation differed somewhat from that presented by General Magruder and myself. He stated that dissatisfaction and disillusionment with present government were widespread and that people no longer trusted promises of Chang Myon cabinet. National constitution had failed to achieve sufficient alleviation of suffering and provide employment in manner which had been promised. Corruption, he felt, was serious and extended to high places within government as testified by tungsten scandal. President said that Korea needed a strong government and that Chang Myon had proven himself incapable of providing such leadership....
> He stated that he had refrained at that time from giving any

commitment to this group but had indicated that should coup expand any further he (President Yun) would step down from his office. President then proceeded to state that in his view solution would have to come in the form of establishing supra-partisan national cabinet including leaders from both within and without national assembly....

General Magruder stated that it important for him to know before returning to his command post whether President approved of calling upon loyal ROK army units to take up positions surrounding Seoul in numbers overwhelming in comparison with coup group so that negotiations with insurgents could be conducted from position of secure government strength. This tactic, he felt, most likely to avoid bloodshed since futility of opposing overwhelming force would be apparent to insurgents. In discussion of this proposal, President stated he not prepared at this time to authorize such move in view of possibility that bloody fighting in Seoul could result. He felt that better solution, if possible, would be persuasion of insurgents to withdraw voluntarily from city and return to normal areas. President noted that some means must be found for saving face of insurgents and some measures of clemency would be required.

By now the repeated arguments by General Magruder and myself against acquiescence in armed coup d'état had taken some visible effect. President Yun professed agreement that any change of government should be accomplished through constitutional means after first removing coup forces from Seoul. (...)

Comment: at beginning of our conversation, President Yun spoke in terms of sympathy for purposes of coup, but he may have been partially convinced as result of our discussions that first problem is to safeguard ROK constitutional processes. I believe he may be committed, however, to securing resignation of Prime Minister Chang and formation of supra-partisan cabinet to lead country following resolution of immediate difficulties.[103]

The meeting between President Yun Boseon, the constitutional commander of the South Korean armed forces, UN Commander Magruder, the commanding authority of the South Korean armed forces, and Chargé d'Affaires Green, the coordinator of all US agencies related to Korea, was an important occasion that could have decided the fate of the coup. Several important matters can be revealed from the meeting.

First, the United Nations commander and the US chargé d'affaires were strongly against the coup d'état. Although North Korea and Pakistan criticized the two men's joint statement as an act of interference in South Korea's domestic affairs and a scheme to hide their involvement in the coup, respectively, the commander and chargé d'affaires were clearly against the coup d'état according to the recorded conversations. The US chargé d'affaires Green tried to persuade President Yun and persisted to the end to obtain the president's consent for suppression.[104]

The second important matter is the United Nation commander's intended method of suppressing the coup. Yun Boseon and Jang Doyeong both worried about possible bloodshed in the process of suppression. However, the UN commander insisted that he could threaten and pressure the coup forces into negotiations by surrounding Seoul with an overwhelming number of troops. Although such a method could also trigger bloodshed, it could also have been the best way to suppress the coup. Moreover, although it may appear to be rather passive, it could have been the only way to avoid street-to-street fighting in Seoul.

The third issue is President Yun Boseon's stance on the coup, which I will discuss in greater detail further in this book.

The quoted telegram clearly indicates that the United Nations commander was strongly against the coup. *Hanguk gunsa hyeongmyeongsa* (History of the Korean military revolution), a book published by the military government after the coup, also emphasized that Commander Magruder had firmly intended to suppress the coup. However, it is worth looking into how strong his intention was as well as the main reason why he opposed the coup.

As can be seen in Magruder's statement and his conversation with President Yun Boseon, Magruder's primary concern was regaining the command of the South Korean military.[105] Because the United Nations commander was only in charge of military matters and not politics, it was, from a political standpoint, an act of arrogation for the UN commander to order the suppression of the coup. Although the United Nations commander was in charge of coordinating American aid to Korea during the 1950s, such responsibility was transferred to the US ambassador in 1959. Because the ambassador seat was vacant, Chargé d'Affaires Green was responsible for matters related to Korean politics at the time of the coup.

General Magruder therefore was not able to suppress the coup against the will of President Yun Boseon, the constitutional commander of the South Korean armed forces, and his superiors at the US Department of Defense. To suppress the coup or to become involved in South Korean politics, Magruder needed a reason to justify his actions. One justification would have been the consent of Yun Boseon, and another would be a directive from Washington.

A full day after the coup started (May 17, 9:00 a.m.), General Magruder sent a report to the Joint Chiefs of Staff on the Korean situation. Was the coup d'état successful?

From General Magruder. My personal summary of the situation after the first twenty four hours is set forth below.

The Prime Minister continues to remain in hiding and does not reveal himself to us. He does not have a reputation for personal courage.

The strength behind the military coup is still unclear but appears to be growing. Only a few troops have moved into Seoul, probably about 3600. They have been essentially unopposed. (...)

A US Army CIC poll of casual bystanders along the streets indicates an average for each ten questioned of four in favor of the uprising, two in favor but consider timing too early, and four opposed.

I am not fully confident in the loyalty of the Chang Myun government of any of the chiefs of staff. Chairman of JCS Kim Chong Oh appears to be neutral with some leaning toward loyalty but exercises little influence. [Air Force Chief of the General Staff] Kim Shin, [Chief of Naval Operations] Lee Sung Ho and [Commandant of the Marine Corps] Kim Sung Eun appear to be neutral. (...)

President Yun Po Sun while giving lip service to the constitution initially, appeared to consider a coup as an acceptable method of getting rid of his political opponent Chang Myun and establishing a new kind of government. He still probably wants to replace Chang Myun and seems to be seeking most legally correct way of achieving this. Both President Yun and Chairman of the House of Councillors George Paik [Baek Nakjun] oppose bringing in troops to suppress

the uprising. (...)
In summary all the powerful men in and around the Seoul government appear to have had knowledge of the plan for the coup and at least have not opposed it. The people appear to be divided for and against but they do not appear to be sufficiently concerned at this time to take any active part.

General Magruder reported the opinions of ordinary citizens, military men, and politicians, and their general opinion was not favorable to Magruder's stance. Magruder calculated that, although they might not be actively supportive of the coup, they were not against it either. Despite their reluctance, Magruder continued to insist on suppression. The only hope was the First Army commander, General Yi Hanrim.

On the advice of General Lee Han Lim in order to help hold the First ROK Army in line and in an effort to stop all the neutrals from going over to the insurgents I have broadcast my support of the constitutionally elected government as has Charge d'Affaires Marshall Green. This appears to have had some effect but it can not be expected to endure indefinitely. ...
We are seeking to undermine the uprising by pressing the responsible commanders, from whose commands came the insurgent troops now in Seoul, to endeavor to get their troops to return to their duty. Success appears probable with the Marine Battalion. It appears improbable with the artillery battalion of the VI ROK Corps. Other troops are still in doubt. ...
Lee Han Lim and his First ROK Army are the force which can probably suppress the uprising by bringing to Seoul such an overwhelming force as to make it hopeless for the insurgents to fight. General Lee states that his troops, with few exceptions, will do as they are ordered. He has four Divisions now in reserve alerted. I believe he would accept and carry out instructions if they were given by Chang Myun to suppress the uprising. I believe he would accept and carry out such instructions if given by me. The longer the above action is delayed the less likely is the prospect of success.

The situation, however, unfolded favorably for the coup forces.

Jang Myeon was missing and Yun Boseon was against mobilization of South Korean forces for the suppression. The coup forces' grip on government power would only grow stronger with time.

The United Nations commander was now in agony. Should he continue to support Jang Myeon and insist on the suppression? Or should he just step back?

If the Prime Minister will assert himself and direct the use of FROKA to suppress the uprising I propose to support him. Unless and until he does, I will seek to hold FROKA available for use. I do not know how long I can hold FROKA in this situation available to support Chang Myun by suppressing the uprising. The longer the Prime Minister remains in hiding the less are his chances of returning to power.

A possible course of action is for me to direct Lee Han Lim to suppress the uprising even though the President, the Chairman of the House of Councillors, the MND and the CS ROKA oppose use of the FROKA for this purpose. If I should do so and were successful we might restore a government with no one to run it and lacking popular support. Basically my mission is to protect Korea from external aggression. To this end the Korean Forces appear to be steadfast. I feel that it is also a part of my mission to protect Korea from internal subversion by the Communists. The uprising does not appear to be Communist inspired although the leader is a former Communist and any uprising against the duly elected government may react to the advantage of the Communists. Accordingly, I do not propose to direct FROKA to suppress the uprising on my own authority only.

Addendum:

Just as the above message was about to be dispatched, I received Lemnitzer›s message of 16 May./1/ This message confirms my intention not to direct FROKA, on my own authority, to suppress the uprising. ...

If the above line of action is not acceptable request further guidance.[106]

Even as matters were proceeding favorably for the coup forces,

Magruder still had a strong intention for suppression. Was he expecting a dramatic return from Jang Myeon and Jang's request for suppression of the coup? Although Magruder referred to the coup forces as "revolutionary" in a telegram sent immediately after the coup started, his wording changed to "insurgent" in a telegram sent the day after the coup's start. Did his negative perception of the coup forces grow stronger? The UN commander also recognized that, as time progressed, the return of the Jang Myeon government and suppression of the coup would become more improbable. He even criticized the Jang Myeon government's return by saying "we might restore a government with no one to run it and lacking popular support."

Unfortunately, there is no available telegram to construe the UN commander's thoughts during the days after the coup. Jang Myeon appeared on May 18, which was already too late for suppression. The First Army commander, General Yi Hanrim, who was initially prepared for suppression, was arrested by the coup forces after declaring his support for the coup d'état on May 17. Sixth Army Corps Commander Kim Ungsu and Eighth Division Commander Jeong Gang, generals under Yi Hanrim who were preparing for suppression, also had to scrap their plans.[107]

As can be seen so far, the United Nations commander possessed a strong will to suppress the coup d'état–the First US Army Corps had ordered the Sixth South Korean Army Corps to do just that on May 17. It is also reported that a US colonel in the Sixth South Korean Army Corps, who was stationed there as a military advisor, also displayed a strong willingness to suppress the coup.[108]

However, several questions remain.

First, given the strong intention of the United Nations commander to suppress the coup, was suppression a possibility? Gregory Henderson, an official of the US Embassy in Seoul, argued that suppression was possible if Magruder willed it.[109] However, could Magruder have suppressed the coup without Yun Boseon's consent or a directive from Washington? Magruder was also nearing his discharge from active duty. His designated successor-to-be General Guy Meloy was already in South Korea as the deputy commander at the time of the coup. According to some testimonies, General Meloy had a more favorable view of the coup forces than

Commander Magruder.[110]

Perhaps, by strongly arguing for suppression, was Magruder trying to display the United Nations commander's power and authority for restoration of commanding authority rather than actually supporting the suppression itself?

Second, why were South Korean commanders indecisive even after the United Nations commander made a public statement against the coup? The UN commander (who is also the commanding general of the Eighth US Army), who had the commanding authority over South Korean armed forces, was a man of great power and authority since the time of the Korean War. He commanded all movements and training of South Korean military units. Moreover, American military advisors were dispatched down to the battalion level of South Korean military units. The UN commander was even involved in the personnel management of the South Korean military. Then why did so many Korean commanders support the coup forces despite the UN commander's statement? Did the US military advisors advise otherwise?

At the time of the coup d'état, Colonel Bang Jamyeong of the Fifteenth Criminal Investigation unit heard of the position of the United States from the Eighth US Army political advisor Kelehon. Keleon informed Bang that, although Magruder was actively against the coup, a directive from Washington ordered the US military commanders to take a "wait-and-see" stance.[111] Would it be possible that South Korean commanders received news of Washington's stance from other channels, such as intelligence personnel like Kelehon, military advisors in the Korean military units, or even CIA agents on the ground? Would it be possible that Washington supported the coup via channels that the UN commander was unaware of?

(5) Is There a Possibility that Washington Approved the Coup?

Gregory Henderson, an official at the US Embassy in Seoul during the time of the coup d'état, revealed a number of important matters related to Washington's stance in a 1987 magazine interview. Below are some parts of Henderson's testimony that are particularly attention worthy:

1. The Jang Myeon government had good relations with us, and we also firmly trusted the Jang Myeon government. Our support for the Jang Myeon government can be proven by the United States Forces Korea Commander Magruder's statement ordering the coup forces to return and supporting the Jang Myeon government as well as the Ambassador [chargé d'affaires] Greene's statement in support of the Jang Myeon government even before receiving a directive from the Department of State. I still remember Mr. de Silva saying that there is much hope for the Jang Myeon government even after the coup's success.

2. Washington sent a directive ordering against suppression. Later I found out that the reason for stopping Magruder's was the aftereffect of the failure of Bay of Pigs invasion three weeks before.

3. Henderson recalled that Magruder's will for suppressing the coup d'état was very strong. If the suppression campaign started after "receiving Yun Boseon's blessings," it would've received ratification of Washington, even as concerned with the scars of the Bay of Pigs.[112]

Paragraph 1 shows the US government stance towards the Jang Myeon government. However, as mentioned before, US officials were not optimistic about the Jang Myeon government's future. Although it was necessary to strengthen it at that moment, cultivating or establishing friendly relations with potential replacements was considered necessary by most American officials on the ground and in Washington.

Paragraph 2 above reveals why the US government did not order the suppression of the coup–the Kennedy administration was still suffering from the aftershock of the Bay of Pigs invasion, an incident in which the US government failed in an attempt to overthrow the Cuban government of Fidel Castro using anti-Castro Cuban exiles, and was hesitant to actively intervene elsewhere. It would have been a significant political burden for the Kennedy administration to intervene elsewhere after such an embarrassing failure.

Then was the suppression order actually given? With the president and secretary of state not yet in their seats in Washington, the chairman of the Joint Chief of Staff was the first one to send a telegram to the United Nations commander in Korea, and he did so on May 16, 11:20 a.m. Washington time (May 17, 12:20 a.m.

Korean time):

1. I have just returned from a White House meeting the purpose of which was to assist in preparing suitable answers to questions on the situation in Korea which were likely to be directed at President's press secretary Salinger at his regular press briefing at 1130 hours today. McConaughy attended also.

2. One of the questions that required most of our time was "Does the President fully indorse the statements released by General Magruder and DCM Green?" As you know, CJCS Kim is reported to have stated that both statements went too far. ...

3. The purpose of this message is to let you know that the consensus of opinion at the White House meeting was that your statement went just about as far as you can possibly go without becoming seriously involved in the internal affairs of the ROK. Therefore, I suggest that insofar as possible you avoid issuing any further statements and concentrate any comments you may have to make on importance of the mission assigned to CINCUNC, i.e., maintenance of the defense of the ROK against Communist attack.[113]

The following is the conversation between Under Secretary of State Chester Bowles and President Kennedy, then staying in Ottawa, on May 16, 6:05 p.m..

The President asked if there was anything on the Korean business. CB [Chester Bowles] said a cable came in a little while ago saying the coup was successful as far as they could see. He said they are aware that we are disturbed and they say full cable will follow tomorrow. The President said he would like to hear their explanation and said he wanted it when he got back. The President asked if there were two statements. CB said Magruder made a statement and the Embassy made one.[114]

Several matters can be perceived from the two telegrams quoted above. First, the statement by the UN commander and Chargé d'Affaires Green was made without Washington's approval. Second, President Kennedy and his aids in the White House nevertheless thought that their statement was not a departure from the US Korea policy.

Third, the chairman of the Joint Chiefs of Staff was displeased with
the UN commander's statement and ordered Magruder not to make
any more. Fourth, within less than twenty-four hours after the coup
d'état broke out, the US under secretary of state already perceived it
to be a success, at a time when the UN commander was still willing
to support suppression.

The most important of the four matters is the final one–
Washington perceived the coup to be a success even before the
US agencies in South Korea did so. According to *The New York
Times* on May 17, 1961, Under Secretary of State Bowles stated to
the members of the Senate Committee on Foreign Relations that
"the coup leaders want to eliminate corruption" and "hope that
the United States will recognize the new military leaders." If *The
New York Times* produced such an article on May 17, the subject
was covered on May 16 American time. What was the basis for
the under secretary of state's reasoning at the time when the UN
commander was leaning towards suppression?

Based on the available documents, it is possible to surmise that
the under secretary of state wholly accepted the contents of certain
telegrams sent early to Washington. On May 16, 2:28 a.m. Korea
time, the second telegram notifying Washington that a coup d'état
had broken out (document number DTG152330Z, Navy Message,
795B.00/5-1661) was sent out. Its author, whose identity is still
unknown to the public, reported that "COUP APPARENTLY
SUCCESSFUL."

However, the under secretary of state could not have declared
the coup to be successful based on a single telegram when other
telegrams presented the situation differently. This was especially
true considering that he was reporting to the president, not just to
his subordinates. He must have felt a great deal of responsibility in
reporting to President Kennedy. The cable Bowles mentioned in the
conversation quoted above with President Kennedy was probably
not the one sent at 2:28 a.m., but another telegram did. However,
none of those telegrams mention the coup's success, although they
do say that the chance of its success is strong.

Therefore, is it possible that a previously undisclosed or
undiscovered telegram exists? If so, was it sent from a location
other than the US Embassy in Seoul? What are its contents?

Another possibility is that the under secretary of state interpreted the telegrams sent from the US Embassy in Seoul in his own way. Bowles had a perspective on US policy toward developing nations that was similar to Rostow's.[115] As a foreign policymaker yearning for the rise of new leadership capable of carrying out reforms in the Third World, Bowles may have seen the May 16 coup as a new hope for South Korea. As mentioned above, Rostow later recollected that he had advised President Kennedy not to suppress the May 16 coup.[116]

After receiving such a report, Kennedy was obviously dissatisfied with the statement of UN commander and chargé d'affaires as it was made in support of a regime on the brink of collapse without considering the circumstances. Such a statement could turn out to be a grave mistake. A telegram sent by the under secretary of state to the US Embassy in Seoul on May 16 at 10:45 p.m. (May 17, 11:45 a.m. Korea time) can be understood in a similar light:

> We recognize desirability of restoring authority of lawful government against reckless challenge of military clique invoking force to upset government freely chosen by Korean people under their own constitutional system. Even though no ideological issue apparently involved, our assessment is that coup attempt undermines stability and reputation of ROK and therefore is contrary to our joint interests.
>
> However, the strange unwillingness of the President, armed forces leaders and other key officials to take any action to suppress coup or to take sides at all, with disappearance from public view of Prime Minister and other members of Cabinet, does not encourage view that Chang government can survive crisis unscathed. Irresolution of those officials who have it in their power to deal with uprising and apparent indifference general public to fate of Chang government provide poor foundation for exertion U.S. influence in behalf Chang Myon.
>
> Therefore cautious attitude of wait-and-see has been adopted pending clarification of situation. We will continue to hope Government can reestablish itself and we will avoid any action which would adversely affect its prospects. On the other hand, in absence some indication government able and willing put forth some effective effort save

itself, we will refrain from additional public identification of U.S.
with fate of what may be a lost cabinet.[117]

In this document, the under secretary of state displays a stance
similar to the chairman of the Joint Chiefs of Staff in requesting a
cessation of further public statements that could indicate possible
American intervention.

An interesting point in this telegram is the response of Walter
McConaughy, who held the posts of assistant secretary of state for
Far Eastern affairs, Korea Task Force chairman, and US ambassador
to South Korea. It also contains the response of Assistant Secretary
of State Cleveland. Cleveland suggested mobilizing the United
Nations force to suppress the coup d'état, and Bowles decided to
discuss matters with McConaughy and Cleveland at a later time to
further assess such a possibility.

> The following morning at the Secretary's staff meeting, McConaughy
> explained that "the President was disturbed by the Green-Magruder
> statements of support for the Chang Government and said the
> President has given Green approval for his exercise of necessary
> discretion but cautioned against further comment." McConaughy
> said that the situation was difficult because the government was
> discredited by weak performance but the coup group did not offer
> promising leadership. Cleveland suggested the use of U.N. machinery,
> and Bowles asked Cleveland and McConaughy to confer with him
> that afternoon.[118]

Certain members of the US State Department viewed the coup
in a negative light. McConaughy also held such a view of the
coup d'état. McConaughy had coordinated US Korea policy at
the time of the April Revolution. As can be seen in Dean Rusk's
telegram (AS-88, January 24, 1961, 795B.00/1-2461) quoted earlier,
Washington evaluated the policy coordination of the US Embassy
in Seoul during the April Revolution as a success. McConaughy
coordinated the honeymoon relationship between the Jang Myeon
government and United States, and such achievements allowed him
to be promoted to assistant secretary of the Department of State.
It is easy to infer how McConaughy, who had helped, advised,

and sometimes pressured the Jang Myeon government, viewed its collapse. In a Korea Task Force meeting held on May 29, thirteen days after the coup, McConaughy expressed his frustration that the draft paper was written as "there was no other choice besides the military government."[119]

It may not be a coincidence that the coup broke out soon after McConaughy left Korea as the US ambassador. The coup forces may have possessed information on McConaughy and carefully planned out the coup accordingly. It is also possible that certain individuals in contact with the coup forces informed them about McConaughy. Or, it could just have been a coincidence. However, what is clear is that if McConaughy stayed in South Korea as the US ambassador at the time of the coup, its fate might have been different, as McConaughy would have been a great help whom Jang Myeon could have relied on.

Chargé d'Affaires Green sent a telegram to the State Department on May 17, 5:37 a.m. (May 17, 6:37 p.m. Korea time), reporting that the coup forces were stabilizing.[120] Although the State Department's midday briefing acknowledged that the state of affairs in South Korea was still in flux,[121] Washington started to believe that the coup was a success. US government officials even started to believe that the establishment of a new and stable government was possible if the current constitution and President Yun Boseon were somehow maintained.[122]

The day Jang Myeon and his cabinet came out of hiding and resigned was May 18, two days after the coup began. By then, the US Department of State acknowledged the coup's success and the resignation of the Jang Myeon government. The answer to the question of why Jang Myeon was "in hiding" can be found here. He was not simply hiding, but rather, stayed in contact with his close associates in the US Embassy in Seoul and his political advisor Whittaker. He must have received the State Department document on the night of May 17.

Jang Myeon by then had no hope. Unless there was a special proposal by the chargé d'affaires or the UN commander, the US agencies on the ground had to support the formation of a new political landscape around the coup forces and Yun Boseon. The Department of State decided on the direction it was going to take forty hours after the coup started. They could no longer just wait and see what would happen.

However, the US wait-and-see policy was itself a clear case of intervention. As mentioned in this book's introductory chapter, the United Nations commander and Washington had the authority to both suppress or (tacitly) approve the coup. By not actively intervening in the coup d'état, the United States created a favorable environment for the coup forces.

When Jang Myeon and his cabinet collectively resigned, Chargé d'Affaires Green began a new task. Green met Yun Boseon on May 19, and Jang met the latter later on that day as well (May 18 Korea time). Jang emphasized in his meeting with Yun that the unity of state must be maintained and a broad-based supra-partisan government with active participation from citizens should be quickly established. He also presented the following six items:

Cooperation with the United States:
1. continued recognition of existing treaties and agreements
2. restoration of operational control of ROK armed forces to CINCUNC
3. return of ROK forces to pre-coup roles and positions
4. release of political prisoners without reprisals
5. anti-corruption and nepotism policies
6. economic stability, development, and efficient use of U.S. aid.[123]

By declaring the fall of the Jang Myeon government and the success of the coup d'état, the United States ended the coup crisis. Unless something radical happened, it was impossible for the United Nations commander to suppress the coup on his own. Did the US government then begin to make efforts to support the military government?

The answer is a decisive no. The secretary of state, as can be seen in the above quoted statement, was trying to pressure the new government into follow US policy. The six provisions Chargé d'Affaires Green presented to President Yun Boseon show what kind of new government the United States wanted. The United States struggled with the new government for more than two years, from 1961 to 1963, to obtain its compliance with American demands.[124]

(6) Was the United States Responsible for the Coup d'État's Success?

What was the actual cause of the coup's success? Did the United States support it behind the scenes? If the United States was not behind the coup, did it have contacts with the coup forces and aid its success by not mobilizing the South Korean army for suppression?

We will review what we have discussed so far in order to avoid confusion. US officials working on Korea issues generally saw the Jang Myeon regime in a negative light. Although they did not argue for its immediate removal, they perceived the need for a replacement in the long run. The Korea Task Force was formed to both strengthen the Jang Myeon regime on the one hand and find and support a replacement on the other. At that point, the coup d'état broke out.

The US president and secretary of state were not at their seats when the coup broke out and the United Nations commander and chargé d'affaires in South Korea issued a public statement in support of the Jang Myeon government without their approval. The UN commander strongly supported the suppression of the coup. However, the South Korean prime minister, who could have given him the support necessary to suppress the coup, disappeared, and President Yun Boseon was clearly against this line of action. In addition, Washington looked askance at the statement by the UN commander and chargé d'affaires.

Based on the disclosed documents, Washington appears to have been perplexed during the initial stage of the May 16 coup d'état. Most importantly, the top people in charge were absent at the time. However, the under secretary of state and the chairman of the Joint Chiefs of Staff nevertheless opposed the UN commander's stance on the coup. They recommended that US officials on the ground in South Korea should refrain from making additional moves and take a wait-and-see approach. The Americans ultimately ended up betting on every possible scenario. Although the UN commander continued to wait for Jang Myeon's reappearance, the US government already concluded that the coup was a success before he and his cabinet showed up again. Then the US government took on a new task.

In summary, it is possible to conclude that the success of the May 16 coup was due to the ambiguous stance of the United

States government. It did not take any action against troops that were removed from its commanding authority and disallowed the opportunity or authority to those who wanted to suppress it. The coup d'état could not but succeed under such conditions. However, this conclusion, which is solely based on a view on the United States and the coup d'état, can be misleading. In addition to the American roles, one should also analyze the actions of South Korean politicians and officials at the time.

This discussion, based on the statement "*ol geosi watguna*" (what we've expected came), is intended to examine the roles played by South Korean politicians and officials. On May 16, 1961, at a meeting with General Park Chung Hee and Colonel Yu Wonsik, President Yun Boseon reportedly said, "*Ol geosi watguna.*" Although Yun Boseon claimed that the specific wording was different, Yu Wonsik, Minister of National Defense Hyeon Seokho,[125] and Kim Jaechun, who was outside waiting for Park Chung Hee, all testified that they heard Yun saying exactly that.

Based on the testimonies so far, at the time of the coup, Yun Boseon appeared to be either favorable to the coup forces, or at least was not for the suppression of it. Although he himself denied such allegations, Yun's stance can be observed in the three-way conversation between the United Nations commander, chargé d'affaires, and President Yun Boseon. On the morning of May 16, instead of suppression, Yun Boseon suggested to the UN commander forming a government for national unity.

As mentioned earlier, a US official later stated that the UN commander would have opted for suppression even without Washington's approval had he had Yun Boseon's "blessing." Would such action on the part of the UN commander been possible? The answer is no. The UN commander could not have suppressed the coup d'état without Washington's consent, as he could not have disobeyed the command structure.

Therefore, Yun Boseon's stance may not have been decisive. However, it nevertheless provided an important legitimization for the coup's success. Telegrams between the chargé d'affaires and the US State Department clearly reveal this aspect. Korean popular indifference to the coup d'état and Korean politicians' hatred toward the Jang Myeon government provided the most important reasons not to suppress the coup. Was an intervention without popular support really necessary? American failures in Panama after successfully kidnapping Manuel Noriega with a few helicopters as well as American inability to "pacify" Iraq even after pouring in so much firepower are due to the lack of popular support in those countries. Right?

Regardless of the success of the coup d'état, the US government wanted Yun Boseon to retain his position. Maintenance of the South Korean president would be a good way to prove to the international world that the constitutional order was being safeguarded in South Korea. Under Secretary of State Bowles argued to the Senate Committee on Foreign Relations that recognizing the new South Korean regime was feasible if President Yun Boseon maintained his position. According to diplomatic custom, there was no need to present a letter of credentials if the head of state remains in his position. International relations can simply continue as they had before. Even when the coup forces asked for a formal recognition, the US government maintained that there was no such need as long as the president remained in power. The US government had already completed a legal examination of this issue by May 22.[126]

(7) A Successful Coup d'État with just 3,500 Men

So far, we have gone over the course of the May 16 coup d'état. Reviewing how it took place is critical given its impact on modern Korean history. In a country with more than six hundred thousand men in its armed forces, how can 3,500 men–less than 1 percent of the entire South Korean military–successfully carry out a coup? Furthermore, the coup succeeded even when it only occupied limited areas in and around Seoul–not the entire country. Although such a fact testifies to how much state power is concentrated in Seoul, it nevertheless leaves many questions unanswered.

The coup forces were not impressive. They could not even mobilize all the units their plans called for. The coup forces also did not expect resistance from the military police when they crossed the Han River into downtown Seoul. There is even testimony contending that Park Chung Hee worried in anguish over whether or not to cross the river. Could this coup d'état attempt, with so many obvious weaknesses, have been successful without US aid?

As I've repeatedly emphasized, according to disclosed US documents, there is no evidence showing that the US government was involved in the coup. With all the documents proving US interventions in Nicaraguan and Iranian politics as well as the American plan to remove Syngman Rhee being disclosed, is there a reason not to reveal the documents proving an American role in the May 16 coup d'état?

But we must also think of the plans the US government established after the plot to remove Syngman Rhee failed as well as when Washington became disillusioned with the Jang Myeon government. Also consider Rostow's plan to carry out social reforms in the so-called Third World. Did the United States not desire to cultivate and support forces that could replace the current leaders in power in those countries?

It is not yet clear exactly how the United States supported such groups. However, what is clear is that the political counselors of the US Embassy in Seoul must have contacted various people in South Korea in search of potential replacements, and the US government must have tried to cultivate such potential candidates. The so-called Kreper incident must have broken out in the midst of this process. Was the US government therefore perplexed because the coup d'état took place while it was trying to build support among another group or groups?

The point I want to emphasize in this section is not whether or not the United States was involved in the coup d'état. What is more important for my purposes is the fact that the forces that successfully carried out the coup were Korean. The priority of US South Korea policy, given its geographic location at the Cold War's frontline, was for South Korea to have and maintain strong leadership. If US-supported South Korea were to collapse not by a foreign invasion but due to its internal complications, it would not only negatively affect American prestige but also cause an enormous problem for the United States in its battle against communism. In addition, if South Korea becomes an anti-American socialist nation through a revolutionary regime change, it would pose a serious security threat to neighboring Japan.

Developments in South Korea during the course of the May 16 coup d'état were of enormous interest to Japan. Japan continued to inquire about the coup forces' inclinations to the United States, even after the military government's establishment. Japan of course was interested in the South Korean coup d'état for its possible consequences to national security.

As revealed in the US Korea policy around the time of the Korean War, although the US was capable of abandoning South Korea, which would not have direct impact on its national interests, the US could not consider abandoning Japan—which formed the center of capitalism in Asia. Therefore, security in the Korean peninsula was of enormous importance to the United States due to its geographic proximity to Japan.

But what the United States observed after the May 16 coup were quiet Koreans and the grumbling of the South Korean president that the current regime was destined to fall. If widespread public opinion in favor of protecting the legitimately elected government existed, could the United States simply have acted as a speculator? What policy did the US government choose after observing the April Revolution and the peak of the Korean democratization movement in June of 1987? Why did the United States sit and watch as China turned red? Although the Jang Myeon and Kuomintang governments are certainly responsible for their failures in cultivating popular support, the ultimate responsibility lies in the hands of most Korean and Chinese citizens who did nothing to stop the regime changes.

Of course, the US government could have supported the coup forces regardless of popular opposition had the US decided that they were favorable to its foreign policy—as the United States did during the "Seoul Spring." However, as will be discussed later, the United States did not wholly trust the coup forces even after the transfer of power to an elected civil government.

3. Taming of the Coup d'État Forces and Park Chung Hee's Tug-of-War

(1) Using Yun Boseon

The chain of events that followed the May 16 coup d'état perplexed not only South Korean citizens but every nation with an interest in South Korea. The prime minister, who was responsible for state affairs, suddenly disappeared after the coup d'état broke out.[127] The

United Nations commander, who possessed commanding authority over South Korean military units, issued a statement in support of the Jang Myeon administration without the South Korean prime minister. President Kennedy expressed his discomfort with the UN commander's statement, which was made without his or the State Department's approval. Although the coup forces attempted to find the prime minister and his cabinet to undertake the power, they were missing.

The most perplexing thing of all was the stance of President Yun Boseon towards the coup d'état. At the meeting with UN Commander Magruder and Chargé d'Affaires Green, President Yun Boseon was not only against suppressing of the May 16 coup d'état, but also described the fall of the Jang Myeon administration as inevitable. Yun spoke of the need to establish a new government.

PRESIDENT THEN PROCEEDED TO STATE THAT IN HIS VIEW SOLUTION WOULD HAVE TO COME IN THE FORM OF ESTABLISHING SUPRA-PARTISAN NATIONAL CABINET INCLUDING LEADERS FROM BOTH WITHIN AND WITHOUT NATIONAL ASSEMBLY (...)
AT THIS POINT WE WERE JOINED BY HOUSE OF COUNCILLORS PRESIDENT L. GEORGE PAIK [Baek Nakjun] WHO STATED VIEW THAT GOVERNMENTAL CHANGES INVOLVING FORMATION OF A MORE RIDIGLY BASED CABINET WERE NEEDED AS BASIC SOLUTION OF PROBLEM POSED BY PRESENT COUP. PRESIDENT YUN LATER COMMENTED THAT HE HAS CABLED SPEAKER KWAK SANG-HUN TO RETURN IMMEDIATELY FROM HIS UNITED STATES VISIT AND INTIMATION WAS THAT CONSULTATIONS FOR FORMATION OF SUCH NEW GOVERNMENT WERE PURPOSE OF KWAK'S RECALL.[128]

On May 4, 1962, about a year after the coup d'état, journalist Yi Manseop of the newspaper *Donga ilbo* received important information from Yu Wonsik of the Supreme Council for National Reconstruction. Yu told Yi that President Yun Boseon had been in contact with Yu Wonsik before the coup and decided to approve the coup d'etat. At the time of the coup, Yu Wonsik met President

Yun with Park Chung Hee before Yun met the United Nations commander, and reportedly asked President Yun to keep his promise. Although Yun later denied this, arguments between Yu Wonsik and Yun Boseon about Yun's prior approval of the coup continued.[129] To summarize the arguments, Yun Boseon appears to have had either a favorable view of the coup forces or was against active suppression of the coup. Although President Yun Boseon denied such allegations, the quoted telegram above displays his stance well.

An important point to note in the midst of these events is that President Yun Boseon was thinking of forming a "supra-partisan national cabinet." President of the House of Councillors Baek Nakjun also argued that the coup d'état crisis should be solved through reorganization of the cabinet and state administration. The Sinmindang[130] president Kim Doyeon, after an emergency staff meeting on May 17, issued a statement urging President Yun to create a supra-partisan government. Reportedly, at a provincial Sinmindang office, certain party members even cheered with joy.[131]

Yun Boseon's stance stems from the conflict between the so-called *sinpa* (new faction) and *gupa* (old faction) of the Democratic Party that had continued since the 1950s, as well as his alienation from the center of power. On April 14, 1961, US ambassador McConaughy stopped by at the Blue House before leaving his post. At his meeting with Yun Boseon, McConaughy noted that Yun's assessment of the conditions in South Korea was even worse than that of the US Embassy in Seoul.[132]

It is clear that Yun Boseon was overly optimistic about the May 16 coup d'état. Yun must have received a report from Park Chung Hee on the morning of May 16 and probably imagined a new power structure uniting the *gupa* of the Democratic Party around him and the coup forces. According to a telegram sent by the US Embassy in Seoul, Park Chung Hee told Yun Boseon on the morning of May 16 that he would soon transfer power to a civil government.[133]

In communicating with the US Embassy in Seoul, Yun Boseon even revealed his plan to set up a de Gaulle–style presidential political system through a supra-partisan cabinet.[134] Yun expected a maximum of six months for a transfer of power to a civil government, if not two to three months. He also expected a direct presidential election to take place in August or September, establishing a supra-partisan cabinet with a strong presidency.[135] The US Department of State perceived Yun's recall of the speaker of the Lower House Gwak Sanghun from his stay in the United States was due to Yun's plans to form a new government.[136]

Magruder was bewildered by Yun Boseon's attitude after the coup d'état, and the State Department also was watchful of President Yun's stance. Under Secretary of State Bowles, temporarily replacing Dean Rusk, ordered the US Embassy in Seoul to take a "cautious attitude of wait-and-see" due to "the strange unwillingness of the President, armed forces leaders and other key officials to take any action to suppress coup or to take sides at all." Bowles simply defined Yun Boseon's attitude as "strange."[137] As time passed by, however, maintenance of Yun Boseon as president and Yun's favorable stance towards the coup d'état became important in smoothing out the relationship between the United States and the Korean military government.

The US government soon had to recognize that the coup forces had seized political power in South Korea.[138] Prime Minister Jang Myeon and his cabinet did not appear, and the coup forces formed the Revolutionary Committee and began seizing government agencies.

Washington was forced to come up with a new stance, as the US government could be condemned domestically and internationally for continuing to support South Korea even after the coup d'état. The US government, which traditionally regarded worldwide realization of American-style democracy as an important moral cause in its foreign policy, could not publicly support a regime established by an illegal coup d'état. Therefore, using the legally elected President Yun Boseon was important in justifying the US stance towards South Korea and the coup forces.

This stance of the US government was most clearly revealed when President Yun Boseon disclosed his intention to resign from his post. Yun Boseon considered resignation a day after Prime Minister Jang Myeon and his cabinet resigned on May 18, 1961, and the military government urged him to stay as a way to legally justify the new regime. The US government was even more eager to keep him.

A political counselor of the US Embassy in Seoul emphasized

that the last vestige of civilian government would be maintained by the office of president, and he contended that Yun Boseon should continue to play a positive role. Accepting this argument, Washington also declared it unnecessary to formally recognize the new regime if President Yun Boseon continued to represent South Korea as the head of state. Ambassador Berger, whom Washington dispatched with significant authority, personally stressed to President Yun Boseon that there was a need for him to remain president.

With the coup d'état's success, the US government decided to use Yun Boseon's position as a way to recognize the military government. As it did in Pakistan and Turkey, the US government decided that it did not need to recognize a new government if the highest ranking official of the previous government retained his position.[139] In a telegram sent to the US Embassy in Seoul the Department of State, made it clear that there was no legal obstacle in recognizing the military government as long as the president remained.[140]

The US government also moved the US ambassador to stop President Yun from resigning when he expressed his intention to do so for the second time in August 1961. The American ambassador communicated Washington's intention that the US government desired that Yun remain president. Yun changed his mind once again, and he resigned at a later date–March 22, 1962.[141]

As seen so far, the US government wanted to maintain Yun Boseon as president in order to smooth out the relationship between the United States and the Korean military government in the international arena as well as to form a new political system using Yun Boseon as a key component. Although highly unlikely, there is evidence in the US documents that indicate that Washington was considering such a possibility.

First, let's examine a telegram sent by the Department of State on May 17, a day after the coup started.

If it is your finding that Chang Myon government has disintegrated irretrievably you are authorized to work along lines which you consider best calculated to encourage early emergence of broadly based, responsible non-partisan government of national unity and of predominantly civilian composition with which we can work constructively and cooperatively in atmosphere of mutual trust. While Revolutionary Committee as presently constituted may appear to offer scant promise of developing in this direction, you are authorized in your discretion to work as you deem necessary with that Committee as starting point, seeking to bring to bear all available moderating, balancing and restraining influences. Possible utility of General Lee Han Lim, Commander First ROK Army, in this connection might be considered.

It is highly important to confer on successor government to maximum attainable extent an aura of legality, continuity and legitimate constitutional succession. Presumably this can best be achieved by continuation in office of Yun Po Sun as President who would use his prestige and office to bring about selection of generally acceptable candidate for Prime Minister.

It our tentative impression here that coup group has no very clear idea exactly where it wants to go after having overthrown Chang government. If this impression correct and Yun Po Sun willing assert leadership inherent in his office at such period of crisis, suggest possibility of Yun calling in coup group leaders together with a few widely respected military and civilian figures of national stature and attempting obtain immediate agreement on selection Prime Minister and full cabinet slate who could reassert governmental authority. Even though such action may not be possible strictly within constitutional framework seems from here some such action within spirit orderly governmental processes might offer best hope of preventing degeneration into chaotic situation which communists might attempt to exploit or into out-and-out military dictatorship. This offered only as suggested line of approach within foregoing framework. There may well be other such lines not apparent to us here.[142]

The United States, previously unable to actively respond to the coup d'état due to President Yun Boseon's "strange" attitude, was now able to formulate new policies based on the maintenance of his position. In other words, the US government aimed to establish a new government uniting civilians and the coup forces using the position and authority of the South Korean president. By displaying a president elected through the constitutional process, the US government could prevent the new regime from appearing as an illegal and dictatorial regime and justify supporting it. This American plan matched the "supra-partisan national cabinet" proposal President Yun suggested to the United Nations commander on the day of the coup.

In addition to the belief that Yun Boseon's authority could have a significant impact, the stances of Korean officials close to the United States also influenced the American position.[143] The South Korean officials the US government contacted immediately after the coup included Cha Gyunhui, Yi Hanbin, and Yi Gihong, all of whom positively viewed the coup's developments.[144] Yi Hanbin even revealed the possibility of forming a temporary cabinet.[145] The US government judged that these officials actually wanted an event like the coup d'état. Kim Jeongnyeom was another South Korean official the US government was paying attention to, and he was staying in the United States after the actualization of the exchange rate undertaken by the Jang Myeon government. He was summoned after the coup d'état, and the US government expected him to play a role as a civilian official in the military government.[146]

The US government appears to have hoped to establish an ideal state structure combining these civilian officials with the military government. As mentioned before, Rostow and other officials of the Kennedy administration emphasized the need for a new ruling class centered on military men so that developing nations could carry out new policies. However, they did not argue that the new ruling class must be made up entirely of military men. For military men to effectively lead a government, they believed, solidarity with intellectuals from other strata, particularly lawyers, academics, and officials, was necessary.[147]

Since the late 1950s, South Korean officials in contact with the US government mostly worked for the Ministry of Finance, Ministry of Reconstruction, and the Industrial Development Commission under the Ministry of Reconstruction. They had experience in drafting an economic development plan. The fact that the coup forces did not have any experience in administrative affairs also justified the need to introduce civilian officials into the military government.[148] A mixture of civilian officials and military men represented the ideal form of government the United States wanted in South Korea.[149]

The American policy is also evident in the US stance towards Choego Hoeuibeop (the Supreme Council law). Chargé d'Affaires Green judged that although the government forming under the Supreme Council law would bring in some civilian officials, power would be concentrated in the Supreme Council for National Reconstruction (SCNR). Green therefore argued that the US government should make a strong case to the coup forces that civilians should not be relegated to advisory or figurehead positions.[150] At a meeting with the South Korean minister of foreign affairs on June 7, Chargé d'Affaires Green displayed his strong disapproval regarding the fact that the Supreme Council law would not grant much authority to civilian officials. Green argued that there was a strong need for civilian officials, and that they should be included at the cabinet level, and that the most pressing need for civilians in the government was in those agencies related to the economy.[151]

Withdrawal of the plan to use Yun Boseon by the US government appears to have occurred at a time when the military government stabilized and it became clear that Yun Boseon was no longer needed. Park Chung Hee's visit to the United States in November 1961 also appears to have played a role. Perhaps the recognition of Park Chung Hee's leadership made Yun Boseon obsolete? By 1962, Yun's usefulness shrank only to issues related to American recognition of the military government. This point is evident in the timing of Yun's resignation.

On January 1, 1962, the South Korean military government released "old" politicians from house arrest. However, the military government nevertheless wanted to prevent them from joining the new government. Yun Boseon expressed his desire to reexamine this restriction against "old" politicians on February 2, 1963, and the Supreme Council for National Reconstruction reacted by directly confronting Yun with the passing of the Jeongchi Hwaldong Jeonghwabeop (Political Activity Purification law) on March 16, 1962. Yun Boseon declared that he would begin preparing for resignation on March 18, 1962 and finally resigned on March 22, 1962. With the Political Activity Purification law, Yun Boseon must have realized that the reorganization of the South Korean political world with himself as the central figure was now impossible.[152]

By then, the American attitude towards President Yun Boseon had changed. Although Ambassador Berger met with Yun and asked him to change his mind, the US stance was not as firm as it once was. In a report to the State Department, Berger merely wrote a short note requesting a review of the resignation. While doing this, Berger also noted that there should be no legal complications because the Supreme Council for National Reconstruction was to succeed the president's authority according to the Supreme Council law. Berger did not try to stop Yun after that.[153]

(2) Forcing "Backroom Boys" to Resign

If the success of the coup d'état and stabilization of the military regime dominated the year 1961, 1962 was the year when conflict between South Korea and the United States on the economic policy issue publicly surfaced. First, the US government expressed its strong dissatisfaction with the military government's economic development plan, which Washington saw as unrealistic and socialist. The US ambassador and the superintendent of the US official delegations to South Korea criticized the economic development plan using various channels and urged Seoul to develop a more realistic one.[154]

Already by July of 1961, the US government dispatched Richard A. Boucher of the US official delegation to South Korea as well as researchers of the Little Company to the military government as economic advisors.[155] They, however, could not change the military government's economic policy.

American dissatisfaction with the military government's economic policy culminated with the June 1962 currency reform. Becoming effective shortly after the so-called stock market suspicion incident, the "Emergency Currency Management Law" (Gingeup Tonghwa Jochibeop) reformed the *hwan* currency to *won* currency and froze bank savings to mobilize domestic capital.[156] Although the military government publicly stated that the currency reform's goal was to curb inflation, the actual purpose was to establish the Industrial Development Corporation, a state investment agency, through the freezing of private bank savings.[157] The Industrial Development Corporation was established so the state could lead investment, which activity had strong elements of a planned economy.

The US government was strongly opposed to currency reform. Although the surface issue was the fact that the US government was unilaterally notified about the reform only forty-eight hours before it took place, the main reason was the suspected possibility that the industrial development plan, accomplished through currency reform, could go "socialistic."[158] Ambassador Berger refused to give an immediate answer when Park Chung Hee requested to meet with him after the currency reform.[159] The Department of State notified Berger that no official statement should be issued before the South Korean government made positive steps.[160] On the same day, Secretary of State Dean Rusk issued a statement declaring that although the South Korean currency reform attempted to follow the 1948 precedent of West Germany, it was fundamentally different from the West German case which sought to create an efficient price system based on a free market system and free distribution of resources.[161] The US Embassy in Seoul even offered the money needed to establish the Industrial Development Corporation in exchange for the freeing of bank savings.[162]

In the end, the South Korean military government was forced to release the frozen bank savings.[163] The Industrial Development Corporation plan was also scrapped.[164] More important than retreating from and modifying policies was the replacement of policymakers themselves. Reporting the Little Company's research on the South Korean economic development plan, Joseph Yager of the State Department strongly emphasized the need to replace Korean economic advisors in addition to modifying state economic policies. Also, the Little Company recommended that the members of the Economic Planning Board should be replaced. The evaluation report of the economic development plan pointed to the estrangement of economic specialists as the fundamental problem of the drafting process of the South Korean economic development plan.[165]

The US government believed that the problem of South Korean economic policy was caused by certain young officers inside the Supreme Council.[166] Economic advisors of the Supreme Council, frustrated with US Korea policy, were not on good terms with James S. Killen, the superintendent of the US official delegations.[167] In the end, the military government replaced Bak Huibeom and other economic advisors who drafted and drove the first five-year economic development plan, as well as Commerce and Industry Subcommittee Chairman Yu Wonsik. Economic specialists were introduced into key policymaking positions as replacements. In addition, the US government actively pressured the South Korean government to remove Kim Yongtae, a close associate of the Korean CIA Director Kim Jongpil, from policymaking.[168]

The US government expected new civilian officials to create a cooperative policymaking environment in the aftermath of the failure of currency reform.[169] Kim Yutaek and Cha Gyunhui, key officials in the Ministry of Finance, Ministry of Reconstruction, and Bank of Korea during the Syngman Rhee administration, were appointed respectively as the minister and deputy minister of the Economic Planning Board after the failure of currency reform. Yu Changsun, who replaced Kim Yutaek as the minister of commerce and industry until February 1963, was the New York chief of the Bank of Korea, vice-minister of the Ministry of Reconstruction during the Jang Myeon government, director of the Foreign Loan Office, and a representative during the normalization talks between Korea and Japan.

Professional bank official Kim Seryeon, Dongguk University faculty member and Kyushu University graduate Hwang Jongryul, and former Bank of Korea and Ministry of Finance official Kim Jeongryeom were appointed as the minister and vice-ministers of the Ministry of Finance. They were all professional economic officials and were appointed after the currency reform. Replacing former military men like Song Yochan, Baek Seonjin, Jeong Raehyeok, Yu Wonsik, and Bak Huibeom, these civilian officials began to participate in economic policymaking.[170]

The US Embassy in Seoul positively evaluated the removal of those who took part in drafting the currency reform and economic development plan.[171] Furthermore, when new economic officials who had studied in the United States or were in contact with the US Embassy in Seoul began to take key economic policymaking positions, the Seoul Embassy reported to the Department of State that they cooperated with US policy.[172]

It appears that worst of current crisis has passed. Undesirable features of monetary reform have been rescinded. Some minor changes in

SCNR have been effected, a new team of economic administrators has taken cabinet office and we are hopeful that more fruitful relationship between Embassy, USOM and their ROKG counterparts can be instituted. At the leadership level an uneasy truce seems to have been achieved but factional clash which pitted Kim Chong-p'il and some of young colonels against combination of Hamgyong and other anti-Kim elements hovers over scene.[173]

We have been having rocky time here during past couple months, and while situation is better in sense that new PriMin and Economic Ministers are working with us in fairly cooperative fashion, I am still not happy about certain aspects of situation.[174]

The change of economic policymakers after a conflict between the US and South Korean governments on the issue of economic policy was easy to predict, and the US government was able to push through a reshuffle of personnel due to currency reform. Although the US government was not directly involved in the details of personnel reshuffling,[175] the South Korean military government nevertheless had to accept the aid-based pressure of the United States.

However, as can be seen in the first of the two quoted telegrams, changes in the administration personnel did not mean that the US government was finished reforming the South Korean government according to its vision. As seen in both telegrams, the problem of factionalism within the military government was an important political task the United States had to resolve in the military government. If the crisis in 1962 was an economic problem centered on currency reform, the 1963 crisis was a political problem focused on the Democratic Republican Party. The American ambassador was "still not happy."

(3) Forcing Kim Jongpil to Resign

Persisting internal conflict within the South Korean military government into the latter part of 1962 surfaced with the so-called anti-revolution (anti–coup d'état) incidents. Prior to the end of 1962, Washington did not take "anti-revolution" incidents seriously. The US government already expected one involving Jang Doyeong immediately after the coup d'état, and it ended with Jang Doyeong's flight to the United States and the collective resignations of those involved. Although most "anti-revolution" incidents turned into nothing more than short reports to the State Department, the US government displayed deep interest in the "anti-revolution" incident involving General Kim Ungsu.

The US government was particularly interested in this "anti-revolution" incident because General Kim Ungsu's attempt to suppress the coup d'état was based on the United Nations commander Magruder's statement. The United States would be placed into an awkward dilemma if Kim Ungsu was punished for following the UN commander's order. Although that part of the story should not have surfaced at all, it became public information during the course of Kim's trial. The court made a point of General Kim Ungsu's circulation of the UN commander's statement to his subordinates.[176]

American officials in South Korea submitted a letter of protest on that point to the Ministry of Foreign Affairs, and it was dropped from the charges against General Kim. The US Embassy in Seoul even considered issuing a public statement. The prosecutor changed his argument regarding Kim Ungsu's action from "attempting to destroy the revolution" to "not following the UN Command's operational control." The incident ended with a ten-year sentence for Kim Ungsu and twelve-year sentence for Jeong Gang.[177]

The "anti-revolution" incidents up to late 1962 were sporadic, and the US government responded to them in a limited fashion. However, in late 1962, the situation became so serious that the US government believed that another such crisis, in this case, the formation of the Democratic Republican Party, could potentially bring down the South Korean military government.

By late 1962, reorganization of the South Korean political world became a key issue for the military government and political circles. Immediately after the coup d'état, Park Chung Hee had declared that a new constitution would be enacted in late 1962. He also declared that political power would be transferred to a civilian government in the spring or summer of 1963. The coup forces therefore were forced to prepare for a transfer of power by the latter part of 1962.

The US government became concerned that several serious problems could further develop during the process of political reorganization–particularly within the military government itself. Observing South Korean conditions through the currency reform and stock market fluctuations, US government officials concluded that the fundamental cause of the South Korean military government's instability centered around the newly created Korean Central Intelligence Agency, its leader Kim Jongpil, and the "young colonels" surrounding him.[178]

> Basic problem is power of Kim Chong Pil and ROK CIA. Kim was given severe shaking and for few days in June and again in July it looked as if his organization was going to be cut back to its basic intelligence mission. Pak gave me [Ambassador Berger] assurances of this on two occasions, but there is no sign this has been done.
>
> ROK CIA has curious set-up. One part devoted to usual activities. Second part consists of political, economic, legislative and public information divisions: which occupy themselves with major policy matters. Numbers employed in latter are large; we have no access to them; and some of their key people have record of past Communist or leftist associations or hold extreme anti-American views. Moreover ROK CIA is in "everything"–appointments, lodging their people in newspapers and business, deriving income from variety of sources from stock market to business deals, etc.
>
> If Pak carries out his assurance to return ROK CIA to its proper function, or if its extra-curricular activities are separated from ROK CIA, we can then deal with Kim Chong Pil on a tidy basis. But there is a real possibility that Kim Chong Pil may continue in the same capacity with the same all-embracing functions, in which case we will have serious problem of whether and how to deal with him.
>
> In a recent conversation with [less than one line of source text not declassified] Political Counselor, Kim Chong Pil expressed his resentment, frustration, and some bitterness [two and a half lines of source text not declassified] at our refusal to accept him as a major direct channel for communication with ROKG on other matters. He [informant] said he [Kim Jongpil] wears two hats which are completely separate, and we were to recognize this and deal with him on all matters, for he [Kim Jongpil] is the real power and

policy maker in the government, and he is going to continue in that capacity. He asked them to convey his desire for direct and regular contact with me. ...

In two conversations with him, once with me in March and once with one of our [less than 1 line of source text not declassified] officers in July, he [Kim Jongpil] said that if it ever becomes necessary to preserve the "revolution," (i.e. preserve his power, which he identifies with the revolution), he will do whatever is necessary, including even "toppling" Pak Chong-hui.[179]

The Department of State agreed with Berger's negative stance, and supported Berger's decision not to see Kim Jongpil other than for business related to the Korean CIA.[180] In a visit to the United States in August 1962, Berger suggested prioritizing the removal of Kim Jongpil.[181] When Kim Jongpil visited the United States in October 1962, the State Department refused his request to have an audience with President Kennedy and other key figures in Washington.[182]

Another document summarizes the characteristics of the group centered on the eighth class of the Korea Military Academy:

A. A "will to power" and a willingness to be ruthless.

B. Frequent rejection of US advice on political matters and tendency to originate and support unsound economic policies.

C. Touchy ultra-nationalism and barely concealed anti-Americanism, which manifest themselves openly whenever we oppose a course of action taken by govt or fail to respond as they may wish.

D. Continued prominence within the group of political advisors with pro-Communist backgrounds who have extraordinary influence. Despite frequent US objection to these individuals and widespread criticism in Korean Govt and political circles, their influence has not diminished and they play an important role in Democratic-Republican Party.

E. Distrust and disregard of independent civilian political forces and of normal democratic processes.

F. Desire to concentrate greater power in hands of narrower leadership group with deliberate elimination of opposing elements within the junta, until in latest move power concentrated almost exclusively in Pak and Kim group.[183]

An interesting point in the quote above is that the US Embassy in Seoul continued to trust Park Chung Hee despite its dislike of Kim Jongpil and the rest of the eighth class of the Korea Military Academy. The US government was well aware that Park Chung Hee could not separate himself from the Kim Jongpil faction and still maintain his power. However, the US government nevertheless identified Park as the only person who could stabilize South Korea.[184]

Ambassador Berger, who emphasized the leading role of Park Chung Hee ever since the coup d'état began, was a key supporter of Park.[185] Other officials at the US Department of State, however, believed that Berger was overly optimistic about Park.[186] Assistant Secretary of State for Far Eastern Affairs William Harriman, Secretary of State Dean Rusk, and National Security Advisor McGeorge Bundy still generally supported Ambassador Berger's stance towards Park.[187]

However, the US government position towards Park Chung Hee became increasingly favorable as the need to find a leader figure capable of replacing or checking Kim Jongpil became increasingly apparent. In a telegram sent to the State Department on December 7, 1962, Ambassador Berger clearly suggested that the US government "should begin to think in terms of a possible need for alternatives for leadership in Korea."[188] Why did Ambassador Berger, who was a strong supporter of Park Chung Hee ever since he was appointed to South Korea, change his mind about Park?

Ambassador Berger expected turbulence and commotion surrounding the founding of the Democratic Republican Party. Berger realized that forces against the "young colonels" existed both within and without the Korean military government, and to avoid instability caused by political conflict, he argued that certain hard-line policies of the South Korean government should be mitigated. Berger also suggested the need to "prepare for the contingency that may require a change in our attitude and policy toward the military regime."[189] He firmly believed that Park Chung Hee and Kim Jongpil would never stray apart.

The fears of the US Embassy in Seoul materialized in 1963, as divisions within the South Korean military government surfaced in public during the course of the Democratic Republican Party's

Ambassador Samuel Berger visiting the South Korean cabinet's controller office in 1963 (the man in the middle). He was one of the key figures who supported Park Chung Hee in the early years of Park's rule.

formation. Kim Jongpil and certain members of the Korean CIA were actively involved in the Democratic Republican Party's founding. The starting point of disruption was the presentation meeting of the Democratic Republican Party at the end of 1962.

On December 23, 1962, Kim Jongpil prepared a presentation meeting for the Democratic Republican Party at the Walkerhill Hotel in Seoul. Led by Kim Dongha and Kim Jaechun, certain members of the Supreme Council resisted Kim Jongpil's move, arguing that he was trying to take over the party. Certain members of the Supreme Council nevertheless joined the Democratic Republican Party as promoters (Kim Dongha, Kim Jaechun, Gang Sanguk, O Jeonggeun, Yi Seokje, Sin Yunchang, Jo Changdae, Jang Dongun, and Seo Sangrin).[190] Finally on January 18, 1963, the meeting of the Democratic Republican Party opened with seventy-eight promoters.[191]

However, Kim Dongha resigned as both Supreme Council member and Democratic Republican Party promoter after releasing a public statement that he was "unable to betray the people" on January 21, 1963. Starting with his resignation, ex–Marine Corps members of the Supreme Council, such as Kim Yungeun, began to unite against Kim Jongpil as well as against the eighth class of the Korea Military Academy.[192] Conflict between the highly cohesive eighth class and their enemies within the military government and the Democratic Republican Party was the most serious internal strife in South Korea since the May 16 coup d'état.

(4) The First US Intervention Surrounding the Transfer of Power to a Civilian Government

The US government expected discord to continue even after the confrontation somehow ended and decided on an intervention, which began on January 17, 1963. Ambassador Berger first met with Park Chung Hee. Refuting an allegation that the US Embassy in Seoul was somehow involved in the former head of the cabinet Song Yochan's criticisms against the Sauth Korean government, Berger displayed his stance towards the Democratic Republican Party's founding:

> **A.** Since split in junta would introduce serious instabilities and dangers, it essential military junta stay united. Such differences as exist must be overcome by compromise.
> **B.** Essential Government party broaden its base to include widest possible representation from all sections and groups.
> **C.** Democratic process requires strong and effective opposition.
> **D.** Essential opposition be formed on broadest possible basis so Korean people can have real choice in election. Essential old enmities be overcome in national interest.
> **E.** Essential there be free debate and discussion during period political activity.[193]

Berger's statements show why the new military government during the early 1980s formed dummy opposition parties such as the Democratic Korea Party and New Korean Citizen Party.

After listening to Berger's stance, Park Chung Hee responded that he could maintain the unity of military government. Berger stated that conflict could be catastrophic and United Nations Commander

Guy S. Meloy may also be forced to intervene.[194] Because of the conflict, Berger also worried that those members of the military government with working relationships with the US government might suffer a drop in their popularity.[195] The United States prioritized maintaining the stability of the South Korean military government.

After speaking with Park Chung Hee, Berger sent the following comments to the Department of State:

> POWER WHICH IS REPRESENTED IN KIM CHONG-P'IL AND HIS SUPPORTERS SHOULD NOT BE DISCOUNTERED. THEIR STRENGTH ARISES NOT ONLY FROM THEIR COHESIVENESS AND THEIR WIDE-RANGING POLICE AND POLITICAL ORGANIZATION. IT ALSO DERIVES FROM THEIR SINGLE-MINDED, REVOLUTIONARY ZEAL AND THEIR DETERMINED QUEST FOR POWER AND AUTHORITY. KIM MAY MAKE COMPROMISES BUT HIS DIRECTION IS NOT EASILY ALTERED NOR HIS CONFIDENCE EASILY SHAKEN.
> YET IN EMBASSY'S VIEW MODIFICATION OF KIM'S PLAN IS NECESSARY. PAK'S RAISING QUESTIONS THAT HE WAS, MAY PROVIDE OPPORTUNITY TO BRING ABOUT THE CHANGE WITHOUT PRODUCING CHAOS IN THESE CRITICAL TIMES. WE BELIEVE PAK RETAINS POWER OF DECISION AND WILL IN FINAL ANALYSIS IF NECESSARY DISPOSE OF SUFFICIENT STRENGTH TO CARRY OUT DECISION EVEN IF IT IS UNPALATABLE TO KIM. THIS MAY ONLY BE TRUE NOW. IT MAY NOT BE TRUE IF KIM CONFIRMS HIS CONTROL OF PARTY.
> PAK'S SUGGESTION THAT JUNTA MIGHT RETURN TO MILITARY LIFE AND WITHDRAW FROM POLITICAL SCENE IS NEITHER FEASIBLE NOR DESIRABLE AND WE THINK PAK WILL COME TO THAT CONCLUSION. WHAT IS FEASIBLE AND DESIRABLE IS INTRODUCING OF LEAVENING ELEMENTS WHICH WILL DISTRIBUTE POWER AMONG CIVILIANS AND MILITARY. THIS WILL MEAN DRASTIC REDUCTION IN THE DECISIVE ROLE PLAYED BY KIM CHONG-P'IL.[196]

Ambassador Berger expected that a military-civilian organization was feasible. As Park Chung Hee suggested, Berger also stated that he would like to see a civilian politician as the party chief if possible. Berger argued that other political forces should coalesce around Park Chung Hee.

On January 21, 1963, four days after meeting Park Chung Hee, Ambassador Berger met with Army Chief of Staff Kim Jongo and further gauged the situation.[197] Berger met with Park Chung Hee again on January 23, 1963. Park Chung Hee requested General Meloy and Ambassador Berger to visit him at his quarters. The conclusions Park Chung Hee reached at this meeting were:

A. KIM CHONG-P'IL WILL RESIGN FROM POLITICAL PARTY AND WILL GO ABROAD UNTIL AFTER ELECTIONS.
B. CERTAIN MEMBERS WILL BE REMOVED FROM SUPREME COUNCIL.
C. REMAINING MEMBERS OF SUPREME COUNCIL WILL BE GIVEN CHOICE OF RETIRING FROM ARMED FORCES AND SUPREME COUNCIL AND JOIN ANY PARTY THEY WANT TO OR STAY ON. THOSE WHO ELECT TO STAY WILL KEEP OUT OF POLITICS AND THEN RETURN TO FORCES WHEN NEW GOVENRMENT TAKES OVER THIS SUMMER.
D. THOSE WHO HAVE BEEN ELIMINATED OR HAVE RESIGNED TO ENGAGE IN POLITICAL ACTIVITIES WILL BE REPLACED BY OFFICERS SELECTED BY REPRESENTATIVE SERVICE CHIEFS.
E. KIM CHONG-P'IL WILL TALK TO HIS SUPPORTERS TO GET THEM TO GO ALONG WITH HIS RETIREMENT FROM POLITICAL ACTIVITIES. HE HAS PROMISED CHAIRMAN THERE WILL BE NO RPT NO TROUBLE.
F. MINDEFENSE AND GENERAL KIM CHONG-O, C/S ARMY, ARE BEING INFORMED BY PAK, AND MIN DEFENSE WILL TELL OTHER THREE CHIEFS OF STAFF AT 1600 HOURS JANUARY 24.
G. FOREGOING PLAN WILL BE REVEALED TO SUPREME COUNCIL AT 1800 HOURS JANUARY 24.[198]

Ambassador Berger and Commander Meloy asked several questions in response. Park Chung Hee responded:

A. SUPREME COUNCIL HAD NOT RPT NOT BEEN INFORMED.
B. HE EXPECS BE ABLE TO PERSUADE SUPREME COUNCIL TO ACCEPT HIS PLAN AT JANUARY 24 MEETING.
C. "REMOVING OF CERTAIN MEMBERS OF SUPREME COUNCIL" MEANS THEY WOULD BE DETAINED AFTER SCNR MEETING AND THEN HELD UNDER HOUSE ARREST. LATER, PERHAPS, THEY MIGHT BE RELEASED TO GO ABROAD POSSIBLE TO US UNTIL AFTER ELECTIONS.
D. SUPREME COUNCIL MEMBERS TO BE REMOVED WERE: BGENT (RET) KANG SANG-UK, MAJGEN KIM YUN-GUN (MARINE), BRIGGEN O CHUNG-GUN (MARINE, RET.) COL PAK WON BUN, COL. CHONG SE-UNG (MARINE) THESE MEN HAD BEEN CONSPIRING TO SEIZE CONTROL OF PARTY APPARATUS AND THEY WILL BE TAKEN INTO CUSTODY BECAUSE OF ANTI-REVOLUTIONARY ACTIVITIES.
E. KIM CHONG-P'IL WOULD RESIGN SOON POSSIBLY TOMORROW. AS FIRST MOVE IN EXECUTION OF PLAN, AND WOULD LEAVE COUNTRY BEFORE LONG.[199]

The American ambassador and commander displayed their bewilderment toward Park's responses. In addition to Kim Jongpil leaving the country, Park's suggestion basically entailed removal of anti–Kim Jongpil forces. The State Department judged that, if Kim Jongpil's supporters were not removed as well, the current crisis would continue and he would control the Democratic Republican Party and Supreme Council.

On the following day, Park Chung Hee presented a revised response to Berger. Although it is difficult to surmise what made Park change his mind as the first four lines of the telegram are erased, Park Chung Hee's revised conclusions were:

A. KIM CHONG-P'IL HAS TENDERED RESIGNATION FROM GOVERNMENT PARTY AND WILL LEAVE KOREA AS SOON AS POSSIBLE PROBABLY NEXT DAY OR TWO. WILL GO TO JAPAN AND THEN POSSIBLY ELSEWHERE.
B. PAK HAS WITHDRWAN PLAN REMOVE FIVE ANTI-KIM OFFICERS FROM SCNR.
C. SCNR AND POLITICAL PARTY WILL BE SEPARATED.

D. PAK WILL RUN FOR THE PRESIDENCY.[200]

In addition, Park Chung Hee notified Berger that O Jeonggeun, Gang Sanguk, and Jeong Se-ung of the anti–Kim Jongpil faction would move to the Democratic Republican Party from the Supreme Council. Such a move was meant to show the ambassador the tangible steps Park Chung Hee was willing to take to check Kim Jongpil. Park Chung Hee told Ambassador Berger that he would, in cooperation with a person whose name is still not disclosed, come up with a plan for the future. There is also a line stating that the undisclosed person would notify Berger the next morning. Based on this, it can be surmised that the undisclosed person was a close informant of the US Embassy in Seoul.

Through different contacts, the US government judged that it was now possible to stop Kim Jongpil and his "young colonels" from taking over the military government and the Democratic Republican Party. A telegram from Secretary of State Rusk, which starts with the line "Congratulations on your success in moderating Pak's plan for settling current crisis within ruling group,"[201] shows how much effort the US Embassy in Seoul and the Department of State put into the political maneuvering in Korea.

However, the State Department popped the champagne too soon. Sixteen hours after receiving the above telegram, the American ambassador sent another telegram to the State Department notifying it that yesterday's report had become "unstuck."[202] Kim Jongpil was not willing to retreat, and he displayed his willingness to maintain control of the party. Breaching a tacit agreement with the opposition, Kim Jongpil opened the party preparation meeting on February 2, 1963. Kim Jongpil became the chairman of the preparation committee, with Jeong Guyeong as vice-chairman.

The State Department responded immediately, emphasizing that there must be a compromise among different factions within the military government. It also recommended a number of measures for political stability. The first recommendation was deleted from the available source document, but the second measure argued, "Military coup by forces opposing Kim Chong-p'il would also be most undesirable." The State Department doubted that anti–Kim Jongpil forces from Hamgyeong Province could win public support even if they seized political power.[203]

The most important part of the January 25 document is the first recommendation, which is still not disclosed. After this specific telegram was sent to the US Embassy in Seoul, most telegrams sent thereafter are unavailable until February 12. Although there are sporadic documents available from the Seoul Embassy that mention a "middle group" interested in compromises, splits within the anti–Kim Jongpil faction,[204] continuation of the close relationship between Park Chung Hee and Kim Jongpil, and the makings of limited compromises while the overall situation was still in a state of flux, most telegrams are still not declassified.[205] Following the period of missing documents, Park Chung Hee stated through the "February 18 declaration" that he would not be part of the civilian administration, and Kim Jongpil left the important post of the Democratic Republican Party and took a leave to the United States as an "ambassador in rotation."

To surmise based on the abovementioned evidence, the undisclosed first recommendation of the January 25 telegram most likely contended for the need to alter Park Chung Hee and Kim Jongpil's stance by pressuring them using different methods, likely amounting to a declaration of a state of emergency and discontinuance of aid to South Korea. According to the February 11 document produced by the US Embassy in Seoul, Berger met with Kim Jongpil, and heard from Kim that Park Chung Hee was dejected and had decided not to run for president. Of course, Berger also directly heard from Kim Jongpil that Kim would go on leave.[206] Conditions in South Korea completely changed during the period of the missing documents. Ambassador Berger asked Park Chung Hee to delay announcing his retreat from politics until he discussed the issue with others, and Park Chung Hee delayed his implementation of the decision made on February 11 until February 18[207]–suggesting strong American pressure during this period.

The US Department of State ordered the US ambassador to South Korea not to recommend or stop Park Chung Hee from declaring himself a presidential candidate, noting that Kim Jongpil would not back down if Park ran for president and that Park should be left alone to make his own decisions.[208] Additionally, the Department of State instructed Ambassador Berger to inform Park Chung Hee

that Kim Jongpil's withdrawal from politics is "the best hope for
political and economic stability."[209]

(5) The Construction of a Moderate Political Party

Contrary to American hopes for political stabilization, the South
Korean political situation continued to deteriorate after Park Chung
Hee's declaration on February 18. Kim Jongpil left the country on
February 25 and an oath-taking ceremony to cement the withdrawal
of the military government took place on February 27.[210] Although
the situation was developing smoothly so far, the so-called
"anti-revolutionary activities of certain elements of the military,"
publicized by the Korean CIA on March 11, reinvigorated political
turbulence in South Korea.

From March 11 to March 13, the Korean CIA arrested twenty
key figures of the anti–Kim Jongpil faction including Kim Dongha,
Bak Imhang, and Bak Changam. On March 13, five high-ranking
military officers including Rear Admiral Kim Yungeun and Major
General Choe Jucheol were arrested by the KCIA for taking part in
a coup d'état conspiracy. Five more civilians were arrested for their
supposed roles in collecting funds and establishing contacts. This
incident is widely known as the "Alaska Suppression."[211] "Alaska"
was a nickname for Hamgyeong Province, and the incident mostly
targeted anti–Kim Jongpil figures who grew up there. Ambassador
Berger described this incident as a fabricated affair to overturn Park
Chung Hee's decision to withdraw from politics.[212]

On March 15, eighty soldiers of the Capital Defense Command
demonstrated in front of the Supreme Council asking for an
extension of military rule. On the night of the same day, Park
Chung Hee conferred with Prime Minister Kim Hyeoncheol and
Ambassador Berger for five hours. On March 16, Park Chung Hee
officially suggested the extension of military rule for four more
years if it was supported by a plebiscite. What happened in January
reoccurred. South Koreans had turned away from the policies they
had told the Americans they would follow.

Following the "secret" intervention from late January to
February 10, another American intervention began. The Kennedy
administration was deeply troubled by the attempt to extend
military rule. The National Security Council, in a document sent to

President Kennedy on March 17, suggested that the US government should not passively observe such developments.[213] In the March 28 document, the National Security Council conjectured that there was a pro–Park Chung Hee coup conspiracy in support of Park's declaration.[214]

In contrast to the previous intervention, the US government intervened publicly following the declaration of the extension of military rule. The US Embassy in Seoul, US Department of State, and President Kennedy all released public statements against it. The US Department of State in particular released three public statements on March 23, 26, and 29.[215] President Kennedy sent a personal letter to Park Chung Hee via Ambassador Berger.

On March 25, Ambassador Berger suggested to Washington that an "interim military-civilian government" was necessary. Ambassador Berger believed that negotiating with opposition leaders and establishing an interim government were the only solutions to the crisis. Park Chung Hee agreed and requested American help in declaring the establishment of an "interim coalition government" in a meeting with Ambassador Berger on March 28.[216]

The State Department, in a directive to the US ambassador to Korea on March 28, declared that there can be no compromise as long as Park Chung Hee insisted on the extension of military rule. The only choice Park Chung Hee had, according to the State Department's view, was to nullify the extension of military rule and meet with opposition leaders to discuss the upcoming election.[217] In addition, the State Department revealed its view that Berger's "interim government" plan should go into effect only for a short duration, that is, until the election.[218] Although the US State Department did not completely agree to the "interim government" plan of Berger and Park Chung Hee, it did acknowledge its validity.

It is not clear whether the "interim government" was the suggestion of Berger or Park. It is clear, however, that both consented to the plan and that Park took concrete measures to execute it. Ambassador Berger reported to Washington that Park Chung Hee was planning to organize "a new transitional military government" made up of fifty individuals (two-thirds to be civilian politicians) as well as an advisory committee made up of thirty elder statesmen.[219]

Park Chung Hee held three conferences between the government and opposition from March 30 to April 1, and it is highly likely that issues related to the "interim government" were discussed in the meetings. However, on April 8, 1963, without sufficient consultation with the opposition, Park Chung Hee released another public statement, an emergency measure deferring the plebiscite; it effectively reversed his declaration of an extension to military rule.

The US State Department did not appear very welcoming to the April 8 statement. Was such a lukewarm response due to prior experience? The State Department informed the US Embassy in Seoul of the need to reduce overt American intervention in South Korea. Because decisions were to be made by Koreans, the State Department recommended that the United States should not appear as overly interventionist.[220] The US Embassy in Seoul, however, had an optimistic expectation towards the April 8 statement.[221]

When the April 8 statement did not materialize due to a compromise with the opposition, Ambassador Berger changed his aim from "interim government" to emphasis on the role of moderates within the military government.[222] The plan to emphasize and create a new party around moderators began around the time the Democratic Republican Party was created in December 1962. At a meeting with Park Chung Hee in July 1962, Berger passed on his opinion that a broad-based ruling party needed to be formed.[223] Although Berger's stance could be interpreted as a suggestion to reform the Democratic Republican Party, it could also mean the creation of a new political party. Although the power and role of Kim Jongpil may be reduced within the party, problems could remain if the party did not receive broad support from anti–Kim Jongpil forces. Arguing for the need for different factions to coalesce around Park Chung Hee also meant that a new political party needed to be created.[224]

On April 10, Park Chung Hee publicly proposed forming a new pan-national party. On April 11, Yi Hurak, the spokesman of the Supreme Council, released a statement declaring that the new party would usher in a new era in Korean politics, and he believed that politicians and young elites would respond positively to it.[225]

A pan-national party was set in motion, and the new Korean CIA Director Kim Jaechun rose as a key figure, replacing Kim Jongpil. Ambassador Berger also considered Kim Jaechun as a key figure among the moderates.[226] It is unknown how much the US was involved in the new pan-national party's activities. However, considering that several members who left the Democratic Republican Party joined the pan-national party,[227] it is likely the case that the US government was secretly involved.

In the end, the pan-national party movement died out in August 1963. The pan-national party was reorganized into the Liberal Democratic Party and attempted to merge with the Democratic Republican Party through Park Chung Hee's mediation. However, the pan-national party eventually crumbled as 742 members of the pan-national party joined the Democratic Republican Party on August 7.[228] Although the United States was able to stop the extension of military rule through open intervention, it was not able to carry out the plan to create a broad-based ruling political party.

Established through a coup d'état, the South Korean military government created a crisis for South Korea-United States relations. The United Nations Command, led by the United States, problematized South Korean military units leaving the commanding authority of the UN commander. As in 1953 when Syngman Rhee freed anticommunist prisoners of war, the most essential issue between the two countries was again the temporary desertion of South Korean military units (for political reasons) from the authority of the UN commander.

However, given the negative assessment of the Jang Myeon government, the United States government could not easily formulate a stance towards the coup forces. It was even more difficult to suppress the coup as major South Korean political figures, including President Yun Boseon, supported the idea of forming a new government. That is the reason why the debate on whether the coup's success depended on the United States or domestic political forces continues to this day in South Korea.

More important was the US policy to "tame" the Korean military government. In the process, the US government made efforts to create a regime that would cooperate with its policy. Although the process was seemingly political, its content included social and economic policies as well. Revision of the first economic development plan in 1962 and criticism against the currency reform in 1963 display the American stance well. Through this process, the United States was able to create a pro-American regime by placing a civilian crust on top of the pro–Park Chung Hee forces.

However, the Park Chung Hee government did not accept all American requests. Park Chung Hee engaged in a tug-of-war between the coup forces and the United States and did not lose his connection with either one of them. Park Chung Hee was only able to play this game well when the ends of the rope were held tight by both sides. Due to his political location in the middle of the two forces, Park Chung Hee's range of movement widened. On the other hand, however, Park was vulnerable to pressures from both sides.

The transfer of power to a civilian government occurred in 1964 when the core members of the military government changed to civilian uniforms. In the process of power transfer, the US government sought to place "trustworthy" leaders around Park Chung Hee and in the center of South Korean politics. Was the American attempt successful? Park Chung Hee, with a relatively weak domestic power base, could not completely eliminate his support base within the military government, and the United States had to accept limited success. Despite American pressures, Park Chung Hee did not let go the hand of his niece's husband (Kim Jongpil), who made a significant contribution to the successful completion of the coup d'état.

Democratic civilian governments began to be established in South Korea beginning in the 1990s, and the emergence of such governments was made possible by the Korean citizens' will and passion for democracy. These governments initially had a "reformist" character, and reformers were appointed to important positions in large numbers during their early days. However, these governments gradually bowed to American pressures and began appointing conservatives at the midpoint of their terms. Instead of playing a tug-of-war between the reformist forces and the United States, leaders of these governments relinquished one connection and opted exclusively for the other. Although such a move may have improved relations with the United States, it severed those governments from domestic reformist forces. Of course, corruption scandals were also important in driving the domestic reformist factions away from the democratic governments. Although it is difficult to define the Kim Jongpil faction as "reformist," these democratic government's choices were different from that of Park Chung Hee, who, despite American pressures, did not give up his connection to domestic forces.

FIVE

Treaty on Basic Relations between Japan and the Republic of Korea and the Plan to Remove Kim Jongpil

Park Chung Hee, who had been walking on a tightrope between the United States on one side and the core members of the military regime on the other, faced another crisis soon after his election victory as a civilian. Although Park had been successful thus far in establishing a new constitution and an elected government, widespread popular resistance against the normalization treaty with Japan (Treaty of Basic Relations between Japan and the Republic of Korea) made everyday governance almost impossible. Under such circumstances, Park had to resort to emergency martial law to maintain control.

To the United States, such developments were perceived as both a crisis and an opportunity. On the one hand, the United States was forced into a position of being criticized for supporting an undemocratic regime and American hopes to mobilize the Park Chung Hee government's leadership to normalize the relationship between Japan and South Korea were also dashed. On the other hand, however, the United States was able to solve many unresolved problems dating from the previous era of military rule (1961-63).

How then did the South Korean and United States governments overcome such a crisis?

1. Possibilities of Another Coup

Following the crisis of the May 16 coup d'état, South Korea-United States relations gradually normalized during the period of 1961-63 due to the Korean military regime's acceptance of American demands, namely, altering its economic policy, removing hawkish officers from the centers of decision making, and introducing professional bureaucrats and intellectuals into the government and the Democratic Republican Party. At a glance, South Korea-United States relations were balmy.

However, on September 21, 1964, the US Joint Chiefs of Staff sent the following telegram to Secretary of Defense Robert McNamara. The telegram suggests a possibility of another coup d'état and how the United States should respond:

4. The Joint Chiefs of Staff recommend that:

a. The following alternative courses of action be approved and coordinated with the Secretary of State:
(1) The US forces remain neutral in any power struggle by noncommunist factions, strive to avoid bloodshed, and maintain responsiveness within the ROK Armed Forces to the United Nations Command.
(2) Through the Military Assistance Program, continue current US support for pro-Western ROK Armed Forces and Government. Through the country team, support the Ambassador, as appropriate, to accelerate social and economic reforms and to eliminate corruption and illegal measures.
(3) In the event of a coup or uprising instigated by communist or other anti-US elements, the United States support the recognized government and/or those elements of the ROK Armed Forces who are unquestionably pro-US.
(4) In the event that the recognized government of the ROK requests release of ROK troops to suppress a coup or uprising, CINCUNC should comply provided it does not, in his judgment, unduly weaken his over-all military posture in Korea.
(5) On the other hand, should anti-Government leaders, even though pro-US and anticommunist, request release of ROK troops from CINCUNC control to aid in the overthrow of the ROK Government, the proposal will be referred to the Joint Chiefs of Staff.
(6) If necessary, CINCUNC as COMUS, Korea, in concert with the country team, should temporarily suspend POL and other items of the Military Assistance Program as the situation warrants.

(7) In carrying out any of the above courses of action, US support must not include the involvement of US military action without prior approval of the Joint Chiefs of Staff, except as authorized by CINCPAC OPLAN 85-63 which has been approved by the Joint Chiefs of Staff.

(8) Approved US military action in support of US unilateral policy should be carried out under COMUS, Korea.

b. A memorandum substantially as contained in Appendix A hereto be forwarded to the Secretary of State.[1]

The telegram begins with the mention of another possible coup attempt, predicting that it will be similar to that of 1961 and carried out by members of the South Korean military. While the chance of it being pro-communist was low, it was likely to be against Park Chung Hee. A telegram six months earlier already mentioned another potential coup d'état. "If pro-U.S. factions requested troops to overthrow the ROK Government, however, troops would be released only after authorization from JCS was received."[2] The first quoted telegram, however, does not completely eliminate the possibility of potential coup being pro-Park Chung Hee.

The first quoted telegram is similar to Plan EVERREADY of 1953. They are different in the sense that while the first telegram emphasizes the need for US neutrality in the case of a coup, Plan EVERREADY sought active US participation in the removal of Syngman Rhee from power. However, they are equally similar in that both plans called for preventive action on the part of the United States to avoid an unfavorable situation. Obviously, the State Department was using the experiences of the 1950s as a lesson for the 1960s. For example, Robert W. Komer of the National Security Council thought that the situation of the 1950s still continued, claiming that instead of urging the South Korean government to be more democratic, "we ought to tolerate a little more dictatorship in this messy fief."[3]

There is a reference to another plan for the establishment of an emergency regime, similar to that of Plan EVERREADY, in the second quoted telegram sent on March 26, 1964. The document included an order "to proceed according to the intentions expressed in paragraphs 16, 17, 18, and 19 of Reference A and in consonance with the instructions of Reference B," and that "[T] hese paragraphs established that troops were to be released to a recognized ROK Government to suppress a coup or an uprising." In addition, it allowed for the possible release of Korean troops in the case of a pro-American coup.[4] This document reveals that other, similar emergency plans were composed following EVERREADY. Unfortunately, however, contents of the "Reference A" and "Reference B" still remain unknown today.

This document also reveals two important facts. First, although Park Chung Hee assumed power with the support of the South Korean military, the United States had other links to the South Korean military beyond Park's knowledge. This reveals that Park Chung Hee did not yet control the entire South Korean military establishment at the time. Someone in the South Korean military likely had informed the United States that the Park Chung Hee government was incompetent, and that is probably the reason why the United States was expecting another coup d'état in South Korea.

This point suggests an important implication in understanding the death of Park Chung Hee and the fall of the Yusin system. If a certain faction in the South Korean military maintained a channel to outside forces (the United States) until 1979, the fall of the Yusin system may not have been the result of a single person. Of course, this is merely a hypothesis and more evidence and testimonies are needed to prove it.

There are numerous instances after 1965 in which American agencies relied on certain Korean agencies or individuals for producing South Korea–related reports. However, the names and posts of informants in the declassified US government documents have been erased, including those documents quoted in this book. Although obscuring the names of informants may have to do with privacy, it is possible to surmise that an unofficial communication link existed and names were removed in order to maintain secrecy.

Another point worthy of note is that the United States government at the time considered the Park Chung Hee government to be in danger of collapse. The first quoted telegram was produced by the US Joint Chiefs of Staff in September of 1964 and aimed at establishing countermeasures for a Park Chung Hee government troubled by widespread protests against the normalization treaty between Japan and South Korea. The US Embassy in Seoul, for example, believed that something similar to the April Revolution (April 19 Revolution) might reoccur.[5] Marshall Green, who experienced the April Revolution in Korea, also believed in the possibility of a popular revolution that could overthrow Park. Green, after analyzing the situation in Korea, reported to the National Security Council that "Pak government be in danger and nothing as good in sight."[6]

The opposition party that led the protests against the normalization treaty actually believed that the Park Chung Hee regime would crumble. Yun Boseon, for example, told the United Nations commander at a meeting that the Park government must be destroyed, with force if necessary.[7] Minister Gang Wonryong, who had many friends in politics, later testified that he had heard that the United States was thinking of replacing the Park Chung Hee regime.[8] The South Korean opposition party even formed a "shadow cabinet" to replace the members of the Park administration. The US Embassy in Seoul and the United Nations Command also learned about this from the Korean opposition. Although the informant's name was not disclosed, there was a request to the United Nations Command not to release control of South Korean military units.[9]

The US government contacted a number of people in order to grasp the level of crisis the Park Chung Hee regime faced. Exchanges with government officials were particularly important in this regard. Conversations with several Korean officials on May 23 and May 24, 1964, reinforced Ambassador Samuel Berger's view that "a serious crisis was rapidly evolving within the Republic of Korea and threatening the existence of the government of President Pak." Samuel Berger also reported in the same telegram that the situation in South Korea is "most grave and fraught with difficulty since the May 16, 1961 coup."[10] After receiving records of the conversations between American officials and the Korean members of the Embassy of the Republic of Korea in Washington, Robert Komer reported to the National Security Council that the Park Chung Hee regime may fall in a matter of weeks.[11]

Based on the first quoted document by the Joint Chiefs of Staff from September 21, 1964, it is highly likely that American agencies in Korea made contacts with certain factions of the South Korean military. It is also likely that they communicated to those South Korean military factions that a countermeasure, another coup d'état, may be necessary if the protests continued. The US Joint Chiefs of Staff, in turn, gave instructions regarding what course of action should be taken in case certain members of the South Korean military launched another coup d'état.

2. How Should the Situation Be Resolved?

What choice should the United States have made? Its decision, of course, was based on the priorities of US Korea policy, most importantly the swift conclusion of the normalization treaty between South Korea and Japan.

> Top priority in NE Asia today is ROK/Jap settlement. This could mean so much more in the way of long-term US dollar saving than a troop cut that there's no comparison. We're still spending over $300 million a year on 20 million ROKs, with no end really in sight. So we've got to find someone to share the long-term burden, and it's logically the Japs. Settlement would pump $.6 to 1 billion of public and private funds into ROK, with more later.
> But many of us fear that if talks (now on brink of success after 11 years) break down once more, Japs will lose interest. They don't need ROKs that much. Also, Jap Diet will adjourn soon.
> We badly need that extra push which might put us over the top. State/AID have a scheme for packing $100 million in DL (which we'd spend anyway) to promise ROKs a bait if they'll sign with Japs. But this should be given oomph by sending a high-level salesman. It would even be worth it to send WPB (though doubtless too busy) or at least Bob Barnett to Seoul and Tokyo. Or how about cranking up Wilson Wyatt?[12]

The normalization of relations between South Korea and Japan was something the United States had insisted on since the 1950s, and, in the 1960s, had become a core policy for a US government desperate for resources to be used in Vietnam and eager to limit spending on South Korea. The solution was to "pass on" South Korea to Japan.

Facing massive popular protests against normalization, there were three possible political options for the United States. One was to encourage the opposition party to seize political power. The Korean opposition had its roots in the Korean Democratic Party, the only Korean political party the United States Army Military Government in Korea (1945–48) had supported. This party urged the restoration of democratic order and was generally more pro-American than the military regime. The opposition also had a record of actively pursuing normalization with Japan as the ruling party of the Second Republic (1960–61). Finally, as mentioned above, the opposition even approached American officials and asked them to support a regime change through the protests.

However, the US government did not choose the opposition party. American agencies in Korea had long been producing negative evaluations of the Korean opposition, and these assessments did not change in the 1960s. As mentioned in chapter 4, the US government believed that the Democratic Party's internal division and lack of leadership were responsible for the success of the May 16 coup d'état. In September 1963, shortly before the presidential election of that year for the reinstitution of civilian government, Ambassador Berger negatively evaluated the opposition's leadership capability and stated that if "by any outside chance opposition succeeded in presidential and Assembly elections, they would be plagued by internal divisions, and there would be a struggle between civilians and the defeated junta with danger of another coup."[13]

The US government therefore saw the opposition-led protests against normalization in a negative light. The US government viewed the protests essentially as an irresponsible means to regain power.

Opposition tactics are to maintain continucus barrage of irresponsible criticism in order capitalize on govt's difficulties and public restlessness in effort bring govt down.[14]

The US government therefore opted for persuading and pressuring the Korean opposition. The position of the US Embassy in Seoul was that the US government should "make every possible effort to influence the opposition to act in responsible fashion."[15] After the failed attempts to regain power through American intervention during the 1952 Busan incident and the 1956 presidential election, the opposition failed once again.

On the other hand, it is important to note that the opposition and students were not against normalization itself. Also, as can be seen in the third option, to be discussed shortly, protesters were not simply targeting Kim Jongpil either. The main reasons behind the normalization protests were the disgraceful and humiliating stance of the South Korean government in the negotiations and suspicions regarding money coming from Japan. After experiencing the "Four Suspicious Incidents" during military rule, the South Korean people suspected again that there was something amiss in the normalization talks. Furthermore, three of the Four Suspicious Incidents had to do with Japan: the "Pachinko Incident," "Saenara automobile Incident," and "Walkerhill Hotel Incident." The opposition and intellectuals believed that Park and the military men, after creating the Democratic Republican Party, were now creating a slush fund to finance their long-term rule through the process of negotiations with Japan.

Why did the US government neglect this aspect? Looking at the records of discussions among the Embassy of the United States in Seoul, the State Department, and the White House, there is almost no analysis of the real reasons behind the protests against normalization. Although it is difficult determine why this was so with the available documents, it is likely the case that the negative view towards the opposition and students on the part of the US government was the main reason.

Some of the protesters displayed anti-American slogans criticizing the United States for meddling in the normalization of relations between South Korea and Japan. Such criticisms were not just simply considered shocking in a country where the American presence was considered to be above criticism, but also caught the attention of American policymakers as well. The US government considered the protests to be instigated by communists, and Ambassador Berger reported to the Department of State that, according to the president of Seoul National University, communists were encouraging them.[16] Also, as mentioned above, the view that irresponsible opposition was using the demonstrations as a means to regain political power probably also influenced the American perception of the protests.

Another possible option for the United States was, as stated in the Joint Chiefs of Staff memorandum produced on September 21, 1964, to support another faction of the South Korean military in the case of a coup d'état. Of course, American support was conditional–the new military group must not be anti-American or pro-communist. In addition, there was also a possibility that the new coup d'état could be a pro-government coup aiming to strengthen Park Chung Hee's power.

A new coup d'état, however, was sure to create daunting problems. Most importantly, it would create a situation in which the constitutional order would be demolished again for the second time since 1961. Here, the prime considerations for the United States were the United Nations and North Korea. Whenever the issue of the Korean peninsula was brought up in the United Nations, the best asset of the United States was the democratic institutions of South Korea, observed and maintained by the United Nations Commission for the Unification and Rehabilitation of Korea (UNCURK). In addition, the fact that the South Korean government was the only government the United Nations recognized further strengthened the American position in the United Nations.

Democracy in Korea was not always the top priority of American Korea policy, the most important being the security of South Korea from the external threat of communism as well as the sources of internal crisis that threatened its viability. In 1964, the normalization of relations between anticommunist South Korea and Japan was vital. Another coup d'état at such a time could put the United States into a difficult situation, as it would be forced to support a government that was founded outside of the constitutional process.

In the end, the only viable choice for the United States was the third option, which entailed suppressing the disruptive forces of society (i.e., protesters) and helping the anticommunist military government regain stability and control. This option essentially involved a repetition of the 1961-63 process–allowing the Park regime to escape public wrath by removing those marked as "troublemakers" from the government.

This option was also chosen during the "Busan Incident" of 1952. Even after the United States government came up with a plan to push Syngman Rhee from power, it only ended up removing a limited number of Rhee's associates for being responsible for the incident, while introducing experienced professional bureaucrats more friendly to the American line into the South Korean government. Following this precedent, if Park Chung Hee was not replaceable, the United States could opt for the introduction of new officials into positions of power, while blaming some of Park's associates for how the normalization treaty was negotiated.

As far as the American agencies in South Korea, the State Department, and the White House could see, there was nobody in South Korea with enough leadership capabilities to replace Park Chung Hee. The opposition was untrustworthy, and another coup d'état could add more burden to the United States by destroying the constitutional order. For the United States, the third option was the only viable one.

3. The Removal of Kim Jongpil

The American agencies in Korea selected the third option and sought to persuade the opposition to remove Kim Jongpil from the center of power, which out of the two objectives, was prioritized by the US Embassy in Seoul. Although repeated American efforts to remove Kim Jongpil during the period of military rule failed, the US government was now given another chance. Kim Jongpil was temporarily removed from the government under American pressure during the establishment of a civilian government in 1963. When Kim Jongpil returned, however, he made a "splendid" comeback as the Democratic Republican Party's chairman. Therefore, the situation in Korea in 1964 was a golden opportunity for the United States to remove Kim Jongpil and regain the initiative in Korea.

Ambassador Berger asserted to the Department of State and Park Chung Hee that Kim Jongpil was entirely responsible for the demonstrations, an effective strategy for targeting him, as the discovery of the so-called Kim-Ōhira memo further strengthened the protesters' position. In addition, developments inside the South

Korean government and the Democratic Republican party would play into the ambassador's plan. Movements to check Kim Jongpil arose within the Park Chung Hee regime. Kim Jongpil was at the center of the military government since the May coup d'état and served as the leader of the Democratic Republican Party. Therefore, there were significant opinions within the government suggesting that Kim Jongpil was to be the "post-Park Chung Hee" in the future. At the same time, a number of important insiders resentful of the power structure centered around Kim sought to create one around Park Chung Hee by separating the two men.[17] The American ambassador's mention of the need for the Democratic Republican Party to be "reconstituted" was also related to the reform of the power structure in South Korea.[18]

Ambassador Berger continued to insist that removing Kim Jongpil would enable the United States to better carry out its Korea policy. Even in the telegram he sent immediately before moving on to the State Department Korea Desk, Berger argued that most of South Korea's problems "during past three years came from activities of Kim Chong-pil."[19] Considering the fact that Berger continued to be promoted in the State Department hierarchy, it is likely that the department trusted him and relied on his views of Korean politics. Due to the bad relationship between Ambassador Berger and Kim Jongpil, Komer commented,

> Berger, who's always detested Kim Chong Pil (and almost seems to carry on personal vendetta against him), is worried. He doubts Pak will dump Kim, but can't see how Pak can cure internal split in DRP without doing so.
> All this clouds prospects for ROK/Jap settlement. Since Kim is great promoter of this (for graft involved, partly) opposition is opposing settlement largely as means of getting at Kim. ROKG in turn is thinking of imposing martial law.[20]

Although Komer suspected that Berger's appraisal of Kim Jongpil may have been a bit personal, he nevertheless agreed that removing Kim Jongpil would appease the South Korean opposition, restore order, and complete normalization between South Korea and Japan. Komer even compared Kim Jongpil to Grigori Rasputin, a man often considered to have contributed significantly to the fall of Imperial Russia.[21]

However, as seen in the telegram quoted above, it was not easy for the United States to remove Kim Jongpil due to his contributions to the normalization negotiations. Kim had thus far single-handedly driven the normalization negotiations forward. Although heavily criticized at home and abroad, had he not carried out secret negotiations with the Japanese minister for foreign affairs Masayoshi Ōhira, the normalization treaty may not have been signed in 1965.

Furthermore, the ruling Liberal Democratic Party of Japan had amicable relationships with both Park Chung Hee and Kim Jongpil. Japanese prime minister Hayato Ikeda had sent a letter to Park Chung Hee in late April of 1963 urging him to run for the presidency,[22] and a number of Japanese businessmen provided political funds to the Kim Jongpil–led Democratic Republican Party.[23] Given Japanese passivity towards normalization, Kim Jongpil's role in the negotiations was indispensable to the US government as well. For instance, Park Chung Hee passed on the opinion of the Liberal Democratic Party vice-president Ōno Banboku to the American Embassy, warning that removing of Kim Jongpil from power would endanger the ongoing negotiations with Japan.[24]

Although Kim Jongpil's role was important to the negotiations, the US government also had to prevent Kim from ruining the normalization itself. As far as the US government could see, protesters targeted Kim Jongpil. Once Kim Jongpil was removed, the US government decided, negotiations would conclude smoothly and the power structure would reorganize around Park Chung Hee. Park Chung Hee, however, was reluctant to remove Kim Jongpil, as he already had significant support within the Democratic Republican Party.[25] Because of Kim's influence, Park was worried that removing him may endanger his own position.

Compromises to overcome the crisis were made between the South Korean and US governments on June 3 and June 6, 1964. American ambassador Samuel Berger, United Nations Commander Hamilton Howze, South Korean president Park Chung Hee, South Korean Joint Chiefs of Staff chairman Kim Jongo, and the minister of national defense Kim Seongeun met together for an

emergency meeting on the night of the "June 3 Incident" to discuss
countermeasures against the sudden surge of demonstrations all
over Seoul.[26] Park Chung Hee asked General Howze to allow the
mobilization of the South Korean Sixth and Twenty-Eighth Divisions
in case there was a need to declare martial law. The request was
accepted under the following conditions:

> I [Ambassador Berger] wanted make clear that President [Park
> Chung Hee] had not asked for our approval but asked for release of
> troops. I wished his govt could avoid any statement that implied our
> approval or agreement. This action was taken by ROK Govt in its
> sovereign capacity. President agreed.[27]

Additional conditions were placed before mobilizing the South
Korean military for martial law. First, in case the protests and chaos
reached the level of the April Revolution, the US government might
withdraw its support for the Park Chung Hee government. Second,
to prevent another revolution, the South Korean government would
remove Kim Jongpil from the center of power, appeasing the
opposition and students engaged in demonstrations.

> Mr. President, I know how painful this subject is but the situation is
> serious, and it is important that we speak frankly. Since March 23 at
> least a dozen Korean leaders, who support you, have told me that if
> martial law is invoked, you and your government will be in serious
> danger unless Kim Chong-pil is removed. I want to make clear that I
> am not saying he should be removed, but this is what some of your
> most loyal supporters are saying.[28]

Park Chung Hee responded that he had personally suggested to
Kim Jongpil that it would be best for him to resign from the post
of chairman of the Democratic Republican Party three days ago.
However, Park also said that the removal of Kim Jongpil would be
difficult at the moment because only Jang Gyeongsun supported it.
Park said that Kim Jongpil probably could not be removed from
party leadership until the summer when the party convention would
be held.

Despite Park Chung Hee's reluctance, the American ambassador and the UN commander were adamant. The two men made it clear that the current crisis could not be solved unless Kim Jongpil stepped down. The emergency meeting produced a five-point agreement. The US government had to clarify and enforce these points in order to avoid being criticized for allowing the mobilization of the South Korean military units:

A. We agreed situation was serious.
B. Invocation of martial law was decision of Korean Govt.
C. We agreed to release of troops at Korean Govt's request.
D. Martial law would not solve basic problems.
E. We hoped President would consider what measures might be announced to deal with popular grievances. In this connection that Kim Chong-p'il must be removed along with martial law had been expressed to me by Korean leaders who supported President.[29]

Although Berger continued to maintain that his demand for Kim Jongpil's removal was not personal, both Park Chung Hee and Kim Jongpil were well aware of the sour relationship that had existed between them since 1962.[30] Although Berger asked Park Chung Hee at another meeting not to inform Kim Jongpil that he had insisted on removing him from power, it is likely the case that Berger's views were communicated to Kim. Therefore, when Kim Jongpil decided to temporarily leave the country on June 7, Kim personally informed Berger of his decision.[31]

Although Kim Jongpil left the Democratic Republican Party leadership, he kept his party membership and seat in the National Assembly. On June 6, 1964, UN Commander Howze even chastised Park Chung Hee, saying that it was Park "who is President and responsible for country," not Kim Jongpil. Pointing to past incidents when paratroopers broke into courts of law and attacked the *Donga ilbo* newspaper office, Howze declared that the US government may consider withdrawing military aid to South Korea if such incidents continued.

In the end, Park Chung Hee asked if it would be feasible for Kim Jongpil to go to the United States to "study." Ambassador Berger responded that it was possible and that the duration of Kim's stay there would have to be at least one to two years. Berger also

stressed the importance of an early departure.[32] The US government
was adamant and even displayed its determination to make Kim's
return to South Korea difficult.

> As we got up to go I [Ambassador Berger] said casually that ten
> minutes before coming to Blue House I had been given a report that
> a list of Assemblymen slated for arrest was being prepared, which
> included a large number of anti-KCP members of the Assembly as
> well as some opposition leaders. I asked if he [President Park Chung
> Hee] knew anything of this. He said he did not. I said he and [I] had
> been caught by surprise several times by actions taken here over the
> last three years which we knew nothing about. I hoped this was not
> going to be repeated. He said with a smile that such arrests would
> require his signature. I smiled back and said if such arrests occurred
> there would real trouble in Korea and we could not remain silent.
> *Comment*: I have no certainty that Pak will follow the lead we have
> given him.[33]

The above quote reaffirms that, by eliminating the pro–Kim
Jongpil faction, the US government was seeking to make Kim's
political comeback difficult even after his return from the United
States. Although Park Chung Hee made it clear that he had no
such plans, Ambassador Berger, aware of the 1963 "anti-revolution
incident" precedent, made it clear that such a development must not
be repeated.

Park Chung Hee met Kim Jongpil on the same day. Although it
is difficult to be sure of the content of their conversation, it is likely
that a compromise was made between the two, as the following
day, Kim Jongpil informed Park that he would leave for the United
States and was interested in obtaining a scholarship from the US
State Department. Although the State Department declined, saying
that he was not an appropriate person to receive a scholarship, it
did offer him the chance through a private fund to attend seminars
led by Henry Kissinger at Harvard University. Berger added that
he hoped that such an opportunity would positively change Kim
Jongpil.[34] Kim left for the United States on June 16, 1964. Ironically
enough, a man removed from power by the United States ended up
going there to study.[35]

In the end, the US government succeeded in removing Kim Jongpil from the center of power. Although Kim came back to Korea earlier than the US government expected–in June 1965–and became the Democratic Republican Party chairman at the party convention in December 1965, his political influence was not as great as it once was. When Kim Jongpil revealed his intention to return to South Korea in December 1964, newly appointed US ambassador Winthrop Brown communicated the Department of State's message to Park Chung Hee that Kim's return would make things in South Korea worse. Park, however, responded that Kim could not affect talks with Japan because "Kim Chong-pil was not all that important."[36]

Important US documents on Korea after 1965 do not mention Kim Jongpil any longer. Although such a development could reflect South Korean government efforts not to provoke the US government, it also signifies that Kim Jongpil was no longer involved in important foreign policymaking processes in Seoul. Indeed, Kim Jongpil's position was different from the one he had when he led the normalization negotiations with Japan.

Park Chung Hee began to conduct state affairs chiefly with Prime Minister Jeong Ilgwon and Secretary–General Yi Hurak. Prime Minister Jeong Ilgwon had argued for Kim Jongpil's leave even before June 1964.[37] According to Yi, Park did not agree with Kim's insistence that the Democratic Republican Party should lead the government.[38] Even within the Democratic Republican Party, people involved with the party's finances, such as Kim Seonggon and Gil Jaeho, were becoming increasingly influential.

However, the United States was heading towards another obstacle. Park Chung Hee, who Ambassador Berger praised as the only hope in South Korea, was becoming the single, dominant center of power. Berger's initial plan was to "educate" and "tame" Park Chung Hee.

We've evaluated Park Chung Hee as someone with fine leadership qualities as well as someone who cares deeply for his country. We wanted to educate him based on the principles of rule.[39]

Before the "education" ended, however, Park Chung Hee became the uncontested ruler of the country, and no one could oppose him.

After the situation following the "June 3 Incident" stabilized, Ambassador Berger received Park's invitation to his villa in Jinhae. After meeting Park, Berger reported to the State Department that "Pak was relaxed, attentive and extremely friendly during all conversations." However, Berger also displayed his fear in his comments: "[W]hat is most worrying is that

Kim Jongpil at a golf outing with Ambassador Habib in summer of 1974 (the man in the far left). By this time, power in South Korea was completely in the hands of Park Chung Hee.

he remains particularly ill-disposed toward opposition and anti-govt press, and his tendency is to think in terms of force rather than compromise."[40]

The American plan to remove Kim Jongpil was successful because the United States was able to play different Korean factions off one another in the midst of the fierce anti-normalization protests. Justifying it as a way of stabilizing the Park Chung Hee regime, the US government was able to get rid of Kim Jongpil, a real thorn in the side of the US government since the era of military rule. Although Kim was able to maintain his position as the second-in-command, he was no longer able to sway the direction of Korean politics.

The removal of Kim Jongpil was something that Ambassador Berger strongly pushed for–to the extent that it made Komer of the National Security Council suspicious of whether his efforts had to do with Berger's personal ills against Kim. However, considering that Berger was promoted as the head of the Department of State's Korea Desk during negotiations with South Korea over the issue of Korean troop deployment to Vietnam, it is likely the case that the decision to remove Kim was supported by others.

However, the success of the plan created another obstacle for the United States as the only person who could check Park Chung Hee's dictatorial power had been removed. There was to be no problem if Park Chung Hee remained obedient to future US Korea policy.

However, given the nature of the power structure in South Korea, this could cause problems in South Korea-United States relations if Park questioned American initiatives in the future. Similar to what happened with the plan to remove Syngman Rhee from power, the United States placed itself into a situation where there was no alternative around which to rearrange South Korean politics.

As will be described in later chapters, divisions in South Korea-United States relations began to show in 1968 when Park Chung Hee and the US government began to have different opinions on important issues between the two countries. By the mid-1970s, the South Korean government was almost uncontrollable. This development was the result of the US policy of removing Kim Jongpil and allowing the overcentralization of power in the hands of Park Chung Hee.

SIX

Tug-of-War between the United States and South Korea over the Dispatch of South Korean Troops to Vietnam

For the South Korean people, the Vietnam War remains a myth–a myth that South Korean economic development would not have been possible without the Vietnam War. Regardless of thousands of young lives lost and vociferous international criticism that the South Korean troops were de facto mercenaries of the United States, what often interests the South Korean people is how much money South Korea made in the war. Most South Koreans at the time perceived the Vietnam War as a business opportunity, similar to the boom the Japanese experienced through the Korean War. When the official documents related to the Vietnam War were recently released by the South Korean government, major media organizations focused almost exclusively on what Seoul sought to attain through its negotiations with Washington and whether or not the South Korean troops in Vietnam were properly compensated as promised.

A number of fundamental questions therefore remain. Why did the South Korean government decide to deploy troops to Vietnam? What did the South Korean government seek to gain? What did it gain? What did it lose? If the South Korean government deployed troops to Vietnam at the request of the United States, did the US-South Korea relationship improve?

1. Crisis of the Park Chung Hee Government and the Offer to Dispatch Troops to Vietnam

(1) The Force Reduction Plan for the South Korean Military and United States Forces Korea (USFK)

Ambassador Berger was appointed as the head of the State Department Korea Desk in August 1964, and Winthrop G. Brown replaced him as the US ambassador to South Korea. Brown had served in Laos with distinction as the American ambassador from 1960 to 1962. On July 31, 1964, before his departure to South Korea, Ambassador Brown met with President Johnson and Robert Komer of the National Security Council at the White House. Two important tasks were given to Brown at this meeting. The first was to meet with politicians of the Korean opposition and dissuade them from fighting against the normalization of the relationship between South Korea and Japan. Another task was to pursue force reduction of the South Korean military. The second task was particularly emphasized given the ongoing developments in Southeast Asia.[1] Why was the issue of force reduction raised at the time when elements of the South Korean military were already operating in Vietnam and with additional South Korean combat troops about to be deployed?

The United States had attempted to reduce the number of South Korean military forces since the 1950s. However, as noted in chapter 3, such attempts were not successful. Korea remained divided, and the fact that Chinese forces were stationed in North Korea until 1958 served as the most important deterrent against force reduction. While the Eisenhower administration's policy to reduce the size of American forces in South Korea resulted in massive reductions, the size of the South Korean military changed only slightly, being reduced from twenty divisions to eighteen. By the late 1950s, when tensions between the United States and the Soviet Union escalated significantly, Eisenhower abandoned the plans for further force reduction in Korea.

The need to reduce US spending in Korea through force reduction became more acute by the time of the Kennedy administration. This need arose from a shift in US foreign policy. The Kennedy administration's economic development aid policy entailed foreign aid on a massive scale. A reduction in the amount of aid to places like South Korea that had already received a significant amount of aid was financially necessary. After the withdrawal of Chinese forces from North Korea in 1958, in particular, Washington even deemed that the South Korean military was ready to handle North Korean forces by itself.[2]

However, the United States could not actively pursue a policy of force reduction in Korea during the era of military government, as the reduction of US forces in Korea and the South Korean military could have threatened the stability of the already precarious Park Chung Hee regime. While Ambassador Berger had composed a detailed plan for force reduction in South Korea (the Berger Plan), he also informed the Department of State that this issue should not be brought up until after the Park Chung Hee regime stabilized.

With the completion of the 1963 election for the transfer of power to a civilian government and the establishment of a South Korean government based on a new constitution in 1964, the United States government began actively pursuing force reduction in South Korea. This policy, of course, was closely related to one of the most important American policy objectives in East Asia, the normalization of relations between South Korea and Japan. What Washington eventually wanted to gain from the normalization was to pass on some of the burden of supporting South Korea to Japan.

The US Korea policy documents dating from 1964 often discuss force reduction in Korea as an important priority. Although the previously mentioned June 3 crisis of the South Korean government temporarily halted this discussion, the issue of force reduction in South Korea continued to appear in American policy documents throughout 1964, becoming even more of a priority after the assassination of President Kennedy in 1963, as the US Congress began raising criticisms against what it thought to be excessive spendings in foreign aid.

With the establishment of the Park Chung Hee government, Berger suggested that Washington bring up the topic of force reduction. Berger noted that, while the South Korean military government had thus far postponed discussions on the issue due to domestic political instabilities, now was the right time to deal with it. While noting that discussing this issue in the midst of widespread popular resistance against South Korea-Japan normalization could provoke additional social unrest to South Korea, Berger nonetheless suggested that Secretary of State Dean Rusk should raise it during his visit to South Korea.[3]

A point worthy of attention here is that, in order to relieve the South Korean government, Ambassador Berger suggested discussing the reduction of South Korean forces first while putting off the issue of US forces in Korea to a later date. Although the South Korean government's "foundation" may weaken due to the reduction of the South Korean military, it was still preferable to the reduction of US forces in Korea, which could give the false impression to the public that US-South Korea relations were souring.

The US government's plan for force reduction at the time was quite extensive and included not only reduction of the number of men in uniform but also the relocation of military bases. The plan was not dissimilar in principle to the ongoing US Global Force Posture Review (GPR). According to Berger, the locations of the US forces in Korea as well as the South Korean military units, which had remained in their postings for the past decade, needed to be rearranged. The heavy concentration of units along the front reduced their ability to quickly respond to crises in other parts of the country. Berger obtained final consent for this plan after submitting it first to the Department of State and the Department of Defense.

A dispute broke out over the issue of force reduction on January 22, 1964, between Robert Komer of the National Security Council, the secretary of state, and the secretary of defense. Secretary of State Dean Rusk was against the reduction of US forces in Korea, as he believed that it could negatively affect the South Korea-Japan normalization process. Rusk thought that popular opinion in both South Korea and Japan were critical of the United States and held that Washington unilaterally sought to reduce its security commitment to their respective countries through the South Korea-Japan normalization

Secretary of Defense Robert McNamara was against prioritizing the reduction of the South Korean forces before the US forces in Korea. McNamara believed that such a policy not only went against the US military aid practice of using "cheaper" soldiers, but there was no justification for reducing the number of local soldiers before sending American troops back home. Considering the fact that the cost of maintaining South Korean forces was relatively cheaper, the Department of Defense argued for the reduction of the US forces in Korea first. Secretary McNamara was also discontented with Washington's "overemphasis" on Northeast Asia, given the larger threats emanating from Southeast Asia.

Despite their differences, the secretary of state and secretary of defense eventually agreed on the course of action for force reduction in Korea. The total numbers to be reduced amounted to 70,000 out of a total South Korean force of 580,000 men and 12,000 Americans from the US forces in Korea. They also agreed with Berger's suggestion of reducing the number of Korean forces before the American troops. They sought to complete their plan before June 30, 1964, and reported on their agreement to President Johnson. According to Robert Komer's report, the Department of Defense and the Department of State agreed through their discussions that the South Korean forces, barring political problems, should be reduced by thirty-five thousand men every year, and that the actual reduction of forces should be completed, without publicization, by the end of 1965. Komer concluded the report to President Johnson by commenting that "any force cuts will always entail some pain."[4]

When Dean Rusk visited South Korea on January 29, 1964,[5] the major points of discussion included the size of military forces, South Korea-Japan normalization, plans for economic stability and development, and the Status of Forces Agreement (SOFA). Of these four issues, Park Chung Hee and Rusk expressed different opinions on the military and the Status of Forces Agreement.[6] The issue of force reduction was particularly thorny. Park Chung Hee requested that the South Korean military remain at its present size and asked for an increase in the Korean Augmentation to the United States Army contingent (KATUSA). Park believed that a reduction of the military's size could result in political instability in Korea.[7]

American resolution on this position, however, was firm. Following Rusk's visit to South Korea, Ambassador Berger composed a list of the most important 1964 US policy objectives in Korea and sent it to Washington.[8] This list included economic issues, such as the actualization of exchange rate, suppression of imports, export promotion, and a plan for achieving financial

stability. The most important issues, of course, were the acceleration
of the normalization process between South Korea and Japan and
the reduction of US and South Korean forces in Korea. While
Berger maintained that the reduction of forces should not take place
in 1964 due to the ongoing normalization talks, the goal for force
reduction itself was fixed.

President Johnson dealt with this issue directly in May 1964
by declaring his intention to withdraw one full US army division
from Korea. While initial plans for such a withdrawal mentioned
its relocation to Hawaii, Johnson later maintained that the troops
could be stationed elsewhere. He ordered that the withdrawal must
start either on June 1, 1964, or December 1, 1964.[9]

An external factor also emerged during the discussions over force
reduction in South Korea–the successful testing of China's first
nuclear bomb. This test caused dissension between the Department
of State and the Department of Defense on the issue of force
reduction. While the Department of Defense maintained that the
withdrawal could be a positive response towards the security threat
from Pyeongyang, the State Department argued that the reduction
of the US forces in Korea could lead to an "errorneous belief" on
the part of Beijing.[10]

Regardless of such variables, the US policy for force reduction
in Korea was carried out with determination. As will be discussed
in greater detail later on, this issue continued to be discussed
even after the South Korean decision to deploy combat troops to
Vietnam. The Park Chung Hee government, which came into being
through a chain of crises, including the disastrous 1962 economic
development plan, currency reform crisis, and the crisis surrounding
the transfer of power to a civilian government, was now faced
with yet another crisis. The Park government, which paraded good
relations with the United States along with solid support from the
South Korean military as the regime's foundation, was faced with
the reduction of US aid. While the crises of the military government
era were problems that could have been solved internally, the 1964
crisis surrounding force reduction entailed changes in US Korea
policy. In other words, this crisis was far more difficult to overcome
than previous ones, as it could not be solved without providing
a reason for the United States to change its Korea policy. USAID

contended that the reduction of aid would create problems for the South Korean military's training schedules, and it even claimed that the South Korean military's unrest could result in a coup d'état or riots that could bring down the Park government itself.[11]

(2) The Dispatch of Troops to Vietnam as a Solution to the Crisis

The Park Chung Hee government responded to the internal threat of popular resistance against the South Korea-Japan normalization and the external crisis of US pressure for force reduction in Korea in a number of ways. The first response was to quickly wrap up the normalization talks between Seoul and Tokyo. The normalization of relations between South Korea and Japan was a top priority in US Korea policy, and a successful conclusion could help guide American Korea policy in a direction more amenable to the Park government's interests.

To achieve quick results, the Park Chung Hee government suggested reaching a partial agreement first. This plan entailed bypassing some of the more contentious issues between the two countries. The South Korean prime minister Jeong Ilgwon first suggested this plan, and the Japanese delegation also agreed at concluding a partial agreement.[12] The issues that the two sides could not reach an agreement on up to this point were the fishery question, Dokdo, and the legal status of Korean residents in Japan.[13]

Despite lowered expectations, however, South Korea-Japan normalization talks failed to reach a compromise. The Japanese delegation displayed a passive attitude and continued to delay the negotiations, citing the popular demonstrations against it in South Korea, while the South Korean side repeatedly requested more active intervention from the reluctant United States. In addition, there was no guarantee that the American plans for force reduction would end with South Korea-Japan normalization, as Washington might pursue force reduction in Korea even more actively in the process of passing on some of the financial burden to Japan. While this American goal was not directly communicated to Seoul, South Korean leaders were nevertheless aware of it. The US aid to South Korea has been declining substantially since 1962.[14]

Another attempt to stop the force reduction was to meet with and persuade the Americans directly. Minister of National Defense

Kim Seongeun visited the United Nations commander on June 17 and 18 to present the following five requests and expressed his intention to visit Washington in order to discuss them.[15] The five requests, in short, were:

1. Do not reduce the number of South Korean military
2. Do not reduce the number of U.S. forces in Korea
3. Increase the American military aid to South Korea
4. The planned transfer of the Military Assistance Program (MAP) should be postponed for at least two more years
5. U.S. should support the increase of South Korean soldiers' wages

The five requests all went against the US Korea policy at the time. The Joint Chiefs of Staff communicated to the UN commander that the United States government could not accept any of the five requests. The UN commander was told to communicate Washington's stance to the South Korean officials without revealing the fact that one division from the US forces in Korea was scheduled to be withdrawn. Park Chung Hee also requested a visit to the United States in September 1964 to stop the American plan for force reduction.

In the end, the Park Chung Hee government presented a proposal that it hoped would change the mind of the US government—the dispatch of South Korean troops to Vietnam. Considering the unfavorable American responses to Syngman Rhee's offers to deploy Korean troops to Southeast Asia in the 1950s as well as Park's offer to dispatch troops to Vietnam during his 1961 visit to the United States as the Supreme Council for National Reconstruction's chairman, his proposal at this time did not appear to be entirely prudent. Washington had flatly rejected the previous offers. It was hard to believe that a country in need of a foreign army to protect itself could deploy its troops elsewhere.

However, Park's 1964 offer was in fact a response to an American request for support in Vietnam in 1963.[16] The American request at the time did not include combat troops, and the South Korean government had decided to only send medics and taekwondo instructors. Under such conditions, former prime minister Kim Hyeoncheol communicated to Ambassador Berger in March

1964 that the South Korean government was ready to deploy three to four thousand soldiers to Vietnam.[17] This offer, however, was not immediately accepted by Washington. The United States was not fully involved in the war in Vietnam at the time, and the South Korean offer was not yet official. In addition, Ambassador Berger also believed that it could negatively impact South Korea-Japan normalization–the Social Democratic Party of Japan and the students who were against normalization could raise further complaints about South Korean involvement in Vietnam.[18]

This offer was nevertheless significant, however, as it became a pretext for the US to request South Korean troops once the United States became fully involved in the Vietnam War. In addition, when Washington did not absolutely turn down the offer, Seoul began making contacts with the South Vietnamese government. Leaders of South Korea's ruling party visited Saigon in March 1964, and South Vietnamese military specialists visited South Korea in April 1964 to research the training of South Korean military units as well as the process of the transfer of power to a civilian government.

The South Korean government first dispatched a medical contingent made up of thirty-four officers, ninety-eight medics, and ten taekwondo trainers on September 11. As this alone could not stop Washington's plan for force reduction, the South Korean government continued to sound out the possibility of deploying troops to Vietnam. The US Department of Defense, however, turned down the South Korean offer claiming that foreign armies are not effective in guerilla warfare.[19]

The South Korean government offered to dispatch South Korean combat troops to Vietnam for the second time through the chairman of the Joint Chiefs of Staff Kim Jongo on November 3, 1964.[20] After returning from his trip to West Germany, Park Chung Hee met with Ambassador Brown along with Executive Secretary Yi Hurak. Park communicated to Brown that Seoul was ready to deploy, if necessary, two combat divisions to Vietnam. Park also mentioned to Brown that, it would not be difficult to create two more combat divisions from the large number of recently discharged veterans in South Korea.[21]

In sum, the South Korean government sought to kill two birds with one stone. Deploying South Korean combat troops to Vietnam would stop the United States from reducing the number of South Korean military units. Forming combat units out of recently discharged veterans would automatically increase the total size of South Korean forces, and additional American aid for the new military units would be a real boon for Seoul.

South Korean combat troops, however, were not included even in the second round of deployment. The two governments entered into a discussion for the additional dispatch of troops beginning on December 25. The US Department of State communicated to the United Nations Command that the number of troops deployed should be around one thousand men,[22] and the size of Korean troops dispatched to Vietnam should increase to around two thousand by early next year.[23] However, South Korea did not send combat troops to Vietnam at this time because it was not a member nation of the Southeast Asia Treaty Organization (SEATO). South Korean forces in Vietnam were mostly made up of military engineers and those involved in transportation and security, and were sent largely for the purpose of supporting construction projects there.

The second round of troop deployment did not end the plans for force reduction in South Korea. However, an important development in US-South Korea relations began to take place at this point. The United States began to (partially) accept South Korean offers to dispatch troops and positively responded to the South Korean conditions and demands. The first example of such development was the US Department of State's favorable response to the South Korean Ministry of Foreign Affair's demand to hold the summit of Asian foreign ministers in Seoul.

The South Korean government first brought up the issue of this meeting on August 31, 1964. The US Department of State initially refused due to doubts about the South Korean minister of foreign affair's abilities as well as the uncertainty of whether or not other foreign ministers would even attend a summit in South Korea. However, the State Department changed its stance immediately after the South Korean government offered to dispatch its troops to Vietnam on November 18. Two weeks later, the Department of State communicated to the US Embassy in Seoul that this meeting would aid South Korea and Taiwan. The Department of State even

Table 5. The South Korean military's deployment conditions

First deployment	September 11, 1964	The Seventh Evacuation Hospital (renamed the First Mobile Surgical Hospital) of 130 men. Taekwondo instructors including one major and nine company officers.
Second deployment (construction support)	March 10, 1965 (Dove Corps)	Corps of 1,022 men consisting of an army engineering brigade, an engineering field support team, an army transport company, a marine engineering company, and one LST. Two more LSTs and supporting crew of around 950 men.
Third deployment (first dispatch of combat troops)	October 3, 1965 (Blue Dragon Corps); October 16, 1965 (Tiger Corps)	Capital Division of 13,672 men (Tiger Corps deployed at Qui Nhon), Second Marine Regiment of 4,130 men (Blue Dragon Corps deployed at Cam Ranh; strength raised to 4,218 men when converted to a brigade).
Fourth deployment (second dispatch of combat troops)	September 25 to September 30, 1966	Capital Division (Twenty-Sixth, Twenty-Eighth, Twenty-Ninth, and Thirtieth Regiments) and the Ninth Division.
Fourth deployment (additory)	August 1967	Marines and other supporting units consisting of 2,963 men, a reinforced infantry battalion (the Fifth Battalion of 957 men), and a marine brigade reorganized as a division.
Fifth deployment (third dispatch of combat troops)	Planned for the summer of 1968	Plan did not materialize.

instructed its embassies around the world to encourage more foreign ministers to attend.[24] In the end, the first Ministerial Meeting for Asian and Pacific Cooperation (ASPAC) was held in Seoul from June 14 to June 16, 1966.

The second example was Washington's positive evaluation of Park Chung Hee's visit to the United States. When Park first proposed visiting the United States in 1964, the US Embassy in Seoul, as well as the US Department of State, were not favorably disposed to his request. They even believed that his visit to the United States prior to South Korea-Japan normalization could be detrimental to the ongoing negotiations. While the South Korean government desired active US intervention in the normalization, Washington feared that such intervention could agitate the Japanese political scene and negatively affect talks.

Such conditions, however, changed with the decision to deploy a second round of troops. Washington decided to accept Park Chung Hee's request for a visit regardless of the outcome of South Korea-Japan normalization talks. The US Department of State was well aware of the fact that Park could silence his opposition's insistence that the United States should withdraw from South Korea if Park gained concessions from that country prior to South Korea-Japan normalization. It would inevitably strengthen Park's domestic political standing.[25] Washington now decided to invite Park.

Park Chung Hee was treated with the utmost respect during his stay in the United States. The US government sent Park a special plane, and allowed Park to enjoy a car parade when he arrived in New York City on May 19, 1965. Men of ministerial caliber routinely attended luncheons and dinner banquets with Park. There was even a farewell party for him the day before he left Washington, and when the secretary of state had to leave early, President Johnson personally provided an excuse. The president met with Park Chung Hee once again before he left Washington and commented that he and Park were like family.

In truth, however, Park Chung Hee is described in a quite interesting way in a document submitted to Johnson before his arrival in the United States:

> Park is a shy, intelligent man born of a farm family, he has spent most of his life in his nation's armed forces. He is said to be self-conscious of his height and therefore initially rather formal and stiff; he can respond to informality, however, once he feels at ease. His one form of recreation is horseback riding.[26]

The treatment Park received in the United States was far beyond anyone's expectation, causing the South Korean newspapers to rave about it. For example, a newspaper argued that the visit irreversibly changed the American understanding about South Korea and resulted in a new Korea policy, and it quoted a Japanese

newspaper article that commented
on the extensive outcomes of the
visit.[27] A large portrait of Park was
hung in front of the Seoul City
Hall on the day he returned from
the United States and a welcoming
party was held at Gyeonghoeru.
Park Chung Hee responded to
the media by claiming that his
"impression of the newspapers has
changed significantly."[28] Of course,
underneath the fine treatment was

President Park Chung Hee visiting New
York City in May 1965. President Park
was well-treated by the U.S. government
after the decision to send South Korean
troops to Vietnam was made.

the American desire to request South Korean troops for Vietnam,
and such information was carefully kept away from the media.

Park Chung Hee was not the only person to receive such
elaborate treatment from the United States. South Korean officials
who played an important role in deploying South Korean troops
were also treated well. From June 22 to June 25, 1966, following
the second deployment of South Korean troops, the US government
invited Minister of National Defense Kim Seongeun for a visit and
presented him a medal. Arriving at the Pentagon, Minister Kim was
greeted by a military parade. He also met with almost all of the
high-ranking figures of the United States Armed Forces.

Park Chung Hee now knew what to do next. He realized that
he could receive even more preferential treatment from the United
States if he dispatched South Korean troops to Vietnam. He also
realized that he could demand more from the United States as the
"price" for South Korean troops. In the end, the Park Chung Hee
government survived the crisis of force reduction through sacrificing
South Korean armed forces in the American war in Vietnam.

2. Deployment of Combat Troopers and the South Korean Government's Responses

(1) South Korean Government's Demand to Deploy Combat Troops

Responding to the South Korean government's continued offers
to dispatch combat troops to Vietnam, the US government began

research on the issue in March 1965. The Department of State composed a document titled, "Probable Communist Reactions to Developments of a ROK Combat Division for Base Security Duty in South Vietnam."[29] According to this document's analysis, the deployment of South Korean combat troops would not lead to invasions by China or North Korea. It did, however, expect a strengthening of the propaganda war.

Such an evaluation, however, appears to be a part of the process of self-justification to rationalize the deployment of South Korean troops. The United States government has a history of producing reports that justify and rationalize changes in its military policies. This specific document appears to be such a case. The report stated that there was no possibility of another battlefront opening in Northeast Asia even when "cheaper" South Korean troops were diverted to fight in Vietnam.[30]

For the United States, the issue of dispatching South Korean combat troops to Vietnam became a priority along with South Korea-Japan normalization. While Johnson proclaimed a "more flags" policy, only a handful of countries joined the US efforts in Vietnam. Furthermore, South Korea was the only country to suggest dispatching combat troops. Aside from the SEATO nations that the United States established relations without active intervention and Australia, which had important geopolitical interests in Southeast Asia, no other country affirmatively responded to American calls to send troops.

South Korean troop deployment was important to the United States for two reasons. One was the justification that other Asians who look similar to the Vietnamese were fighting in Vietnam. Another was the cheap price of South Koreans. Gradually, the South Korean deployment of combat troops became an even more important issue than South Korea-Japan normalization.[31] When the South Korea-Japan normalization became a fait accompli after the Japanese minister of foreign affairs Shiina Etsusaburō released a public apology for the Japanese occupation of Korea, the South Korean deployment of combat troops became a greater priority for the United States than South Korea-Japan normalization. With the visit of Henry Lodge to South Korea on April 27, 1965 as the special envoy of President Johnson, the deployment of South Korean combat troops became the most important issue of US-South Korea relations at the time.[32]

Now, the Park Chung Hee government was in a place where it was receiving an American "request" for a favor. While it is difficult to judge whether or not "pressure" is a better description than "request" for such issues, the United States was now asking for South Korea's favor for the first time in the history of US-South Korea relations. While recognizing that South Korea at the time was not in a position to "help" another nation, Washington nevertheless had to ask South Korea for a favor.[33]

It is particularly important to note that the US request for the deployment of combat troops came at a time when the South Korean government was facing a political crisis in the form of widespread resistance to South Korea-Japan normalization. The US Department of State judged that it was not easy for Seoul to deploy combat troops to Vietnam at the time.[34] Therefore, the United States had to make its request cautiously.

In reality, however, the Park Chung Hee government does not appear to have been in a crisis. Instead, it sought to kill two birds with one stone through deploying combat troops. Of course, Park also believed that troop deployment would bring political stability. There was no guarantee that Park would win the upcoming 1967 election unless the crisis generated by the South Korea-Japan normalization was resolved. This is why Park continued to actively insist on dispatching combat troops to Vietnam. In a meeting with President Johnson in Washington on May 17, 1965, Park expressed his desire to dispatch troops saying, while "people in Korea were worried whether they might not invite further activity from North Korea if they weakened the line by sending too many troops to Viet-Nam," Park himself "would like to send more troops to Viet-Nam."[35] Such conversations, of course, remained secret–Park publicly denied any plan to send combat troops at a press conference following his return to Seoul.[36]

The South Korean government judged that the US government was increasingly in a situation where it could not readily refuse the South Korean demands. This first became evident during the negotiation process with the United States for the February 1965 deployment of South Korean troops. During the negotiations, the

American side began displaying its willingness to positively consider South Korean demands for a pay raise.[37] The fact that pay for South Korean military officers were raised by 83.5 percent less than a month after Park discussed this issue with President Johnson during his visit to the United States further supports this judgment.

Seoul made a number of other demands as a reward for dispatching combat troops.[38] Perhaps two of the most important ones were the ending of the US plan for force reduction in Korea and receiving a security guarantee equaling that of the North Atlantic Treaty Organization (NATO) member nations. Since the time of the Syngman Rhee administration, the South Korean government was discontent over the fact that their mutual defense treaty with the United States lacked the "automatic intervention" clause. According to the US-South Korea treaty, each party was to "act to meet the common danger in accordance with its constitutional processes" when the other party was attacked. Such wording meant that, without the "coming through" of such processes, one did not have to intervene for the other's sake. In addition, the US Congress often opposed active American intervention overseas. Perceiving dispatching combat troops to Vietnam as a chance for rectification, the South Korean government demanded that the United States elevate the conditions of the mutual defense treaty to the level of those enjoyed by the NATO member nations.

Second, Seoul sought to modify the Status of Forces Agreement (SOFA) to its favor. The SOFA issue has been a "hot potato" for the two countries since the 1950s. The obvious unfairness of the agreement was used as political rhetoric for the South Korean opposition when it criticized the government. The voices arguing for the revision of SOFA remained loud. For example, the main goal of the first mass student protest during the military government era was the revision of SOFA.

While the Park Chung Hee government sought to revise SOFA on more favorable terms, the American stance on the issue remained firm. The US government refused to budge to the South Korean demands on criminal jurisdiction and the labor dispute adjustment period (seventy days) for Korean nationals hired by the Eighth United States Army (US Forces in Korea).[39] The US Joint Chiefs of Staff was even set on limiting South Korea's option to exercise jurisdiction to definitive categories of cases (for example, rape, murder, and robbery). The Joint Chiefs of Staff quoted rampant corruption and bribery as the reasons for such limitation.[40] Ambassador Brown also added that, while the SOFA of the Philippines was more favorable to the host country than in the case of South Korea, the US could not give into Korean demands anymore.[41]

When Park visited the United States, however, Washington ended up recognizing the right of Korean employees to strike if a labor dispute was not resolved by the end of a seventy-day period.[42] Korean media judged that Park Chung Hee already had won half the victory by revising SOFA.[43] When the second American request for troop deployment came in January 1966, Seoul demanded that Washington reopen discussions for the revision of SOFA. Washington agreed.[44]

The third demand was to expand South Korean exports to Vietnam. Claiming that South Korea must gain from Vietnam what Japan gained from the Korean War, the South Korean minister of national defense Kim Seongeun requested that South Korea be given a favorable stance in offshore procurement in the war effort in Vietnam. While Washington maintained that the principles of commerce and competition must be upheld, it also could not flatly reject the South Korean demands given their active participation in the war. The US government therefore expressed the opinion that it could grant preferential treatment to the products South Korean producers excelled at, such as tires and rubber tubes.[45]

This issue was put forth again when the United States placed the second request for combat troops. When Vice President Hubert Humphrey visited South Korea on January 1, 1966, Park Chung Hee strongly requested that South Korean exports to Vietnam through offshore procurement be significantly increased.[46] When Washington made its third request for combat troops, the South Koreans asked for US aid in expressway construction, ignoring the principle that issues of economic aid were not to be discussed at such meetings.

(2) The Park Chung Hee Government Takes Control of the Negotiation Process

The normalization treaty between South Korea and Japan was

signed immediately after Park's return from the United States, with an American request for South Korean combat troops in Vietnam following soon after. With the beginning of negotiations for further troop deployment, based on past experience, the South Korean delegation sought to take control of the negotiations. Of course, an important premise here was the United States' pressing conditions in the Vietnam War. On July 10, 1965, the US ambassador to Korea sent the following telegram when the South Korean decision to dispatch combat troops was made.

1. If Korea provides a combat division for RVN this will add a new dimension to our relationship.

2. Korea, a small country bordering on the Communist world, will be in actual combat in one of the most active areas of RVN against Communist forces. It will have provided very substantially greater combat manpower than any other free world country great or small except the United States. This is a decision of great import for any country to make.

3. It comes at a rather crucial period for Korea, a sort of watershed in its current history. ... [I]t can save us a great deal in blood and treasure.[47]

Now the issue of dispatching combat troops became easily the most important one in US-South Korea relations.[48] In order to take control of the negotiation process, the South Korean government used the following methods.

First, the South Korean government emphasized that it was making a difficult decision in dispatching troops to Vietnam due to political conditions at home. While the South Vietnamese government sent an official message of gratitude to the South Korean government for deploying combat troops to South Vietnam,[49] Park Chung Hee told the American ambassador that the South Korean government had not yet made the decision to do so. Park added that, given the pending ratification of the South Korea-Japan normalization treaty in the South Korean National Assembly, the issue of combat troops should not be publicized at this time.[50] At that time, however, the US Military Assistance Command Vietnam (MACV) commander William Westmoreland had already requested for South Korean marines to be deployed in other combat areas. Washington soon became impatient with the South Korean government. When the United States government requested additional deployment of combat troops in December 1965, Prime Minister Jeong Ilgwon continued to refer to the difficulties they had with the political opposition at home.[51]

Such a stance on the part of the South Korean government was different from what Park had promised during his visit to the United States–the swift approval of both South Korea-Japan normalization and deployment of combat troops to Vietnam. After experiencing the crisis of widespread opposition to South Korea-Japan normalization, the Park Chung Hee government began to use the domestic opposition to its advantage in dealing with the United States. In the end, however, the Democratic Republican Party was able to use its position as the majority party to ratify the deployment of combat troops to Vietnam in the National Assembly on August 13, 1965. In protest, the Korean opposition did not participate in the voting. As listed in table 5, the first deployment of South Korean combat troops to Vietnam took place in October of the same year.

The second method the South Korean government employed was manipulating the media to its advantage. Minister of National Defense Kim Seongeun publicized the records of negotiation with the United States on the matter of the South Korean troops' pay to the media. The records included comparisons in pay with other nations that dispatched troops to Vietnam. Ambassador Brown immediately protested that the release of such information could be detrimental to the war effort in Vietnam. While Kim Seongeun publicly apologized,[52] this was just the beginning of the South Korean government's manipulation of the media to its advantage. Immediately after receiving Minister Kim Seongeun's apology, Ambassador Brown reported to Washington that, unless the United States took South Korean demands seriously, it might be severely criticized by the South Korean media and public.[53] This is yet another good example of how the Park Chung Hee government manipulated the media.

What the South Korean government used most extensively was the rumor that the "US expects flesh and blood from Korea while concentrating its purchases of war materials in Japan to the advantage of Japanese economy."[54] The May 3 and June 29, 1965 issues of *Chosun ilbo* included articles arguing that Japan was enjoying an economic boom through the Vietnam War. Sparking off a Japan-related controversy was the easiest way to manipulate the Korean media, and was used to divert the South Korean media's attention away from criticisms of the government. Such a strategy was used repeatedly during the issue of repatriation to North Korea in the 1950s, the espionage incident involving Korean residents in Japan, the Mun Segwang incident in the 1970s, and the Japanese textbook and Dokdo issues from the 1980s onward. Ambassador Berger claimed in a report to the US State Department that, due to the widespread rumor that Japan was making a great profit from this war, Washington should give the impression that South Korea was also profiting economically from the dispatch of combat troops.[55] Executive Secretary Yi Hurak also emphasized to Ambassador Berger that the South Korean public needed to be convinced that South Korea was profiting more from the Vietnam War than Japan.[56]

The South Korean government was now in a place where it could ask the United States how many more troops it wanted.[57] Again, the South Korean government manipulated the media. When Minister of Foreign Affairs Yi Dongwon visited the United States in early December 1965, soon after the first deployment of combat troops to Vietnam took place in October, the Korean newspapers collectively contended that the United States would ask for the deployment of additional Korean troops.

The more the United States asked for, the stronger the South Korean position became and the more control it had over the negotiations. When the talks for the second round of combat troop deployment took place in the end of 1965, the South Korean government more actively began demanding rewards for its troops and contended that it could not dispatch additional ones without them. The South Korean government even asked for "immaterial" benefits, such as political measures to strengthen Park Chung Hee's power.

While the United States claimed that there would not be any more requests for further deployments after the first dispatch of combat troops (this claim was made during the third round of

negotiations, which included discussions over noncombat personnel),
the US government requested additional combat troops on
December 16, 1965.[58] In an effort to galvanize public support for
the deployment, Prime Minister Jeong Ilgwon requested a visit from
the US secretary of state or secretary of defense to South Korea and
an invitation for South Korean congressmen and reporters to travel
to South Vietnam at Washington's expense.[59] Vice President Hubert
Humphrey visited South Korea on January 1, 1966.

The moment Seoul recognized that it could fully control the
negotiations was during the negotiation for the second deployment
of combat troops in January of 1966. The South Korean
government had no need to rush. The United States government, on
the other hand, was faced with increasingly hostile public opinion
over the war. "Importing" the South Korean troops was the only
way to increase the number of combat troops on the ground in
Vietnam without agitating the American public. Faced with a
presidential election a year later, Park Chung Hee of course also had
to gain something from the United States.[60] While Park had already
obtained the American promise of $150 million worth of loans, it
was not enough for him. While the US government needed combat
troops on the ground in April of that year, Park Chung Hee could
wait. The US government was therefore pressed for time.

At this moment, the South Korean government presented a list
of largely unacceptable demands entitled "Economic and Financial
Supports Suggested for Review by USG." The list included the
following:

(1) Additional budget costs from sending troops, including death and
disability payments and provision new division to re- place Tiger
division already in SVN (estimated by ROKG at 3 billion won).

(2) U.S. budget support for three quarters of military budget until
1971 (end next 5 year development plan).

(3) Compensation for land and building requisitioned by UNC (estimated
at 4.6 billion won through 1963).

(4) $10 million special assistance from "U.S. Presidential Contingency
Fund" for cultural, educational, welfare projects.

(5) Variety of OSP proposals under MAP and AID. Also priority to
Korea over Japan and other Asian countries. Expansion and full use

Korean facilities for producing military supplies and repair services. Abolish application aid [garble] American policy to OSP for Vietnam (e.g., iron and steel). Process PL 480 wheat and cotton for Vietnam in Korea. Use Korean technicians in Vietnam and train Vietnamese technicians in Korea.

(6) Variety of development loan requests: Allocation $100 million DL year for six years 1966 through 1971; accelerate approval of projects under $150 million commitment; finance steel plant, machine shop; approve thermal power loans Ulsan and Yongdong areas before end 1966; support port expansion Inchon, Yosu, Phohang, Masan, Pusan to enable start of work before end 1966....

(7) To finance commodities for economic stabilization, export promotion, and domestic capital mobilization, $50 million program loan in 1966 and $20 million per year from 1967.

(8) 150,000 tons of cargo ships by grants-in-aid and loans in kind.

(9) Encouragement Korean exports to U.S. Lift U.S. quota on Korean textiles.

(10) January 7 paper on military requirements includes counter-infiltration assistance (affecting AID and MAP), item (2) above, suspension MAP transfer through 1971, and MAP for construction barracks and welfare facilities.[61]

This list was supposedly agreed upon by the South Korean president, prime minister, deputy prime minister, minister of national defense, minister of foreign affairs, and executive secretary. Former US ambassador to Korea and the director of Korea Desk Samuel Berger expressed his "disappointment" that "the mendicant period of Korean history" still did not appear to be over, and Ambassador Brown also argued that such demands were "extremely unreasonable." The concerned US agencies on the ground agreed that these demands not only went against the principles set by the United States in foreign relations, but South Korea itself did not yet have the ability to effectively utilize such aid.[62] Ambassador Brown, however, did communicate his opinion that additional troop deployment from South Korea may be difficult if South Korea did not receive a preferential position in the Vietnam War's offshore procurement vis-à-vis Japan.

The US government did, however, display its willingness to

accept the South Korean demands to a certain extent. The costs, in the end, were "small in comparison with the cost of doing the job ourselves."[63] Despite the South Korean government's pressure, Washington perceived that it would be possible to accept the South Korean demands by only slightly increasing the aid that was going to be given in the first place.[64] Regardless of such a forecast, the pay and death compensation for the South Korean troops sent to Vietnam nevertheless increased. Providing of weapons for the South Korean troops on the ground was granted, and additional American aid came for the organization of combat divisions in South Korea. Additionally, the United States promised the South Korean government that it would stimulate South Korean export of items, such as zinc and steel, and aid Korean entry into the South Vietnamese market "within the capability of Korean industry."[65]

The South Korean government was overjoyed. While suggestions three and four were flatly ignored, the rest were nevertheless accepted by the United States. During the negotiations, the South Korean government intentionally delayed the publicization of it in order to give the impression that the negotiations were long and difficult—a decision made by Park Chung Hee. The US ambassador, on the other hand, gave off the impression that he conceded to the South Korean government more than he should have.[66]

(3) Background to the South Korean Control of the Negotiations

It was not diplomatic power that allowed Seoul to dominate the negotiations. After declaring its intention to fully intervene in Vietnam in 1965, the United States needed to deploy more troops in order to turn the tide. While the war's development continued to the disadvantage of the United States since the beginning of its bombings of North Vietnam, Washington was convinced that it could turn the war around with greater supply of troops and bombs. On December 30, 1965, President Johnson declared that persuading South Korea to dispatch additional combat troops to Vietnam was a matter of "utmost importance."[67]

Until 1965, the US government generally declined excessive South Korean demands by referring to established principles. By 1966, however, the United States changed its stance by accepting some of the South Korean demands in order to obtain the commitment of combat troops to Vietnam. The 1966 "Brown Memorandum" was written in this context. By January of 1966, immediately after the second request for South Korean combat troops was made, the US government already had decided (internally) to provide compensation to South Korea in a package form.[68] While the date on which the South Korean government submitted its own demands to the US Embassy in Korea was January 10, 1966, the US government had already decided to compensate South Korea with a package deal before January 5. In other words, it was not South Korean diplomatic prowess that won such concessions from Washington.

The third round of negotiations for combat troops in 1966 was an urgent matter for the United States. There even existed the opinion within the US Department of Defense that, given the plan to deploy approximately 20 percent of the US army to Vietnam by mid-1967, South Korea should match that number by deploying some one hundred thousand men there. Also, given the upcoming presidential election, which additional American requests for combat troops could negatively affect,[69] the US Department of Defense ordered the United Nations commander to obtain South Korean verbal commitment before the election.[70] This sense of urgency allowed the South Korean side to dominate the negotiations.

In addition, there were claims that the American compensation, including the "Brown Memorandum," were inadequate. In other words, some critics argued that the US government did not concede much. The $150 million worth of loan Park received during his visit to the United States in 1965 was a regular loan scheduled for three years. Furthermore, the loan was "subject to applicable legislation and appropriations."[71] The $14 million worth of loans for the 1967 fiscal year the "Brown Memorandum" promised to South Korea was actually just a $5 million increase from the previously planned loan package.[72] USAID also stated that, while the content of the "Brown Memorandum" would be carried out according to the standards of American aid overseas, the president's ratification was still necessary in case the plan for financial stability (to combat inflation) failed.[73] Out of the $15 million of the loan, $12 million was delivered to the Korea Development Bank (KDB). The US government included the condition that the money sent to the KDB should be used by small to medium-sized South Korean businesses to buy American capital goods.[74] The development loan, granted in order to aid Park Chung Hee's reelection, also required, by US government insistence, that the money be used to buy American power plant equipment.[75] In addition, the US government had already planned to substantially reduce military aid to South Korea once its contributions to the Vietnam War ended.[76]

The plan for force reduction in Korea was still carried out even after the South Korean deployment of combat troops to Vietnam. The US agencies on the ground were considering an 18 percent reduction of US forces in Korea during the negotiation process for the first request for combat troops.[77] Johnson's promise to Park Chung Hee that the US government would not reduce forces in Korea was merely conditional. Johnson had merely told Park that he would first inform the Korean president if conditions changed.[78] Even at the point of having requested the first round of South Korean combat troops, the Department of State and the Department of Defense continued to carry out discussions to reduce the US Seventh Infantry in Korea.[79] After the second round of South Korean combat troops were deployed to Vietnam, the US government told Minister of National Defense Kim Seongeun to reduce the number of South Korean armed forces to the level that fit the South Korean economy as well as its North Korean counterpart.[80]

In fact, the US forces in Korea were partially reduced in number during the time South Korean combat troops were fighting in Vietnam. The size of US forces in Korea at the end of November 1966 stood at around forty-three thousand.[81] This number was significantly lower than what the US government promised to South Korea on paper: fifty-one thousand. The United States was unable to maintain the number it promised to South Korea due to the Vietnam War.

Revision of the mutual defense treaty also did not materialize. Despite the renegotiation and the South Korean government's wish to be treated at the level of a NATO member nation, the SOFA agreement did not improve beyond the level of West Germany due to the resistance on the part of the US Department of Defense.[82] Although the criminal jurisdiction, claims, and labor articles of SOFA were slightly modified at the time when the United States requested the third round of combat troops, another revision on July 9, 1966, led to a reversion to its previous unfair state by requiring American consent in exercising its jurisdiction.[83]

None of these plans were reported to the South Korean government. Without knowing about them, the South Korean government falsely believed that it was dominating the negotiations with the United States. I believe that the South Korean government also believed that such perceived dominance had more to do with their own diplomatic power than luck.

3. The South Korean Government's Overreaction and Changes in US-South Korea Relations

(1) Rise of Security Crisis

As mentioned above, the South Korean government appears to have thought that it dominated the negotiations with the United States. Therefore, it responded even more actively when the third request for combat troops was made. It is worth noting that the South Korean government's response at this time actively created new circumstances for US-South Korea relations.

The South Korean government focused particularly on the security of the Korean Peninsula. Having experienced the strengthening of the South Korean military through the negotiations for the second round of combat troop deployment, the South Korean government decided to further strengthen its armed forces by bringing up the security issue during the negotiations for the third round of troop deployment. The South Korean government must have calculated that the United States could not afford to divert South Korean armed forces to Vietnam with a security crisis on the Korean Peninsula. To put it differently, the South Korean government sought to demand that the United States guarantee South Korea's security as a price for being able to utilize "cheap" South Korean soldiers in Vietnam.

Of course, it is also possible that the South Korean government made this decision without much calculation. Or this decision could have been made in conjunction with the aggressive handling of the increasingly frequent clashes across the Korean Demilitarized Zone.[84]

In any case, it is clear that the South Korean government sought to use such developments to its advantage in the negotiations with the United States. While past South Korean responses were passive and limited under the UN Command, the South Korean government now believed that active responses were now possible. Therefore, although carried out as a retaliatory measure for earlier provocations, the South Korean side sometimes began to attack the North first. Such attacks also took place during times when important negotiations with the United States were being carried out. The point in time when the South Korean government started its active responses also matches the time when Senator Richard B. Russell first suggested the withdrawal a US army division from Korea (October 1966).

In June 1966, US agencies on the ground in South Korea recommended not raising the issue of additional troop deployment to the South Korean government due to the domestic political conditions in the country. At that time, the US ambassador worried about two issues: the South Korean presidential election being less than a year away and the concern that the third request for combat troops could negatively affect US-South Korea relations. He particularly emphasized that the US request for combat troops should not place Park Chung Hee in a difficult position before the upcoming election.[85]

Although the US government declined the South Korean ambassador Kim Hyeoncheol's request to have the US secretary of state or secretary of defense visit South Korea to "aid" Park's reelection, the US government still displayed its support for Park by dispatching the State Department's assistant secretary George Ball along with representatives of twenty-three US companies and three US banks. President Johnson also invited and subsequently met with the South Korean prime minister, minister of national defense, and minister of commerce and industry in Washington.[86] A developmental loan amounting to US$34.7 million was also promised by the US government two days before the election. As can be seen, the US government sought to "reelect" Park Chung Hee by avoiding the mention of further requests for troops that could have a detrimental impact on Park's campaign.

However, Park Chung Hee most likely received the information

Table six. The number of North Korean provocations against the South

	1965	1966	1967
Major events in the Demilitarized Zone	42	37	423 (286)
Major events south of the ceasefire line	17	13	120
Combat engagements at the Demilitarized Zone	23 (29)	19 (30)	117 (132)
Combat engagements south of the ceasefire line	6	11	95
North Korean forces killed south of the ceasefire line	4 (34)	43	224 (146)
North Korean forces captured south of the ceasefire line	51	19	50
United Nations forces deaths	21 (40)	35 (39)	122 (75)
United Nations forces wounded	6 (49)	29 (34)	279 (175)
South Korean police/civilian deaths	19	4	22
South Korean police/civilians wounded	13	5	53

Source: *Chosun ilbo*, November 4, 1967. The numbers inside of the parentheses are the numbers reported by the United Nations forces to the US Department of State.

that the US government was going to request another round of troop deployment to Vietnam by June 1966 at the latest. In response, the South Korean minister of national defense claimed that the South Korean government could send additional troops to Vietnam during his visit to the United States. Of course, the additional troops for Vietnam would be selected from among recently discharged veterans. This plan was similar to Park's earlier offers in 1961 and 1964.

Another noteworthy point is that at this time a number of military attacks against the North were carried out by South Korean military forces.[87] North Korean forces launched a series of attacks against the United Nations forces during President Johnson's official visit to South Korea from October 31 to November 2, 1966. In one attack, carried out on the morning of November 2, seven US soldiers and one South Korean soldier were killed.[88] According to the United Nations Command's research, however, such attacks on the part of the North Korean forces were in fact retaliation for a South Korean attack carried out on October 26.[89] In other words, the North Korean attacks were not necessarily launched because of President Johnson's visit to South Korea.

Ambassador Brown strongly protested to President Park Chung Hee and Prime Minister Jeong Ilgwon on November 3 and 17, soon after President Johnson returned to the United States. The United Nations commander Charles H. Bonesteel also notified the South Korean government that while he agreed on the need to respond to recent North Korean provocations, he was nevertheless against using radical measures, such as preemptive strikes.[90] However, another case of South Korean attacks against the North was reported to the United Nations Command around November 12.[91]

Such reciprocal actions between North and South Korea generated a security crisis in Korea. Physical clashes between the two increased tenfold from 1966 to 1967 (see table 6), meaning that, on average, there was a physical clash between North and South Korea every single day in 1967, as clashes in the Demilitarized Zone increased from forty-two instances in 1965 to four hundred instances in 1967. A major clash of June 1967 resulted in the deaths of thirteen South Korean soldiers and seven North Korean soldiers. The US Central Intelligence Agency received information that North Korea was planning to assassinate Park Chung Hee in the latter part of June 1967, more than six months before the Blue House raid of January 21, 1968. Another intelligence source argued that the North Korean government was considering guerilla warfare to stop the South Korean deployment of troops to Vietnam.[92] United Nations Commander Bonesteel believed that a serious security crisis was looming in the Korean Peninsula at the time.[93]

The South Korean government made two requests to the United States at this point. One was the introduction of additional military equipments that could help the South Korean forces fight infiltration from the North. Another was dispatching new military units made of recently discharged veterans as well as civilian experts and workers to Vietnam. The two requests, sent before the US government made its third request for South Korean combat troops, became core considerations for negotiations even after the US government's official request for South Korean troops.

While the second South Korean request continued to generate controversy, it was difficult for the United States government to refuse the first request because it was the basic premise in justifying the deployment of South Korean combat troops to Vietnam. In other words, the United States had to contain the security crisis in Korea, in particular, as security problems in Korea would not only make further deployment of South Korean troops difficult, but may also cause a media outcry for those troops already dispatched to Vietnam to return home.[94] Park Chung Hee presented these proposals to Johnson before the official US requests for South Korean troops.[95] In particular, he hoped for equipment, such as helicopters and navy destroyers, which could be used to deter infiltrations from the North.

However, such overly active strategies on the part of the Park Chung Hee government began to make the relevant US agencies worry about developments in Korea. Such a feeling of crisis was largely generated by the actions of the South Korean government itself. It was also true that the Park Chung Hee government put too much pressure on the US government over the issues of the deployment of South Korean troops and the security crisis in Korea. Opinions were beginning to be raised inside of the US government that the Park Chung Hee government's demands were excessive.

The telegram sent by Ambassador Brown immediately before his departure from his Seoul post illustrates this perspective well. He argued that, while requesting South Korean troops was unavoidable given the state of the American war in Vietnam, it was necessary to be cautious with the South Korean government. He warned that the US government could be in trouble if it forced Park Chung Hee to give a yes-or-no answer on the question of troop deployment.[96]

Brown's perspective was reiterated by his successor William Porter. Ambassador Porter had to negotiate with the South Korean government over the issue of combat troop deployment immediately after taking office. On September 4, 1967, Park Chung Hee told Porter that the feasibility of troop deployment depended on how much military equipment the United States would provide.[97] While Porter defined his goals as sending as many South Korean troops as possible to Vietnam, minimizing the US financial burden that the deployment of South Korean troops would generate, and improving domestic political difficulties faced by the South Korean government,[98] Porter started to feel that there were an increasing number of problems as the negotiations progressed.

While some of Porter's worries arose from his perusal of the past records of negotiations with Seoul, perhaps a more important source of discomfort was the strong reaction of Park Chung Hee during the negotiations. Porter had several rules he sought to abide by in the negotiations: no mentioning of economic issues (unlike the negotiations for the second deployment) and persuading the South Korean government to strengthen its military capabilities as military aid to South Korea would decrease after the Vietnam War's conclusion.[99] Ambassador Porter's stance was therefore less friendly to South Korea than that of Ambassador Brown. It is likely the case that the US State Department instructed Porter to take a harder line based on experiences from the last round of negotiations over troop deployment.

The South Korean government, however, reacted strongly, insisting that it would not take part in negotiations unless it could reap substantial rewards. When there was a clash between North and South Korea at the Demilitarized Zone, Park Chung Hee publicly declared that he would retaliate against all provocations despite the US suggestions to the contrary.[100] While Ambassador Porter protested strongly when he heard the news that the South Korean military forces attacked North Korea in the midst of US-South Korea negotiations on September 4, 1967, Park continued to insist that retaliatory actions must be carried out. When the United Nations commander told Park to discuss the issues of retaliation with the US president's representative, Ambassador Porter, Park strongly warned the UN commander instead:

> He said that he respects the fact that Republic of Korea forces are under the operational control of the United Nations Command and therefore retaliations will never be done without due coordination with the Command. However, unless the United Nations Command undertakes strong measures, the people of Korea will complain increasingly against the Korean Government. We have, he said, almost 600,000 men in the armed forces. If no counter-measures are taken, the people's patience will wear very thin. The President then said he would be very grateful if General Bonesteel would tell him what countermeasures the United Nations will take if the enemy continues and intensifies his attacks. ...
> Certainly the wisest course would not be to totally abandon to the

Communists the full initiative to do what they wished, but it was a fact that it would be hard to preserve and continue the United Nations Command in Korea if the Command were party to violating the armistice. ...

Porter concluded from his comments that Pak intended to put the U.S. "on notice that northward actions by ROK personnel will continue at a greater pace and with greater vigor than in the past, with or without U.S. cooperation." The United States could expect to be informed of South Korean incursions after they occurred, so that U.S. forces in Korea could be prepared for possible retaliation by North Korea. Porter recommended reminding Pak of U.S. disapproval of ROK incursions and requesting "ROK discuss with UNC means of making North Korean actions more costly for NK elements as they occur." (Telegram 1483 from Seoul, September 22; ibid.) Bundy concurred with Porter's recommendation and stated that the matter was being given "urgent attention" in Washington.[101]

While such a stance by Park Chung Hee was an expression of his determination to stand up to North Korean provocations, it was also a method which Park used to pressure the United States. Not only did Park ask what sort of alternatives the United Nations commander had when he objected to the policy of retaliation, Park also threatened the preservation of the United Nations Command in Korea itself.

While it was merely a way of pressuring the United States, the United States government saw it as a potential threat against the foundation of its foreign policy in Northeast Asia. The United States already had experienced threats of unilateral northward advance from South Korea during the 1950s, and it had stopped Syngman Rhee's threat by providing massive aid and supporting the enormous South Korean military establishment. But Park's threat, however, was unprecedented. While Rhee's threats remained largely rhetorical, Park's retaliations against the North were currently being actualized.

If US-supported South Korea started trouble (read war) first, then Washington could no longer justify supporting South Korea. The mutual defense treaty between the United States and South Korea would also lose its efficacy. Furthermore, the South Korean forces already had attacked North Korea a number of times. In

Washington's eyes, Park Chung Hee may have been crossing a line that he never should have. While the US State Department continued to believe that such clashes were unlikely to spark a full-scale war, it nevertheless did believe that there was a chance for a war if South Korean retaliations continued.[102]

Despite US opposition and pressure, however, Park Chung Hee did not back down from his stance that strong retaliation was necessary. When the third US request for South Korean troops was made, the United Nations commander received information suggesting that the South Korean government may be preparing for even stronger attacks against North Korea. The US government had to prepare for the worst.

A meeting between the South Korean prime minister Jeong Ilgwon and US vice president Hubert Humphrey on October 31, 1967 further exacerbated the critical situation plaguing the US-South Korea relationship.

1. After an exchange of greetings, the Prime Minister stated that during his recent visit to Washington President Johnson had voiced concern about North Korean infiltration into South Korea. At that time the Prime Minister understood that a bill authorizing three destroyers for Korea had passed the House of Representatives, and been forwarded to the Senate Armed Services Committee. He has recently learned that the request for two of these destroyers was cancelled by the Armed Services Committee of the Senate. This will have unfortunate political repercussions in Korea as these three destroyers are badly needed to patrol their 600-mile coastal area. In view of the relationship of Korean public opinion to the Vietnamese war, the loss of the two destroyers is actually less important than the decline in the morale of the Korean people. If the Korean Government should in the future attempt to increase its troop strength in Vietnam, the opposition can effectively use this destroyer issue to criticize the government and weaken its position.

2. The Vice President stated that he would check into this matter of destroyers carefully. The U.S. has received a number of requests for destroyers and for modern jet airplanes recently, including requests from a number of South American countries. There has been a general reaction in the Congress against excessive military assistance

in the past, and this has resulted in a tendency to refuse all requests. The Vice President counseled patience and stated that he believed the matter could be worked out. ...

The Vice President asked the Prime Minister directly if the U.S. is failing to provide anything the Koreans expected. Is the U.S. keeping up with shipments of equipment to the regular forces in Korea?

5. The Prime Minister expressed appreciation for the continued presence of U.S. forces in Korea, and expressed the hope that deliveries on the equipment promised–such as trucks and jeeps could be speeded [up]....

6. [sic] The Vice President expressed the gratitude of American Government and the American people for the Korean participation in the Vietnam war. He is aware that Ambassador Porter has been talking to President Park about the possibility of additional troops for Vietnam. He knows of the political problems that this might cause and has not been sent by President Johnson to make any request for additional troops. ...

Korea will stay with the U.S. till the final victory in Vietnam and this is important not only for Vietnam but for Korea and the United States.

8. The Prime Minister referring to the recent demonstrations in Washington against the war, stated that we might want to send those demonstrators to Korea and have them brainwashed there. Perhaps at the next Seven Nation Conference it would be well to mobilize 200,000 people in all the nations in support of the war to offset the demonstrations against the war.

9. The Vice President stated that the U.S. is aware of the great problem presented by the infiltration from North Korea. But South Korea must not respond unilaterally, must not act without consultations with General Bonesteel or if necessary Ambassador Porter. On this matter, as on all others, we must think and act in concert. We are aware of the pressures to respond to these provocations, but unilateral action can only lead to misunderstanding. He asked the Prime Minister to pass on this message to President Park. The Prime Minister made no response to the Vice President's remarks on this subject.

10. The Prime Minister expressed concern about the possibility of restrictions on the importation of Korean goods into the U.S. For the

past 18 years, U.S. officials have encouraged Korea to increase its exports. Korea has succeeded in doing this and now its exports total $350 million. They hope to continue increasing their trade so they can eventually end their reliance on U.S. economic assistance. But to be self-sustaining they must have the possibility of increased trade. ...

14. Addressing General Westmoreland, the Prime Minister asked if it might be possible for the American logistics command in Vietnam to hire Koreans for maintenance positions from the groups of Koreans who have completed their military service in South Vietnam. This has now become a problem for Korean veterans returning from Vietnam who do not always have suitable opportunities for employment in Korea.

15. The Prime Minister stated that he had been told that the U.S. is agreeable but that the GVN is opposed to this. He had discussed this with Prime Minister Ky in Feb. and although he agreed in principle, nothing has happened. This has been discussed many times during the past year but with no results. General Westmoreland responded that he had recently instructed his staff to look into this matter. With a new government coming into power, and a new draft law which would absorb 65,000 more men, he believes that the situation is now more hopeful. He has the matter under detailed study and believes it possible that something can be worked out in the near future.

16. In conclusion, Westmoreland expressed to the Prime Minister his great admiration for the performance of Korean soldiers in Vietnam and for their leaders. He specifically praised General Chae and presented the Prime Minister with a highly favorable report on the Korean forces which had been prepared by his staff.[103]

The content of this conversation suggests that the South Korean government's actions may be crossing over the bounds set by the United States. Ambassador Porter was particularly irritated by how South Korean newspapers reported that Vice President Humphrey promised three navy destroyers to South Korea.[104] In response, Ambassador Porter reported to Washington that the South Korean government was using its media outlets to blackmail the United States. Some of the US policy documents around this time began displaying an understanding that the South Korean government was using domestic political opposition to its advantage.[105]

When the newly appointed South Korean minister of foreign affairs Choe Gyuha visited Washington on November 13, 1967, Secretary of State Dean Rusk strongly requested that the South Korean government stop the provocations. Rusk sought to persuade Choe by saying that South Korea should always be the victim of aggression in order to win the international community's support and sympathy.[106] While the South Korean government's strategy was to win as much as it could from the United States and display its confidence to North Korea, the execution of that strategy was something the United States could no longer tolerate. Ambassador Porter believed that Seoul's desire for "special treatment" from the United States arose from it thinking of its fifty thousand soldiers in Vietnam as an "Aladdin's lamp."[107]

Ambassador Porter argued that the United States should not request any more troops from South Korea, believing that increased South Korean participation in the Vietnam War would only delay the reduction of US forces in Korea. While Porter's suggestion did not directly translate into policy, the role of the US ambassador in US-South Korea relations is nevertheless substantial. While much of Porter's negative view stemmed from Park Chung Hee's ill-mannered attitude,[108] perhaps the most important factor in shaping Porter's position was the South Korean government's supercilious stance in the negotiations.

This stance on the part of the South Korean government negatively impacted the meeting between President Johnson and Park Chung Hee in Canada on December 21, 1967. Desperate over the developments in Vietnam, Johnson told Park that he would accept much of the South Korean government's demands so that additional South Korean troops could be deployed there. Park, however, sarcastically commented, "Sometimes when we decide to do something, we can do it quicker than you."[109] While Johnson ended up ignoring this display of arrogance, it is easy to surmise how members of the United States government felt given the history Park Chung Hee had with the United States. When President Johnson requested that South Korean troops be dispatched in March, "Park said he would ask his Defense Minister how soon he could get his forces in and he replied April was the earliest possible." Annoyed, Johnson told Park:

That's why you've got Presidents: to make Defense Ministers work harder. It is a President's job to do the impossible. The possible is easy. It is the impossible that Presidents must deal with.[110]

Negative reactions on the part of President Johnson to Park's display of arrogance vis-à-vis the United States is clear in the records of their conversation. Such responses occurred for the first time since South Korea began dispatching combat troops to Vietnam.

The United States government, from this point on, began distancing itself from South Korea in negotiations. While the US government had to request favors from South Korea, it nonetheless began to flatly refuse some of the South Korean demands. Washington declined the South Korean request for aid in building an expressway. It also declined the South Korean request to allow its prime minister and minister of national defense to visit the United States prior to the South Korean National Assembly's approval of the deployment of troops to Vietnam.[111] Even though South Korea agreed to deploy troops, US-South Korea relations were heading into yet another crisis.

When the topic of the third deployment of South Korean troops came up within the US government after the second dispatch of South Korean troops, Ambassador Brown had warned that untimely calls for South Korean forces could produce "unfortunate consequences."[112] While Brown was referring to the domestic political difficulties of the Park Chung Hee regime, this request did produce the seeds of unfortunate consequences for US-South Korea relations as well, featuring Park Chung Hee and Ambassador Porter at center stage. These seeds of misfortune led to the conflict in the US-South Korea relationship of the 1968 security crises. It also marked a starting point for the conflicts that arose in the 1970s.

(2) The 1968 Security Crisis and the Bankruptcy of the US-South Korea Relationship

The ensuing conflict between the United States and South Korea beginning in 1967 intensified with the 1968 security crises, including the Blue House raid on January 21, 1968 and the *Pueblo* Incident on January 23, 1968, which led to a cooling of their relationship. What is interesting is that the series of incidents that broke out in 1967 almost appear to be preludes for what followed in 1968. The

General Woodward, in charge of negotiating for the USS Pueblo, holding a press conference in January 1969. The Pueblo incident chilled the US-South Korea relations.

year 1968 saw a number of serious incidents that rocked the relations between North Korea, South Korea, and the United States in the Blue House raid, the *Pueblo* Incident, and the North Korean infiltrations of the Uljin and Samcheok areas. The Blue House raid appeared akin to the infiltration of North Korean special forces in June of 1967, and the *Pueblo* Incident seemed similar to the news articles published on December 26, 1967, on the North Korean capture of an American spy boat. There were also rumors that North Korea was planning to create a "second front" of the Vietnam War on the Korean Peninsula at the end of 1967. While the United Nations commander denied the possibility of a second front, the infiltrations at Uljin and Samcheok gave the impression that North Korea was indeed trying to create a second front. Fifteen days before the Blue House raid on January 6, 1967, Park Chung Hee warned military officers to be prepared for a North Korean infiltration. The North Korean raid materialized only fifteen days later.[113]

On the other hand, the South Korean government now sought to retaliate against North Korea to an unprecedented level beyond the "limits" set by the United States. Evidently angry at the North Korea's Blue House raid, Park Chung Hee planned for a massive retaliatory campaign. His detailed plans even included coordinated attacks against six locations where the North Korean military trained its guerillas.[114] While Park Chung Hee thanked Lyndon Johnson for bringing up the Blue House raid at the United Nations, Park also grumbled via the South Korean media that the United States' did not respond to it as strongly as it did the *Pueblo* Incident.[115]

The South Korean government informed Ambassador Porter

via the South Korean prime minister about the widespread South Korean public opinion against the secret conference between North Korea and the United States over the return of the USS *Pueblo*. The prime minister even threatened that the continuation of secret conferences with North Korea would make the South Korean government reconsider the very foundations of the US-South Korea relationship.[116] Park Chung Hee, despite the strong objection of President Johnson, maintained his plan for retaliations against North Korea.[117] On February 9, United Nations Commander Bonesteel was informed via the South Korean Air Force that Park Chung Hee may order a raid amounting to a "suicide" attack against North Korea.[118] Park Chung Hee strongly argued that Seoul should be included in the secret conference between North Korea and the United States. Park also informed Ambassador Porter that Seoul would launch immediate retaliations against North Korea in case of another provocation against the South. Porter judged that such actions could result in the resumption of the Korean War.[119]

The United States government also planned for comprehensive retaliation against the North, including dispatching special units into North Korea. Such a plan, however, was eventually abandoned due to past results—the spy infiltration missions in 1963 had less than a 50 percent success rate. Only one spy infiltration mission had succeeded during the period between 1965 and 1967, and independent South Korean infiltration missions into North Korea had a low success rate. The US government also judged that such plans could even strengthen North Korea's security capabilities.[120]

The US government expressed its displeasure at the South Korean government's continued insistence for retaliation, as it would not only make the United States lose its justification for supporting South Korea, but would also endanger the negotiations for the return of the USS *Pueblo*'s crew. Washington also judged that retaliation might mean North Korea's rejection of South Korean participation in the negotiations over the USS *Pueblo*, eradicating the only means of communication it possessed with the North. In addition, the United States did not want to divert its attention from its policy priorities in Vietnam.

Concerned, the United States Pacific Command (USPACOM) warned that South Korea would suffer a great deal if its enmity against the North continued. On February 6, the secretary of state, in a telegram to Ambassador Porter, disdainfully referred to (South) Koreans as the "Irish of the Far East" and stated that the recent developments in South Korea were becoming more difficult than those the United States had experienced with Syngman Rhee.[121] Commander Bonesteel also reported that South Korean public opinion was heavily manipulated by its government, something that the US government took seriously.

Tension between South Korea and the United States reached its peak on February 10, twenty days after the Blue House raid. Ambassador Porter met Park Chung Hee in Seoul on that day. During their meeting, Porter stated that, in his judgment, South Korean government officials were losing their capability of prudent analysis. Porter reported to Washington that Park Chung Hee responded by yelling at him and attempted to send a letter filled with rash staements to President Johnson.[122] After meeting with Park, Porter met with the South Korean minister of foreign affairs. Not only did that minister request the return of a part of the operational control of South Korean military units, but he also requested that President Johnson be granted the power to intervene in Korea without the approval of the US Congress.[123] Washington subsequently determined that no progress could be made through contacts between the South Korean government and the American agencies on the ground in South Korea.

President Johnson sent a letter to Park Chung Hee informing him that he would be sending Cyrus Vance as the president's special envoy to South Korea. Vance visited South Korea from February 11 to February 15. The United States government gave Vance the following responsibilities:

1. To persuade President Park that we attach as much importance to the North Korean provocations against South Korea as we do to the return of the USS Pueblo and crew.

2. To make Park understand we do not see the issue in Korea as a double problem, one involving the U.S. in its attempts to obtain the release of the USS Pueblo and its crew, and one involving the Republic of Korea in the face of North Korean provocations. The provocations against the Republic of Korea are a problem for both

countries, not just the Republic of Korea, and the USS Pueblo is not just our problem but requires South Korean cooperation to be resolved.

3. To explain to Park that we are committed to using peaceful means to resolve both sets of problems and until we have clearly abandoned hope for a peaceful settlement we must reserve judgment as to further courses of action.

4. To ask Park publicly and privately to associate himself with our view that he too seeks a peaceful solution.[124]

While Vance was able to stop the Park Chung Hee government from launching attacks against the North, the overall mission was not successful. The two sides merely re-recognized their differences of opinion. Recalling the unsuccessful mission of Assistant Secretary of State for Far Eastern Affairs Walter S. Robertson to South Korea immediately after the armistice, the South Korean government insisted that the meeting should bear fruit, but the two sides could not resolve their differences. A particularly thorny issue was the continued presence of South Korean troops in Vietnam. When Prime Minister Jeong Ilgwon threatened to pull them out, Vance reacted by saying that the US government might withdraw its forces from Korea.[125] While Vance ultimately obtained the South Korean government's promise not to launch retaliatory attacks against North Korea without first consulting with the United States, he nevertheless reported the following to Johnson:

They are also angry about the Pueblo. They wanted us to take out Wonsan and not doing so was in their opinion a loss of face.

One of their guys, the Defense Minister, is an absolute menace. He has organized a very elite anti-infiltration unit under his command which has been conducting raids across the border against North Korea.

So there is blame on all sides.

There is a very strong danger of unilateral action by Pak.

Pak controls the whole country. Nobody will tell him what he does not want to hear. He is moody, volatile and has been drinking heavily. He is a danger and rather unsafe. ...

I made it very clear to Pak that were they even to consider removing

troops from South Vietnam we would pull ours out of Korea.
In summary, the prospects for the future are not good.

Vance concluded his report by saying,

I do not know if Pak will last. In the past, South Korea has been a
showcase for the United States, but we must look at the cold hard
facts. There is no longer a perfect showcase.[126]

The conversation that followed Vance's presentation is a
noteworthy one that shows the subsequent flow of the US-South
Korea relations:

The President: Is Pak's drinking irrationally something new?
Mr. Vance: No, this has been going on for some time. He hit his wife
with an ash tray. He has thrown ash trays at several of his assistants
and I was fully prepared for that.
The President: What does he want us to give him?
Mr. Vance: He has a large shopping list. ...
The President: What do you think the consequences are of the 600
raids that have taken place this year? Have they hurt the South
Koreans much?
Mr. Vance: No, not except for the Blue House raid.
The President: Was the Blue House raid intended for our Ambassador
too?
Mr. Vance: No. The one infiltrator who was captured was told to say
that he was after Ambassador Porter. But he really wasn't. ...
The President: Did they say anything about Vietnam?
Mr. Vance: No, they did not.
Secretary Rusk: Did Ambassador Porter say we would pull out our
troops in South Korea if they pull out their troops from Vietnam?
Mr. Vance: No, I do not know if Porter said that. I made it clear to
Pak that he should not persist in that attitude. I told him that any
talk of that would have grave impact on the future of relations of
our two countries.
Secretary Rusk: If we had started this consultation earlier, would we
have had all these problems? Or were they inherent in Pak before
this happened?

Mr. Vance: They were inherent in the situation with Pak.

Under Secretary Katzenbach: Do they continue to think we should take Wonsan?

Mr. Vance: Yes, they went through a list of things with me that they would do if certain events were to happen. ...

Secretary McNamara: How about our [their?] raids into the North?

Mr. Vance: They are conducting about two a month.

The President: Do we have a clear idea of what they have done?

Mr. Vance: They have been operating two a month raids recently. The anti-infiltration units are under the command of the Defense Minister. They took out a division headquarters in recent attacks. An attack no later than March is planned across the DMZ again.

There is much talk in military circles about this.

The numbers are not clear. They have about 200 anti-infiltration troops trained with each division upon the DMZ and have an additional group being trained by these men now.

On the other side, there are some highly trained guerrilla units. They estimate there are 2400 of these in 30 man teams. ...

Secretary Rusk: Now that we have made a case of the 570 raids across the DMZ aren't we in a difficult position if any of this information comes to light about South Korean raids into the North?[127]

Secretary McNamara: We do not have adequate knowledge of this.

Mr. Vance: Here is a list of items right here. There have been eleven raids between 26 October and December.

The Vice President: When did they start?

Mr. Vance: I do not know, although I think it has been at least a year.

General Wheeler: General Bonesteel had rumors of this from his advisors who are with the Korean units. Hard information is difficult to get.

The President: What is the purpose of these raids?

General Wheeler: They are punitive. ...

Secretary Rusk: We had the same problem with Syngman Rhee 20 years ago. How much do we give him when he is having to strike the North?

Clark Clifford: I am most distressed about President Pak's instability. Does he have power to start major action on his own?

Mr. Vance: The generals would let us know and would drag their feet. But if he said go, they would have to go.

One general told General Bonesteel that he was terrified of the possibility of unilateral action, but he said that if he is given the order, they will have to respond. ...

Mr. Vance: President Pak will issue all sorts of orders when he begins drinking. His generals will delay any action on them until the next morning. If he says nothing about those orders the following morning then they just forget what he had told them the night before.

The President: Where do we get this information from?

Mr. Vance: General Bonesteel gets it. The military have the greatest amount of respect for the UN Commander and for his position.

Clark Clifford: Did you get any threat at all, even a veiled threat, about withdrawing troops from South Vietnam?

Mr. Vance: The Prime Minister mentioned that the legislature might ask for that. I told him very bluntly that we would remove our troops from South Korea if that happened. The Prime Minister turned ashen. It really shook him. ...

The President: Who is watching the situation on our behalf?

Mr. Vance: Ambassador Porter is watching the President. General Bonesteel will step in at any time.

General Wheeler: As I understand it, General Bonesteel focuses on the Defense Minister and the ROK Joint Chiefs.

General Taylor: It goes back 20 years when the military was a restraining force against Syngman Rhee. The senior military will talk frankly.

Mr. Vance: That is why we meet with them.

The content of this conversation shows that the US officials began to perceive Park Chung Hee and his aids as untrustworthy. In a letter to Assistant Secretary of State Bundy, Porter noted that the US government should recognize that it has "concurrently been nourishing a tiger." Porter stated that he was even willing to receive help from Sun Myung Moon of the Unification Church if he could help Porter restrain the South Korean government.[128]

The above conversation shows how dangerous the Korean Peninsula was at the time. Clashes between North and South Korea were breaking out at a time when the leader of South Korea was behaving irrationally and the armistice had ceased functioning. If the content of this conversation is true, it is almost surprising that these clashes did not lead to war.

Such conflict, however, did not end US-South Korea cooperation. Given the deployment of South Korean troops in Vietnam, the United States had to resolve some of its differences with South Korea by partially accepting some of its requests of aid. In fact, President Johnson continued to request combat troops from South Korea even after the Blue House raid and the *Pueblo* Incident. When fulfilling some of the requests for anti-infiltration military equipment, Johnson reiterated that such support was conditional upon the South Korean promise to dispatch troops to Vietnam.[129] He also judged that, if the North Korean strategy was to obstruct South Korean participation in the Vietnam War, deployment of additional South Korean troops to Vietnam meant a strategic failure on North Korea's part.[130] However, the real rationale behind the request for South Korean troops had more to do with American anxiety following the Tet Offensive in 1968.

However, the South Korean government's excessive demands once again plunged the negotiations into trouble. At a meeting with Ambassador Porter on March 8, 1968, Prime Minister Jeong Ilgwon requested American aid to transform three South Korean reserve divisions into fully armed divisions and seven reserve divisions in the rear into regular reserve divisions in exchange for deploying two or more South Korean army divisions to Vietnam. Jeong also requested transferring the US base in Okinawa to Jeju Island if Prime Minister Satō Eisaku of Japan requested that those bases be returned to Japan.[131]

While Johnson and Park Chung Hee met on April 17, 1968, at Honolulu to further discuss the issue of troop deployment, no progress was made. The US government did not accept the South Korean government's excessive demands, and Park Chung Hee judged that Johnson, who already had forgone the possibility of another term in office, did not have the political power to demand additional Korea aid from US Congress. In other words, both governments implicitly came to an agreement that there would be no additional deployment of South Korean troops to Vietnam.[132]

The Johnson administration no longer kept its promises to the

South Korean government. Johnson had agreed that it would consult with the South Korean government if US forces in South Korea were to be reduced. However, when the US Department of Defense decided on a plan to do just that, no consultations were made with Seoul. This plan entailed withdrawal of the US Second Infantry Division in 1971 and the Seventh Infantry Division in 1973 as well as a complete shutdown of all aid to South Korea by 1975.[133] The plan was adopted by the Nixon administration in 1967 and 1970 with some revisions. In addition, the South Korean request to dispatch five thousand noncombat agents to Vietnam, as a way to ameliorate the problem of unemployment in South Korea, was also rescinded.[134]

The United States government could no longer trust the South Korean government. In the worst-case scenario, the South Korean government could ruin the US Northeast Asia policy in its entirety. The South Korean government did not hide its disappointment with the United States government that seemed only to focus on the *Pueblo* Incident and not on retaliations against the North for its aggressive actions. The US-South Korea relationship therefore entered into an era of crisis.

Much of it was caused by the United States. Through the plan to remove Kim Jongpil and the process of deploying South Korean troops to Vietnam, the US government helped make Park Chung Hee the undisputed leader of South Korea. Park Chung Hee soon became uncontrollable, even for the United States. Such development meant that the US government was now faced with a situation similar to what it had faced with Syngman Rhee back in the 1950s.

The South Korean government gained much from its participation in the Vietnam War. First, it was able to overcome a political crisis through the careful manipulation of domestic politics and media. Money that the South Korean government received from the United States for its participation in the Vietnam War and exports to South Vietnam allowed it to fund its own economic development plan. The overall effects of such gains were much greater considering that US Korea aid had been declining over the years. The South Korean military establishment, the strongest base of support for Park Chung Hee, was also strengthened. Not only did the South Korean military units acquire combat experience, but many reserve divisions were

turned into combat divisions and one additional quasi-combat
division was added.

However, let's think of what South Korea actually gained.
What it could receive from the United States was clearly limited.
Perhaps more importantly, the United States did not think of the
rewards South Korea received as rightful compensation for its
efforts–Washington viewed the South Korean demands as something
more akin to begging. Furthermore, South Korean reprisals against
the North made the United States government hesitant to provide
additional military aid. In other words, Washington believed that
additional military aid to South Korea may provide it the ability to
launch more attacks against the North.[135]

What Park Chung Hee desired the most–for South Korea to
receive the same level of treatment as Japan did from the United
States–was ultimately not attained. Park Chung Hee wanted to
display to domestic and international audiences the close and
special relationship between the United States and South Korea by
dispatching troops to Vietnam, regardless of international skepticism
and criticism against the war there.[136] However, the aggressive
reaction on the South Korean government's part at the third US
request for South Korean combat troops drove the US-South Korea
honeymoon into an "unfortunate" state. In the end, US-South Korea
relations did not rise to the level as had been hoped, despite South
Korea responding to US needs.

Instead, the South Korean and the US governments lost trust in
each other. Four months after the Blue House raid, the US State
Department judged that, while there was little chance of North
Korea starting a full-scale war, massive South Korean retaliations
against small provocations from the North could spark off a real
war. The State Department therefore recommended that it was
more important to control the South Korean government than the
North.[137] The US government could not trust the South Korean
government as much as it could trust North Korea.

Many years later, the South Korean government dispatched
troops to Iraq at the United States government's request. What
did the South Korean government expect to gain? What sorts of
"learning effect" did the South Korean people, who believed that
dispatching troops to Iraq was in its "national interest," gain from

the Vietnam War? As many South Koreans did think of participating in the Vietnam War as a business opportunity, are the people of South Korea thinking the same for the Iraq War?[138] Considering the American attitude in the negotiations with South Korea during the Vietnam War, however, one must reflect on what South Korea could gain from its participation in the Iraq War. If the goal of participating in the Iraq War is to attain a normal diplomatic relationship with the United States or elevate the status of US-South Korea relations to the level of that between the United States and Japan, the example of the Vietnam War negotiations show that such wishes were unattainable. The deployment of South Korean troops to Iraq cannot be an "Aladdin's lamp" for South Korea.

Considering that the ongoing negotiations between the United States and South Korea over the issue of wartime operational control of the South Korean military are closely tied to the concomitant global relocation of American military forces abroad as well as the transformation of the US forces in Korea into a quick reaction force, lessons from the Vietnam War can be even more valuable for South Korea. The South Korean deployment of troops to Vietnam has its roots in the American intention to reduce US forces in Korea, and the transformation of the US forces in Korea into a quick reaction force had been discussed as early as in 1964.[139] Therefore, the issue of the South Korean dispatch of troops to Vietnam is definitely something to be studied in the future, particularly with the recent declassification of relevant South Korean documents.

SEVEN

The United States-South Korea Relations of the 1970s and the "Learning Effect"

The United States could no longer unilaterally guide and dominate South Korea. While this change had much to do with the fact that the United States was in a position where it sometimes had to ask favors from South Korea, it also had to do with South Korea's economic and social growth and development during the 1960s. The US-South Korea relationship during the 1970s was not smooth. Conflicts between the United States and South Korea were sometimes serious and went beyond anything to be had between allies. What meanings do such phenomena have for the US-South Korea relationship? A qualitative change? Could the US decision to reduce and withdraw the American forces from South Korea without any prior consultation as well as the South Korean decision to pursue self-reliance in national defense be seen as "normal" in a military alliance?

1. Learning Effect from the Negotiations for Troop Deployment

(1) New Foreign Policy: *Realpolitik*

The Nixon Administration brought new and major changes to American foreign policy, the most noticeable and important of which was limited intervention in the affairs of allies and an attempt to reduce costs, which was the result of increased government expenditures from the war in Vietnam. Nixon's policy was therefore in a way similar to the New Look policy of Eisenhower back in the 1950s. The conservative fiscal policy of the Eisenhower administration, especially vis-à-vis South Korea, reduced American foreign intervention and brought the Korean War to a close. To further reduce costs, the Eisenhower administration withdrew some American forces from South Korea. The Nixon administration followed suit by reducing the number of members of the American armed forces in South Korea as well as other parts of Asia.

Such a change in foreign policy was also caused by transformations in the international arena. First, the economic growth of Japan and Europe ended the American monopoly of the dollar. On August 15, 1971, President Nixon declared his decision to cancel direct convertibility of the US dollar to gold. Under the Bretton Woods system (and the International Monetary Fund system), the US government had guaranteed an exchange rate of thirty-five US dollars to an ounce of gold since 1944. The gold standard, however, could no longer be maintained due to the rapid economic growth of Europe and Japan that placed the American economy at a disadvantage, accumulated a trade deficit, and caused inflation in the United States.[1]

Another factor was China's growth. So far, the US government had viewed the Soviet Union as the sole leader of the communist world. This stance, however, could no longer be maintained due to China's rise. The beginning of the Sino-Soviet split beginning in the late 1950s made it difficult for the United States to control the communist world solely through dealing with the Soviet Union. There was an even greater need to directly negotiate with China after its first successful test of nuclear weapons in 1964.

China now had the power to threaten other nations around it without Soviet support. With the United States now considering withdrawal from Vietnam, the China factor became even more important given the Chinese border with Southeast Asia. The United States had maintained a hostile stance toward China since the Korean War, which had translated into the American veto against China's attempt to replace Taiwan (the Republic of China) as a veto-wielding permanent member of the United Nations Security Council. A change, however, was not inevitable. A compromise with China was also a way of encouarging a schism within the communist world.

Reduction of foreign aid was also a priority. While foreign intervention needed to be reduced in order to reduce foreign aid, unilateral action in this area was difficult given the US government's commitments and relationships with its allies. To justify and legitimize reduction of foreign aid, the United States needed to reduce the level of security threat its allies faced. The US government also worked to avoid giving the impression that the United States was taking a step back in its competition against the Soviet Union.

Through such changes in international conditions, the United States made a transition from its ideological commitment to the Cold War to a pursuit of practical interests. To uphold its cause, the United States would have needed to take a hard line against the communist world while actively intervening in the Third World to stop the spread of communism. The United States, however, had paid a high price in the Vietnam War, learning that its ability to follow such policy was limited.

The Nixon administration's foreign policy change was led by National Security Advisor Henry Kissinger. His theory of foreign policy, generally referred to as *Realpolitik* in the American context, displayed a new understanding of the Cold War system. He emphasized the balance of power and believed that the United States and the Soviet Union did not monopolize international relations. This understanding is similar to that of Kennan–particularly in his designation of strategically important regions around the globe. In short, Kissinger believed that there is no fixed international order. Defying the previous paradigm of containment, Kissinger believed that the United States needs to avoid playing a zero-sum game in foreign policy and recognize the limits to its power.[2]

Kissinger, in particular, focused on China's growth, the Sino-Soviet split, and the limits of Soviet power. This aspect is also similar to Kennan. Kissinger pursued a policy of détente, which entailed a normalization of relations with China and negotiations for arms reduction with the Soviet Union. If the United States could reduce tension with the communist world, it could also reduce its aid to its allies as well as its military expenditures–which were astronomically high due to its competition with the Soviet Union. Kissinger led American foreign policy under the Nixon and Ford administrations carrying the banner of *Realpolitik*.

The Nixon administration's new policy shocked South Korea.

Soon, the Nixon Doctrine was declared.

> Now, one other point I would make very briefly is that in terms of this situation as far as the role we should play, we must recognize that there are two great, new factors which you will see, incidentally, particularly when you arrive in the Philippines–something you will see there that we didn't see in 1953, to show you how quickly it has changed: a very great growth of nationalism. ...
>
> The second factor is one that is going to, I believe, have a major impact on the future of Asia, and it is something that we must take into account. Asians will say in every country that we visit that they do not want to be dictated to from the outside, Asia for the Asians. And that is what we want, and that is the role we should play. ...
>
> But as far as our role is concerned, we must avoid that kind of policy that will make countries in Asia so dependent upon us that we are dragged into conflicts such as the one that we have in Vietnam. This is going to be a difficult line to follow. It is one, however, that I think, with proper planning, we can develop. ...
>
> I believe that the time has come when the United States, in our relations with all of our Asian friends, be quite emphatic on two points: One, that we will keep our treaty commitments, our treaty commitments, for example, with Thailand under SEATO; but, two, that as far as the problems of internal security are concerned, as far as the problems of military defense, except for the threat of a major power involving nuclear weapons, that the United States is going to encourage and has a right to expect that this problem will be increasingly handled by, and the responsibility for it taken by, the Asian nations themselves. ...
>
> Asia for the Asians. And that is what we want, and that is the role we should play.[3]

The Nixon Doctrine, proclaimed on July 29, 1969, was a declaration of the "Vietnamization" of the Vietnam War and the "Koreanization" of the Korea problem. People of the regions themselves, instead of the international community, would have to tackle their own problems. While existing alliances would still be maintained and the changes would not take place immediately, the people of these regions themselves would have to start taking up a greater share of the responsibilities. On the Korea issue, this reflected the American determination to reduce or withdraw US forces from South Korea as well as to create an international atmosphere that would eliminate the "need" for US forces there.

Considering the fact that, since the 1950s, the US Department of Defense and the Joint Chiefs of Staff saw the US forces in Korea not only as a deterrent against North Korea but also against China, a reduction of tension between the United States and China would further rationalize the reduction and eventual withdrawal of US forces from Korea. From the 1960s, the US government deemed South Korea to be strong enough to be able to handle North Korean forces in a war. A US Department of State document from 1968 evaluated the South Korean armed forces as superior to North Korean forces in all areas except the air force.

Another important factor was the successful normalization of South Korea-Japan relations, which the US government had prioritized since the 1950s in order to shift some of its burdens and responsibilities in East Asia to Japan. This policy, meant to magnify the Japanese presence in Asia, was realized in the 1960s with normalization and the establishment of the Asian Development Bank.[4] While the United States government had planned to reduce both the number of the US forces in Korea as well as its Korea aid after South Korea-Japan normalization, this plan was delayed due to South Korea's participation in the Vietnam War.

With the impending American decommitment from Vietnam, however, there was no more reason to delay a Japan-centered regional order. Kissinger's *Realpolitik* also emphasized the role of Japan in Asia. Japan also took an active approach vis-à-vis Korea due to its security concerns with North Korea and China. While there were shifts, in general, the South Korean government prioritized economic goals while the Japanese government prioritized security in the South Korea-Japan summit talks.[5]

The concurrence between Japan and the United States was expressed in the "Korea clause" of a joint statement released by President Nixon and Prime Minister Satō of Japan:

The President and the Prime Minister specifically noted the continuing tension over the Korean peninsula. The Prime Minister deeply appreciated the peacekeeping efforts of the United Nations in the area and stated that the security of the Republic of Korea was essential to Japan's own security.[6]

Satō further elaborated on the Korea security issue at a speech at the press club immediately after the summit:

> In particular, if an armed attack against the Republic of Korea were to occur, the security of Japan would be seriously affected. Therefore, should an occasion arise for United States forces in such an eventuality to use facilities and areas within Japan as bases for military combat operations to meet the armed attack, the policy of the government of Japan towards prior consultation would be to decide its position positively and promptly on the basis of the foregoing recognition.[7]

What Satō meant is that the US forces in Japan could move based on the situation in Korea without prior consultation in case of a war there. On the one hand, it was an expression emphasizing the importance of security in Korea. On the other hand, however, it implied that Japan would follow the United States in intervening in Korea in case of a war. The tripartite alliance between South Korea, Japan, and the United States was now active in the realm of security. This long-term US policy goal first pursued by the Eisenhower administration now began to bear fruit. Furthermore, as stated in the Nixon Doctrine, the United States had now created international conditions in which it could substantially reduce its forces in Korea without threatening its security.

(2) The July 4 Joint Statement and Collision with Yusin

A month after the declaration of the Nixon Statement in Guam, President Nixon met with President Park Chung Hee on August 22, 1969 and released a joint statement. The two men probably did not know at the time that this meeting would mark the beginning of ensuing troubles between the two countries throughout the 1970s. Or perhaps only Park Chung Hee was not aware of it, as their meeting ended cordially.

Park Chung Hee stressed to Nixon the security threat presented by the North Korean attacks. The heads of state agreed that the South Korean military forces and the US forces in Korea must continue to cooperate in fending off North Korean aggression based on the mutual defense treaty. They also agreed that the newly formed South Korean homeland reserve forces were contributing to the stability in South Korea. However, Park continued to stress security while Nixon emphasized the need for an appeasement policy to reduce the level of crisis. Despite their differences of opinions, a joint statement was nevertheless concluded on an ambiguous note.

Park Chung Hee and Richard Nixon meeting in San Francisco on August 22, 1969. Park's stern facial expression sharply contrasts with Nixon's rather relaxed look.

On March 20, 1970, less than a year after the joint statement, the Nixon administration decided to withdraw one of the two US divisions stationed in Korea. Since the state of peace was to be maintained through the status quo, the Second Infantry Division of some twenty thousand men was scheduled to be withdrawn from South Korea by March of 1971.[8]

Park Chung Hee was informed of the unilateral plan for withdrawal in July 1970. In August of the same year, Vice President Spiro Agnew visited South Korea. Agnew's visit had two purposes: to explain the US stance on the withdrawal and to give a political gift to Park Chung Hee prior to the presidential election in 1971.

As noted, the South Korean government was not consulted over plans for withdrawal, meaning that President Johnson's promise that Seoul was to be notified beforehand was not going to be kept. Park Chung Hee was most displeased with this. Such unilateral action on the part of the United States government also shows that the US-South Korea relationship did not change qualitatively through South Korea's participation in the Vietnam War.

Perhaps the South Korean government's most important goal in its participation in the Vietnam War, in addition to economic gains, was to "normalize" US-South Korea relations. The Park Chung Hee government also endeavored to shape the US-South Korea relationship into one between bona fide allies. This point is most evident in Park's intention to transform South Korea into "another Japan" through the deployment of South Korean combat troops to Vietnam.

As shown in chapter 6, however, the South Korean government's excessive attempts to dominate the negotiations estranged the US government to the point that such "normalization" became impossible. Of course, given the presence of US forces in Korea, the mutual defense treaty, and the fact that the United States was shouldering much of South Korea's security burden, it would have been difficult to normalize the US-South Korea relationship into one based on equality under any scenario. Looking at the example of Japan, which also relied heavily on the United States for its security, however, the "normalization" of US-South Korea relations should not have been entirely impossible. In conclusion, the unilateral notification of the reduction of US forces in Korea is a representative example that the deployment of South Korean combat troops to Vietnam did not change the nature of US-South Korea relations.

Of course, reduction of the US forces in Korea would have taken place regardless of improvements in US-South Korea relations due to the general direction of Nixon's foreign policy. However, the main issue here is whether or not consultation with the South Korean government had taken place before a policy change that could impact South Korean society in grave ways. When the South Korean military government carried out the 1962 currency reform, the US government was critical of the fact that it had not been consulted beforehand and threatened Seoul with the slashing of aid. However, in the process of reducing American forces in Korea, Washington made no attempts to consult with the South Korean government beforehand. At the same time, this unilateralism on the part of the United States government may have to do with the "learning effect" from the past that prior consultation may result in the South Korean government generating a security crisis on the

Korean Peninsula.

After some discussions, the South Korean and the US governments issued a joint statement on February 6, 1971, on the reduction of US forces in Korea. It included a proclamation of the withdrawal of the US Seventh Infantry Division and three air force squadrons, as well as the relocation of the US Second Infantry Division from its prior location along the Demilitarized Zone to the rear.[9] Park Chung Hee was deeply shocked. Given that some South Korean forces were still stationed in Vietnam and the presidential election was a year away, the reduction of American forces in Korea came across as a political threat. As can be seen in the example from 1967, the two most important pillars of the Park Chung Hee regime were the economic development plan and support from the United States.

The Park Chung Hee regime's first response was to seek to persuade Washington to change its mind through an emphasis on security issues. While the South Korean governments of 1949 and 1967 created security crises to obstruct the American plans for withdrawal or reduction, it could not do the same in 1970. As mentioned in chapter 6, the United States government made it clear to Seoul that South Korean provocations of the North, instead of being a method of persuasion, could bankrupt US-South Korea relations. Vance at the time even threatened to withdraw all US forces from Korea.

In a letter addressed to President Nixon on September 16, 1971, Park Chung Hee stated that there would not be any more aggression against the North. He reiterated the defensive posture the United States and South Korean forces were assuming at the time, and that the US forces in Korea remained the most effective deterrent against the resumption of war in Korea. This stance was indeed a retreat from Park's previous position in which he emphasized the need to retaliate against all forms of aggression from the North. Newly appointed Ambassador Philip Habib also believed that the South Korean government would not launch attacks against the North in the name of retaliation. The South Korean government now sought ways other than active aggression against the North to change American policy. Park Chung Hee sent a personal letter to Nixon, the South Korean National Assembly passed a resolution accusing the United States of betraying South Korea despite the presence of the South Korean combat troops on duty in Vietnam, and the South Korean cabinet even declared its willingness to resign en masse. At the Third Annual Security Consultative Meeting, which lasted from July 22, 1970, to July 21, 1970, the South Korean government even threatened to withdraw South Korean troops from Vietnam in reprisal.[10] Of course, the South Korean government had no actual intention to withdraw from Vietnam given the benefits it was accruing there. While such a move was logically similar to the US threats to cut off economic and military aid to South Korea during the 1960s, it did not work the other way around. Moreover, given the American decision to "localize" the war in Vietnam, the South Korean threats had even less of an effect on Washington.

Another response on the part of Park Chung Hee was to urge the US Congress to change Nixon's Korea policy. This attempt took place in secret using illegal political funds. As can be deduced from the findings on "Koreagate," the South Korean government began its lobbying activities with a number of American congressmen from both houses with the ascension of the Nixon administration. Most of the funds probably came from the Korea Central Intelligence Agency. Congressmen with Korea interests–those whose constituencies exported to South Korea–were lobbied in an attempt to generate policies favorable to the South Korean government in as Congress. Such a move, however, not only failed to generate expected results, it eventually tainted the image of South Korea through scandals, such as Koreagate in 1976, which was an embarrassing application of a Korean method of politics–buying politicians with money.

The Nixon administration continued to push for the reduction of US forces in Korea and ways to defuse tension on the Korean Peninsula. While the majority opinion within the South Korean government was that Seoul was still too weak to engage in direct contact with the North Korean government,[11] the US Department of State and Ambassador Porter continued to emphasize the need for the South Korean government to talk to the North Korean government to reduce tension, as that would not only legitimize reduction of American forces in Korea, but also prevent the South Korean government from pressuring the United States with security issues.

The determination of Washington at this time was strong. Ambassador Porter, who argued for the necessity of firmer methods in the telegram in February 1972, again displayed his strong will in the following telegram sent immediately after the presidential election on April 27:

> I think that we should be little less passive, little less permissive on this question. Elsewhere in world we are actively seeking ways to reduce tension with communist powers. With US troops committed to Korea we have direct interest in finding ways to reduce tension on peninsula and we cannot let ROK hold us both in position of rigid hostility. ....[I]n absence of satisfactory ROK reactions or initiatives, we inform them that we will take steps ... to find channels for private discussions between ourselves and North Koreans.[12]

Ambassador Porter believed that such an American policy would have widespread support from the South Korean people.[13] He further pressured the South Korean government by stating that US grants to South Korea would end in 1975.

South Korea had no choice but to follow along, as the US government carried out its Korea policy without any prior consultation with Seoul. This again was a "learning effect" Washington gained from its dealings with the South Korean government during the Vietnam War. This point is particularly evident in the strong stance of Ambassador Porter, who held a particularly negative view towards the South Korean demeanor during the Vietnam War negotiations. The American pressure eventually resulted in the North-South Red Cross meeting in 1971 and the July 4 Joint Statement in 1972.[14]

It was yet another crisis for Park Chung Hee.[15] Given the relative parity in per capita income between North Korea and South Korea at the time, there was no guarantee that South Korea could beat North Korea in a competition outside of a war. In addition, the threat of war, the most effective method for controlling and mobilizing the people, could no longer be used by Park to govern. Of course, North Korea had a similar sense of crisis, leading to it adapting a socialist constitution in 1972 and naming of the successor in the mid-1970s.

Park Chung Hee was concerned with a security crisis even to the point of proclaiming the July 4 Joint Statement.[16] No longer able to generate a security crisis to its advantage, the Park Chung Hee government opted for another strategy. His alternative plan was to systematize South Korean society for the rapid mobilization of its resources. Park had already explored his long-term plan and vision for a mobilization system in a speech related to "the Second Economy" prior to the security crisis on January 15, 1968.[17] Park began to further develop this vision.

Park first declared a state of national emergency on December 6, 1971. Framing it as a preparatory measure for the upcoming North-South contacts, the South Korean government justified its call as a response to the international changes generated by China joining the United Nations and its impact upon the Korean Peninsula, as well as North Korea's military preparations against the South. Following the July 4 Joint Declaration, Park declared the Yusin System on October 17.

(3) The Nonintervention and Two-Korea Policies

Such responses on the part of Park Chung Hee were significant for the US-South Korea relationship in two ways. First, it was a direct challenge to the US policy of emphasizing democratic institutions in South Korea. Second, it was a way of taking advantage of the power vacuum generated by the Nixon Doctrine. While the United States has emphasized institutional democracy for all of its allies over the years, the Nixon administration never intervened against a dictatorship. General Lon Nol of Cambodia carried out a coup d'état in 1970, and the military regime in Thailand dissolved its national assembly and declared martial law in November of 1971. Ferdinand Marcos also declared martial law in the Philippines in September of 1972. The United States, however, did not intervene in any of these events. And, despite expressions of concern, the United States also did not intervene against the South Korean government and the declaration of the Yusin system.

Ambassador Habib, who succeeded Porter, sent his overview of the conditions of South Korea at the time as well as his opinions and suggestions for the US government:

Referendum approval of the amendments is certain, and a one-man authoritarian regime will be established with all of the institutional checks and balances built into the old constitution completely eliminated. This retrogressive step is more complex than a simple palace coup or power grab. Park Chung Hee and the group around him which has governed Korea for the past 12 years are convinced that only Park can lead the country and protect Korean national interests in confronting the dual challenges and uncertainties of negotiating with the North and the big power détente. ...

It is clear, that Park has turned away from the political philosophy which we have been advocating and supporting in Korea for 27 years. The characteristics of the discarded system which he regarded as weaknesses, -the limitations on executive power, the dissent and inherent uncertainties which arise in direct Presidential elections-we regard as strengths. Because of our historic relationship with Korea, our security commitments, and the presence of a substantial number of American troops, we are confronted with the problem of our reaction to these developments.

An effort to persuade Park to abandon completely this course of action and return to the old constitution must be discarded at the outset as impractical. Only specific and drastic sanctions could turn him around (i.e., immediate termination of all military and economic support). We would, however, have won a pyrrhic victory. We would either destroy Park or make future cooperation with him impossible.

A second possible course of action would be to try to persuade Park to soften the more repressive aspects and modify the more egregious violations democratic principles and procedures while accepting the basic structure of the reorganization. ...

The third, and in our judgment preferred course of action, would be to adopt a policy of disassociation. We have already made clear, both in Washington and Seoul our disappointment and disagreement with the martial law proclamation. Having stated privately our strong general reservations about the reorganization, we should make no comment on its specific measures. After announcement of the Constitutional amendments on the 27th, the department should state publicly that ROKG is taking actions with which we are not associated. Department's statement should also note that we were not consulted and, referring to earlier bray statement, state we see no need for these actions. Afterwards we would seek not to involve ourselves at any stage in the reorganization process. We would, however, protest if Park should embark on a program of flagrant personal repression.

In following such a course, we would be accepting the fact that the US cannot and should no longer try to determine the course of internal political development in Korea. We have already begun a process of progressively lower levels of U.S. engagement with Korea. This progress of disengagement should be accelerated.[18]

As can be seen here, instead of actively intervening as it did in the cases of the Busan Incident of 1952 and the 1963 transfer of power to a civilian government, the United States government chose not to intervene.

The reason why the Nixon administration chose not to intervene on the Yusin system was that it began formulating a policy different from the past model of pursuing a South-led unification of Korea via the United Nations. Instead, the Nixon administration sought the peaceful coexistence of North and South Korea within a peaceful international order in Northeast Asia. Kissinger's *Realpolitik* emphasized the limits of American power and the need for maintaining the status quo, and the Korea policy was no exception.

Korean policy has since 1950 remained largely unchanged and postulated on cold war assumptions that are increasingly anachronistic. The primary elements of this policy–aimed at deterring renewed conflict and buttressing the ROK–have consistently remained a mix of:
1) A US Treaty commitment to Korea, backed by the stationing of substantial US forces in Korea.
2) US support for the modernization of ROK military forces and broader international aid to its economy.
3) A UN role in Korea through UNCURK and the UN Command, with the ROK holding a privileged position vis-à-vis Pyongyong in the UN and elsewhere in the international community.
4) Support for the goal of peaceful unification under conditions favorable to the ROK.
The reduction of cold war tensions and the progress toward

normalization of US-PRC relations have over the past year eroded this policy and left elements in it increasingly anachronistic. A general consensus among the four major powers involved–US, USSR, PRC and Japan–has evolved favoring accommodation of both sides in minimizing the risk of North-South conflict. Even the ROK and North Korea have given recognition to this trend by opening bilateral talks.

In recent months, the pressure for new arrangements on Korea looking to a two-Korea "provisional" accommodation have accelerated, despite the clear lack of progress in North-South talks. The recent developments giving new impetus to Korean policy reconsideration are: ...

Policy Objective: Aid to Korea Accommodation

The goal of US policy towards Korea should be to formalize and consolidate a two-Korea accommodation between the North and the South for an indefinite period, while leaving as an ultimate goal the eventual reunification of Korea.

Policy Guidelines:

1) The US should actively encourage through all means, diplomatic and otherwise, a two-Korea accommodation.

The basic question is the degree of U.S. involvement in seeking a two-Korea accommodation. Under the present circumstances, any posture less than active encouragement would permit the situation to drift to our disadvantage. At the present time, even the ROK seems likely to seek an active American role. ...

Actions for Immediate Decision:

A. Reciprocal Recognition

B. Dual UN Membership

C. Normalization of US-NK relations

While we are probably in a position to withhold formal recognition of North Korea until a later date, there is a strong case for beginning the process of normalizing our relations with the North. In particular, informal secret contacts with the North seem increasingly necessary to provide us with direct information and perspective on Pyongyang's policies, as well as a step toward bringing Pyongyang into a more constructive relationship with the West. Short of any formal contacts, we could signal our intention by changing our travel regulations and stimulating unofficial contacts. These steps, particularly any contacts with the North, will require very close consideration of ROK sensitivities.[19]

Maintaining of the "status quo" was the cheapest foreign policy. Although the United States already had experimented with this in order to reduce foreign aid during the Eisenhower administration with the "New Look" policy, it could not recognize North Korea during the 1950s with its ongoing confrontation with China. The 1970s was a different time. As can be seen in the quote above, the two-Korea policy meant a fundamental change in US Korea policy reflecting the transformation of international conditions over the past two decades.

Since 1948, two important policy objectives appeared in US policy papers related to Korea. One was maintaining a stable democratic order in South Korea and the other was unifying the Korean Peninsula under the South Korean system with UN help. The quote above shows that such policy objectives were no longer maintained.

Furthermore, a particularity of the US Korea policy–the tendency to involve the United Nations in carrying out its Korea policy–was also partially withdrawn at this time. This aspect was actualized following repeated Chinese requests to dissolve the United Nations Commission for Unification and Rehabilitation of Korea and the United Nations Command, first of which the United States finally decided to do in 1973. As for the United Nations Command, the United States government decided to reduce its role through the establishment of Combined Forces Command and the conclusion of a nonaggression treaty between North and South Korea.[20]

The US-South Korea relationship, on the surface, appeared to be normal again. The United States reaffirmed its noninterventionism and chose a policy for the status quo in Korea. Such changes were significant compared to the time before the 1970s. Problems, however, remained. Conflicts between the United States and South Korean governments continued throughout the 1970s, and the United States was placed in a position in which it had to intervene into South Korea before the decade closed.

2. Gwangju: Whose Fault Was It?

(1) Whirlpool of the mid-1970s

The US-South Korea relationship appeared to normalize with the ascension of President Gerald Ford after Nixon's resignation following the Watergate scandal. Ford emphasized security more so than Nixon, and Ford also took an active stance on the security issue of Korea when South Vietnam fell.[21] Ford's stance was that, while maintaining détente, the United States was to actively support the security and self-reliance of its allies in order to maintain a strong system of international security.[22]

The Park Chung Hee government, given its uncomfortable relationship with the Nixon administration, was hopeful that the ascension of Gerald Ford to the presidency could mark a new turning point in the US-South Korea relationship.[23] Park Chung Hee's expectations became even higher with Ford's official visit to South Korea. While preparing for his trip to Korea, eight American congressmen requested that Ford make contacts with opposition figures during his trip in order to pressure the South Korean government in the realm of human rights.[24] Ford returned to the United States after reaffirming the defense pledge and stating that there would be no further reduction in the number of US forces in Korea.[25] President Ford's visit was widely publicized in South Korea to the point that it made the top ten news of 1974, and his visit elevated the South Korean government's prestige, which had taken a dive after the reduction of US forces in the Nixon years.

The effect of South Vietnam's communization, however, did not last long. The first problem was the deterioration of South Korea-Japan relations. The kidnapping of Kim Daejung in 1973 and the Mun Segwang incident in 1974 drove South Korea-Japan relations to a low point. President Ford wrote President Park Chung Hee in order to persuade him to prevent the further deterioration of South Korea-Japan relations. The US Embassies in South Korea and Japan also had to work extra hard to normalize relations between the two countries.[26] The United States had to readjust its Northeast Asia policy in case a serious problem arose because of conflict between South Korea and Japan. Perhaps the Park Chung Hee government sought to pressure the United States for its criticisms about human rights problems in South Korea.

While South Korea and Japan reached an agreement that enabled them to maintain their relationship through political means, a series of events in 1976 led to the deterioration of US-South Korea relations. While the South Korean government sought to further emphasize the importance of the Korean security issue through the Axe Murder Incident at Panmunjeom on August 18, 1976, the American public elected Jimmy Carter, who pledged to withdraw American forces stationed abroad, as the thirty-ninth president of the United States. US-South Korea relations further worsened through the aforementioned Koreagate scandal in 1976. After the election of Carter, who emphasized human rights and ethics, the US Congress even formed a special committee for investigation of human rights abuses.

In addition, the illegal activities of the South Korean Embassy in Washington began to be exposed. The South Korean Embassy oversaw the Korea Central Intelligence Agency's illegal inspection against Korean Americans involved in anti-Yusin activities in the United States. It was also involved in the illegal lobbying of American politicians. This fact was revealed by the congressional testimonies of South Korean Embassy personnel as well as the former director of the Korea Central Intelligence Agency Kim Hyeonguk. Bak Dongseon, who played a leading role in the Koreagate scandal, had not left South Korea at the time, and the South Korean government denied his role in the lobbying.[27]

While the Koreagate scandal was settled via a political compromise,[28] the South Korean government could not thereafter actively respond to the Carter administration's policy of withdrawing US forces from Korea, which was one of Carter's presidential election pledges and therefore something he could not easily back away from. While a number of major figures of the Carter administration, including the secretary of state, were against the withdrawal, President Carter strongly pushed for it. He ordered a preparatory plan for the withdrawal immediately after his election in a presidential review memorandum (PRM 13) in which he involved a number of related departments and agencies. On May 5, 1977, the plans for withdrawal were prepared through a presidential directive. Carter's plan entailed an immediate withdrawal of one combat brigade of six thousand men from the Second Infantry Division by 1978. Another brigade as well as all noncombatants of nine thousand men were to be withdrawn from South Korea by the end of June 1980. The remaining forces, the United States Command in Korea, and nuclear weapons were to be completely withdrawn by 1982.[29]

The card Park Chung Hee chose to play at this point was the development of nuclear weapons.[30] Park's logic was that if a problem arose in the security alliance between South Korea and the United States, there was no choice for South Korea but to develop nuclear weapons of its own. While the South Korean government had joined, with the cooperation of President Ford, the Nuclear Non-Proliferation Treaty in 1975,[31] it now sought to secretly develop nuclear weapons.

From the US government's perspective, however, this move amounted to a crossing of the Maginot Line. The United States government could not foresee the consequences of a nuclear South Korea without the ability to control Park Chung Hee. The Park Chung Hee government had already launched a series of attacks against North Korea in the late 1960s. The United States, about to conduct Strategic Arms Limitation Talks (SALT) with the Soviet Union and internationally strengthen the Nuclear Non-Proliferation Treaty, had to stop South Korea from developing nuclear weapons.

Another problem was the clash between the "human rights diplomacy" of the Carter administration with the Yusin system. Carter made it clear that he would pressure the South Korean government in the realm of human rights using all available means. Carter even made it clear that the plan for the withdrawal of US forces from Korea was connected to the Yusin system.[32] While a number of Carter administration officials criticized his human rights diplomacy as endangering the security of the United States and its allies, Carter did not back down from his criticism of the Yusin system's suppression of human rights in South Korea. In conclusion, Carter's decision to pressure the South Korean government through the withdrawal of US forces in Korea also meant that the United States was attempting to intervene in South Korea's internal matters.

(2) Was the United States behind the October 26 Incident?

Observing the sequence of events from the election of Carter to the October 26 Incident (the assassination of Park Chung Hee), it is easy to gain the impression that the United States may have been behind assassination. While absent from official records, rumors claiming that Kim Jaegyu testified that he had American backing did not cease. The question of the possibility of American involvement naturally arises given the conflicts between the Park Chung Hee government and the Carter administration over the issues of human rights and nuclear weapons. The United States government had established plans to remove key South Korean leaders in 1952 and 1963-64 and had intervened through coups d'état many times in the Third World. It is therefore not unreasonable to surmise that the United States could have been behind the assassination of Park Chung Hee.

The developments of 1979, however, took place in a way that leads to a different conclusion as the relationship between Carter and Park Chung Hee stabilized in that year. In particular, Carter's postponing of the plan to withdraw American forces from Korea in February 1972 and Park Chung Hee's abandonment of his plan to develop nuclear weapons, as well as signs of improvement in the realm of human rights in South Korea, served as impetuses for the improvement of relations. The South Korean government publicly presented the US decision to postpone withdrawal due to the South Korean government's efforts. The report that the ambassador to the United States Kim Yongsik strongly fought for the postponement of withdrawal while he was in the United States and the report that an American research institute produced a report that the South Korean government would develop nuclear weapons in case US forces withdrew from Korea are representative examples.[33] However, the decision for postponement came from the Carter's acquiescence to the opinions of US officials who were against the plan in the first place.

The Carter administration's foreign policy therefore assumed a duality in its execution. While it emphasized human rights diplomacy, the Carter administration was also filled with cold warriors. One example is Zbigniew Brzezinski, who had a Polish background and was working in the White House at the time. Similarly, Harold Brown, who carried out the bombing of North Vietnam as secretary of the air force during the Vietnam War, became secretary of defense.[34] Therefore, there existed a conflict within the Carter administration between those who supported human rights diplomacy and those who argued for active intervention in the Third World and a hard-line approach to the Soviet Union. The establishments of anti-American regimes in Nicaragua and Iran in 1979 and the strengthening of Soviet intervention in Afghanistan finally shifted the Carter administration's foreign policy vis-à-vis the Third World to a hard-line position.

Furthermore, a mid-term US congressional election in November 1978 saw a substantial advance of conservative forces in politics, with liberals in the Democratic Party also becoming more conservative in response to changes in the international arena.[35] In particular, they believed that working relationships with the Third World anticommunist regimes did not contradict American liberal policies. Such thought had been expanded by Rostow and Huntington since the 1960s, and they believed that dictatorships in the developing nations could even aid American interests there.

According to Rostow, political democracy may be a luxury for the people of developing nations. As examined in chapter 4 of this book, Rostow argued that the leaders of developing nations should place greater emphasis on building national power through economic growth rather than political democratization, meaning that the hasty application of American-style democracy could be harmful to the Third World. This line of argument became further elaborated in political science through Samuel Huntington and economics through Simon S. Kuznets's work on distribution. Major aspects of the US foreign policy towards the Third World can be summarized as the following:

1. Developing nations desire economic growth more than political democracy. Therefore, a forcing of democratization based on American liberalism can trigger anti-Americanism in the Third World.
2. Such developments are due to historic differences between developed nations, including the United States, and developing nations. These countries typically feature strong nationalism as well as statism. The key, therefore, is to prevent nationalism and statism

from turning into socialism while using them as the engines for economic growth.

3. These countries may develop dictatorships in the process of capitalistic economic development. While such phenomena may not conform to American-style democracy, they may create leadership necessary in generating economic growth in developing nations.

4. Democratic institutions can automatically be attained after attaining economic growth. Disparities in wealth also can change into a more balanced distribution of wealth once a certain level of economic growth is achieved.

The rising power of such views resulted in the weakening of Carter's human rights diplomacy. Eventually the United States government sought a certain compromise with Park Chung Hee in 1979, resulting in the US-South Korea summit talks and the revision of plans for the withdrawal of US forces from Korea. Policy documents from the US State Department expressed this development as the normalization of the US-South Korea relations.[36]

Such a policy on the part of the United States government is evident in the document composed by the US Embassy in Seoul.[37] This document includes a number of important facts. One is that the South Korean government began gradually accepting elements of a democratic order from the latter part of 1978. This did not mean, however, that the South Korean government was introducing a democratic system—instead it signifies that it was becoming more lenient in its handling of dissidents. Second, the attempts of the opposition to express itself as an important political force essentially failed. Despite the inability of the ruling party to obtain a majority in the South Korean National Assembly through the 1978 election, the South Korean government was still able to control the National Assembly.[38]

In conclusion, the US Embassy in Seoul argued that the people of South Korea still felt the need to accept a strong government for historical and cultural reasons and was willing to live within the limitations placed by the Yusin system for the foreseeable future. It also argued that the people of South Korea would resent the United States for any pressure it exerted against the South Korean system. Moreover, it concluded that human rights in South Korea had the potential for gradual improvement over time, and the best thing the United States government could do was to give "friendly" advice. This evaluation on the part of the United States Embassy in Seoul shows the enormous gap between American and Korean understandings of the conditions in South Korea at this time, and, along with similar evaluation on the part of other US agencies, most likely played a part in American support of the new military government during the Seoul Spring.

The US Embassy's evaluation included clear distortions of facts. Popular resentment of the Yusin system was on the rise in 1979 and was already evident in the general election of 1978. The oil shocks and double-price system endangered people's livelihoods. In addition, a series of incidents that amounted to suppression of human rights broke out in early 1979: the Hampyeong Potato Incident, Christian Academy Incident, and the South Korean National Liberation Front Preparatory Commission Incident.

However, a document composed on May 25, 1979 judged that the Yusin government continued to enjoy popular support.[39] The joint statement released as a result of the US-South Korea Summit from June 31, 1979, to July 1, 1979, between Carter and Park Chung Hee minimized issues related to human rights and democracy while focusing on military and economic cooperation between the two countries. While it briefly mentioned human rights, its main focus was the delay or even the abandonment of the plan to withdraw American forces from South Korea. The scene of President Carter jogging with American servicemen in Korea was widely publicized in South Korea through both televisions and newspapers.

The US ambassador to Korea William H. Gleysteen was at the center of this conservative US Korea policy. Considering Ambassador Gleysteen's stance and President Carter's visit, there is almost no chance that the United States was behind the October 26 Incident. The United States government intentionally judged the Yusin system in a highly positive light. Ambassador Gleysteen also reported immediately after the October 26 Incident that, although he had met with Kim Jaegyu prior to the assassination, he never once insinuated that Park Chung Hee was becoming an obstacle to US-South Korea relations. Gleysteen stated as much in a telegram sent on November 19, 1979:

Ambassador Gleysteen in an official meeting with President Park Chung Hee in July 1978. Conservative in policy choices, Ambassador Gleysteen remained in his post in Seoul until August 1981.

I can honestly say that none of us have indicated anything similar to the ending of Park regime or that we somehow condone the removal of President Park to Kim Jaegyu or anyone else. ... I am not crazy enough to bring up delicate issues such as the President Park's political future.

Even so, it is difficult to say that the United States had nothing to do with the fall of the Yusin system. While the South Korean government (1) released eighty-six violators of the emergency measure in a Constitution Day special pardon, (2) permitted Yi Taeyeong, a lawyer and human rights activist, to leave the country, (3) reinstated a number of expelled students to their respective schools, and (4) released another fifty-three violators of the emergency measure in a special National Liberation Day pardon, US-South Korea relations quickly cooled down after President Carter's visit. This was due to the conflict between the two governments over the YH Incident of August 11 and the confirmation of the removal of Kim Young Sam from the post of New Democratic Party chairman. At a meeting between the South Korean ambassador to the United States Kim Yongjik and the assistant secretary of state for East Asian and Pacific affairs Richard Holbrooke on September 11, 1979, Holbrooke notified Kim of the US government's desire that the South Korean government stop intervening in the New Democratic Party's internal affairs. Minister Bak Dongjin met with Assistant Secretary Holbrooke on September 27, 1979, and Holbrooke warned him that the United States government could hinder the South Korean government's loan application to the Asian Development Bank through vetoing it or abstaining from the vote.

The Park Chung Hee government went ahead and banned Kim Young Sam from politics on October 4, 1979. The Carter administration responded with a public complaint and the recall of the American ambassador. After returning to the United States, the US ambassador to Korea met with State Department officials and congressional leaders with Korean interests to discuss future Korea policy.

The US Department of State pressured the South Korean government through indirect methods. On October 9, 1979, the United States ambassador to Japan Michael Mansfield declared in a press interview that South Korea lay outside of the American defense perimeter. While this was not the Department of State's official stance, such a reference to security could destroy US-South Korea relations.[40]

When the Busan-Masan demonstrations broke out, Ambassador Gleysteen met with Park Chung Hee and informed him of the US government's concerns. While Park Chung Hee told Gleysteen that he would not use violence to suppress them, Park eventually declared martial law in Busan and Masan. Thus, US-South Korea relations entered a turbulent period following Carter's visit.

According to US policy papers, the United States government was already considering options for the post-Park Chung Hee era by the middle of 1979.[41] US government officials even discussed this issue with Kim Jaegyu.[42] While the content of the conversation with Kim Jaegyu was limited to how the absence of a designated successor to Park Chung Hee could disrupt South Korean society, there was clearly room for misinterpretation.

However, such facts are not enough to conclude that the United States was behind the assassination of Park Chung Hee. However, one possible scenario based on the available facts is that Kim Jaegyu, acting by himself, wanted to stop the US-South Korea relationship from degenerating irreversibly by killing Park Chung Hee. In other words, it is possible that Kim Jaegyu, through a number of meetings with Ambassador Gleysteen, came to the realization that the existence of Park Chung Hee threatened US-South Korea relations, and consequently, the Republic of Korea (South Korea) itself.

In the document sent by Gleysteen on October 28, 1979, he

suggests that Kim Jaegyu may just be one of many people who believed that Park Chung Hee's hard-line policy threatened South Korea.[43] Might this belief have turned into a conviction for Kim Jaegyu through his meeting with American officials in South Korea? Assumptions can be dangerous in the writing of history, and it is therefore hard to conclude anything about the assassination without sufficient facts. However, this issue, along with the Gwangju Incident, is of central importance to US-South Korea relations.

(3) Pro-Democracy Forces cannot be Trusted

Existing research on US Korea policy and US-South Korea relations during the period between 1979 and 1980 argue for American responsibility in the emergence of a new military government in South Korea and the massacre in Gwangju. Surveying the US policy documents from this period, one can easily see that the United States government went from supporting the restoration of democratic institutions immediately after assassination to supporting the new South Korean military government for the sake of "stability."[44] The United States also played a role in suppressing the "Seoul Spring" by permitting the movement of South Korean military units to put down student protests even before the Gwangju Democratization Movement.[45] The United States government even approved the introduction of South Korean military units into Gwangju to violently crush opposition there.

The reason why there has been considerable attention to the issue of American involvement in Gwangju is that the initial American explanation of the introduction of South Korean military units there turned out to be false. The following is a summary of the initial explanation given by the US Department of State on the issue of American responsibility in the massacre in Gwangju:

> The United States government did not have prior information on the chain of events from October 26th to May 17th. After finding out, we have protested against the mobilization of troops on December 12th and the expansion of martial law on May 17th to General Chun. We also recommended that he use non-military measures in entrance and suppression of Gwangju. Therefore, the United States is not responsible.

In spring of 1980, however, Gleysteen sent the following telegram to the US Department of State:

> 2. ROK Military has advised U.S. Command of Following troop movements for contingency purposes. On May 8 the 13th special forces brigade, now in the combined field army(CFA) area, will be moved to the special warfare center southeast of Seoul for temporary duty. On May 18 the 11th special forces brigade, now in the first Republic of Korea Army(FROKA) area, will he moved to the Kimpo Peninsula and co-located for temporary duty with the first special forces briggade. These two brigades, in total about 2,500 people, are being moved to the Seoul Area to cope with possible student demonstrations.
> 3. U.S. Command also alerted to the possibility that the first ROK Marine division in Pohang might be needed in the Taejon/Pusan Area. First marine division is opcon(operational control) to CFC and U.S. approval would be required for movement. There was been no request for such approval yet, but CINCUNC would agree if asked.[46]

As can be seen in the quote above, the US government was well aware of the movements of South Korean military units for the purpose of suppressing opposition, which it was ready to approve if such request came from the new South Korean military government. Of course, the US ambassador to Korea and the US Department of State expressed their anger toward the new military government for its arrest of students and politicians as well as the expansion of martial law to the rest of the country on May 17, 1980. However, the main reason behind the US government's protest was that the new South Korean military government did not consult or inform the United States prior to its actions.[47]

US intervention was even more clear during the unfolding of the Gwangju Democratization Movement. First, the United States commander John A. Wickham agreed to the new military government's request to declare DEFCON (defense readiness condition) 3 and prepare against a potential invasion from North Korea.[48] When airborne troops alone could not suppress the demonstrators, Wickham approved the introduction of the South Korean Twentieth Army Division into Gwangju at the new military government's request.[49]

When the issue of responsibility for deploying suppression forces into Gwangju came up, Gleysteen repeatedly testified that he delayed the introduction of military forces from May 25 to May 27. The White House, however, already decided not to obstruct the introduction of the Twentieth Army Division by May 22, 1980 for the suppression of opposition. While the United States government urged restraint, it also did not rule out the use of force.

Commander Wickham testified about this issue:

High-ranking South Korean military leaders including the Army Chief of Staff visited the Combined Forces Command and asked for the commanding authority of the 20th division for the purpose of riot suppression drill. We've allowed their request under the condition that heavy armaments such as artillery stay faced against North Korea. ...

Although we have approved the introduction of the 20th division (to Gwangju), such approval was made legally by the South Korean government's request.

Given the stances of the United States government, the US Embassy in Seoul, and the US commander, the South Korean people naturally inquired about American involvement and responsibility, and such issues continue to be one of the most important matters of concern in US-South Korea relations. There was also much criticism against President Ronald Reagan, who invited Chun Doo Hwan to the White House immediately after Chun became the twelfth president of South Korea.

Yi Samseong, a well-known historian of this era, concluded the following regarding the issue of American responsibility:

The reason why the repeat of American demeanor before December 12, 1979 is clearly noticeable is because it gives off the impression that the US decisions at the critical junctures of modern Korean history in the December 12 Incident and the tragedy in Gwangju were premeditated.[50]

However, could the United States government have so easily

approved the new South Korean military government had the prodemocracy activists and the South Korean people themselves acted differently? In June 1987, at the peak of Reagan's hard-line policy, how did the Reagan administration respond to the Chun Doo Hwan government's plan for martial law? How did the Eisenhower administration, which even gave up the plan to reduce the number of South Korean military forces due to the aggressive Soviet foreign policy, react to the April Revolution?

The problem I would like to present here is not the issue of American responsibility, but that of Korean politicians in the opposition. I do not argue that the United States has no responsibility for the killings in Gwangju and the suppression of students and other citizens who fought for democracy in South Korea. What I want to ask is whether or not the opposition politicians themselves are free of blame.

The US policy papers from 1979 to 1980 reveal an interesting perspective on the South Korean opposition and the pro-democracy forces in South Korea. Here are some of the expressions the US agencies used to describe them: "society of garlic and pepper eating combatants" (in a telegram sent by Gleysteen to the Department of State), "a handful of Christian extremist dissidents" (in a telegram sent by Assistant Secretary Holbrooke to Ambassador Gleysteen), "hardbitten confrontationalists in opposition," "supplicants,"[51] and "obstructionists."[52]

The US government and the US Embassy in Seoul at the time had a very negative impression of the South Korean opposition and prodemocracy activists in South Korea. They brushed off the YMCA Wedding Incident, which was instigated by the pro-democracy opposition to speed up the democratization process after the assassination of Park, as being caused by a handful of Christian extremist dissidents. Noting that no influential clergymen participated, the US government judged these Christian extremists as merely provoking South Korean authorities. The fault, therefore, was with the pro-democracy forces.[53]

The members of the US government, of course, cannot be free from the charges of Orientalism in their view of the South Korean opposition at this time. Commander John Wickham, for example, referred to the South Korean opposition politicians as "rats" immediately after the massacre in Gwangju. Such thinking is in line with a foreign news reporter who claimed in the 1950s that establishing democracy in Korea was like a rose growing out of a garbage can.

However, there clearly was a share of responsibility on the part of South Korean opposition politicians. The most noteworthy example can be found in the following document composed by Gleysteen immediately after the October 26 Incident.

> Different factions in South Korea will, for their purposes, attempt to benefit from American influence in Korea. Already several factions have approached me, and I expect additional contacts from military generals, dissidents, and politicians in the opposition.[54]

Gleysteen judged that, despite the valid chance for democracy, the South Korean opposition was solely occupied with grabbing power for themselves:

> They are divided into Kim Young Sam and Kim Dae Jung factions. While the two Kims have publicly stated that they will support each other after doing their best in becoming nominated as the presidential candidate, each of them believe that only he has the legitimate right to become the opposition leader in the first real opportunity to seize power via popular voting. Both of them only want to work with their followers and do not want division of power. Once the presidential candidate, they are highly unlikely to appoint those from the other side to any position of significance. Because of the fierce campaigning within the party, resulting damages may be almost irrecoverable. We are not ruling out the possibility of a split within the opposition.[55]

The quote above sounds like a foretaste of things to come in the South Korean political scene after June 1987. How would the US government agencies on the ground in South Korea judge South Korean opposition politicians who relied on the United States at moments of danger and were only interested in grabbing power for themselves?

Such an understanding is not limited to this period alone.

Politicians who asked the United States to support the opposition at the time of the Busan Incident of 1952, those who fled in fear of Syngman Rhee's suppression at the time the United States government was contemplating removing Rhee from power, those who lined up to meet with the US ambassador to Korea prior to the 1956 presidential election, and those who fled when the May 16 coup d'état broke out all collectively contributed to the American perception of the South Korean opposition.

The US ambassador to Korea Samuel Berger concluded that the opposition's leadership was hopeless at the moment of civilian power transfer in 1963. Berger argued, "If by any outside chance opposition succeeded in presidential and Assembly elections, they would be plagued by internal divisions, and there would be a struggle between civilians and the defeated junta with danger of another coup."[56] Such evaluation was not based on Berger's preference for Park Chung Hee. Berger was well aware of factionalism within the South Korean opposition from the Democratic Party era of 1960–61 and the election of 1963.

Even during the protests against South Korea-Japan normalization, Berger believed that "[o]pposition tactics are to maintain continuous barrage of irresponsible criticism in order capitalize on govt's difficulties and public restlessness in effort bring govt down."[57] Berger's opinion in fact came from speaking to the South Korean politicians who went to the US Embassy at the time of protests and requested that the United States remove Park Chung Hee.

In conclusion, in 1980, the United States judged that the ascension of the opposition could drive South Korean society into a crisis–a crisis that would threaten the two goals of the US Korea policy–establishment of a strong anticommunist regime and the long-term establishment of a democratic system. Of course, the hard-line policies of the Carter and Reagan administrations at the time were the fundamental basis of their recognition of the new South Korean military government. However, their negative perceptions of the South Korean opposition also played an important role.

If this is the case, why did the South Korean opposition receive such a negative evaluation from the United States government? This issue is not unrelated to the post-1990s issue of "democracy after democratization." Why did the pro-democracy forces, who went through many difficulties in capturing state power, make the same mistakes as the dictatorships they fought against?

While the reasons here are numerous, one is the series of crackdowns they experienced during the process of their struggles against the dictatorships. The opposition and pro-democracy forces themselves, who endured every forms of suppression imaginable, entered into a vicious cycle in which they could not trust anyone else. The dictators had engaged in countless instances of manipulation to divide the opposition. The report Kim Jaegyu submitted after the October 26 Incident shows that in addition to the Korea Central Intelligence Agency, the South Korean Office of Presidential Security was also involved in political maneuvering. Therefore, once in power, the South Korean opposition essentially reverted to the cronyism of those who they replaced. Despite their criticism of the dictatorships, however, members of the South Korean opposition were nevertheless influenced by the tarnished legacy of their predecessors.

Another reason for negative American views is the opposition's overreliance on the United States. In fact, the South Korean opposition and prodemocracy forces, due to their own weaknesses, could not effect a regime change without American support. Moreover, the South Korean opposition and some of the pro-democracy forces in South Korea were sometimes even more conservative than their political enemies on issues related to the United States. While this had in part to do with the fact that the roots of South Korean opposition were in the Korean Democratic Party from the days of the US military government in Korea, a more fundamental reason was that the South Korean opposition did not have the capacity to obtain widespread popular support from its people. Unable to come up with ideological and policy goals that could replace that of the dictatorships, the South Korean opposition fought only under the banner of "democratization" and believed that the dictatorships could only be destroyed with American support. The fact that a number of opposition politicians had a history of collaboration with the Japanese also must have weakened them.

This reliance upon the United States may have had to do with the South Korean opposition's experience with the power the United States exercised over Korean society and government over the years. To win the support of the people who were largely concerned with security, politicians had to give off the public impression that they had American support. The experiences of the 1950s and 1960s, when the South Korean government could not function without American aid, must have provided the opposition with a sufficient "learning effect" of the importance of US support. They therefore sought to build a cooperative working relationship with the United States while criticizing the dictatorships that were at times in conflict with Washington.

In conclusion, acts of irresponsibility on the part of the South Korean opposition comprised one reason why the United States opted for a new South Korean military government during the "Seoul Spring." This fact is also evident in the American "selection" of the coup forces over the Democratic Party politicians who irresponsibly fled at the time of the May 16 coup.

CONCLUSION

1. Without a Day of Peace: US-South Korea Relations

Since the establishment of South Korea in 1948, the South Korean people have typically viewed the United States as its closest ally. Following the Korean War, the mutual defense treaty and the stationing of US forces in Korea became tangible guarantees of security for South Korea, which confronted the North Korean regime supported by the giant communist powers of the Soviet Union and China. Therefore, even when South Korea was put into an unfavorable position in its dealings with the United States or forced to acquiesce to an unreasonable demand from Washington, South Koreans typically perceived acceptance of such situations as the means of "repaying" America for the grace and favor it had bestowed.

However, US-South Korea relations were not always smooth. As has been shown throughout this book, a large number of crises and conflicts broke out between the two countries from 1945 to 1980, and have continued after this period to the present day. Even now, points of conflict, such as the relocation of American military bases in South Korea, strategic flexibility of US forces in Korea, the US-South Korea Free Trade Agreement, and solutions to the North Korea nuclear crisis, continue between the United States and South Korea. US-South Korea relations were smooth only during two brief periods: around the year 1965 when South Korea began to deploy troops to Vietnam and in early 1980 when the new South Korean military government became established.

Why was there so much conflict between the United States and

South Korea? International relations obviously involve clashes of interests, entailing discord and contention. However, were not the United States and South Korea allies? Why were there then so many conflicts between them?

So far, I have identified two causes of this contentious relationship. First, the United States, as an "empire," forced its policy upon South Korea against the latter's will. US foreign policy was almost "imperialistic" in its determined will to intervene in the internal matters of so-called developing nations such as South Korea. Of course, such interventionist policies took place in regions that the United States considered to be geopolitically important, including South Korea. While the Korean Peninsula may have meant less to the United States than Japan or China, its location between these two countries, which were pivotal to American foreign policy in the Pacific, made it significant. The ongoing debate in Washington on whether or not to abandon South Korea had more to do with its location between China and Japan than the Korean Peninsula itself. The United States therefore did not give up on South Korea.

US interventions in Korea were most visible through the US forces stationed there. The size and character of US forces in Korea were determined more by American interests than what South Koreans hoped for. In 1947, 1953, 1964, 1970, 1979, 1990, and even to the present time, Washington considered reducing or entirely withdrawing US forces from Korea. While the size and nature of the American forces in Korea have changed over time, the period from July 1949 to June 1950 was the only time since 1945 when US forces were not stationed there. In addition, its headquarters directly intervened in military-related matters in South Korea by retaining control of South Korean military units.

The size of American forces in Korea and the operational control of South Korean military units are closely related and influence policy debate. The outright withdrawal or significant reduction of the size of US forces in Korea would endanger an important rationale for the American operational control of the South Korean military. The ongoing discussion on this issue is closely related to the strategic relocations of US forces abroad. Voices for the return of wartime operational control of South Korean military forces are likely connected to the ongoing transformation of the US forces in

Korea into a "quick reaction force."

US intervention in South Korea took place not only in the military, but in politics, the economy, and society as well. As can be seen in former ambassador Berger's 1966 assertion that the US government should cultivate "alternatives" to the current policymakers in Seoul,[1] the US government actively intervened in South Korean politics. The suppression of the political left and support for right-wing conservatives during the era of the United States Army Military Government in Korea (1945–48), the US plans to remove Syngman Rhee from power, and the US insistence on purging Kim Jongpil are good examples of such interventions. US aid, loans, and trade became methods for economic intervention, and education aid and study abroad support acted in the same way in the social and cultural spheres. Such soft power–based intervention, as opposed to the older methods of imperialism, illustrates the United States' status as a "new empire."

Because of the American commander's control of South Korean military units, a policy of nonintervention could amount to de facto intervention. The circumstances surrounding the May 16 coup are a good example. US commander Carter Magruder gave no orders to the coup forces or the units that sought to suppress the coup. He did not intervene at all. However, the South Korean military units that sought to suppress the coup forces could not move without Magruder's approval, and nonintervention therefore effectively amounted to intervention on behalf of the coup forces. The developments in South Korea from the night of December 12 to the morning of December 13 in 1979 echoed what happened some twenty years ago.

Another cause of contention in US-South Korea relations was poor decision making by the South Korean government. As discussed in this book, the South Korean government responded to US Korea policy in a number of different ways. Actions taken by the South Korean government, such as the Busan Incident of 1952, the unilateral release of anticommunist POWs in 1953, the suggestion of dispatching South Korean troops to Southeast Asia in the late 1950s, the 1963 reversal of the promise to transfer power to a civilian government, the deployment of South Korean troops to Vietnam, the security crisis of the mid-1960s, the declaration of the Yusin system in 1972, the attempt to develop a nuclear weapon in the mid-1970s, and the Koreagate of 1976 are all representative examples of the various ways it responded to US Korea policy.

Such responses on the South Korean government's part, however, resulted in conflict with the United States, leading the US government to seek to prevention of conflict through pressure. Into the 1960s, the United States frequently threatened to reduce or cut off US aid and loans, which the South Korean government could not survive without. Therefore, with a few exceptions, such as the economic development plan and the deployment of troops to Vietnam, the South Korean government had no choice but to give in to US threats.

In the end, the South Korean government's responses produced conflicts in its relationship with the United States. That being the case, it is important to evaluate whether such responses were appropriate or not. Had the South Korean government responded in more appropriate ways, some of the conflict between the United States and South Korea could have been avoided. From Washington's perspective, however, the South Korean government's responses were often inappropriate and were sometimes considered to be acts of brinkmanship. Moreover, the South Korean government sometimes created unnecessary conflicts by crossing over what the United States government considered to be the "Maginot Line." The unilateral release of anticommunist POWs and the deliberate cultivation of security crises are good examples.

Certain researchers have positively evaluated such acts from the perspective of nationalism. However, such responses on the part of the South Korean government often prioritized regime security and did not consider national interest or security at the level of the "nation." The 1953 release of the anticommunist POWs, for example, displayed the will to continue the war that could result in the destruction of the Korean nation. The attempt to develop nuclear weapons in the mid-1970s was not very different. The dispatch of South Korean troops to Vietnam was merely a means of regime survival at the cost of the invaluable lives of young men.[2]

Additionally, the South Korean government's responses often directly opposed the principles of democracy. The Busan Incident of 1952, the 1963 reversal of the promise to transfer power to a civilian government, and the establishment of the Yusin system resulted in significant retreats for human rights and democracy in South Korea. Could we still label such acts as being under the umbrella of democracy?

2. The United States as Myth

Excessive intervention by the United States and inappropriate responses by the South Korean government resulted in contention within the US-South Korea relationship. Despite its status as a world hegemon, however, the United States did not intervene in the affairs of all nations, and other nations do not always respond to American interventions in unsuitable ways. Why then did the US and South Korean governments repeatedly engage in inappropriate interventions and responses?

The fundamental foundation of such conflicts has to do with the fact that the South Korean government (until recently) was not established upon the principles of democracy. While the South Korean state maintained the formality of constitutional democracy, there was no real democratic government in South Korea until the 1990s. While "elections" continued to display that the people of South Korea supported their dictatorial governments, they were often rigged. Even at times when the elections showed the "will" of South Korea's people, that is, popular opinion, it had often been distorted by the powerful state's careful manipulation. The conditions of the late 1950s, the period immediately following the May 16 coup, the time under the Yusin rule, and the era of new military government during the 1980s are all good examples of times when public opinion itself was deliberately molded by the government's domination of the media.

Such rash decisions in the US-South Korea relationship could have been avoided had there been a democratic government in South Korea during the periods under discussion. In other words, had the South Korean people at large been informed of the excesses of American intervention and the inappropriate responses of the South Korean government, it is likely the case that US-South Korea relations could have been more "normal." Under a dictatorial power, however, the United States remained a "myth" in South Korea, a legacy that continues to this day.

Nations with "normal" relationships with the United States often have institutionalized democracy. India, Japan, and the Philippines are good examples. The Philippines, for instance, did not have a "normal" relationship with the United States during the dictatorial rule of Ferdinand Marcos. This is because, generally speaking, the democratic political system entails an additional "cost" in the process of collecting public views. Therefore, authoritarian and fascist governments are sometimes seen as more "efficient" in decision making. A democratic system, however, is a source of enormous power in foreign relations, as it is difficult to intervene against a government that has been established with widespread public consensus. In such a case, "regime security" rests on a foundation made up of democratic institutions and broad support of its people. Governments without public consensus, however, often seek outside sources of regime security. There are many examples of authoritarian and fascist regimes dating from the nineteenth century that sought to attain national unity through external expansion rather than social reform.

Lacking public support and consensus, it is not surprising that the dictatorial governments of South Korea often sought national unity and popular support through radical measures, such as the so-called Marching North Campaign, deployment of troops abroad, manipulation of anti-Japanese sentiment, and the cultivation of regional security crises. In fact, the dictatorial regimes sought legitimization through "security crises" more often than democratic means. Therefore, the "security" of South Korean dictatorial governments often came from the United States, which functioned as the "security umbrella" of South Korea. Such an analysis could also be applied to the case of the North Korean regime, which maintains its grip on power through the crisis generated by its confrontation with the United States. Outside pressures are often utilized as a way of strengthening internal unity. This point leads to the valid questioning of the George W. Bush administration's North Korea policy.

Certain researchers find the source of the "special" nature of US-South Korea relations in the matter of external security. However,

South Korea and Japan are not so different in this regard. Of course, the case of Japan differs from the case of South Korea in that it does not have a standing "military" force of its own. On the other hand, however, the two cases are similar in the sense that they are both under the American security umbrella and US forces are stationed within their national borders. Still, while US-Japan relations have been (relatively) mutually complementary, the US-South Korea relationship has been marred by conflict with unilateral notifications being more frequent than meaningful dialogues.

I want to emphasize here that an alliance with a powerful nation is not the exclusive source of "real" national security. The US interim ambassador Green's statement on the morning of May 16, 1961 in discussing the coup d'état reminds us of the true source of national security.

> Coups invited further coups. I further remarked on effect which success of such coup would have on Korea's international standing and emphasized that Korea's democratic institutions and free-elected government are her greatest assets in confrontation with Communist totalitarianism in North.[3]

There are two types of national security: external and internal. External security has to do with defense from an outside threat, and internal security has to do with preserving social stability through maintaining internal cohesion. The two reinforce each other. While dictatorial regimes seek to maintain internal security through external crisis, democratic governments can obtain internal security through democratic order and public consensus.

The difference between a dictatorial regime and a government based on democratic principles is evident in the discussions surrounding the 1965 normalization of South Korea-Japan relations. The South Korean government at the time desired active American intervention in the negotiations, believing that was the only way to silence the South Korean people's widespread resistance to normalization. The Japanese government, on the other hand, believed that an active American intervention could lead to the failure of normalization. The Japanese government predicted that the overt intrusion of a foreign power into the process of normalization

A photograph of people running away from the American helicopter during the Korean War. Are abnormalities in US-South Korea relations rooted in widespread Korean perceptions of the United States as a myth?

could lead to a widespread backlash in Japanese society.

Here, we can discern another reason for the abnormality of US-South Korea relations–the "myth" of the United States as understood by the people of South Korea, who continue to see this ongoing abnormal relationship as somehow natural. The Korean people began to perceive the United States in a generally positive light in the late nineteenth century, and this "myth" became stronger through liberation in 1945 and the Korean War. The United States was not just another country that South Korea had a diplomatic relationship with. The relationship with the United States was special.

This society-wide perception in South Korea was strengthened through the anticommunist ideology–based domestic policies of the Cold War's context. There is no other country with a history of significant interactions with the United States that continues to display such a lack of anti-American sentiments than South Korea. While criticisms against the United States and its foreign policies are (recently) beginning to take place in South Korea, such a discourse cannot be seen as "genuine" expressions of anti-Americanism. In South Korea, the United States still remains the "beautiful" country to be learned from and modeled after. Criticism against the United States prior to the 1990s was almost considered to be a criminal act similar to that of praising communism.

The Republic of Korea's citizens therefore did not consider the American control of their military forces, one of the primary elements of national sovereignty, as a source of discomfort despite the fact that the Republic of Korea is a sovereign state. In addition, the support of the United States government has long been one of the barometers for the South Korean people for judging the competence of their government. Presidents of South Korea have often visited the United States as an expression of "friendship" between the two countries, and such "friendship" was widely publicized through Korean media outlets.

However, due to the fact that the South Korean military forces' operational control has remained in the hands of the US commander in Korea, South Korea's political sovereignty has been compromised in significant ways. No illegal coups could be effectively suppressed because the American commander's acquiescence was necessary for the timely movement of military units to put them down. Sometimes the US command had more control over the South Korean military establishment than the South Korean government. The US government was able to formulate its Korea policy during the 1952 Busan Incident, the 1953 signing of armistice, and the 1962 coup d'état knowing that the South Korean military was more loyal to it than the South Korean government.

Another important issue is the South Korean vision of US-South Korea relations through a "social Darwinist" lens that remains at the center of its international relations. To put it differently, most South Koreans continue to prioritize obtaining "benefits" in diplomacy in order to survive in what they see as a world where the law of the jungle prevails. This point is evident in the way that the primary focus of South Korean diplomacy has always been on the so-called major powers, including the United States. This perception is also evident in the South Korean stance on deploying troops to Vietnam. Of course, we cannot conduct a survey to examine how people thought some forty years ago. However, the conclusion the US Embassy in Seoul made after several interviews with South Korean officials and intellectuals was that, through its participation in the Vietnam War, South Korea wanted to obtain the kinds of "benefit" Japan had obtained through the Korean War. While other nations generally shied away from participating in the "illegitimate" war in Vietnam, the South Koreans were primarily pursuing "practical benefits" regardless of international criticism of South Korean combat troops as America's "mercenaries."

Controlled and distorted information and education must have influenced the thought of the South Korean people at large. However, South Korea's foreign policy has not changed much and will not change in the future as long as such thinking has widespread currency. Why were the South Korean forces dispatched to Iraq? Why did so many of the voices raised against participation in the Iraq War eventually fall silent? Could this move reflect a society-wide desire to obtain security on the Korean Peninsula as well as business opportunities in the Middle East through the deployment of Korean troops–a thought process similar that of South Korea during the Vietnam War? Are the people of South Korea still chasing after the "myth" that they too can become an "empire" through the dispatching of troops to Iraq?

3. Was There a Learning Effect?

Let us now go back to the fundamental question of this book: how can we define the US-South Korea relationship? Are the United States and South Korea allies? Do US-South Korea relations represent a subordinate relationship between the core and a periphery? Could US-South Korea relations be defined as something between an empire and a puppet state, similar to the relationship between Imperial Japan and Manchukuo? If these examples are not suitable, how about what researchers of international relations often describe as a patron-client relationship? As was mentioned in the introduction, many works of research have been carried out in an attempt to define the US-South Korea relationship by applying a number of theoretical concepts. So far, however, an accurate description of the US-South Korea relations have been difficult to formulate.

In this book, I sought to identify some of the basic premises of the US-South Korea relationship after 1945 through historical analyses. Unfortunately, however, the conclusion I can draw from this book is that developing a catch-all description of US-South Korea relations is not possible. In other words, US-South Korea relations exhibited different characteristics at different eras in history.

Each of the theories listed above represents an era in US-South Korea relations. The US-South Korea relationship at the time of the US military government was like that of an imperial power and a colony. As an organization, the United States Army Military Government in Korea (USAMGIK) was similar to the Japanese colonial government. The US military government sought a deliberate reorganization of the Korean political scene for the sake of American Korea policy through its governing of southern Korea. While this attempt was not entirely successful, it did enable those who were favored by the United States to rise in the political scene because it was believed that they would act in accordance with US Korea policy to seize political power.

The US-South Korea relationship of the 1950s can be best characterized as that of a patron and a client. The South Korean government could not have survived without US aid–all it could do was militarily confront the Communist Bloc under the American security umbrella. South Korea's security was (barely) maintained through the unstable armistice and the mutual security treaty with the United States. The South Korean government placed much of its energy and focus on the exchange rate policy in order to obtain as many dollars as it could from the United States.

The US-South Korea relationship of the 1960s is a classic example of the core-periphery relationship. The core country intervened deeply into the internal affairs of the periphery using the operational control of military forces and loans. The periphery's leadership and economic policy were transformed according to the core's interests. Even in the realm of diplomacy, the normalization of relations between a periphery (South Korea) and a semi-periphery (Japan) was carried out according to the core's interests. While the normalization may have had long-term benefits for both South Korea and Japan, it would have been difficult without US intervention and exhortation. In addition, the periphery nation even dispatched combat troops abroad despite the fact that it had a hard time maintaining its own security.

Furthermore, some of the policies Japan had carried out in Manchukuo before 1945 were reproduced in US Korea policy in the 1960s. In addition to creating a military base, Japan's Manchukuo policy also sought to create a "showcase" to advertise its imperialist policies to the world. Similar to the example of Japan-Manchukuo, the United States also sought to create a "showcase" for the so-called free world on the Korea Peninsula, the frontline of the Cold War.

US-South Korea relations of the 1970s acquired greater complexity than the periods before. In other words, the US-South Korea relationship of the 1970s could no longer be theoretically explained using the abovementioned models. The South Korean government in the 1970s began to display a greater ability to maintain internal control and implement its own policies in the face of American pressure. While these abilities remained limited, an increasing number of US policy papers began to recognize that older forms of pressure against Seoul would not be as effective as they once were.

US-South Korea relations developed while displaying various particularities and characteristics over time. The United States sometimes actively intervened to change the internal landscape of South Korea. In other times it displayed a wait-and-see attitude. While the South Korean government at times displayed a willingness to obey and follow, at other times it actively resisted American intervention.

My conclusion therefore is that US-South Korea relations cannot be easily explained by a single theory or model. I can, however, conclude that the nature of the US-South Korea relationship has changed over time in dynamic ways. US-South Korea relations of the 1950s differ from that of the 1970s, which in turn differ with that of the present. Along with the changes of individual conditions that influence US-South Korea relations, their content has also changed with time. US-South Korea relations from the time when a dictatorial regime was in power in South Korea differ from the time when a democratic government was in power in Seoul. And they should be different.

One other issue I want to mention here is the "learning effect" in US-South Korea relations. I have written of the "learning effect" in analyzing US Korea policy and South Korean government responses. What is striking, however, is that there is hardly a trace of any "learning effect" in the South Korean government's foreign policies.

The US government learned a great deal from its interactions with South Korea. US diplomatic papers often feature historical analyses of US-South Korea interactions from the past, which are then applied to devising future Korea policies. At the time of the June 3 Incident of 1964, the Johnson administration carefully examined US-South Korea relations around the time of the 1961 April Revolution. When the dictatorial power of Park Chung Hee was on the rise in 1968, the US State Department reexamined Plan EVERREADY of 1953, including its shortcomings. In formulating its Korea policy, the Nixon administration of 1969 and 1970 obtained important "learning effects" from US dealings with South Korea over the deployment of South Korean troops to Vietnam several years ago. The negative perception of South Korean opposition held by the US Embassy in Seoul at the time of the Seoul Spring was based on the American understanding of the conservative Korean opposition dating from the 1950s. The Reagan administration found lessons from the nightmare of Gwangju in 1980 when it responded to the Chun Doo Hwan regime's willingness to invoke the garrison act in 1987.

All appointed American ambassadors to South Korea studied the history of US-South Korea relations in detail. The best example of this tendency, as seen in diplomatic papers, is Ambassador William Porter, who served in Korea from 1967 to 1971. Before negotiating with the South Korean government on the matter of deploying South Korean troops to Vietnam, Ambassador Porter carefully examined past negotiations with South Korea. Through this analysis, Ambassador Porter reported to Washington that the negotiations with South Korea would not be easy and that requesting troops from South Korea might not be the best option for the United States.

On the other hand, what sort of a "learning effect" did the South Korean government obtain from past US-South Korea relations? Examining the South Korean government's responses so far, I am doubtful that it learned anything from history. While inappropriate responses to the Moscow Conference of Foreign Ministers and the fission of political forces during the US military government era resulted in the country's division, there were almost no Korean "learning effects" from such experiences. The fragmentation of Korean political forces at the time of the hardening of US Korea policy had harsh consequences. The Democratic Party of South Korea became fragmented as the Kennedy administration strengthened its interventionism vis-à-vis South Korea, and the South Korean president denied responsibility when the United Nations commander urged for the suppression of the coup forces at the time of the May 16 coup.

Despite the history of the American rejection of South Korean offers under the Syngman Rhee administration to dispatch troops to Southeast Asia to prevent the reduction of US forces in Korea, the Park Chung Hee government later repeated the same offer. Of course, given the new international developments surrounding Vietnam, the US government accepted it. However, the offer to deploy troops arose from the South Korean resolve to escape from its own crisis instead of US desperation, and therefore negatively affected negotiations, preventing the South Korean government from obtaining what it ultimately wanted.

The South Korean government did not learn from this history that overly active responses can result in negative consequences. The South Korean plan to develop a nuclear weapon in the mid-1970s, like the security crisis card played by the Park Chung Hee regime in the late 1960s, went directly against US Korea policy as well as American world policy. The suppression of human rights under the Yusin system also ignored the lessons from the Busan Incident of 1952. Did the South Korean government even try to learn from past US-South Korea relations? If it did, were there any misunderstandings or misinterpretations?

The problem of "learning effect" persists to this day. An article published by a major newspaper a few years ago displays this tendency well. Pointing out that it has been forty years since the assassination of President John F. Kennedy, this article positively evaluated his legacy. Of course, Kennedy promoted a "frontier" spirit and sought to expand American values and principles of democracy abroad. The article, however, does not mention the "learning effects" from the Kennedy administration years. The Kennedy administration deeply intervened in the policies of developing nations, and it is not an exaggeration to say that it essentially began American involvement in Vietnam. It was Kennedy who ordered the Bay of Pigs Invasion to overthrow Fidel Castro. The theoretical justification to legitimize US support for dictatorial regimes abroad was also established during the Kennedy years, and it was also during his administration that US interventionism vis-à-vis South Korea reached its apex.

Leaving aside judgments from the US point of view, the Kennedy administration's foreign policy was not something South Korea should welcome or use as a model for its own. What would happen if the South Korean government of today followed Kennedy's precedent in formulating its foreign policy vis-à-vis the Third World? While the ultimate results may vary, such policy most likely would not result in the creation of a positive image of South Korea in the Third World.

How about the issue of South Korean participation in the Iraq War? Would not South Korean participation be a revelation that the South Korean government learned little from the experience of participating in the Vietnam War? South Korea certainly did gain from its participation in the Vietnam War. However, it ultimately did not gain what it should have–the normalization of US-South Korea relations. Despite its deployment of the third largest force to Iraq, the US president has not thanked the South Korean government as much as he thanked Japan, despite its much smaller contribution.

Let us take a look at US-North Korea relations. Was South Korea able to save itself from destruction by dispatching forces to Iraq? One could make the argument that the deployment of South Korean troops to Iraq may have prevented another war from breaking out on the Korean Peninsula. US-North Korea relations, however, still have not improved, and there is no tangible signs that they will in the future. Both the United States and North Korean governments are using, if not enjoying, the conflicts between them.

A security crisis in Northeast Asia could be an important legitimization for the United States in its quest to continue box china in. Given its failed economy, the North Korean regime has found that ongoing tension with the United States is useful in maintaining internal security and cohesion. The South Korean government's complacent decision to obtain "security" on the Korean Peninsula in return for dispatching troops to Iraq can therefore be read as a result of not studying past US-South Korea interactions during the time of the Vietnam War. In other words, the South Korean government's belief that it could gain something through participation in the Iraq War as it did for the Vietnam War stems from historical ignorance.

Lastly, I want to emphasize that the grasp of "social Darwinist" thought over South Korean society's understanding of international relations should be broken. The law of the jungle continues to play a central role in shaping diplomacy in South Korea to this day. Our diplomacy has always prioritized the so-called great powers. Given the newly found status of South Korea, however, the vision of our diplomacy should also expand. We also should recognize that such thought will produce negative consequences in our dealings with the Third World, as Rostow repeatedly emphasized would happen on account of the coercive posture of the United States in the Third World.

South Korean foreign policy is largely based on the still-prevalent "social Darwinist" thought of its people. The South Korean people will not be able to pully criticize the Japanese colonization of Korea as long as they continue to subscribe to such thought. Certain segments of Japanese society argue that Japan had to colonize Korea in order to escape its own colonization, and, as a result, Korea eventually became more developed than the Joseon dynasty. If the South Korean people view international relations from the perspective of the law of the jungle, such Japanese claims are certainly not wrong. South Korea, all the while criticizing Japan, has been assuming the same perspective vis-à-vis the less developed countries of the world.

Tangible benefits are important in international relations.

However, morals and humanity's universal values–peace and human rights–are more important than short-term benefits. While "social Darwinist" thought may be useful in obtaining immediate gains, universal values may prove to be more beneficial in the long run. This may be the most important "learning effect" of US-South Korea relations of the twentieth century.

NOTES

Introdution

1) "Letter from the Ambassador of Korea (Brown) to the Assistant Secretary of State for Far Eastern Affairs (Bundy)," August 26, 1966, in *Foreign Relations of the United States, 1964–1968* (hereafter *FRUS*), ed. David S. Patterson, vol. 29, part 1, *Korea*, ed. Karen L. Gatz (Washington, DC: Government Printing Office, 2000), document no. 84.

2) "Memorandum of Conversation," December 19, 1966, *FRUS, 1964–1968*, vol. 29, part 1, document no. 106.

3) Choe Sangyong, *Migunjeong gwa Hanguk minjokjuui* (Seoul: Nanam, 1988).

4) Bruce Cumings, *The Origins of the Korean War*, vol. 1, *Liberation and the Emergence of Separate Regimes, 1945–1947* (Princeton, NJ: Princeton University Press, 1981).

5) Bruce Cumings, "The Origins and Development of the Northeast Asian Political Economy: Industrial Sectors, Product Cycles and Political Consequences," *International Organization* 38, no. 1, 1984.

6) Park Tae Gyun, "1945~1946 nyeon Migunjeong ui jeongchi seryeok jaepyeon gyehoek gwa Namhan jeongchi gudo ui·byeonhwa," *Hanguksa yeongu* 74 (1991): 109–60; Jeong Byeongjun, "1946~1947 nyeon jwau hapjak undong ui jeongae gwajeong gwa seonggyeok byeonhwa," *Hanguksaron* 29 (1993): 249–305; Do Jinsun, *Hanguk minjokjuui wa nambuk gwangye: Yi Seungman, Kim Gu sidae ui jeongchisa* (Seoul: Seoul Daehakgyo Chulpanbu, 1997); Jeong Yonguk, *Haebang jeonhu Miguk ui dae Han jeongchaek: Gwado jeongbu gusang gwa jungganpa jeongchaek eul jungsim euro* (Seoul: Seoul Daehakgyo Chulpanbu, 2003).

7) Hong Seokryul, "Hanguk jeonjaeng jikhu Miguk ui Yi Seungman jegeo gyehoek," *Yeoksa bipyeong* (Autumn 1994): 138–69; Park Tae Gyun, "1956~1964 nyeon Hanguk gyeongje gaebal gyehoek ui seongnip gwajeong: gyeongje gaeballon ui hwaksan gwa Miguk ui dae Han jeongchaek byeonhwa reul jungsim euro" (PhD diss., Seoul Daehakgyo, 2000); Yi Cheolsun, "Yi Seungman jeonggwongi Miguk ui dae Han jeongchaek yeongu, 1948~1960" (PhD diss., Seoul Daehakgyo, 2000); Jeong Iljun,

"Miguk ui dae Han jeongchaek byeonhwa wa Hanguk baljeon gukga ui hyeongseong, 1953~1968" (PhD diss., Seoul Daehakgyo, 2000); Sin Ukhui, "Gihoe eseo gyochak sangtaero – Detangteu sigi Han-Mi gwangye wa Hanbando ui gukje jeongchi," *Hanguk jeongchi oegyosa nonchong* 26, no. 2 (2005): 253–85.

8) Yi Samseong, *Hyeondae Miguk oegyo wa gukje jeongchi* (Seoul: Hangilsa, 1994).

9) The most notable example is Yi Jongwon (Rī Jonwon), *Higashi Ajia reisen to Kan-Bei-Nichi kankei* (Tokyo: Tokyo Daigaku Shuppankai, 1996).

10) Victor D. Cha, *Alignment despite Antagonism: The US-Korea-Japan Security Triangle* (Stanford, CA: Stanford University Press, 2000).

11) Ibid., 186–89.

12) This book was published in 2006 in South Korea.

Chapter One

1) Kim Ilyeong, *Geonguk gwa buguk: Hanguk hyeondae jeongchisa gangui* (Seoul: Saenggak ui namu, 2005).

2) Arthur J. Brown, *The Mastery of the Far East: The Story of Korea's Transformation and Japan's Rise to Supremacy in the Orient* (New York: Charles Scribner's Sons, 1919), 471.

3) Bak Jeongyang, "Miguk jeongwon daesin huihwanhu ipsi yeonseol," in *Bak Jeongyang jeonjip*, ed. Hangukhak Munheon Yeonguso (Seoul: Asea Munhwasa, 1984), 6:page numbers.

4) *Gojong sillok*, vol. 26, July 24, 1891.

5) Han Cheolho, "Chodae ju Mi jeongwongongsa Bak Jeongyang ui Migukgwan – *Misok seubyu* (1888) reul jungsim euro," *Hanguk hakbo* 18 (1992): 1053–91.

6) Bruce Cumings, *Korea's Place in the Sun: A Modern History* (New York: W.W. Norton, 1997), 129.

7) Homer B. Hulbert, *The Passing of Korea* (New York: Doubleday, Page, 1906), 9.

8) Brown, *The Mastery of the Far East*, 46.

9) "United States Policy regarding Korea (Part 2), 1941–45," 611.95/5/150, May 1950.

10) "Roosevelt-Stalin Meeting," February 8, 1945, *FRUS*, vol. 5, *The Conferences of Malta and Yalta, 1945*, 770.

11) "Benninghoff to Secretary of State," September 15, 1945, *FRUS: Diplomatic Papers, 1945*, vol. 11, *British Commonwealth, the Far East*, 1049–53.

12) Song Namheon, *Haebang 3 nyeonsa* (Seoul: Kkachi, 1985), 1:81–82.

13) "The Assistant Secretary of War (McCloy) to the Under Secretary of State (Acheson)," November 13, 1945, *FRUS, 1945*, 6:1123.

14) "The Acting Political Adviser in Korea (Langdon) to the Secretary of State," November 20, 1945, *FRUS, 1945*, 6:1130–31.

15) "The Political Adviser in Korea (Benninghoff) to the Secretary of State," September 15, 1945, *FRUS, 1945*, 6:1053.

16) Jeong Byeongjun, "Haebang jikhu Yi Seungman ui gwiguk gwa Donggyeong hoehap," in *Hanguk minjok undongsa yeongu*, ed. Usong Jo Donggeol Seonsaeng Jeongnyeon Ginyeom Nonchong Ganhaeng Wiwonhoe (Seoul: Nanam, 1997).

17) "The Acting Political Adviser in Japan (Atcheson) to the Secretary of State," October 15, 1945, *FRUS, 1945*, 6:1091–92.

18) "The Acting Political Adviser in Korea (Langdon) to the Secretary of State," November 20, 1945, *FRUS, 1945*, 6:1130.

19) Jeong Byeongjun, "Ju Han Migunjeong ui 'Imsi Hanguk Haengjeongbu' surip gusang gwa dongnip chokseong jungang hyeobuihoe," *Yeoksa wa hyeonsil* 19 (1996): 135–74.

20) Jeong Byeongjun, "Yi Seungman ui dongnip noseon gwa jeongbu surip undong" (PhD diss., Seoul Daehakgyo, 2001), 185–86.

21) "The Charge in the Soviet Union (Kennan) to the Secretary of State," January 25, 1945, *FRUS, 1946*, vol. 8, *The Far East*, 617–18.

22) Park Tae Gyun, *Hanguk jeonjaeng–Kkeunnaji aneun jeonjaeng, kkeunnaya hal jeonjaeng* (Seoul: Chaek gwa Hamkke, 2005), 86–92.

23) Park Tae Gyun, *Hyeondaesa reul bego sseureojin geoindeul: Song Jinu, Yeo Unhyeong, Jang Deoksu, Kim Gu* (Seoul: Jiseongsa, 1994).

24) "Memorandum of Conversation with Major General A.V. Arnold," October 9, 1946, *FRUS, 1947*, vol. 7, *The Far East, China*, 743.

25) "SWNCC 176/18," January 28, 1948.

26) Foreign Affairs House of Representatives, June 6, 1946, 13.

27) Park Tae Gyun, chap. 3 of *Jo Bongam yeongu* (Seoul: Changjak gwa Bipyeongsa, 1995).

28) Park Tae Gyun, chap. three of *Hyeondaesa reul bego sseureojin geoindeul*.

Chapter Two

1) John Lewis Gaddis, chaps. 2 and 3 in *Strategies of Containment: A Critical Appraisal of Postwar American National Security Policy* (Oxford: Oxford University Press, 1982).

2) "The United States Assistance to Other Countries from the Standpoint of National Security," JCS 1769-1, April 29, 1947, in *Containment: Documents on American Policy and Strategy, 1945–1950*, ed. Thomas H. Etzold and John Lewis Gaddis (New York: Columbia University Press, 1978), 71–84.

3) SWNCC was created in 1947 to coordinate American foreign policy. As the US Air Force did not exist at the time, the Army, Navy, and Department of State worked together to coordinate US foreign policy. With the founding of the Air Force in 1948,

its name was changed to the State–Army–Navy–Air Force Coordinating Committee (SANACC). It was later expanded to the National Security Council (NSC) in 1948. The CIA, Department of Treasury, and Department of Commerce often participated in NSC meetings, and other executive departments also joined in as needed. The post-1945 US policy papers with the SWNCC, SANACC, and NSC headers refer to policy papers that went through a coordination between these departments. The number added on the document after a slash (/1, /2) refer to the number of editing.

4) Bruce Cumings, *The Origins of the Korean War*, vol. 2, *The Roaring of the Cataract, 1947–1950* (Seoul: Yeoksa bipyeongsa, 2002), 54–57, 61.

5) "Report by the National Security Council on the Position of the United States with respect to Korea," April 2, 1948, *FRUS, 1948*, vol. 6, *The Far East and Australasia*, 1164–69.

6) Ibid.

7) "Oral History Interviews with John J. Muccio," by Jerry N. Hess, Harry S. Truman Library & Museum, February 10 and 18, 1971, 26, http://www.trumanlibrary.org/oralhist/muccio1.htm.

8) "740.0019 Control (Korea)/5-0148," Bunce to Edwin Martin, in *Daehan Minguksa jaryojip*, vol. 25, ed. Guksa Pyeonchan Wiwonhoe (Gwacheon, Gyeonggi, South Korea: Guksa Pyeonchan Wiwonhoe, 1995), page number(s).

9) "Memorandum by President Truman to the Secretary of State," August 25, 1948, *FRUS, 1948*, 6:1288–89.

10) "Memorandum by the Assistant Secretary of State for Occupied Areas (Saltzman): Future Economic Assistance to Korea," September 7, 1948, *FRUS, 1948*, 6:1292–98; "Marshall to Hoffman," September 17, 1948, *FRUS, 1948*, 6:1303–5.

11) Harry Bayard Price, *The Marshall Plan and Its Meaning* (Ithaca, NY: Cornell University Press, 1955), 184; Robert A. Packenham, *Liberal America and the Third World: Political Development Ideas in Foreign Aid and Social Science* (Princeton, NJ: Princeton University Press, 1973), 33–35.

12) *Korean Aid: Hearings Before the Committee on Foreign Affairs, House of Representatives: Eighty-First Congress, First Session, on H.R. 5330, a Bill to Promote World Peace and the General Welfare, National Interest, and Foreign Policy of the United States by Providing Aid to the Republic of Korea*, 81st Cong. 2 (1949) (*Foreign Affairs, House of Representatives* hereafter).

13) *Foreign Affairs, House of Representatives*, 7–10.

14) "Gyeongje wonjo wa saneop geonseolchaek," *Jubo* 58, May 11, 1950.

15) CIA, "Prospects for Survival of the Republic of Korea," ORE 44-48, October 28, 1948, in "Burok C: Hanguk ui gingeup gyeongje munje," *Haebang jeonhu Miguk ui dae Han jeongchaeksa jaryojip*, ed. Jeong Yonguk and Yi Gilsang (Seoul: Darakbang, 1996), 58–73.

16) *Foreign Affairs, House of Representatives*, 71.

17) *Foreign Affairs, House of Representatives*, 23; Gukhoe Doseogwan Ipbeob

Josaguk, ed., *Gukje Yeonhap Hanguk Wiwondan bogoseo 1949 (A/936)* (Seoul: Daehan Minguk Gukhoe Doseogwan, 1965), 64–65.

18) Korean translation.

19) "Memorandum on Economic Condition in Korea," 895.50/2-2846, February 28, 1946, General Records of the Department of State, Record Group (RG hereafter), National Archives and Records Administration (NARA hereafter); "Special Interdependent Committee Memo," February 25, 1947, *FRUS, 1947*, vol. 6, *The Far East*, 609–18; no title, Bunce to Martin, 895.00/2-1247, February 12, 1947, General Records of the Department of State, RG 59, Decimal File 1945–49, NARA; "The Acting Secretary of State to the Secretary of War (Patterson)," March 28, 1947, *FRUS, 1947*, 6:621–23; "Memorandum by the Assistant Secretary of State (Hilldring) to the Secretary of State," August 6, 1947, *FRUS, 1947*, 6:742–43.

20) Bruce Cumings, "The Origins and Development of the Northeast Asian Political Economy," 7.

21) *Foreign Affairs, House of Representatives*, 13. Paul Hoffman argued that South Korea was a core outpost for democracy (see page 10).

22) Robert A. Packenham, *Liberal America*, 33–34 and 43–49. US ambassador to Korea Muccio later recalled that the ECA aid was carried out through "point 4." "Oral History," by Jerry N. Hess, 21.

23) *Foreign Affairs, House of Representatives*, 12, 80, 99–100.

24) "740.0019 Control (KOREA)/2-2048," Whitman to Pearson, in *Daehan Minguksa jaryojip*, 24:page number(s); "The Special Representative in Korea (Muccio) to the Secretary of State (Acheson)," November 12, 1948, *FRUS, 1948*, 6:1325–27; "The Special Representative in Korea (Muccio) to the Secretary of State (Acheson)," January 27, 1949, *FRUS, 1949*, vol. 7, *The Far East and Australasia*, 947–52.

25) CIA, "Prospects for Survival of the Republic of Korea," in *Haebang jeonhu*, ed. Jeong Yonguk and Yi Gilsang, 58–73.

26) "Jungang Jeongbobu bimangnok," June 19, 1950, in *Hanbando ginjang gwa Miguk: 25 nyeon jeon gwa oneul*, ed. and trans. Seo Donggu (Seoul: Daehan Gongnonsa, 1977), 134–36.

27) W. D. Reeve, *The Republic of Korea: A Political and Economic Study* (London: Oxford University Press, 1963), 106.

28) Paul Hoffman, "Recovery," in *Foreign Affairs, House of Representatives*, 10 and 15.

29) Harry S. Truman, Public Papers (1949), 546–47.

30) "Gyeongje wonjo wa saneop geonseolchaek," *Jubo* 58, May 11, 1950.

31) The ECA proposal was rejected by one vote in the US House of Representatives on January 19, 1950. *Chosun ilbo*, January 22, 1950, and January 23, 1950.

32) James E. Webb, "Implementation of NSC 8/2 during the Period from August 1, 1949 through December 31, 1949," NSC Progress Report 3, February 10, 1950, in *Hanguk jeonjaeng jaryo cheongseo*, vol. 1, *Mi Gukga Anjeon Bojang Hoeui munseo /*

Documents of the National Security Council: Korea (1948–1950), ed. Gukbang Gunsa Yeonguso (Seoul: Gukbang Gunsa Yeonguso, 1996).

33) For the plan for fiscal year 1951, see Division of Historical Policy Research, Office of Public Affairs, Department of State, "United States Policy Regarding Korea: Part 3, December 1945–June 1950," Research Project No. 252, December 1951, in *Miguk ui dae Han jeongchaek, 1934–1950*, ed. Hallimdae Asia Munhwa Yeonguso (Chuncheon, Gangwon, South Korea: Hallym University Press, 1987), 42–48.

34) Yi Jongwon, *Nihon to shokuminchi 8: Ajia no reisen to datsushokuminchika* (Tokyo: Iwanami Shoten, 1993), 8–9.

35) Cumings understood that the Japan-centered regional strategy was established around the time of NSC-48. Considering the content of NSC-48/2, however, such understanding needs to be revised. NSC-48/2 argues that a Japan-centered strategy should be considered after the peace treaty.

36) Yi Jongwon, 11–12.

37) US Senate Committee on Foreign Relations, *Economic Assistance to China and Korea 1949–1950* (New York: Garland Publishing, 1979), 159–60.

38) Yi Jongwon, 27–28.

39) Ibid., 29–30.

40) "The Ambassador in Korea (Muccio) to the Secretary of State," January 18, 1950, *FRUS, 1950*, vol. 7, *Korea*, 8–11; John Merrill (Jon Meril), "Hanguk ui naeran 1948~1950–Hanguk jeonjaeng ui gukjijeok baegyeong," in *Hanguk jeonjaeng gwa Han-Mi gwangye 1943~1953*, by Bruce Cumings (Beuruseu Keomingseu) et al., trans. Bak Uigyeong (Seoul: Cheongsa, 1987), 192.

41) *Jubo* 49, March 9, 1950.

42) A. I. Bloomfield and J. P. Jensen, *Banking Reform in South Korea* (New York: Federal Reserve Bank of New York, March 1951).

43) Gukhoe Doseogwan Ipbeob Josaguk, ed., *Gukje Yeonhap Hanguk Wiwondan bogoseo 1949–1950* (Seoul: Gukhoe Doseogwan Ipbeob Josaguk, 1965), 286–87.

44) Division of Historical Policy Research, Office of Public Affairs, Department of State, "United States Policy Regarding Korea: Part 3, December 1945–June 1950," in *Miguk ui dae Han jeongchaek, 1934–1950*, ed. Hallimdae Asia Munhwa Yeonguso, 42–48.

45) "Daechung jageum ui sayong gyeoljeong–minguk bongni reul wihaya(ginyo saeob e yuchul)," *Jubo* 61, May 25, 1950.

46) Bank of Korea, *Josa wolbo*, September 1954, 55.

Chapter Three

1) "Conversation between General of the Army MacArthur and Mr. George F. Kennan," March 5, 1948, *FRUS, 1948*, 6:699–706.

2) "Strategic Evaluation of the United States Security Needs in Japan: NSC 49," June 15, 1949, in *Containment: Documents on American Policy and Strategy, 1945–1950*, ed. Etzold and Gaddis, 231–33.

3) Bruce Cumings, *The Origins of the Korean War*, vol. 2, *The Roaring of the Cataract, 1947–1950* (Princeton, NJ: Princeton University Press, 1990), 46.

4) Ibid., 82–97.

5) "A Report to the President Pursuant to the President's Directive of January 31, 1950," April 7, 1950, *FRUS, 1950*, vol. 1, *National Security Affairs, Foreign Economic Policy*, 252.

6) Ibid., 282.

7) Ibid., 258–59.

8) Ibid., 258.

9) Ibid., 258–59.

10) Todd G.Buchholz, chaps. 9 and 10 in *New Ideas from Dead Economists: An Introduction to Modern Economic Thought* (New York: Plume, 1989).

11) "The Joint Chiefs of Staff to the Commander in Chief Far East (Clark)," June 25, 1952, *FRUS, 1952–1954*, vol. 15, *Korea*, 358–60.

12) "The Commander in Chief, United Nations Command (Clark) to the Joint Chiefs of Staff," July 5, 1952, *FRUS, 1952–1954*, 15:377–79.

13) "The Ambassador in Korea (Muccio) to the Assistant Secretary of State for Far Eastern Affairs (Allison)," February 15, 1952, *FRUS, 1952–1954*, 15:50–52.

14) "The Charge in Korea (Lightner) to the Department of State," May 27, 1952, *FRUS, 1952–1954*, 15:252–56.

15) "Paper Submitted by the Commanding General of the United States Eighth Army (Taylor)," May 4, 1953, *FRUS, 1952–1954*, 15:965–68.

16) "Memorandum of Conversation, by the Assistant Secretary of State for Far Eastern Affairs (Robertson)," *FRUS, 1952–1954*, 15:933–35.

17) "The Ambassador in Korea (Griggs) to the Department of State," April 26, 1953, *FRUS, 1952–1954*, 15:938–40.

18) "The Ambassador in Korea (Briggs) to the Department of State," May 25, 1953, *FRUS, 1952–1954*, 15:1100–1102.

19) Hong Seokryul, "Hanguk jeonjaeng jikhu Miguk ui Yi Seungman jegeo gyehoek," 153.

20) "Telegram: The Ambassador in Korea (Briggs) to the Department of State," April 14, 1953, *FRUS, 1952–1954*, 15:906.

21) "Memorandum of Conversation, by the Director of the Office of Northeast Asian Affairs (Young)," April 8, 1953, *FRUS, 1952–1954*, 15:898–99.

22) "The Chief of Staff, United States Army (Collins) to the Commander in Chief, Far East (Clark): South Korean Attitude toward Armistice," May 29, 1953, *FRUS, 1952–1954*, 15:1119–23.

23) "Letter to the Ambassador in Korea (Briggs) to the Department of State," June 7,

1953, *FRUS, 1952–1954*, 15;1148.

24) "A Letter of the Secretary of State to the President of the Republic of Korea (Rhee)," June 22, 1953, *FRUS, 1952–1954*, 15:1238–40.

25) Hong Seokryul, "Hanguk jeonjaeng jikhu Miguk ui Yi Seungman jegeo gyehoek," 159–67.

26) "Memorandum of the Substance of Discussion at a Department of State–Joint Chiefs of Staff Meeting," July 3, 1953, *FRUS, 1952–1954*, 15:1318.

27) "The Commander in Chief, United Nations Command (Hull) to the Chief of Staff, United States Army (Ridgeway)," *FRUS, 1952–1954*, 15:1913.

28) "Memorandum by the Joint Chiefs of Staff to the Secretary of Defense (Wilson)," *FRUS, 1952–1954*, 15:1932–33.

29) Gang Wonyong, "Yi Seungman, Jo Bongam sai eseo yangdari geolchin Miguk," interview by Park Tae Gyun, *Sindonga*, January 2004, 502–553.

30) "Organization and Development of the Democratic Party," 795B. 00/2-1356, Feb 13, 1956, General Records of the Department of State, RG 59, Decimal File, 1955–59, NARA.

31) Park Tae Gyun, *Hanguk jeonjaeng: Kkeunnaji aneun jeonjaeng, kkeunnaya hal jeonjaeng*, 304–11.

32) "The Chief of the United Command Mission to Korea (Meyer) to the Secretary of State," May 24, 1952, *FRUS, 1952–1954*, 15:238–42.

33) Kim Yeonsu et al., *Jaegye hoego*, vol. 7, *Yeokdae gyeongje bucheo janggwan*, 389–90.

34) Steven Hugh Lee, "The Political Economy of US-ROK Relations, 1954–1960," Paper prepared for presentation at the international conference "Toward an Industrial Society in Korea," Centre for Korean Research, University of British Columbia, 1996, 13–15, 24–32.

35) Yi Wondeok, *Han-Il gwageosa cheori ui wonjeom: Ilbon ui jeonhu cheori oegyo wa Han-Il hoedam* (Seoul: Seoul Daehakgyo Chulpanbu, 1996), 84–89; Park Tae Gyun, "Han-Il hoedam sigi cheonggugwon munje ui giwon gwa Miguk ui yeokhal," *Hanguksa yeongu* 131 (2005): 37–47.

36) "Letter from the Assistant Secretary of State for Far Eastern Affairs (Robertson) to the Assistant Secretary of Defense for International Security Affairs (Sprague)," July 8, 1958, *FRUS, 1958–1960*, vol. 18, *Japan, Korea*, 424.

37) "Telegram from the Assistant Secretary of Defense for International Affairs (Sprague) to the Commander in Chief, United Nations Command (Decker)," December 11, 1957, *FRUS, 1958–1960*, 18:525–27.

38) While Syngman Rhee initially argued against the reduction of the South Korean military, the US Department of Defense convinced Rhee to reduce the number to around 630,000 men by promising him M-47 tanks, 120-millimeter AAA guns, M-33D flamethrowers, and tractor engines. The US Department of Defense soon after sent a congratulatory telegram to UN Commander Decker. "Telegram from the Department of

Defense to the Commander in Chief, United Nations Command (Decker)," March 28, 1958, *FRUS, 1958–1960*, 18:449–51.

39) "Letter from the Assistant Secretary of Defense for International Security Affairs (Sprague) to the Assistant Secretary of State for Far Eastern Affairs (Robertson)," January 21, 1958, *FRUS, 1958–1960*, 18:431.

40) *Chosun ilbo*, January 28, 1958.

41) "Memorandum by the Joint Chiefs of Staff to the Secretary of Defense," June 11, 1954, *FRUS, 1952–1954*, 15:1806–7.

42) "The Ambassador in Korea (Briggs) to the Department of State," June 23, 1954, *FRUS, 1952–1954*, 15:1813–14.

43) "Security of State to the Embassy in Korea," November 8, 1954, *FRUS, 1952–1954*, 15:1910–11.

44) *Chosun ilbo*, May 26, 1954.

45) *Chosun ilbo*, August 13, 1955.

46) *Chosun ilbo*, November 15, 1955.

47) *Chosun ilbo*, August 17, 1955; *Chosun ilbo*, August 31, 1955.

48) *Chosun ilbo*, August 30, 1955.

49) "United States Summary Minutes of the Fourth Meeting of the United States–Republic of Korea Talks," July 30, 1954, *FRUS, 1952–1954*, 15:1857.

50) "Draft Statement of Policy on U.S. Objectives and on Courses of Action in Korea (National Security Council Report, NSC 5514)," February 25, 1955, *FRUS, 1955–1957*, vol. 23, *Japan, Korea*, 44–48.

51) "Memorandum of a Conversation, Department of State," April 7, 1955, *FRUS, 1955–1957*, 23:64.

52) "Telegram from the Department of State to the Embassy in Sweden," May 1, 1956, *FRUS, 1955–1957*, 23:255.

53) "Memorandum of a Conversation, Department of State," May 4, 1956, *FRUS, 1955–1957*, 23:257–62.

54) *FRUS, 1955–1957*, 23:274n4.

55) *Chosun ilbo*, September 7, 1955. There was an incident in which the Polish representatives died in an airplane accident prior to the withdrawal of inspectors. Three Polish representatives heading back to Panmunjeom for change of personnel via a US military plane all died in an accident on November 7, 1955. *Chosun ilbo*, November 9, 1955.

56) *Chosun ilbo*, September 7, 1955.

57) *FRUS, 1955–1957*, 23:15n3.

58) "Telegram from the Department of the Army to the Commander in Chief, United Nations Command (Hull)," February 5, 1955, *FRUS, 1955–1957*, 23:27.

59) "Memorandum from the Deputy Assistant Secretary of State for Far Eastern Affairs (Sebald) to the Deputy Under Secretary of State for Political Affairs (Murphy)," February 23, 1955, *FRUS, 1955–1957*, 23:38–39.

60) "Memorandum of Discussion at the 240th Meeting of the National Security Council," March 10, 1955, *FRUS, 1955–1957*, 23:56–58.

61) Ibid., 68–71.

62) "Memorandum of Conversation," June 3, 1955, *FRUS, 1955–1957*, 23:111–12.

63) "Memorandum of Discussion at the 248th Meeting of the National Security Council," May 12, 1955, *FRUS, 1955–1957*, 23:92–94.

64) "Record of a Meeting," January 18, 1957, *FRUS, 1955–1957*, 23:387–89.

65) "Memorandum of a Conversation," June 18, 1955, *FRUS, 1955–1957*, 23:114–16.

66) *FRUS, 1955–1957*, 23:126n4. Ironically, the introduction of MiGs into North Korea became known because the MiGs were part of a sortie in response to US reconnaissance missions. However, given that the area was in Manchuria, it is difficult to be sure where the MiGs actually flew from. *FRUS, 1955–1957*, 23:103n2.

67) *Chosun ilbo*, May 27, 1955; July 6, 1955; December 31, 1955; October 20, 1956; December 14, 1956; May 8, 1957.

68) "Editorial Note," *FRUS, 1955–1957*, 23:432–33.

69) "Editorial Note," *FRUS, 1955–1957*, 23:460–61; *Chosun ilbo*, June 22, 1957.

70) John Lewis Gaddis, *Strategies of Containment*, 3–4.

71) Park Tae Gyun, "Miguk ihae e ttara gyeoljeongdoen ju Han Migun ui unmyeong," *Wolgan jungang*, August 2000.

72) Park Tae Gyun, "1950~60 nyeondae Miguk ui Hangukgun gamchungnon gwa Hanguk jeongbu ui daeeung," *Gukje jiyeok yeongu* 9, no. 3 (2000).

73) Ibid., 35–36.

74) "National Security Council Report (NSC 5702)," January 14, 1957, *FRUS, 1955–1957*, 23:374–84. Previous works of research have often emphasized NSC-5702/2 of August 1957 because it had to do with South Korean economic development. The draft version of NSC-5702, however, includes various options regarding the reduction of South Korean military forces. This means that the plans for South Korean economic development, from their inception, were closely tied to the plans for reduction of forces in South Korea. By viewing NSC-5702/2 as an entirely new strategy for economic development, the works of Yi Jongwon and Meredith Jung-En Woo overlook the context from which NSC-5702/2 arose.

75) "Telegram from the Commander in Chief, United Nations Command (Lemnizer) to the Department of the Army," January 30, 1956, *FRUS, 1955–1957*, 23:209–13.

76) "Memorandum of Discussion at the 245th Meeting of the National Security Council," April 21, 1955, *FRUS, 1955–1957*, 23:68–71.

Chapter Four

1) Criticisms against Rostow can be categorized as follows: First, Rostow did not

provide mechanisms that could provide a logical connection between the five stages of economic growth he suggested. Second, Rostow did not adequately explain the reason why traditional societies must change to societies capable of "take-off." Third, although Rostow provided preconditions to specific stages of growth, he did not explain which direction it must develop in or even why it must develop. Charles P. Oman and Ganeshan Wignaraja, *The Postwar Evolution of Development Thinking* (London: Macmillan in association with OECD Development Centre, 1991), 12–13.

2) Bak Huibeom, *Hanguk gyeongje seongjangnon* (Seoul: Goryeo Daehakgyo Asea Munje Yeonguso, 1968), 298–326; Byeon Hyeongyun, "Roseutou doyak iron ui Hanguk gyeongje e daehan jeogyong munje," in *Hanguk gyeongje baljeon ui iron gwa hyeonsil*, ed. Naegak Gihoek Jojeongsil (Seoul: Naegak Giheok Jojeongsil, 1969), 36–51.

3) For Bak's activities immediately following the May 16 coup d'état, see Park Tae Gyun, "1961~1964 nyeon gunsa jeongbu ui gyeongje gaebal gyehoek sujeong," *Sahoe wa yeoksa* 57 (2000): 113–46.

4) John Lodewijks was the first researcher to analyze Rostow's thought as a policymaker. However, Lodewijks's work only focuses on a limited number of Rostow's publications and Rostow's work related to the Vietnam War and antiguerilla warfare. In this book, I'd like to approach Rostow's thought more holistically to reveal how it sought to change the Third World. John Lodewijks, "Rostow, Developing Economies, and National Security Policy," in "Economics and National Security: A History of Their Interaction," ed. Craufurd D. Goodwin, annual supplement, *History of Political Economy* 23 (1991): 285–310.

5) John Lodewijks, 285.

6) John K. Galbraith, *A Life in Our Times* (Boston: Houghton Mifflin, 1981), 241.

7) John Lodewijks, 286–87.

8) Walt W. Rostow, "My Life Philosophy," *American Economist* 30, no. 2 (1986): 3–13.

9) "Walt W. Rostow Oral History Interview," by Richard Neustadt, April 11 and 25, 1964, John F. Kennedy Library Oral History Program, John F. Kennedy Presidential Library & Museum (hereafter JFKL), 113, 149.

10) Walt W. Rostow, *Eisenhower, Kennedy, and Foreign Aid* (Austin: University of Texas Press, 1985).

11) "Walt W. Rostow Oral History Interview," 46–47, 80.

12) Rostow, while working on the Policy Planning Council of the Department of State, produced important policy documents such as "Basic National Security Paper" and "Reflection on National Security Policy at April 1965." "Basic National Security Policy (S/P Draft)," March 26, 1962, Lyndon B. Johnson Papers, Vice Presidential Security Files, Box 7, Lyndon B. Johnson Library & Museum (henceforth LBJL); John Lewis Gaddis, *Strategies of Containment*, 200–201.

13) Eugene Rostow, Walt Rostow's older brother, was appointed under secretary for political affairs in September 1966.

14) Arthur M. Schlesinger, Jr., *A Thousand Days: John F. Kennedy in the White*

House (Boston: Houghton Mifflin, 1965), 341.

15) Thomas Parker, *America's Foreign Policy, 1945–1976: Its Creators and Critics* (New York: Facts on File, 1980), 143–46.

16) Max F. Millikan and W. W. Rostow, *A Proposal: Key to an Effective Foreign Policy* (New York: Harper & Brothers, 1957), 4–5.

17) Ibid., 18.

18) W. W. Rostow, *The Stages of Economic Growth, a Non-Communist Manifesto* (Cambridge: Cambridge University Press, 1960), 23, 41. For the idea of "Communism cannot be destroyed. It can only be replaced," see Rostow, *An American Policy in Asia* (Cambridge, MA: Technology Press of Massachusetts Institute of Technology and John Wiley & Sons, 1955), 6.

19) Millikan and Rostow, *A Proposal*, 34–35.

20) Ibid., 10.

21) Rostow, *The Stages of Economic Growth*, 23–25.

22) Millikan and Rostow, *A Proposal*, 30.

23) "The Role of the Military in the Underdeveloped Areas," RG 59, Department of State, 1960–1966: Policy Planning Council, 1962–1963, Box 6, NARA.

24) Millikan and Rostow, *A Proposal*, 6–8.

25) "The Challenge of Democracy in Developing Nations," keynote address by the Honorable Walt W. Rostow, counselor and chairman of the Policy Planning Council, Department of State, at the Seminar on Democracy, Mérida, Venezuela, Sunday, January 26, 1964, 4:00 p.m., Entry 5041, Records on the Policy Planning Council, 1963–1964, Lot 79D199 NND, Box 267, NARA.

26) Millikan and Rostow, *A Proposal*, 38–39.

27) Rostow, *An American Policy in Asia*, 10–11.

28) John Lewis Gaddis, chap. 5 in *Strategies of Containment*.

29) A number of Keynesians from the Truman administration continued to work in the Kennedy administration, and an active fiscal policy of increased spending to stimulate the economy was also carried out in the Kennedy administration. Certain scholars called the new policy of the Kennedy administration a "Keynesian Revolution." See Gaddis, *Strategies of Containment*, 213–32.

30) Paul Hoffman, "Recovery," in *Foreign Affairs, House of Representatives*, 10, 15.

31) Millikan and Rostow, *A Proposal*, 55.

32) Ibid., 81–85.

33) "The Challenge of Democracy in Developing Nations," Record of Policy Planning Council, 1963–64, Lot 70D199 NND 979524, Box 267, NARA.

34) Millikan and Rostow, *A Proposal*, 97.

35) "Memorandum from Robert H. Johnson and George Weber to Rostow," February 22, 1961, NSF: M&M: Staff Memoranda, Walt W. Rostow, Foreign Aid, International Aid for Underdeveloped Countries, 2/21/61–2/23/61, Box 324, JFKL.

36) *Daehak sinmun*, May 3, 1965.

37) Millikan and Rostow, *A Proposal*, 114.

38) Kim Jonghwan, "Roseutou baksa ui gaebal yeondae bihwa–na ui chunggo e ttara Kenedi neun Bak Jeonghui reul dopgiro gyeolsimhaetda," *Wolgan Joseon*, December 1992.

39) Park Tae Gyun, "1950 nyeondae gyeongje gaeballon yeongu," *Sahoe wa yeoksa* 61 (2002).

40) Park Tae Gyun, chap. 4 in "1956~1964 nyeon Hanguk gyeongje gaebal gyehoek ui seongnip gwajeong."

41) Walt W. Rostow, *The Prospects for Communist China* (Cambridge, MA: Technology Press of Massachusetts Institute of Technology and John Wiley, 1954).

42) "Memorandum of Conversation: Japan's World Responsibilities," S/P File, May 13, 1963, RG 59, NND 979524, US-Japanese Security Relation Documents (microfiche), Harvard University Lamont Library.

43) "The Joint U.S.-Japan Committee on Trade and Economic Affairs: The Southeast Asia Regional Development Program," S/P File, July 3, 1965, RG 59, NND 979519, U.S.-Japanese Security Relation Documents (microfiche), Harvard University Lamont Library.

44) For the Japanese stance on the Asian Development Bank, see "Ilbon ui Asia jiyeok gyeongje gaebal wonjo Asia Gaebal Eunhaeng–Miguk ui dae Il jeongchaek eul jungsim euro," unpublished paper, The University of Tokyo, Institute of Oriental Culture, June 30, 2003.

45) Rostow, *An American Policy in Asia*, 13; "Department of State Policy on the Future of Japan," June 26, 1964, U.S.-Japanese Security Relation Documents (microfiche), Harvard University Lamont Library.

46) Rostow, *An American Policy in Asia*, 45–46.

47) "Report by Hugh D. Farley of the International Cooperation Administration to the President's Deputy Special Assistant for National Security Affairs (Rostow)," March 6, 1961, President's Office Files: Countries Series (henceforth "CO"), Korea, Security 1961–1963, JFKL. Farley argued that his report was submitted at the request of Arthur Schlesinger, who had a discussion on the issue with the United States National Security Advisor McGeorge Bundy. *FRUS, 1961–1963*, vol. 22, *Northeast Asia*, 424.

48) On social reform, the Farley report argued for American involvement in South Korean social reform, claiming that it would result in an anti-American wave if social reform was carried out entirely by Koreans. At the same time, Farley also argued that South Korea's crisis constituted a great opportunity for the United States and most South Koreans were waiting for American intervention. Farley argued for an indirect intervention on the part of the United States, and suggested the one-year anniversary of the May 16 coup d'état as the most opportune time to begin it.

49) Yi Jaebong, "4 wol hyeongmyeong gwa Miguk ui gaeip," *Sahoe gwahak yeongu* 18 (1995).

50) "Embassy Telegram [henceforth "Embtel"] No. 1142," March 11, 1961,

795B.00/3-1161, General Records of the Department of State, RG 59, Central Decimal File, 1960–1963, Box 2181, NARA (henceforth "Box 2181, Decimal File, 1960–1963"); "Memorandum from Sheppard to Labouisse," March 10, 811.0095B/3-861, Box 2181, Decimal File, 1960–1963; "Memorandum from the Under Secretary of State for Economic Affairs (Ball) to the President's Deputy Special Assistant for National Security Affairs (Rostow)," March 20, 1961, *FRUS, 1961–1963*, 22:429. "Mr. Bacon to FE Mr. Steeves: For Meeting on Monday, March 13, at ICA concerning the Hugh Farley Matter," March 19, 1961, RG 59, Bureau of Far Eastern Affairs, NND 959269, Box 5, NARA; "Hugh Farley's Views on the U.S. Program in Korea," March 16, 1961, RG 59, Bureau of Far Eastern Affairs, NND 959269, Box 5, NARA.

51) "Memorandum from the President's Deputy Special Assistant for National Security Affairs (Rostow) to President Kennedy," March 15, 1961, *FRUS, 1961–1963*, 22:428–29.

52) "Note by Battle (Executive Secretary)," March 15, 1961, 795B.00/3-1561, Box 2181, Decimal File, 1960–1963.

53) "Memorandum," March 15, 1961, NSF: CO, Korea, General, 1/61–3/61, JFKL.

54) "NSC Meetings No. 483," NSF: M&M: NSC meetings, May 5, 1961, JFKL (quoted in *FRUS, 1961–1963*, 22:448). President Kennedy approved the Korea Task Force organization with National Security Action no. 2421. Although *FRUS* officially contends that there were no documents produced by the Korea Task Force during its discussions, the Gardener files from the US National Archives and Records Administration suggest that at least twenty-three officials participated. They represented the Department of State (ten officials), Department of Defense (three officials), CIA (unknown), International Cooperation Administration (three officials), Bureau of Public Affairs (three officials), Department of the Treasury (two officials), National Security Council (one official), and Bureau of the Budget (one official).

55) "First Draft Report to the Korea Task Force," May 15, 1961; "Third Draft-Report of the Korea Task Force," May 22, 1961; "Walter P. McConaughy to Members of Task Force: Fourth Draft-Report of the Korea Task Force," June 1, 1961, Gardener files.

56) "Summary and Revision of Recommendations of Task Force: Report on Korea: For Discussion at Meeting at White House at 4 P.M. on June 12, 1961," President's Office Files: CO, Korea, Security, 1961–1963, Box 120, JFKL; "Summary and Revision of Recommendations of Task Force Report on Korea: Walter F. McConaughy to Members of the Task Force on Korea," June 13, 1961, Gardener files.

57) L. L. Lemnitzer (chairman of Joint Chiefs of Staff), "Strategic Appraisal of US Position in Korea 1962–1970 (U)," April 10, 1962, RG 59, Records of the Policy Planning Council, 1963–1964, Box 281, NARA.

58) "Walter P. McConaughy to Members of Korea Task Force: Meeting of Korea Task Force," May 12, 1961, Gardener files.

59) "Presidential Task Force on Korea: Report to the National Security Council," June 5, 1961, President's Office Files: CO, Korea, Security, 1961–1963, Box 120, JFKL.

60) "Telegram from the Embassy in Korea to the Department of State," July 23, 1962, *FRUS, 1961–1963*, 22:581–85.

61) *FRUS, 1961–1963*, 22:549n2. Samuel Berger, McConaughy, and Bundy agreed to it.

62) "Editorial Note," *FRUS, 1961–1963*, 22:656–57.

63) Robert Komer, "Relative Priority of Military vs. Reconstruction: Focus in Korea," June 12, 1961, President's Office Files: CO, Korea, Security, 1961–1963, Box 120, JFKL.

64) "National Intelligence Estimate (14/2/42-61)," September 7, 1961, *FRUS, 1961–1963*, 22:521.

65) As the content of US aid changed from outright grants to loans, the military government needed to make up for the difference. Two laws were passed on July 31, 1962, for a more flexible use of foreign capital, and the law for introduction of foreign capital was passed on August 31, 1966. See, Gyeongje Gihoegwon, ed., *Gaebal yeondae ui gyeongje jeongchaek: Gyeongje Gihoegwon 30 nyeonsa (1961 nyeon~1980 nyeon)* (Seoul: Miraesa, 1994), 396–97.

66) "Rusk to Samuel Berger," August 1, 1961, FG 84, NND 948813, Korea, General Records, Box 27, NARA.

67) "The First Draft Report of the Korea Task Force," written on May 15, 1961, points to corruption as the most pressing issue of the day. It also views the problem of corruption in Korea thusly, "Corruption has been deeply engrained in Korean society for centuries."

68) "Statement by Embassy Seoul: Korean Government and Business Are Riddled with Graft and Corruption" and "Statement by Embassy Seoul: General Conclusions and Recommendations on Measures to Cope with Corruption and Nepotism in Korea," no dates, Gardener files.

69) "Memorandum for Mr. Rostow: This Afternoon's Meeting on Korea," July 12, 1961, NSF: CO, Korea, General, 6/61, Box 127, JFKL.

70) "General Statement of AID Policy," August 1, 1962, *Agency for International Development Manual*, Records of Government Agencies, AID, Reel 18, JFKL.

71) "Walter P. McConaughy to Members of Korea Task Force: Meetings of Korea Task Force," May 12, 1961, Gardener files.

72) Documents that display prejudices against Koreans well are "Donald S. Macdonald (Korean Desk Officer) (State) to Members of Task Force: Economic Policy Recommendations Excerpted from Recent Communications from Embassy Seoul," May 10, 1961, Gardener files; "Statement by Embassy Seoul: General Conclusions and Recommendations on Measures to Cope with Corruption and Nepotism in Korea," no date, Gardener files.

73) Walt W. Rostow, "The Future of Foreign Aid," *Foreign Service Journal*, 38, no. 6 (1961): 30–35; Im Daesik, "1950 nyeondae Miguk ui gyoyuk wonjo wa chin Mi elliteu ui hyeongseong," in *1950 nyeondae Nambukhan ui seontaek gwa guljeol* (Seoul: Yeoksa Bipyeongsa, 2004).

74) Richard Pells, *Not Like Us: How Europeans Have Loved, Hated, and Transformed American Culture Since World War II* (New York: Basic Books, 1997), 58–63.

75) "Memorandum to the President: Crucial Issues in Foreign Aid," February 28, 1961, NSF: M&M: Staff Memoranda, Walt W. Rostow, Foreign Aid, 2/24/61–2/28/61, Box 324, JFKL.

76) Yi Jongwon (Rī Jonwon), "Kannichi kokkō seijōka no seiritsu to Amerika ichisen kyūhyaku rokujū kara rokujūgonen," in *Sengo gaikō no keisei*, ed. Kindai Nihon Kenkyūkai (Tokyo: Yamakawa Shuppansha, 1994).

77) "National Security Action Memorandum No. 151," April 24, 1961, NSF: M&M: Staff Memoranda, Arthur M. Schlesinger, 7/62–6/63, Box 327, JFKL.

78) "Walter P. McConaughy to Members of Korea Task Force: Meetings of Korea Task Force," May 12, 1962, Gardener files.

79) Department of State (Policy Planning Council), "Brief Foreign Policy Statements," March 5, 1963, RG 59, Lot 70D199, Records of the Policy Planning Council, 1963–1964, Box 243, NARA.

80) "Department of State Guidelines for Policy and Operations," October, 1961, RG 59, Bureau of Far Eastern Affairs, NND 959269, Box 20, NARA; "Japanese Aid to the Developing Areas," March 1, 1962, RG 59, Bureau of Far Eastern Affairs, NND 959269, Box 20, NARA.

81) "Agenda," National Security Council Standing Group Meeting, International Situation Room, The White House, May 18, 1962, NSF: M&M, NSC meetings, 1963 Standing Group Meetings, 5/18/62–8/3/62, Box 314, JFKL.

82) "Some Comments on a Far East Strategy," Department of State, 1960–1966: Roger Hilsman, General, 1963–1966, Box 8, JFKL.

83) "Korean-Japanese Relations," background paper for use in connection with the meeting of the NSC Standing Group, May 18, 1962, NSF: M&M, NSC meetings, 1963 Standing Group Meetings, 5/18/62–8/3/62, Box 314, JFKL.

84) Jeong Changhyeon, "5.16 kudeta neun Miguk i judohaetda," *Wolgan mal*, April 1993.

85) The so-called Kreper incident was reported by a Korean person, and the exact spelling of the name "Kreper" is unavailable.

86) Jo Seonggwan, "Miguk jeongbo gigwan, Jang Doyeong chudaehayeo Jang Myeon jeongbu dwieopeuryeo haetda: Kim Jongpil jeongbo bujang gwa Samuel Beogeo ju Han Mi daesa ui miryak e uihae 30 nyeongan deopeojyeo watdeon Keurepeo (daeryeong) sageon," *Wolgan Joseon*, August 1993.

87) "A Proposal to the Presidential Task Force on Korea," May 12, 1961, Gardener files.

88) Coincidently, the approval date of the Korea Task Force was on May 16, 1961, the day of the coup. Data for the meeting, however, were being assembled since April by officials in South Korea. A draft for discussions was submitted on May 9, 1961, and the

first meeting was convened on May 12, 1961.

89) Jeong Daecheol, *Jang Myeon eun wae sunyeowon e sumeo isseonna* (Seoul: Donga Ilbosa, 1997), 107–22.

90) Cheon Huisang, "5.16 kudeta 30 nyeon–Bak Jeonghui ui jaejomyeong: Bak Jeonghui–Kim Jongpil–Maegeurudeo bimil hoedam girok; 5.16 jikhu Hanguk-Miguk sunoebu sai e ogogan eunmilhan iyagi ga 30 nyeonman e gonggaedoenda," *Wolgan Joseon*, May 1991.

91) "Memorandum from Director of Central Intelligence to President," May 16, 1961, *FRUS, 1961–1963*, 22:456–57.

92) An informant disguised as a potato vender stationed in front of Park's house observed Park's movements. Yi Yeongsin, "Jang Doyeong silgak, yuksa 5 gi wa 8 gi ui galdeung," *Sindonga*, May 1984.

93) "Outline for Discussion," Presidential Task Force on Korea, May 9, 1961.

94) "First Draft Report of the Korea Task Force," May 15, 1961, Gardener files.

95) A directive from Secretary of State Dean Rusk on April 17, 1961, displays a similar view. Although Rusk pointed to the flaws of Jang Myeon's leadership, he nevertheless argued that the US government should continue to support Jang's government. "State Department Telegram (henceforth "Deptel") No. 1123," 795B.00/4-161, Box 2181, Decimal File, 1960–1963.

96) Yi Hanrim was a Catholic, as was Jang Myeon. Yi Hanrim was also recommended as chief of staff by Kim Cheolgyu, a Catholic priest who was supporting Jang Myeon behind the scenes.

97) Hong Seokryul, "5.16 kudeta ui wonin gwa Han-Mi gwangye," *Yeoksa hakbo* 168 (2000).

98) However, Green's telegram was not the first one on the coup d'état. Telegrams written by the Embassy officials and the US Forces Korea reached Washington around two to three o'clock in the morning (Korea time).

99) Gukga Jaegeon Choego Hoeui, Gunsa Hyeongmyeongsa Pyeonchan Wiwonhoe, ed., *Hanguk gunsa hyeongmyeongsa I-A* (Seoul: Donga Seojeok Jusik Hoesa, 1963), 260. The only news report stating that the UN commander was not going to mobilize US forces is an article from the *New York Times* on May 16, 1961. It states that "General Magruder sent orders to his units throughout Korea, including those manning the armistice line about thirty miles north of the capital, to take appropriate measures to strengthen their security." However, General Magruder also "restricted United States troops to their compounds and told them to take a hands-off policy." United Press International, "Fighting in Seoul," *New York Times*, May 16, 1961.

100) "Telegram from the Commander in Chief, U.S. Forces Korea (Magruder) to the Joint Chiefs of Staff," May 16, 1961, *FRUS, 1961–1963*, 22:449–51.

101) "Embtel No. 1530," May 16, 1961, 795B.00/5-1661, Box 2181, Decimal File, 1960–1963.

102) Ibid.

103) "Embtel No. 1536," section one of two, section two of two, May 16, 1961, 795B.00/5-1661, Box 2181, Decimal File, 1960–1963.

104) The testimony of Presidential Secretary Hong Gyuseon well recalls the content of the above conversation. Hong testified that the UN commander Magruder passed on the suppression plan using the First Army to President Yun three times, and Yun repeatedly refused to follow it. Hong Gyuseon, "Dangsi Cheongwadae biseogwan ui 5.16 gwanchal girok–Yun Boseon daetongnyeong ui 24 si," *Wolgan Joseon*, June 1991.

105) Magruder's main interest during a talk with Park Chung Hee and Kim Jongpil after Jang Myeon's resignation and the establishment of the Supreme Council for National Reconstruction was the return of commanding authority of the South Korean armed forces. "Embtel No. 1663," 795B.00/5-2561, Box 2181, Decimal File, 1960–1963; "Embtel No. 1676," 795B.00/5/2761, Box 2181, Decimal File, 1960–1963.

106) "Telegram from the Commander in Chief, United Nations Command (Magruder) to the Chairman of the Joint Chiefs of Staff (Lemnitzer)," May 17, 1961, *FRUS, 1961–1963*, 22: 458–61.

107) Mun Myeongho, "Kim Ungsu inteobyu–5.16 kudeta jinap jwajeol ui jinsang," *Sindonga*, May 1986; Gang Seongjae, "Kim Ungsu inteobyu–Jagiman aegukjaran saenggak eun gollan," *Sindonga*, October 1987; Yi Cheong, "Biun ui janggun Jeong Gang," *Wolgan Joseon*, June 1993.

108) Jeong Yongseok, "20 nyeonman e gonggaehanun 4.19, 5.16 bihwa–Masyeol Geurin dangsi ju Han Mi daeri daesa bonji dokjeom inteobyu," *Sindonga*, April 1982.

109) Kim Jeonggi, "5.16 dangsi Mi daesagwan munjeonggwan Geuregori Hendeoseun ui hoego–Kenedi, 5.16 jinap geonui reul muksal," *Sindonga*, May 1987.

110) Bang Jamyeong, "Uri neun 5.16 kudeta jeoji e silpaehaetda," *Sindonga*, May 1984. Although the United Nations commander position is typically considered as a stepping-stone for higher posts in the US Army, Commander Magruder nevertheless went into the reserve soon after the May 16 coup. Although some argue that his discharge was a punishment for his stance against the coup, others argue that his discharge was already decided on before the May 16 coup.

111) Ibid.

112) Kim Jeonggi, "5.16 dangsi," 222–25.

113) "Telegram from the Chairman of the Joint Chiefs of Staff (Lemnitzer) to the Commander in Chief, U.S. Forces Korea (Magruder)," May 16, 1961, *FRUS, 1961–1963*, 22:451–52.

114) "Telegram from the Chairman of the Joint Chiefs of Staff (Lemnitzer) to the Commander in Chief, U.S. Forces Korea (Magruder)," May 16, 1961, *FRUS, 1961–1963*, 22:451–52.

115) Bowles graduated from Yale University. He was a foreign policy specialist of the Democratic Party and served as Connecticut governor from 1948 to 1950 and US ambassador to India from 1951 to 1953. He worked as a policymaker on the Third World from 1960 to 1961.

116) Kim Jonghwan, "Roseutou baksa." .

117) "Telegram from the Department of State to the Embassy in Korea," May 16, 1961, *FRUS, 1961–1963*, 22:455–56.

118) Ibid.

119) "Meeting of Korea Task Force," May 29, 1961, Gardener files.

120) "Embtel No. 1454," 795B.00/5-1761, Box 2181, Decimal File, 1960–1963; "Embtel No. 1545," 795B.00/5-1761, Box 2181, Decimal File, 1960–1963.

121) "Deptel No. 1320," 795B.00/5-1761, Box 2181, Decimal File, 1960–1963.

122) "Telegram from the Department of State to the Embassy in Korea," May 17, 1961, *FRUS, 1961–1963*, 22:461–62.

123) "Embtel No. 1579," 795B.00/5-1851, Box 2181, Decimal File, 1960–1963; *FRUS, 1961–1963*, 22:462.

124) Park Tae Gyun, chap. 2 in "1956~1964 nyeon Hanguk gyeongje gaebal gyehoek ui seongnip gwajeong."

125) Hyeon Seokho testified that Yun Boseon said, "As far as I can see, this is the only way to save the country. What else should we do now that the military revolution has occurred?" Hyeon Seokho, "5 wol 16 il 10 si ui Yun Boseon ssi," *Wolgan jungang*, July 1970. Hyeon Seokho was close to Jang Myeon and also a Catholic.

126) "Embtel," 795B.00/5-2261, Box 2181, Decimal File, 1960–1963.

127) According to Jeong Daecheol, Prime Minister Jang Myeon attempted to meet Chargé d'Affaires Green at the ambassador's residence but was stopped by security. See Jeong Daecheol, 272.

128) "Embtel No. 1536," section one of two, section two of two, 795B.00/5-1661, Box 2181, Decimal File, 1960.

129) Yi Sangu, "Yun Boseon, Yu Wonsik nonjaeng ui jinwi," *Jeonggyeong munhwa*, November 1983. Choe Deoksin, South Korean ambassador to South Vietnam, also suspected that Yun Boseon was involved in the coup d'état planning. "Embtel No. 1784," 795B.00/5-2361, Box 2181, Decimal File, 1960–1963.

130) Sinmindang was a new political party created by the so-called *gupa* (old faction) of the Democratic Party. Jang Myeon belonged to the so-called *sinpa* (new faction), which had the control of government.

131) Jo Sehyeong, "5.16 gwa Seodaemun hyeongmuso," *Wolgan Joseon*, December 1985.

132) "Embtel No. 1337," 795B.00/4-1461, Box 2181, Decimal File, 1960–1963.

133) "Embtel No. 1627," 795B.00/5-2261, Box 2181, Decimal File, 1960–1963.

134) "Embtel No. 1727," 795B.00/6-361, Box 2181, Decimal File, 1960–1963.

135) "Embtel No. 1627," 795B.00/5-2261, Box 2181, Decimal File, 1960–1963.

136) "Memorandum from State Department to General Consul in Geneva," 795B.00/5-1761, Box 2181, Decimal File, 1960–1963.

137) "Telegram from the Department of State to the Embassy in Korea," May 16, 1961, *FRUS, 1961–1963*, vol. 29, 455–56.

138) Although the US government did not recognize the coup's success and military government's existence until late May when the prime minister and his cabinet resigned and the commanding authority of South Korean armed forces returned to the United Nations commander, it nevertheless made statements implying its success since the coup started.

139) "Embtel," 795B.00/5-2261, Box 2181, Decimal File, 1960–1963.

140) "Deptel No. 1421," 795B.00/6-361, Box 2181, Decimal File 1960–1963.

141) Yi Sangu, "Yun Boseon, Yu Wonsik nonjaeng ui jinwi."

142) "Telegram from the Department of State to the Embassy in Korea," May 17, 1961, *FRUS, 1961–1963*, 29:461–62.

143) Certain counselors of the US Embassy in Seoul had held regular seminars with a number of South Korean officials since the late 1950s. They assessed Korea's present and future and discussed different issues regarding the Korean economy, politics, and society. The Department of State believed that economic issues between the United States and South Korea, which were causing friction between the two countries in the 1950s, could be solved through its relationships with them. Park Tae Gyun, "1956~1964 nyeon Hanguk."

144) "Embtel," 795B.00/5-1961, Box 2181, Decimal File, 1960–1963.

145) "Deptel," 795B.00/5-2061, Box 2181, Decimal File, 1960–1963. Yi Hanbin and Yi Gihong were in the United States to negotiate a loan for the Jang Myeon government's economic development plan when the May 16 coup d'état broke out. The above document is a report of the conversation between Yi Hanbin, Yi Gihong, and Assistant Secretary of State for Far Eastern Affairs McConaughy. Yi Hanbin argued against forming a temporary cabinet with older officials and suggested forming a temporary one with vigorous young officials in their thirties and forties. The persons Yi recommended included Jeong Inuk, Na Ikjin, Jang Junha, Yi Yonghui, Seo Seoksun, Kim Sanghyeop, Jeong Ilgwon, Son Wonil, Jeong Namgyu, Cha Gyunhui, Jang Giyeong, Yu Changsun, O Jaegyeong and Sin Eunggyun. It was essentially a civilian-centered cabinet with some military men included.

146) "Foreign Exchange and Stabilization," December 11, 1961, RG 84, NND 948813, Korea, General Records, Box 29, NARA.

147) Park Tae Gyun, "W. W. Rostow and Economic Discourse in South Korea in the 1960s," *Journal of International and Area Studies* 8, no. 2 (2001).

148) "From Director, CIA to President: Current Situation in South Korea," May 18, 1961, NSF: CO, Korea, 4/11/61–5/17/61, Box 128, JFKL; "Background Paper on the Korean Military Government. May 16–August 15, 1961," NSF: CO, Korea, Cables, 8/61–9/61, Box 128, JFKL.

149) Although not on record, it is likely that the US government was involved in Cha Gyunhui's appointment as the deputy minister of the Economic Planning Board. There is a State Department document produced immediately before the coup d'état that positively evaluates Cha Gyunhui's role. "Objectives of ROK Economic Working Group,"

895B.00/5-961, Box 2181, Decimal File, 1960–1963. Although this document is a record of the conversation with Yi Hanbin, Yi Gihong, and Kim Yeongrok during their stay in the United States, it also mentions the role Cha Gyunhui played in South Korea.

150) "Embtel No. 1725," 795B.00/6-361, Box 2181, Decimal File, 1960–1963.

151) "Embtel No. 1738," 795B.00/6-761, Box 2181, Decimal File, 1960–1963.

152) A CIA report written shortly before the 1963 presidential election theorized that Yun Boseon resigned after realizing that Park Chung Hee had no interest in allowing Yun Boseon's supporters to join the government. "Special Report: Background for Elections in South Korea, by Central Intelligence Agency (SC No. 00613/63C)," October 11, 1963, NSF: CO, Korea, General Box 127, JFKL.

153) "Embtel, No. 1055," March 20, 1962, NSF: CO, Korea, Cables, 1962, Box 128, JFKL. An interesting point to note is that Syngman Rhee expressed his willingness to return to South Korea at this time. Berger made it clear in this cable that Yun's resignation was not connected to the issue of Syngman Rhee's return.

154) Park Tae Gyun, "1961~1964 nyeon gunsa jeongbu ui gyeongje gaebal gyehoek sujeong." At a meeting with Park Chung Hee, Berger directly criticized the five-year plan as something economists unrealistically made up at the Supreme Council's request. No title, August 22, 1961, RG 84, NND 948813, Korea, General Records, 1961, Box 28, NARA.

155) "Mr. McConaughy to Leonard L. Bacon: Current Economic Situation in Korea," July 24, 1961, RG 59, Bureau of Far Eastern Affairs, NND 959269, Box 5, NARA; "Proceedings of Meeting of Working Level Task Force on Korea," Room 5714, October 4, 1961, RG 59, Bureau of Far Eastern Affairs, NND 959269, Box 5, NARA.

156) "Gingeup Tonghwa Jochibeop gongpo," *Seoul gyeongje sinmun*, June 10, 1962. Currency reform was also aimed at mobilizing the bank savings of Chinese Koreans. Cheon Byeonggyu, *Cheonma chowon e nolda*, ed. Dongbaek Cheon Byeonggyu Gohui Jajeon Ganhaeng Wiwonhoe (Seoul: Dongbaek Cheon Byeonggyu Gohui Jajeon Ganhaeng Wiwonhoe, 1988), 204.

157) "Saneop gaebal jageumhwa," *Seoul gyeongje sinmun*, June 17, 1962;Yi Wanbeom et al., *1960 nyeondae ui jeongchi sahoe byeondong*, ed. Hanguk Jeongsin Munhwa Yeonguwon, Hanguk hyeondaesa ui jaeinsik 10 (Seoul: Baeksan Seodang, 1999), 97–98.

158) "Mr. Gordon from Albert E. Pappano," July 31, 1962, RG 84, Classified General Records, NND 948833, Box 34, NARA; "Embtel No. 1306," June 17, 1962, RG 84, Classified General Records, NND 948833, Box 34, NARA.

159) "Embtel, No. 1306," June 17, 1962, RG 84, Classified General Records, NND 948833, Box 34, NARA.

160) "Embtel, No. 1171," June 27, 1962, NSF: CO, Korea, Cables, 1962, Box 128, JFKL.

161) "Comparison of Recent ROK Currency Conversion with That in Western Zones of Germany in 1948 (A-102)," June 23, 1962, RG 84, Classified General Records, NND

948833, Box 34, NARA.

162) Yi Wanbeom et al., 99.

163) "Bongswae gyejeong eul jeonmyeon haeje," *Seoul gyeongje sinmun*, July 14, 1962.

164) "Gaebang ongsabeoban pyegidoel deut," *Seoul gyeongje sinmun*, December 12, 1962.

165) "From Joseph A. Yager to FE Avery F. Peterson: Arthur D. Little Company Report–Reconnaissance Survey of Economic Development Planning in Korea," July 26, 1962, RG 59, Bureau of Far Eastern Affairs, NND 959269, Box 5, NARA.

166) "Embtel, No. 1312," 795B.00/6-1962, Box 2181, Decimal File, 1960–1963; "Memorandum of Discussion at a Department of State/Joint Chiefs of Staff Meeting," June 15, 1962, *FRUS, 1961–1963*, 22:575–76; "Telegram from the Embassy in Korea to the DOS," July 23, 1962, *FRUS, 1961–1963*, 22:581–85.

167) "*Gyeongu* bangdam–6, 70 nyeondae ui tteugeowotdeon gyeonghyeop jeonjaeng," *Gyeongu*, November 1990, 66. The US government believed that "a small group around President Pak" was playing a monopolistic role in economic policymaking. Department of State, "National Policy Paper: Republic of Korea, Part One: U.S. Policy," September 9, 1965, NND 979519, RG 59, Box 306, NARA (materials in possession of Dr. Jeong Iljun).

168) Kim Yongtae, *Kim Yongtae jaseojeon* (Seoul: Jimmundang, 1990), 162.

169) "Telegram from the Embassy in Korea to the DOS," July 23, 1962, *FRUS, 1961–1963*, 22:581–85; "Telegram from the Embassy in Korea to DOS," July 27, 1962, *FRUS, 1961–1963*, 22:589–90.

170) Although not directly mentioned in US documents, US pressure may have influenced the replacement of Supreme Council Finance and Economy Chairman Kim Dongha with former chief officer of the Korean Embassy in Washington Yu Yangsu. Ever since the coup d'état first broke out, Yu Yangsu played a key role in putting the coup forces and Washington in contact.

171) "Telegram from the Embassy in Korea to the DOS," July 23, 1962, *FRUS, 1961–1963*, 22:581–85.

172) "Telegram from the Embassy in Korea to DOS," July 27, 1962, *FRUS, 1961–1963*, 22:589–90.

173) "Telegram from the Embassy in Korea to the Department of State," July 23, 1962, *FRUS, 1961–1963*, 22:581–82.

174) "Telegram from the Embassy in Korea to the Department of State," July 27, 1962, *FRUS, 1961–1963*, 22:589.

175) With the exception of *Kim Yongtae jaseojeon*, there is no evidence of the US Embassy in Seoul or the United Nations commander pointing to a specific person. In the case of Yu Wonsik, Yu later recollected that he resigned from the position of his own free will due to his conflict with the decision made by Park Chung Hee. Kim Yongtae, *Kim Yongtae jaseojeon*; Yu Wonsik, *Hyeongmyeong eun eodiro ganna: 5.16 birok* (Seoul:

Inmul Yeonguso, 1987), 344.

176) "From Macdonald to Tori Block," March 21, 1961, 795B.00/1-2462, Box 2181, Decimal File, 1960–1963.

177) "Embtel, No. 876," January 16, 1962, NSF: CO, Korea, Cables, 1/62, Box 128, JFKL.

178) At a meeting with Kim Jongpil in late October of 1962, Ambassador Berger suggested to him that he should not become involved in the "Walkerhill Hotel incident," stock market fluctuations, and currency reform. "Airgram from Embassy in Seoul to the Department of State," October 23, 1962, NSF: CO, Korea, Cables, 9/62–12/62, Box 129, JFKL.

179) "Telegram from the Embassy in Korea to the Department of State," July 27, 1962, FRUS, 1961–1963, 22:589–91.

180) "Telegram from the Department of State to the Embassy in Korea," August 5, 1962, FRUS, 1961–1963, 22:594–596.

181) "Memorandum from Robert W. Komer of the National Security Council Staff to the President's Special Assistant for National Security Affairs (Bundy)," August 17, 1962, FRUS, 1961–1963, 22:595.

182) "Deptel, No. 321," 795B.00/10-16, RG 59, Box 8985, Decimal File 1960–1963. Although requests for an official meeting were declined, Kim Jongpil nevertheless visited the CIA and privately met with the secretary of state as well as Chairman Rostow of the Policy Planning Council.

183) "Telegram from the Embassy in Korea to the Department of State," July 15, 1963, FRUS, 1961–1963, 22:653–54.

184) "Telegram from the Department of State to the Embassy in Korea," August 5, 1962, FRUS, 1961–1963, 22:591–95.

185) "Telegram from the Embassy in Korea to the Department of State," July 9, 1962, FRUS, 1961–1963, 22:496–98. In this document, Berger emphasized that there is no substitute to Park Chung Hee.

186) "Deptel," 795B.00/1-1062, Box 2181, Decimal File, 1960–1963; "Deptel," 795B.00/1-1862, Box 2181, Decimal File, 1960–1963.

187) "Memorandum from the President's Special Assistant for National Security Affairs (Bundy) to President Kennedy," June 20, 1962, FRUS, 1961–1963, 22:578; "Informal Visit of Korean Junta Leader, Lt, General PAK Chong-hui," September 1, 1961, RG 59, Bureau of Far Eastern Affairs, NND 959269, Box 5, NARA.

188) "Airgram from the Embassy in Korea to the Department of State (A-399)," December 7, 1962, FRUS, 1961–1963, 22:616–17.

189) "Airgram from the Embassy in Korea to the Department of State (A-399)," December 7, 1962, FRUS, 1961–1963, 22:616–17.

190) Twelve people signed up as promoters at the promotion meeting on January 10, 1963: Kim Jongpil, Kim Donghwan (member of the coup forces), Kim Jeongryeol (retired general), Jo Eungcheon (retired general), Bak Hyeonsuk, Kim Wonjeon (former member

of the Liberal Party), Kim Jaesun (former member of the Democratic Party led by Jang Myeon), Seo Taewon, Yun Ilseon (an academic), Kim Seongjin, Yi Wonsun, and Yun Juyeong. Jungang Seongeo Gwalli Wiwonhoe, ed., *Daehan Minguk jeongdangsa*, rev. ed. (Seoul: Jungang Seongeo Gwalli Wiwonhoe, 1968), 262.

191) Yi Sangu, *Je 3 gonghwaguk*, vol. 1, *5.16 eseo 10 wol yusin kkaji* (Jungwon Munhwa, 1993), 59–62.

192) Jungang Seongeo Gwalli Wiwonhoe, ed., *Daehan Minguk jeongdangsa*, 262–63.

193) "Embtel, No. 503," January 17, 1963, NSF: CO, Korea, Cables, Box 129, JFKL.

194) It is unclear why Ambassador Berger stated that UN Commander Meloy may need to be involved, as certain documents remain classified. General Meloy resigned from the post of UN commander after the transfer of power to a civilian government, and General Hamilton H. Howze succeeded him. There is no evidence connecting the timing of General Meloy's resignation and the conflicts surrounding the power transfer.

195) "Embtel, No. 503," January 17, 1962, NSF: CO, Korea, Cables, 1/63, Box 129, JFKL.

196) "Embtel, No. 504," January 17, 1963, NSF: CO, Korea, Cables, Box 129, JFKL.

197) The Department of State and the US Embassy were counting on Kim Jongo. They understood that Kim Jongo was a rising leader in the military and the only person there who asked for Park Chung Hee's withdrawal from politics. "Telegram from the Department of State to the Embassy in Korea," March 28, 1963, *FRUS, 1961-1963*, 22:637–38.

198) "Embtel, No. 517," January 23, 1963, NSF: CO, Korea, Cables, Box 129, JFKL.

199) "Embtel, No. 517," January 23, 1963, NSF: CO, Korea, Cables, Box 129, JFKL.

200) "Embtel, No. 521," January 24, 1963, NSF: CO, Korea, Cables, Box 129, JFKL.

201) "Deptel," January 24, 1963, NSF: CO, Korea, Cables, Box 1129, JFKL. The time the US Embassy in Seoul's telegram 521 reached the Department of State was 6:00 p.m., and the time the Department of State sent this telegram to the US Embassy in Seoul was 6:10 p.m.. This indicates that Secretary of State Rusk was waiting for the results of the conversation with Park Chung Hee even after the time the department usually closed, and he sent an immediate response.

202) "Embtel, No. 526," January 25, 1963, NSF: CO, Korea, Cables, Box 129, JFKL.

203) "Deptel," January 25, 1963, NSF: CO, Korea, Cables, Box 129, JFKL.

204) "Embtel, No. 527," January 26, 1963, NSF: CO, Korea, Cables, Box 129, JFKL.

205) "Embtel, No. 529," January 27, 1963, NSF: CO, Korea, Cables, Box 129, JFKL. This document states that Park Chung Hee will turn to the Kim Jongpil faction and create an "antirevolution" incident against the Hamgyeong Province faction, the "antirevolution" incident will involve Prime Minister Song Yochan and former Supreme Council member Yu Wonsik, relationship between Park Chung Hee and Kim Jongpil will not change, as Park needs Kim as much as Kim needs Park.

206) *FRUS, 1961–1963*, 22:622n1. It is likely the case that Park Chung Hee's feeling of dejection was due to American pressure.

207) *FRUS, 1916–1963*, 22:625n3.

208) "Telegram from the Department of State to the Embassy in Korea," February 14, 1963, *FRUS, 1961–1963*, 22:625.

209) "Editorial Note," *FRUS, 1961–1963*, 22:627.

210) Yi Sangu, 24–25. The State Department expressed strong disapproval for the February 27 declaration. The declaration forbade the political activity of those who "negated basic principles of liberal democracy, obstructed revolutionary activities, haven't returned the money after being convicted of corruption, and were in hiding to avoid prosecution," and the State Department understood those provisions as reflecting Park Chung Hee's unwholesome intention. "Telegram from the Department of State to the Embassy in Korea," March 28, 1963, *FRUS, 1961–1963*, 22:637.

211) Kim Dongha argued that this incident was a fabrication, and called it the "Alaska Suppression." Yi Yeongseok, "5.16 hyeongmyeong gwa banhyeongmyeong ui noegwan," *Jeonggyeong munhwa*, May 1984. According to the information the US Embassy received from Prime Minister Kim Hyeoncheol, it was a coup attempt by certain members of the rightist "ChokChong" (Jokcheong, National Association of Young Men). According to Kim, this attempt was aimed at assassinating Park Chung Hee, and threw South Korean politics into a panic. "Telegram from the Embassy in Korea to the Department of State," March 14, 1963, *FRUS, 1961–1963*, 22:628.

212) *FRUS, 1961–1963*, 22:628n1. UN Commander Meloy had a different opinion than Berger as he.contended that an antirevolutionary coup conspiracy actually existed. *FRUS, 1961–1963*, 22:635n3. The trials of the Kim Dongha faction and Bak Imhang faction were conducted separately. Although the Kim Dongha faction argued that the incident itself was fabricated, the Bak Imhang faction acknowledged the prosecution. Yi Yeongseok, "5.16 hyeongmyeong."

213) "[Enclosure] Intelligence Note: Memorandum from Michael V. Forrestal of the National Security Council Staff to President Kennedy," March 17, 1963, *FRUS, 1961–1963*, 22:634.

214) "Memorandum from Michael V. Forrestal of National Security Council Staff to President Kennedy," March 28, 1963, *FRUS, 1961–1963*, 22:640.

215) For statements released by the State Department, see National Security Council, "US Relations with the Korean Military Junta," March 28, 1963, NSF: CO, Korea, General, Box 127, JFKL.

216) *FRUS, 1961–1963*, 22:636n1 and 3.

217) The State Department, expecting opposition to forming the government in the near future, directed the US Embassy to strengthen its contacts with opposition leaders. "Telegram from the Department of State to the Embassy in Korea," March 28, 1963, *FRUS, 1961–1963*, 22:637.

218) "Telegram from the Department of State to the Embassy in Korea," March 28, 1963, *FRUS, 1961–1963*, 22:637. However, Michael Forrestal of the National Security Council contended that an "interim government" could be in the best interest of the

United States. "Memorandum from Michael V. Forrestal of National Security Council Staff to President Kennedy," March 28, 1963, 22:640.

219) *FRUS, 1961–1963*, 22:640n2.

220) "Telegram from the Department of State to the Embassy in Korea," April 8, 1963, *FRUS, 1961–1963*, 22:642.

221) *FRUS, 1961–1963*, 22:642n1.

222) "Telegram from the Embassy in Korea to the Department of State," April 29, 1963, *FRUS, 1961–1963*, 22:643–44. The ambassador discovered the significance of moderates in the midst of the conflict between the Kim Jongpil and anti–Kim Jongpil factions.

223) *FRUS, 1961–1963*, 22:617n1.

224) "Embtel, No. 504," January 17, 1963, NSF: CO, Korea, Cables, Box 129, JFKL.

225) Yi Sangu, "Janggundeul ui chungdol."

226) "Telegram from the Embassy in Korea to the Department of State," July 15, 1963, *FRUS, 1961–1963*, 22:652.

227) Yi Sangu, *Je 3 gonghwaguk*, 1:77–78.

228) Jungang Seongeo Gwalli Wiwonhoe, *Daehan Minguk jeongdangsa*, 281. Although the Liberal Democratic Party attempted to survive on its own and nominated Song Yochan as its presidential candidate, it collapsed when Kim Jaechun was forced to take a leave.

Chapter Five

1) "Memorandum from the Joint Chiefs of Staff to Secretary of Defense McNamara (JCSM-815-64): Alternative US Courses of Action in Korea Under Certain Contingencies," September 21, 1964, *FRUS, 1964–1968*, vol. 29, pt. 1, *Korea*, document no. 22.

2) "Telegram from the Commander in Chief, United Nations Command, Korea (Howze) to the Chairman of the Joint Chiefs of Staff (Taylor)," March 26, 1964, *FRUS, 1964–1968*, vol. 29, pt. 1, document no. 6.

3) "Memorandum from Robert W. Komer of the National Security Council Staff to the President's Special Assistant for National Security Affairs (Bundy)," March 26, 1964, *FRUS, 1964–1968*, vol. 29, pt. 1, document no. 7.

4) *FRUS, 1964–1968*, vol. 29, pt. 1, document no. 6.

5) "Memorandum from Robert W. Komer of the National Security Council Staff to the President's Special Assistant for National Security Affairs (Bundy)," April 21, 1964, *FRUS, 1964–1968*, vol. 29, pt. 1, document no. 8.

6) *FRUS, 1964–1968*, vol. 29, pt. 1, document no. 7. In a document Komer sent to Bundy a month later analyzing the Korean situation, he argued that another "student revolt" would occur if even a few students were killed by the police. *FRUS, 1964–1968*, vol. 29, pt. 1, document no. 8.

7) "Telegram from the Embassy in Korea to the Department of State," July 21, 1964, Pol 15-1 Kor S, Subject-Number Files 1964–1966.

8) Gang Wonryong, "'Bak Jeonghui chukchul' dajimhaetdeon Miguk, Beteunam pabyeong daega ro jeonggwon bojang," interview by Park Tae Gyun, *Sindonga*, February 2004.

9) *FRUS, 1964–1968*, vol. 29, pt. 1, document no. 6.

10) "Telegram 1534 from Seoul, May 24; National Archives and Records Administration," RG 59, Central Files 1964–1966, Pol 23-8 Kor S in "Editorial Note," *FRUS, 1964–1968*, vol. 29, pt. 1, document no. 11.

11) "Memorandum from Robert W. Komer of the National Security Council Staff to the President's Special Assistant for National Security Affairs (Bundy)," June 3, 1964, *FRUS, 1964–1968*, vol. 29, pt. 1, document no. 12.

12) "Memorandum from Robert W. Komer of the National Security Council Staff to the President's Special Assistant for National Security Affairs (Bundy)," May 19, 1964, *FRUS, 1964–1968*, vol. 29, pt. 1, document no. 342. Wyatt was an American representative during oil negotiations with Indonesia.

13) "Telegram from the Embassy in Korea to the Department of State," September 2, 1963, *FRUS, 1961–1963*, vol. 22, document no. 313.

14) "Telegram from the Embassy in Korea to the Department of State," January 21, 1964, *FRUS, 1964–1968*, vol. 29, pt. 1, document no. 1.

15) "Airgram from the Embassy in Korea to the Department of State," February 13, 1964, *FRUS, 1964–1968*, vol. 29, pt. 1, document no. 4.

16) "Telegram from the Embassy in Korea to the Department of State," June 3, 1964, *FRUS, 1964–1968*, vol. 29, pt. 1, document no. 13.

17) The military officers of the military government who went through the purges during military rule, as well as politicians, businessmen, and intellectuals who joined the Democratic Republican party, wanted to check Kim Jongpil out of fear of being purged.

18) "Telegram from the Embassy in Korea to the Department of State," June 4, 1964, *FRUS, 1964–1968*, vol. 29, pt. 1, document no. 14.

19) "Telegram from the Embassy in Korea to the Department of State," June 6, 1964, *FRUS, 1964–1968*, vol. 29, pt. 1, document no. 15.

20) *FRUS, 1964–1968*, vol. 29, pt. 1, document no. 8.

21) *FRUS, 1964–1968*, vol. 29, pt. 1, document no. 7.

22) "Telegram from the Embassy in Korea to the Department of State," May 2, 1963, Pol 14 Kor S, Subject-Number Files 1963.

23) CIA, "Special Report," March 18, 1966.

24) "Telegram from the Embassy in Korea to the Department of State," May 20, 1964, *FRUS, 1964–1968*, vol. 29, pt. 1, document no. 10.

25) Ibid.

26) *FRUS, 1964–1968*, vol. 29, pt. 1, document no. 13.

27) Ibid.

28) Ibid.

29) Ibid.

30) Berger's insistence has to do with the order he received from the Department of State, as it instructed him not insist too strongly on the removal of Kim Jongpil. Ibid.

31) "Telegram 1621, June 7; National Archives and Records Administration," RG 59, Central Files 1964–1966, Pol 15-1 Kor S, in "Editorial Note," *FRUS, 1964–1968*, vol. 29, pt. 1, document no. 16.

32) *FRUS, 1964–1968*, vol. 29, pt. 1, document no. 15.

33) Ibid.

34) "Editorial Note," *FRUS, 1964–1968*, vol. 29, pt. 1, document no. 16.

35) On July 2, 1964, less than a month after Kim Jongpil's departure, Park Chung Hee informed Samuel Berger at Jinhae that Kim was interested in coming back to Korea. Berger was adamantly against it and told Park that the country would be thrown into another crisis if Kim returned. The State Department agreed with Berger. "Telegram from the Embassy in Korea to the Department of State," July 6, 1964, *FRUS, 1964–1968*, vol. 29, pt. 1, document no. 18.

36) "Telegram 551 from Seoul, December 19 (in Telegram from the Embassy in Korea to the Department of State)," December 21, 1964, *FRUS, 1964–1968*, vol. 29, pt. 1, document no. 29.

37) In May 1964, Jeong Ilgwon informed the American ambassador of his view that Kim Jongpil should be removed within two months. *FRUS, 1964–1968*, vol. 29, pt. 1, document no. 10.

38) "Memorandum of Conversation: Brown and Yi Hu-rak," October 13, 1965, Box 2, Bureau of Far Eastern Affairs, Office of the Country Director for Korea, Records Relating to Korea 1952–1966, RG 59, NARA.

39) Samuel D. Berger, "The Transformation of Korea: 1961–1965," January 7, 1966, RG 59, NND 979519, Subject Files of the Assistant Secretary of State for East Asian and Pacific Affairs 1961–1974, Box 305, NARA.

40) *FRUS, 1964–1968*, vol. 29, pt. 1, document no. 18.

Chapter Six

1) "Memorandum from Robert W. Komer of the National Security Council Staff to President Johnson," January 2, 1964, *FRUS, 1964–1968*, vol. 29, pt. 1, document no. 2.

2) "National Intelligence Estimate (14.2/42-61)," September 7, 1961, *FRUS, 1961–1963*, 22:521.

3) "Telegram from the Embassy in Korea to the Department of State," January 21, 1964, *FRUS, 1964–1968*, vol. 29, pt. 1, document no. 1.

4) *FRUS, 1964–1968*, vol. 29, pt. 1, document no. 2.

5) "Memorandum from Robert W. Komer of the National Security Council Staff to

President Johnson," January 22, 1964, *FRUS, 1964–1968*, vol. 29, pt. 1, document no. 3.

6) "Airgram from the Embassy in Korea to the Department of State: Aide-Memoire from ROKG in Connection with Secretary of State's Visit," February 5, 1964, *FRUS, 1964–1968*, vol. 29, pt. 1, document no. 3.

7) Prior to Rusk's visit, the South Korean government had passed on its own views to the US Embassy on January 29. "Memorandum from Robert W. Komer of the National Security Council Staff to President Johnson," January 22, 1964, *FRUS, 1964–1968*, vol. 29, pt. 1, document no. 3n2. Also, the South Korean government expressed its bias against Korean residents in Japan. "The Korean Government maintains that the question of legal status of the Korean residents in Japan must be solved with due consideration of the historical background that has led to their presence in Japan and they should be given a special legal status and more favorable treatments than those accorded to ordinary aliens in Japan. Since it is expected that the solution of this question in line with the above principles would stimulate the affiliation of the Communist-inclined Korean residents in Japan to democratic camp, especially during the Tokyo Olympic games, it is desired that the Japanese Government would favorably consider the Korean position on this question." Ibid., note 11.

8) "Airgram from the Embassy in Korea to the Department of State: Proposed U.S. Objectives in the Republic of Korea for 1964," February 13, 1964, *FRUS, 1964–1968*, vol. 29, pt. 1, document no. 4.

9) "National Security Action Memorandum No. 298: Study of Possible Redeployment of U.S. Division now Station in Korea," May 5, 1964, *FRUS, 1964–1968*, vol. 29, pt. 1, document no. 9. While Johnson argued for the completion of the relocation plan by May 26, the due date was postponed for some reason, which was likely South Korea's instability.

10) "Draft Memorandum from Secretary of State Rusk to President Johnson: Study of Possible Redeployment of U.S. Division Now Stationed in Korea," June 8, 1964, *FRUS, 1964–1968*, vol. 29, pt. 1, document no. 17.

11) "Memorandum from the Deputy Assistant Secretary of State for Far Eastern Affairs (Barnett) to the Chief of the Military Assistance Division of the Agency for International Development (Black): Comments on Proposed Reduction of FY 1965 MAP for Republics of Korea and China," October 5, 1964, *FRUS, 1964–1968*, vol. 29, pt. 1, document no. 25.

12) "Telegram from the Embassy in Korea to the Department of State," June 6, 1964, *FRUS, 1964–1968*, vol. 29, pt. 1, document no. 15.

13) While there is still a need for a deeper analysis of more recently released documents, the South Korea-Japan normalization treaty was signed without mentioning the question of Dokdo, the fishery issue, cultural artifacts, and Korean residents in Japan. According to researchers who have delved into recently declassified documents, the South Korean government did sincerely attempt to solve the abovementioned issues while the American side focused mostly on how the normalization process could aid

the Park regime politically by bypassing such sensitive issues in order to quickly reach an agreement. The issue of Korean residents in Japan continued to cause problems in Japan into the 1990s and the fishery issue has remained a problem in South Korea-Japan relations to this day.

14) Park Chung Hee invited Ambassador Berger to his villa in Jinhae on July 2, 1964, to request additional aid for new projects, including the building of highways, but Berger flatly refused Park's request. "Telegram from the Embassy in Korea to the Department of State," July 6, 1964, *FRUS, 1964–1968*, vol. 29, pt. 1, document no. 18.

15) "Memorandum from the Joint Chiefs of Staff to Secretary of Defense McNamara: Guidance to the Commander in Chief, United Nations Command (U) (JCSM-683-64)," August 11, 1964, *FRUS, 1964–1968*, vol. 29, pt. 1, document no. 19.

16) Assistant Secretary William Bundy had communicated to the United States ambassador to Korea that it would be desirable to have South Korean troops in Vietnam by January 15. "'Wollam pabyeong munje' eseo goryeodoeeoya hal munjejeom," January 6, 1964, Daetongnyeong Biseosil munseo, report no. 65, vol. 7, Gukga Girogwon Jeonsisil jeonsi munseo, Daejeon.

17) "Editorial Note," *FRUS, 1964–1968*, vol. 29, pt. 1, document no. 5. The US decision to dispatch its own troops to Vietnam came in March 1965. The Korean offer to deploy its troops to Vietnam came a year before that. The popular perception that the deployment of South Korean troops to Vietnam came at the American behest needs to be reconsidered.

18) Ibid.

19) Ibid.

20) "Memorandum of Conversation," *FRUS, 1964–1968*, vol. 29, pt. 1, document no. 28n3.

21) Ibid.

22) Ibid.

23) "Telegram from the Embassy in Korea to the Department of State," December 30, 1964, *FRUS, 1964–1968*, vol. 29, pt. 1, document no. 30.

24) "Editorial Note," *FRUS, 1964–1968*, vol. 29, pt. 1, document no. 20.

25) "Memorandum from James C. Thomson of the National Security Council Staff to President Johnson: Your Meeting at 5 P.M. with President Park," May 17, 1965, *FRUS, 1964–1968*, vol. 29, pt. 1, document no. 47.

26) Ibid.

27) *Chosun ilbo*, May 21, 1965, and May 30, 1965.

28) *Chosun ilbo*, May 28, 1965.

29) "Special National Intelligence Estimate (SNIE 10-4-65): Probable Communist Reactions to Developments of a ROK Combat Division for Base Security Duty in South Vietnam," March 19, 1965, *FRUS, 1964–1968*, vol. 29, pt. 1, document no. 35.

30) This document notes that "Viet Cong terrorist efforts and military harassment might be directed against the ROK forces in the hope that casualties would cause

discontent in South Korea and also serve as a warning to other potential foreign contingents." This reminds one of the ongoing situation in Iraq.

31) "Telegram from the Embassy in Korea to the Department of State," March 30, 1965, *FRUS, 1964–1968*, vol. 29, pt. 1, document no. 36.

32) "Memorandum from the Assistant Secretary of Defense for International Security Affairs (McNaughton) to the Deputy Secretary of Defense (Vance)," April 13, 1965, *FRUS, 1964–1968*, vol. 29, pt. 1, document no. 38.

33) "Telegram from the Embassy in Korea to the Department of State: ROK Troops for Vietnam," April 15, 1965, *FRUS, 1964–1968*, vol. 29, pt. 1, document no. 39.

34) Ibid.

35) "Memorandum of Converation: U.S.-Korean Relations," May 6, 1965, *FRUS, 1964–1968*, vol. 29, pt. 1, document no. 48.

36) *Chosun ilbo*, June 4, 1965.

37) "Editorial Note," *FRUS, 1964–1968*, vol. 29, pt. 1, document no. 32.

38) "Letter from Secretary of State Rusk to Secretary of Defense McNamara," March 22, 1965, *FRUS, 1964–1968*, vol. 29, pt. 1, document no. 36.

39) Ibid. In this document, Secretary of Defense McNamara argued that the SOFA in South Korea and Taiwan should follow the West German precedent. He also pointed out that, unlike South Korea and Taiwan, the Philippines had successfully revised its SOFA in terms more favorable to itself.

40) "Memorandum from the Assistant Secretary of Defense for International Security Affairs (McNaughton) to the Deputy Secretary of Defense (Vance): Chinese and Korean Status of Forces Negotiations–Criminal Jurisdiction," April 13, 1965, *FRUS, 1964–1968*, vol. 29, pt. 1, document no. 38.

41) "Telegram from the Embassy in Korea to the Department of State," May 14, 1965, *FRUS, 1964–1968*, vol. 29, pt. 1, document no. 44.

42) "Memorandum of Conversation: Joint Communique to Be Issued by President Johnson and Park," May 18, 1965, *FRUS, 1964–1968*, vol. 29, pt. 1, document no. 50.

43) *Chosun ilbo*, May 26, 1965.

44) "Telegram from the Embassy in Korea to the Department of State: SOFA Negotiations," January 6, 1966, *FRUS, 1964–1968*, vol. 29, pt. 1, document no. 70.

45) "Memorandum of Conversation," May 6, 1965, *FRUS, 1964–1968*, vol. 29, pt. 1, document no. 42. Minister of National Defense Kim Seongeun also requested 75 percent increase in the defense budget and an increase of $30 million. and Ambassador Brown flatly rejected these requests.

46) "Memorandum from Vice President Humphrey to President Johnson: Korea," January 5, 1966, *FRUS, 1964–1968*, vol. 29, pt. 1, document no. 48.

47) "Telegram from the Embassy in Korea to the Department of State," July 10, 1965, *FRUS, 1964–1968*, vol. 29, pt. 1, document no. 57.

48) "Telegram from the Embassy in Korea to the Department of State," December 22, 1965, *FRUS, 1964–1968*, vol. 29, pt. 1, document no. 63n2.

49) In order to better justify the deployment of South Korean troops to Vietnam, Washington always had the South Vietnamese government itself request them from the South Korean government.

50) "Telegram from the Embassy in Korea to the Department of State: ROK Troops to Vietnam," June 14, 1965, *FRUS, 1964–1968*, vol. 29, pt. 1, document no. 55.

51) "Telegram from the Embassy in Korea to the Department of State: Troops for Vietnam," December 28, 1965, *FRUS, 1964–1968*, vol. 29, pt. 1, document no. 65.

52) "Telegram from the Embassy in Korea to the Department of State," June 23, 1965, *FRUS, 1964–1968*, vol. 29, pt. 1, document no. 56.

53) *FRUS, 1964–1968*, vol. 29, pt. 1, document no. 57.

54) Ibid.

55) "Memorandum from the Assistant Director of the United States Operations Mission to Korea (Brown) to the Director of the United States Operations Mission to Korea of the Agency for International Development (Bernstein): Procurement in Korea for Vietnam," September 23, 1965, *FRUS, 1964–1968*, vol. 29, pt. 1, document no. 59. In this document, Ambassador Brown argued that increased aid to Korea would still cost less than deploying a US division to Vietnam.

56) "Telegram from the Embassy in Korea to the Department of State," January 5, 1966, *FRUS, 1964–1968*, vol. 29, pt. 1, document no. 48.

57) "Memorandum of Conversation," January 5, 1966, *FRUS, 1964–1968*, vol. 29, pt. 1, document no. 48.

58) Washington requested the deployment of a division by July 1, 1966, and then sought the dispatch of a brigade by October 1, 1966.

59) "Telegram from the Embassy in Korea to the Department of State: Additional Korean Troops for South Vietnam," December 22, 1965, *FRUS, 1964–1968*, vol. 29, pt. 1, document no. 63.

60) "Korean Troops for Vietnam," January, 15, 1966, 0630Z, RG 59, Central Files 1964–1966, Pol 27-3 Viet S, in *FRUS, 1964–1968*, vol. 29, pt. 1, document no. 72.

61) "Telegram from the Embassy in Korea to the Department of State," January 10, 1966, *FRUS, 1964–1968*, vol. 29, pt. 1, document no. 71.

62) Secretary of Defense McNamara noted that while the South Koreans want "about $600–700 million worth of cumshaw" for additional troops, the United States may be willing to give around "something on the order of $70 million worth of extra equipment and payments." Ibid.

63) "Telegram from the Embassy in Korea to the Department of State: Troops for RVN," January 21, 1966, *FRUS, 1964–1968*, vol. 29, pt. 1, document no. 73.

64) For example, while the South Korean Ministry of National Defense requested $65 million worth of equipment, Assistant Secretary McNaughton reported to Secretary of Defense McNamara that an additional $6 million to the already established military "modernization" package for South Korea would suffice. "Memorandum from the Assistant Secretary of Defense for International Security Affairs (McNaughton) to

Secretary of Defense McNamara," January 27, 1966, *FRUS, 1964–1968*, vol. 29, pt. 1, document no. 74.

65) "Telegram from the Department of State to the Embassy in Korea: Korean Troops for South Viet-Nam," January 27, 1966, *FRUS, 1964–1968*, vol. 29, pt. 1, document no. 76. With some editing of secret content, the American proposal was communicated to the South Korean media as the "Brown Memorandum" on March 8.

66) "Telegram from the Embassy in Korea to the Department of State," February 1, 1966, *FRUS, 1964–1968*, vol. 29, pt. 1, document no. 77.

67) "Telegram from the Embassy in Korea to the Department of State," December 30, 1965, *FRUS, 1964–1968*, vol. 29, pt. 1, document no. 67.

68) "Telegram from the Embassy in Korea to the Department of State," January 5, 1966, *FRUS, 1964–1968*, vol. 29, pt. 1, document no. 48.

69) Park Chung Hee stated in a closed press conference on November 10, 1966, that no more South Korean combat troops would be dispatched to Vietnam. "Telegram from the Embassy in Korea to the Department of State," November 22, 1966, *FRUS, 1964–1968*, vol. 29, pt. 1, document no. 91.

70) "Memorandum from the Executive Secretary of the National Security Council (Smith) to the President's Special Assistant (Rostow)," January 19, 1967, *FRUS, 1964–1968*, vol. 29, pt. 1, document no. 107.

71) "Memorandum from James C. Thomson of the National Security Council Staff and the President's Special Assistant for National Security Affairs (Bundy) to President Johnson: Development Loan Commitment to Korea," May 14, 1965, *FRUS, 1964–1968*, vol. 29, pt. 1, document no. 44.

72) "Memorandum from the President's Special Assistant for National Security Affairs (Bundy) to President Johnson: Sweetener for Another ROK Division in Vietnam," February 3, 1966, *FRUS, 1964–1968*, vol. 29, pt. 1, document no. 78. In this document, Bundy reported to Johnson that an additional $5 million would allow Park to buy the voters.

73) "Memorandum from the Administrator of the Agency for International Development (Bell) to the President's Special Assistant for National Security (Bundy): A.I.D. Commitments to Korea in Connection with the Negotiations on Additional Korean Troops for Vietnam (Attach 4)," January 25, 1966, in ibid.

74) "Memorandum from William J. Jorden of the National Security Council Staff to President Johnson: $12 Million Loan to Korean Reconstruction Bank," August 15, 1966, and "Memorandum from the President's Special Assistant for National Security Affairs (Bundy) to President Johnson: Sweetener for Another ROK Division in Vietnam," February 3, 1966, *FRUS, 1964–1968*, vol. 29, pt. 1, document no. 89.

75) "Memorandum from the President's Special Assistant (Rostow) to President Johnson: Loans to Korea for Power Development," May 1, 1967, and "Memorandum from the President's Special Assistant for National Security Affairs (Bundy) to President Johnson: Sweetener for Another ROK Division in Vietnam," February 3, 1966, *FRUS, 1964–1968*, vol. 29, pt. 1, document no. 115.

76) "Telegram from the Embassy in Korea to the Department of State," March 15, 1965, and "Memorandum from the President's Special Assistant for National Security Affairs (Bundy) to President Johnson: Sweetener for Another ROK Division in Vietnam," February 3, 1966, *FRUS, 1964–1968*, vol. 29, pt. 1, document no. 128.

77) "Telegram from the Embassy in Korea to the Department of State," March 15, 1965, *FRUS, 1964–1968*, vol. 29, pt. 1, document no. 33.

78) "Memorandum of Conversation: U.S.-Korean Relations," May 17, 1965, *FRUS, 1964–1968*, vol. 29, pt. 1, document no. 46.

79) "Telegram from the Embassy in Korea to the Department of State," June 4, 1965, *FRUS, 1964–1968*, vol. 29, pt. 1, document no. 54. An interesting piece of information contained in this document is that the South Korean government deployed its police officers at US bases in Korea. The South Korean government ordered the police officers to observe the movements of US forces.

80) "Memorandum of Conversation," June 22, 1966, *FRUS, 1964–1968*, vol. 29, pt. 1, document no. 119.

81) "Letter from the Ambassador to Korea (Brown) to the Assistant Secretary of State for East Asian and Pacific Affairs (Bundy): U.S. Army Strength in Korea," December 13, 1966, *FRUS, 1964–1968*, vol. 29, pt. 1, document no. 105.

82) "Letter from the Assistant Secretary of Defense for International Security Affairs (McNaughton) to the Assistant Secretary of State for Far Eastern Affairs (Bundy)," April 9, 1966, *FRUS, 1964–1968*, vol. 29, pt. 1, document no. 83. This document also includes the judgment that the people of South Korea would continue to complain about SOFA regardless of revision.

83) "Editorial Note," *FRUS, 1964–1968*, vol. 29, pt. 1, document no. 88.

84) The reason why clashes increased in the Korean Demilitarized Zone after 1966 has not been clearly explained. According to an article by Mitchell Lerner, the reason for the escalation was the active policy on the part of North Korea. Mitchell Lerner, "A Dangerous Miscalculation: New Evidence from Communist-Bloc Archives about North Korea and the Crises of 1968," *Journal of Cold War Studies* 6, no. 1 (Winter 2004): 3–21. However, I believe that the active strategy taken by North Korea was a way of responding to the South Korean deployment of troops to Vietnam. Some researchers explain the escalation as a response to the American efforts to open another front on the Korean Peninsula. Hanguk Yeoksa Yeonguhoe, Hyeondaesa Yeonguban, "Bukhan ui sahoejuui geonseol gwajeong gwa jaju noseon," *Hanguk hyeondaesa*, vol. 3, *1960,70 nyeondae Hanguk sahoe wa byeonhyeok undong* (Seoul: Pulbit, 1991), 243–80. However, I believe, based on a comprehensive analysis of American documents, that it was an attempt by North Korea to stop the South Korean deployment of troops to Vietnam and respond to the strengthening of South Korean armed forces.

85) "Telegram from the Embassy in Korea to the Department of State: Troops for RVN," March 18, 1966, *FRUS, 1964–1968*, vol. 29, pt. 1, document no. 82; "Telegram from the Embassy in Korea to the Department of State," October 19, 1966, *FRUS*,

1964–1968, vol. 29, pt. 1, document no. 93; "Telegram from the Embassy in Korea to the Department of State," November 22, 1966, *FRUS, 1964–1968*, vol. 29, pt. 1, document no. 101.

86) "Memorandum of Conversation," March 14, 1967, *FRUS, 1966–1968*, vol. 29, pt. 1, document no. 110.

87) Park Tae Gyun, "1960 nyeondae jungban anbo wigi wa je 2 gyeongjeron," *Yeoksa bipyeong*, Fall 2005, 250–76.

88) Because of this, the US government reexamined the level of security in South Korea prior to the congratulatory visit of Vice President Humphrey for the inauguration of Park Chung Hee. "Report Prepared by the Office of National Estimates of the Central Intelligence Agency: SECURITY CONDITIONS IN SOUTH KOREA," June 23, 1967, *FRUS, 1966–1968*, vol. 29, pt. 1, document no. 120.

89) "Intelligence Memorandum: ARMED INCIDENTS ALONG THE KOREAN DMZ," November 8, 1966, *FRUS, 1966–1968*, vol. 29, pt. 1, document no. 98.

90) Bonesteel reported to Washington that preemptive strikes may be necessary to protect United Nations forces in November of 1966. "Memorandum of Conversation: Mr. Bundy's Meeting with Mr. Colby," December 1, 1966, *FRUS, 1964–1968*, vol. 29, pt. 1, document no. 104.

91) "Telegram from the Commanding General, United States Eighth Army, Korea, and the Commander in Chief, United Nations Command, Korea (Bonesteel) to the Chairman of the Joint Chiefs of Staff (Wheeler)," November 10, 1966, *FRUS, 1964–1968*, vol. 29, pt. 1, document no. 99.

92) "Memorandum of Conversation: Mr. Bundy's Meeting with Mr. Colby," September 15, 1967, *FRUS, 1964–1968*, vol. 29, pt. 1, document no. 127.

93) "Memorandum from Alfred Jenkins of the National Security Council Staff to the President's Special Assistant (Rostow): Bonesteel's 'Eye Only' of July 21," July 26, 1967, *FRUS, 1964–1968*, vol. 29, pt. 1, document no. 123.

94) *FRUS, 1964–1968*, vol. 29, pt. 1, document no. 107.

95) *FRUS, 1964–1968*, vol. 29, pt. 1, document no. 110.

96) "Telegram from the Embassy in Korea to the Department of State," June 7, 1967, *FRUS, 1964–1968*, vol. 29, pt. 1, document no. 117.

97) "Editorial Note," *FRUS, 1964–1968*, vol. 29, pt. 1, document no. 126.

98) "Telegram from the Embassy in Korea to the Department of State: Additional ROK Forces for Vietnam," September 19, 1967, *FRUS, 1964–1968*, vol. 29, pt. 1, document no. 128.

99) Ibid.

100) "Telegram from the Embassy in Korea to the Department of State. Internal Security: Views of President Park," September 19, 1967, *FRUS, 1964–1968*, vol. 29, pt. 1, document no. 129.

101) Ibid.

102) "Special National Intelligence Estimate (SNIE 14.2-67): NORTH KOREAN

INTENTIONS AND CAPABILITIES WITH RESPECT TO SOUTH KOREA," September 21, 1967, *FRUS, 1964–1968*, vol. 29, pt. 1, document no. 134.

103) "Telegram from the Embassy in Korea to the Department of State: Vice President's Meeting with Prime Minister of Korea," October 31, 1967, *FRUS, 1964–1968*, vol. 29, pt. 1, document no. 132.

104) *Chosun ilbo*, November 1, 1967.

105) "Telegram from the Embassy in Korea to the Department of State: Additional ROK Troop Contribution to Vietnam," November 25, 1967, *FRUS, 1964–1968*, vol. 29, pt. 1, document no. 134.

106) "Memorandum of Conversation: North Korean Harassment and U.S. Commitments," November 13, 1967, *FRUS, 1964–1968*, vol. 29, pt. 1, document no. 133. While Choe Gyuha conveyed South Korea's desire to increase its exports to South Vietnam at this meeting, the US representatives did not approve this request. Berger claimed that US$60 million had been remitted back to South Korea during the first half of 1967 alone, which was almost the same amount as that for the entire year of 1966. Choe did not deny this fact. Berger also declined the request to have South Korean troops in Vietnam wear South Korea–made underclothes, claiming that it was not part of the Brown memorandum.

107) "Telegram from the Embassy in Korea to the Department of State: Additional ROK Troop Contribution to Vietnam," November 25, 1967, *FRUS, 1964–1968*, vol. 29, pt. 1, document no. 134.

108) During the meeting on December 6, Park Chung Hee broke the traditional mode of contact and negotiation by telling Ambassador Porter to discuss the matters of troop deployment with the South Korean minister of national defense. This would have seemed rude to Ambassador Porter. "Telegram from the Embassy in Korea to the Department of State," December 6, 1967, *FRUS, 1964–1968*, vol. 29, pt. 1, document no. 137.

109) "Telegram from the Embassy in Australia to the Department of State," December 21, 1967, *FRUS, 1964–1968*, vol. 29, pt. 1, document no. 139.

110) "Notes on Conversation Between President Johnson and President Pak," December 21, 1967, *FRUS, 1964–1968*, vol. 29, pt. 1, document no. 140.

111) "Memorandum from the President's Special Assistant (Rostow) to President Johnson: More Korean Troops for Vietnam," January 5, 1968, *FRUS, 1964–1968*, vol. 29, pt. 1, document no. 142.

112) *FRUS, 1964–1968*, vol. 29, pt. 1, document no. 82.

113) *Chosun ilbo*, June 15, 1967, December 7, 1967, and January 7, 1967; "Editorial Note," *FRUS, 1964–1968*, vol. 29, pt. 1, document no. 143.

114) "Telegram from the Embassy in Korea to the Department of State," January 24, 1968, *FRUS, 1964–1968*, vol. 29, pt. 1, document no. 145.

115) "Telegram from the Commanding General, United States Eight Army, Korea, and the Commander in Chief, United Nations Command, Korea (Bonesteel) to the

Chairman of the Joint Chiefs of Staff (Wheeler)," January 27, 1968, *FRUS, 1964–1968*, vol. 29, pt. 1, document no. 148.

116) "Telegram from the Embassy in Korea to the Department of State," February 6, 1968, *FRUS, 1964–1968*, vol. 29, pt. 1, document no. 156.

117) "Telegram from the Embassy in Korea to the Department of State," February 3, 1968, *FRUS, 1964–1968*, vol. 29, pt. 1, document no. 150.

118) "Telegram from the Commander in Chief, Pacific (Sharp) to the Chairman of the Joint Chiefs of Staff (Wheeler)," February 9, 1968, *FRUS, 1964–1968*, vol. 29, pt. 1, document no. 165. Commander Bonesteel reported that the South Korean generals were playing out the Mad Hatter's tea party, a reference to *Alice's Adventures in Wonderland*, meaning that South Korean generals were supportive of Park's wish to advance northward.

119) "Telegram from the Embassy in Korea to the Department of State," February 8, 1968, *FRUS, 1964–1968*, vol. 29, pt. 1, document no. 161.

120) *FRUS, 1964–1968*, vol. 29, pt. 1, document no. 165.

121) "Embtel No. 4034: National Archives and Records Administration," RG 59. Central Files 1967–1969, Pol 33-6 Kor N-US, in "Telegram from the Department of State to the Embassy in Korea," February 7, 1968, *FRUS, 1964–1968*, vol. 29, pt. 1, document no. 160.

122) "Telegram from the Embassy in Korea to the Department of State," February 10, 1968, *FRUS, 1964–1968*, vol. 29, pt. 1, document no. 171.

123) "Telegram from the Embassy in Korea to the Department of State," February 10, 1968, *FRUS, 1964–1968*, vol. 29, pt. 1, document no. 174.

124) "Memorandum Prepared by the Department of State," February 9, 1968, *FRUS, 1964–1968*, vol. 29, pt. 1, document no. 169.

125) "Telegram from the Embassy in Korea to the Department of State," February 14, 1968, *FRUS, 1964–1968*, vol. 29, pt. 1, document no. 179.

126) "Notes of the President's Meeting with Cyrus R. Vance," February 15, 1968, *FRUS, 1964–1968*, vol. 29, pt. 1, document no. 180.

127) In a letter sent on the same day, Vance mentioned that other South Korean officials were not aware of the retaliatory raids against North Korea because the minister of national defense did not release that information. He also mentioned that while South Korean special forces blew up a division headquarters in North Korea in November 1967, it probably did not influence the decision to launch the Blue House raid in 1968. "Memorandum from Cyrus R. Vance to President Johnson," February 20, 1968, *FRUS, 1964–1968*, vol. 29, pt. 1, document no. 181.

128) "Letter from the Ambassador to Korea (Porter) to the Assistant Secretary of State for East Asian and Pacific Affairs (Bundy)," February 27, 1968, *FRUS, 1964–1968*, vol. 29, pt. 1, document no. 182.

129) *FRUS, 1964–1968*, vol. 29, pt. 1, document no. 160.

130) "Telegram from the Embassy in Korea to the Department of State," February

12, 1968, *FRUS, 1964–1968*, vol. 29, pt. 1, document no. 176.

131) "Telegram from the Embassy in Korea to the Department of State," March 8, 1968, *FRUS, 1964–1968*, vol. 29, pt. 1, document no. 186.

132) "Intelligence Information Cable from the Central Intelligence Agency (TDCSDB-315/01422-68)," April 23, 1968, *FRUS, 1964–1968*, vol. 29, pt. 1, document no. 195.

133) "Paper Prepared by the Policy Planning Council of the Department of State," June 15, 1968, *FRUS, 1964–1968*, vol. 29, pt. 1, document no. 201.

134) "Information Memorandum from the President's Special Assistant (Rostow) to President Johnson," June 19, 1968, *FRUS, 1964–1968*, vol. 29, pt. 1, document no. 202.

135) "Telegram from the Embassy in Korea to the Commander in Chief, Pacific (Sharp)," April 16, 1968, *FRUS, 1964–1968*, vol. 29, pt. 1, document no. 191.

136) "Memorandum from Vice President Humphrey to President Johnson," January 5, 1966, *FRUS, 1964–1968*, vol. 29, pt. 1, document no. 48.

137) "Special National Intelligence Estimate (SNIE 14.2-68)," May 16, 1968, *FRUS, 1964–1968*, vol. 29, pt. 1, document no. 200.

138) *FRUS, 1964–1968*, vol. 29, pt. 1, document no. 56.

139) "Draft Memorandum from Secretary of State Rusk to President Johnson: Study of Possible Redeployment of U.S. Division Now Stationed in Korea," June 8, 1964, *FRUS, 1964–1968*, vol. 29, pt. 1, document no. 16.

Chapter Seven

1) Jeong Seongjin, "21 segi Miguk jegukjuui," *Sahoe gyeongje pyeongnon* 20 (2003). Of course the end of the gold standard meant a collapse of the dollar-centered international monetary system leading the United States to create a new system in which it could control the world economy by selecting the flexible exchange rate system centered on the US dollar in 1973.

2) John Lewis Gaddis, *Strategies of Containment*, 276–83.

3) "Informal Remarks in Guam with Newsmen," July 25, 1969, in Gerhard Peters and John T. Woolley, *The American Presidency Project* (Santa Barbara: University of California, Santa Barbara, 2012), http://www.presidency.ucsb.edu/ws/?pid=2140.

4) Bak Taeho and Park Tae Gyun, "1960 nyeondae Asia Gaebal Eunhaeng ui changnip gwajeong e daehan yeongu," *Gukje jiyeok yeongu* 13, no. 2 (2004).

5) Park Tae Gyun, "Han-Il hyeopjeong gwajeong eseo natananeun Miguk gwa Ilbon ui ihae gwangye wa geu teukjing," in *Han-Il gwangyesa yeongu nonjip*, vol. 10, *Haebang hu Han-Il gwangye ui jaengjeom gwa jeonmang*, ed. Han-Il Gwangyesa Yeongu Nonjip Pyeonchan Wiwonhoe (Seoul: Gyeongin Munhwasa, 2005).

6) Ilbon Yeongusil, ed., *Han-Il gwangye jaryojip* (Seoul: Goryeo Daehakgyo, Asea Munje Yeonguso, 1977), 643–46.

7) Victor D. Cha, *Alignment despite Antagonism.*

8) Through a national security decision memorandum (NSDM), Nixon ordered the withdrawal of one of the two divisions stationed in South Korea. While he mentioned the Second Infantry Division, the Seventh Division ended up being withdrawn. Bak Geonyeong, Bak Seonwon, and U Seungji, "Je 3 gonghwaguk sigi gukje jeongchi wa Nam-Buk gwangye," *Gukga jeollyak* 9, no. 4 (2003): 70.

9) Cha, *Alignment despite Antagonism.*

10) Cha, *Alignment despite Antagonism.*

11) "Embtel to Department of State: Conversation with General Kim Hyung Wook, Former Director, ROK CIA," January 2, 1970.

12) "Proposal for Increased Display of U.S. Interest in Dialogue between ROK and North Korea." February 18, 1971.

13) Ambassador Porter argued that the general sentiment of the South Korean people toward the lessening of tension on the Korean Peninsula could be seen in their support of Kim Daejung, who pledged to reduce military forces in the seventh presidential election.

14) The July 4 Joint Statement was not entirely the result of American pressure. To fully explain the July 4 statement to the public, the widespread popular hope for unification as well as the desire to escape the shadow of war needed to be taken into account. However, in this work, I have relied on the existing body of research that has viewed the July 4 statement from the perspective of US-South Korea relations.

15) To escape this predicament, Park Chung Hee even considered a mutual defense treaty with Japan. Cha, *Alignment despite Antagonism.*

16) "President Park's View of North Korea Threat," April 16, 1972, Frm: Amembassy Seoul to Secstate.

17) Park Tae Gyun, "1960 nyeondae jungban anbo wigi wa je 2 gyeongjeron."

18) "U.S. Response to Korean Constitutional Revision," October 23, 1972, Pol 15 Kor S, Records of the US Department of State Relating to the Internal Affairs of Korea, 1970–1973, NARA.

19) "Korean Policy Reconsideration: A Two-Korea Policy," Pol 32-34 Kor/UN, DOS Central Files: Korea, 1970–1973, NARA.

20) "NSDM 251," March 29, 1974, Winston Lord Files, Box 376.

21) Following the communization of South Vietnam, President Ford even requested $5 million of special aid to South Korea.

22) *Chosun ilbo*, August 14, 1974.

23) The *Chosun ilbo* even described the conditions at the time as a "new era of harmony" between the United States and South Korea. *Chosun ilbo*, November 23, 1974.

24) *Chosun ilbo*, November 6, 1974.

25) *Chosun ilbo*, November 22, 1974, and November 23, 1974. The South Korean government mobilized 1.8 million people to welcome President Ford during his visit.

26) Cha, *Alignment despite Antagonism.*

27) *Chosun ilbo*, January 6, 1976. Bak Dongseon had been working as a lobbyist and frequented the Blue House and the Korea Central Intelligence Agency since the early 1970s.

28) More research is necessary on the topic of Koreagate and its ramifications on US–South Korea relations. While some documents on the topic have been released, many more remain classified.

29) Cha, *Alignment despite Antagonism.*

30) There are many facts waiting to be uncovered on the issue of South Korean nuclear weapons development.

31) *Chosun ilbo*, April 23, 1975.

32) Cha, *Alignment despite Antagonism.*

33) *Chosun ilbo*, January 18, 1979, and April 28, 1979.

34) Yi Samseong, "Gwangju haksal, Miguk singunbu ui hyeopjo wa gongmo-choegeun Miguk oegyo munseo reul tonghae bon 5.17 kudeta, Gwangju haksal gwa Miguk ui dae Han jeongchaek," *Yeoksa bipyeong*, Autumn 1996, 95.

35) Yi Samseong, *Hyeondae Miguk oegyo wa gukje jeongchi*, 252–72.

36) Ibid., 99.

37) Ibid., 100–101.

38) The South Korean government was able to control the National Assembly through the organization called the Yujeonghoe (short for Yusin Jeonguhoe), which allowed the government to appoint one-third of all assembly members. The US Embassy report did not mention this.

39) Jo Dongjun, "Jeon Duhwan, Kateo reul nongnak hada: 1979~80 nyeon Mi Gungmubu bimil oegyo munseo 4 cheon peiji cheoljeo bunseok," *Wolgan Joseon*, August 1996, 339.

40) Ibid., 343.

41) Ibid., 334.

42) Ibid., 345.

43) Ibid., 348.

44) Bak Seongwon, "Miguk, singunbu e kkeullyeo danyeotda," *Sindonga*, May 1996, 120.

45) Ibid., 120–21.

46) "From Gleysteen to Secretary of State: ROK Shifts Special Forces Units," May 1980, 07096Z.

47) "From Gleysteen to Secretary of State: Crackdown in Seoul," May 1980, 1716730Z; "From Christopher to Gleysteen: Crackdown in Seoul," May 1980, 180008Z.

48) "From Gleysteen to Secretary of State: The Kwangju Crisis," (1980.5) 210932Z.

49) Ibid.

50) Yi Samseong, 117.

51) Byeon Changseop, "Hangugin eun gugeolkkun, Miguk ui oman gwa pyeongyeon,"

Sisa jeoneol, March 14, 1996, 34.

52) Tim Sherok and Kim Jaeil, "80 nyeon 6 wol, Jeon Duhwan deunggeuk injeong," *Sisa jeoneol*, March 21, 1996.

53) "Choe Gyuha neun jeongchi minjuhwa kkumdo motkkwotda," *Nyuseu meikeo*, March 1996, 35.

54) "Choe Gyuha, jipjeong budamseureowo haetda," *Nyuseu meikeo*, March 1996, 35.

55) "Mi yang Kim ssi bunyeol yecheukhaetda," *Nyuseu meikeo*, April 1996, 67.

56) "Telegram from the Embassy in Korea to the Department of State," September 2, 1963, *FRUS, 1961–1963*, 22:657–61.

57) "Telegram from the Embassy in Korea to the Department of State," January 21, 1964, *FRUS, 1964–1968*, vol. 29, pt. 1, document no. 1.

Conclusion

1) "Transformation of Korea 1961–1965," January 7, 1966, RG 59, NND 979519, Subject Files of the Assistant Secretary of State for East Asian and Pacific Affairs, Box 305, NARA.

2) The American efforts to obtain and retain the control of South Korean military forces from the time of the Korean War had to do with restraining a belligerent dictatorial regime that risked war even before 1950. This consideration continued throughout the entire period discussed by this book.

3) "Embtel No. 1536," May 16, 1961, Box 2181, Decimal File 1960–1963.

BIBLIOGRAPHY

Chosun ilbo.
Daehak sinmun.
Daetongnyeong biseosil munseo.
Foreign Relations of the United States.
Gardener files.
Gojong sillok.
Foreign Affairs, House of Representatives.
Josa wolbo.
Jubo.
National Archives and Records Administration.
New York Times.
Nyuseu meikeo.
Seoul gyeongje sinmun.
Sindonga.
Sisa jeoneol.
Wolgan jungang.
Wolgan mal.
The American Presidency Project.

Bak, Huibeom. *Hanguk gyeongje seongjangnon.* Seoul: Goryeo Daehakgyo Asea Munje Yeonguso, 1968.

Bak, Jeongyang. "Miguk jeongwon daesin huihwanhu ipsi yeonseol." In *Bak Jeongyang jeonjip*, edited by Hangukhak Munheon Yeonguso. Seoul: Asea Munhwasa, 1984.

Bak, Seonwon and U Seungji. "Je 3 gonghwaguk sigi gukje jeongchi wa Nam-Buk gwangye." *Gukga jeollyak* 9, no. 4 (2003): 70.

Bak, Taeho and Park Tae Gyun. "1960 nyeondae Asia Gaebal Eunhaeng ui changnip gwajeong e daehan yeongu." *Gukje jiyeok yeongu* 13, no. 2 (2004).

Byeon, Hyeongyun. "Roseutou doyak iron ui Hanguk gyeongje e daehan jeogyong munje." In *Hanguk gyeongje baljeon ui iron gwa hyeonsil*. Edited by Naegak Gihoek Jojeongsil.Seoul: Naegak Giheok Jojeongsil, 1969, 36-51.

Bloodfield, A. I. and J. P. Jensen.*Banking Reform in South Korea*. New York: Federal Reserve Bank of New York, March 1951.

Brown, Arthur J.*The Mastery of the Far East: The Story of Korea's Transformation and Japan's Rise to Supremacy in the Orient*. New York: Charles Scribner's Sons, 1919.

Buchholz, Todd G. *New Ideas from Dead Economists: An Introduction to Modern Economic Thought*. New York: Plume, 1989.

Cha, Victor D. *Alignment despite Antagonism: The US-Korea-Japan Security Triangle*. Stanford, CA: Stanford University Press, 2000.

Choe, Sangyong.*Migunjeong gwa Hanguk minjokjuui*. Seoul: Nanam, 1988.

Containment: Documents on American Policy and Strategy, 1945-1950. edited by Thomas H. Etzold, and John Lewis Gaddis. New York: Columbia University Press, 1978.

Cumings, Bruce. *Korea's Place in the Sun: A Modern History*. New York: W.W. Norton, 1997.

Cumings, Bruce. "The Origins and Development of the Northeast Asian Political Economy: Industrial Sectors, Product Cycles and Political Consequences." *International Organization* 38, no. 1, 1984.

Cumings, Bruce. *The Origins of the Korean War, vol. 1, Liberation and the Emergence of Separate Regimes, 1945-1947*. Princeton, NJ: Princeton University Press, 1981.

Cumings, Bruce. *The Origins of the Korean War, vol. 2, The Roaring of the Cataract, 1947-1950*. Seoul: Yeoksa bipyeongsa, 2002.

Daehan Minguksa jaryojip, edited by Guksa Pyeonchan Wiwonhoe. Gwacheon, Gyeonggi, South Korea: Guksa Pyeonchan Wiwonhoe, 1995.

Daehan Minguk jeongdangsa. Edited by Jungang Seongeo Gwalli Wiwonhoe. Seoul:

Jungang Seongeo Gwalli Wiwonhoe, 1968.

Do, Jinsun.*Hanguk minjokjuui wa nambuk gwangye: Yi Seungman, Kim Gu sidae ui jeongchisa*. Seoul: Seoul Daehakgyo Chulpanbu, 1997.

Gaddis, John Lewis. *Strategies of Containment: A Critical Appraisal of Postwar American National Security Policy*. Oxford: Oxford University Press, 1982.

Gaebal yeondae ui gyeongje jeongchaek: Gyeongje Gihoegwon 30 nyeonsa (1961 nyeon~1980 nyeon). Edited by Gyeongje Gihoegwon. Seoul: Miraesa, 1994.

Galbraith, John K. *A Life in Our Times*. Boston: Houghton Mifflin, 1981.

Gukga Jaegeon Choego Hoeui.*Hanguk gunsa hyeongmyeongsa I-A*. Edited by Gunsa Hyeongmyeongsa Pyeonchan Wiwonhoe.Seoul: Donga Seojeok Jusik Hoesa, 1963.

Gukje Yeonhap Hanguk Wiwondan bogoseo 1949 (A/936). Edited by Gukhoe Doseogwan Ipbeob Josaguk. Seoul: Daehan Minguk Gukhoe Doseogwan, 1965.

Gukje Yeonhap Hanguk Wiwondan bogoseo 1949-1950. Edited by Gukhoe Doseogwan Ipbeob JosagukSeoul: Gukhoe Doseogwan Ipbeob Josaguk, 1965.

Haebang jeonhu Miguk ui dae Han jeongchaeksa jaryojip. Edited by Jeong Yonguk and Yi Gilsang. Seoul: Darakbang, 1996.

Han, Cheolho. "Chodae ju Mi jeongwongongsa Bak Jeongyang ui Migukgwan - Misok seubyu (1888) reul jungsim euro." *Hanguk hakbo* 18 (1992): 1053-91.

Han-Il gwangye jaryojip. Edited by Ilbon yeongusil. Seoul: Goryeo Daehakgyo, Asea Munje Yeonguso, 1977.

Hanguk jeonjaeng jaryo cheongseo, vol. 1, Mi Gukga Anjeon Bojang Hoeui munseo / Documents of the National Security Council: Korea (1948-1950). Edited by Gukbang Gunsa Yeonguso. Seoul: Gukbang Gunsa Yeonguso, 1996.

Hanguk jeonjaeng gwa Han-Mi gwangye 1943~1953. Edited by Bruce Cumings and translated by Bak Uigyeong. Seoul: Cheongsa, 1987.

Hanguk Yeoksa Yeonguhoe Hyeondaesa Yeonguban, "Bukhan ui sahoejuui geonseol gwajeong gwa jaju noseon." *Hanguk hyeondaesa, vol. 3, 1960,70 nyeondae Hanguk sahoe wa byeonhyeok undong*. Seoul: Pulbit, 1991, 243-80.

Hong, Seokryul. "5.16 kudeta ui wonin gwa Han-Mi gwangye." *Yeoksa hakbo* 168 (2000).

Hong, Seokryul. "Hanguk jeonjaeng jikhu Miguk ui Yi Seungman jegeo gyehoek." *Yeoksa bipyeong* (Autumn 1994): 138-69.

Hulbert, Homer B. *The Passing of Korea*. New York: Doubleday, 1906.

Im, Daesik. "1950 nyeondae Miguk ui gyoyuk wonjo wa chin Mi elliteu ui hyeongseong." In *1950 nyeondae Nambukhan ui seontaek gwa guljeol*. Seoul: Yeoksa bipyeongsa, 2004.

Jeong, Byeongjun. "1946~1947 nyeon jwau hapjak undong ui jeongae gwajeong gwa seonggyeok byeonhwa." *Hanguksaron* 29 (1993): 249-305.

Jeong, Byeongjun. "Haebang jikhu Yi Seungman ui gwiguk gwa Donggyeong hoehap." In *Hanguk minjok undongsa yeongu*, edited by Usong Jo Donggeol Seonsaeng Jeongnyeon Ginyeom Nonchong Ganhaeng Wiwonhoe. Seoul: Nanam, 1997.

Jeong, Byeongjun. "Ju Han Migunjeong ui 'Imsi Hanguk Haengjeongbu' surip gusang gwa dongnip chokseong jungang hyeobuihoe." *Yeoksa wa hyeonsil* 19 (1996): 135-74.

Jeong, Byeongjun. "Yi Seungman ui dongnip noseon gwa jeongbu surip undong." Ph.D. diss., Seoul Daehakgyo, 2001.

Jeong, Daecheol.*Jang Myeon eun wae sunyeowon e sumeo isseonna*. Seoul: Donga Ilbosa, 1997.

Jeong, Iljun. "Miguk ui dae Han jeongchaek byeonhwa wa Hanguk baljeon gukga ui hyeongseong, 1953~1968." Ph.D. diss., Seoul Daehakgyo, 2000.

Jeong, Seongjin. "21 segi Miguk jegukjuui." *Sahoe gyeongje pyeongnon* 20 (2003).

Jeong, Yonguk.*Haebang jeonhu Miguk ui dae Han jeongchaek: Gwado jeongbu gusang gwa jungganpa jeongchaek eul jungsim euro*. Seoul: Seoul Daehakgyo Chulpanbu, 2003.

Kim, Ilyeong.*Ganguk gwa buguk: Hanguk hyeondae jeongchisa gangui*. Seoul: Saenggak ui namu, 2005.

Kim, Yongtae.*Kim Yongtae jaseojeon*. Seoul: Jimmundang, 1990.

Lerner, Mitchell. "A Dangerous Miscalculation: New Evidence from Communist-Bloc Archives about North Korea and the Crises of 1968." *Journal of Cold War Studies* 6, no. 1 (Winter 2004): 3-21.

Lodewijks, John. "Rostow, Developing Economies, and National Security Policy." In "Economics and National Security: A History of Their Interaction." Edited by Craufurd D. Goodwin, annual supplement, *History of Political Economy* 23 (1991): 285-310.

Miguk ui dae Han jeongchaek, 1934-1950. Edited by Hallimdae Asia Munhwa Yeonguso. Chuncheon, Gangwon, South Korea: Hallym University Press, 1987.

Millikan, Max F. and W. W. Rostow.*A Proposal: Key to an Effective Foreign Policy*. New York: Harper & Brothers, 1957.

Oman, Charles P. and Ganeshan Wignaraja.*The Postwar Evolution of Development Thinking*. London: Macmillan in association with OECD Development Centre, 1991.

Packenham, Robert A.*Liberal America and the Third World: Political Development Ideas in Foreign Aid and Social Science*. Princeton, NJ: Princeton University Press, 1973.

Park, Tae Gyun. "1950 nyeondae gyeongje gaeballon yeongu." *Sahoe wa yeoksa* 61 (2002).

Park, Tae Gyun. "1950~60 nyeondae Miguk ui Hangukgun gamchungnon gwa Hanguk jeongbu ui daeeung." *Gukje jiyeok yeongu* 9, no. 3 (2000).

Park, Tae Gyun. "1956~1964 nyeon Hanguk gyeongje gaebal gyehoek ui seongnip gwajeong: gyeongje gaeballon ui hwaksan gwa Miguk ui dae Han jeongchaek byeonhwa reul jungsim euro." Ph.D. diss., Seoul Daehakgyo, 2000.

Park, Tae Gyun. "1945~1946 nyeon Migunjeong ui jeongchi seryeok jaepyeon gyehoek gwa Namhan jeongchi gudo ui byeonhwa." *Hanguksa yeongu* 74 (1991): 109-60.

Park, Tae Gyun. "1960 nyeondae jungban anbo wigi wa je 2 gyeongjeron." *Yeoksa bipyeong* (Fall 2005): 250-76.

Park, Tae Gyun. "1961~1964 nyeon gunsa jeongbu ui gyeongje gaebal gyehoek sujeong." *Sahoe wa yeoksa* 57 (2000): 113-46.

Park, Tae Gyun.*Hanguk jeonjaeng-Kkeunnaji aneun jeonjaeng, kkeunnaya hal jeonjaeng*. Seoul: Chaek gwa Hamkke, 2005.

Park, Tae Gyun. "Han-Il hoedam sigi cheonggugwon munje ui giwon gwa Miguk ui yeokhal," *Hanguksa yeongu* 131 (2005): 37-47.

Park, Tae Gyun. "Han-Il hyeopjeong gwajeong eseo natananeun Miguk gwa Ilbon ui ihae gwangye wa geu teukjing." In *Han-Il gwangyesa yeongu nonjip, vol. 10, Haebang hu Han-Il gwangye ui jaengjeom gwa jeonmang.* Edited by Han-Il Gwangyesa Yeongu Nonjip Pyeonchan Wiwonhoe. Seoul: Gyeongin Munhwasa, 2005.

Park, Tae Gyun.*Hyeondaesa reul bego sseureojin geoindeul: Song Jinu, Yeo Unhyeong, Jang Deoksu, Kim Gu.* Seoul: Jiseongsa, 1994.

Park, Tae Gyun. *Jo Bongam yeongu.* Seoul: Changjak gwa Bipyeongsa, 1995.

Park, Tae Gyun. "W. W. Rostow and Economic Discourse in South Korea in the 1960s." *Journal of International and Area Studies* 8, no. 2 (2001).

Parker, Thomas. *America's Foreign Policy, 1945-1976: Its Creators and Critics.* New York: Facts on File, 1980.

Pells, Richard. *Not Like Us: How Europeans Have Loved, Hated, and Transformed American Culture Since World War II.* New York: Basic Books, 1997.

Price, Harry Bayard.*The Marshall Plan and Its Meaning.* Ithaca, NY: Cornell University Press, 1955.

Reeve, W. D. *The Republic of Korea: A Political and Economic Study.* London: Oxford University Press, 1963.

Rowstow, Walt W. *An American Policy in Asia.* Cambridge, MA: Technology Press of Massachusetts Institute of Technology and John Wiley & Sons, 1955.

Rostow, Walt W. *Eisenhower, Kennedy, and Foreign Aid.* Austin: University of Texas Press, 1985.

Rostow, Walt W. "My Life Philosophy," *American Economist* 30, no. 2 (1986): 3-13.

Rostow, Walt W. "The Future of Foreign Aid." *Foreign Service Journal* 38, no. 6 (1961): 30-35.

Rostow, Walt W. *The Prospects for Communist China.* Cambridge, MA: Technology Press of Massachusetts Institute of Technology and John Wiley, 1954.

Rostow, Walt W.*The Stages of Economic Growth, a Non-Communist Manifesto.* Cambridge: Cambridge University Press, 1960.

Schlesinger, Jr., Arthur M.*A Thousand Days: John F. Kennedy in the White House.* Boston: Houghton Mifflin, 1965.

Sin, Ukhui. "Gihoe eseo gyochak sangtaero - Detangteu sigi Han-Mi gwangye wa Hanbando ui gukje jeongchi." *Hanguk jeongchi oegyosa nonchong* 26, no. 2 (2005): 253-85.

Song, Namheon.*Haebang 3 nyeonsa.* Seoul: Kkachi, 1985.

US Senate Committee on Foreign Relations.*Economic Assistance to China and Korea 1949-1950.* New York: Garland Publishing, 1979.

Yi, Cheolsun. "Yi Seungman jeonggwongi Miguk ui dae Han jeongchaek yeongu, 1948~1960." Ph.D. diss., Seoul Daehakgyo, 2000.

Yi, Jaebong. "4 wol hyeongmyeong gwa Miguk ui gaeip." *Sahoe gwahak yeongu* 18 (1995).

Yi, Jongwon (Ri Jonwon).*Higashi Ajia reisen to Kan-Bei-Nichi kankei.* Tokyo: Tokyo Daigaku Shuppankai, 1996.

Yi, Jongwon (Ri Jonwon). "Kannichi kokko seijoka no seiritsu to Amerika ichisen kyuhyaku rokuju kara rokujugonen." In *Sengo gaiko no keisei.* Edited by Kindai Nihon Kenkyukai. Tokyo: Yamakawa Shuppansha, 1994.

Yi, Jongwon (Ri Jonwon).*Nihon to shokuminchi 8: Ajia no reisen to datsushokuminchika.* Tokyo: Iwanami Shoten, 1993.

Yi, Samseong. "Gwangju haksal, Miguk singunbu ui hyeopjo wa gongmo-choegeun Miguk oegyo munseo reul tonghae bon 5.17 kudeta, Gwangju haksal gwa Miguk ui dae Han jeongchaek." *Yeoksa bipyeong*(Autumn 1996).

Yi,Samseong.*Hyeondae Miguk oegyo wa gukje jeongchi.* Seoul: Hangilsa, 1994.

Yi, Sangu.*Je 3 gonghwaguk, vol. 1, 5.16 eseo 10 wol yusin kkaji.* Seoul: Jungwon Munhwa, 1993.

Yi, Sangu. "Yun Boseon, Yu Wonsik nonjaeng ui jinwi."*Jeonggyeong munhwa*(November 1983).

Yi, Wanbeom et al.*1960 nyeondae ui jeongchi sahoe byeondong, ed. Hanguk Jeongsin Munhwa Yeonguwon, Hanguk hyeondaesa ui jaeinsik 10*. Seoul: Baeksan Seodang, 1999.

Yi, Wondeok.*Han-Il gwageosa cheori ui wonjeom: Ilbon ui jeonhu cheori oegyo wa Han-Il hoedam*. Seoul: Seoul Daehakgyo Chulpanbu, 1996.

Yi, Yeongseok. "5.16 hyeongmyeong gwa banhyeongmyeong ui noegwan." *Jeonggyeong munhwa*(May 1984).

Yu, Wonsik.*Hyeongmyeong eun eodiro ganna: 5.16 birok*. Seoul: Inmul Yeonguso, 1987.

INDEX